CHARACTER DESIGN ESSENTIALS

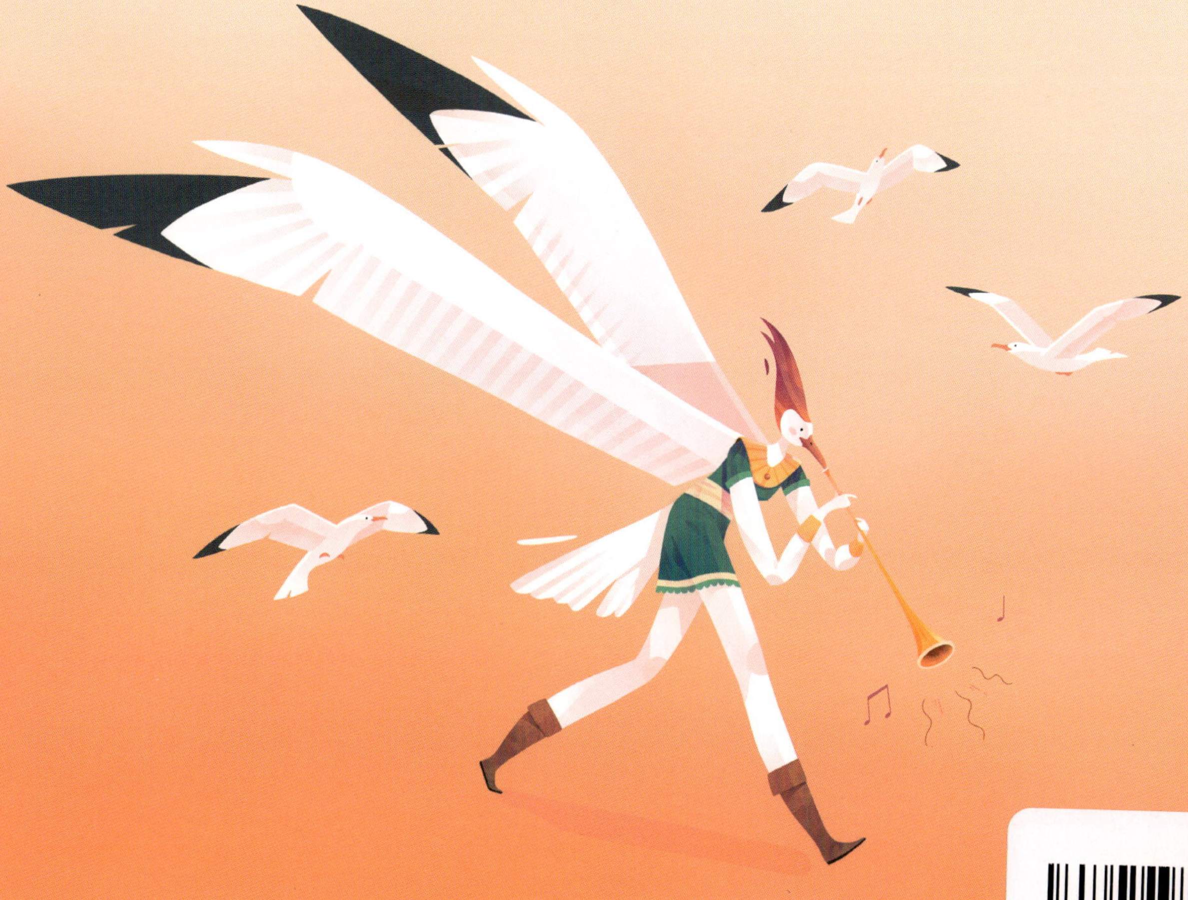

3dtotalPublishing

3dtotal Publishing

Correspondence: **publishing@3dtotal.com**
Website: **store.3dtotal.com**

First published in the United Kingdom, 2026, by 3dtotal Publishing.

Address: 3dtotal.com Ltd,
6 Sansome Street, Worcester,
WR1 1UH, United Kingdom.

Soft cover ISBN: 978-1-915992-45-1

Printed and bound in Shanghai, China, by KS Printing.

Visit **store.3dtotal.com** for a complete list of available book titles.

Editor: Sam Draper
Designer: Fiona Tarbet
Lead Editor: Rhiannon Joseph
Lead Designer: Joseph Cartwright
Studio Manager: Simon Morse
Managing Director: Tom Greenway

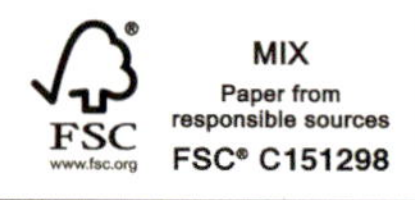

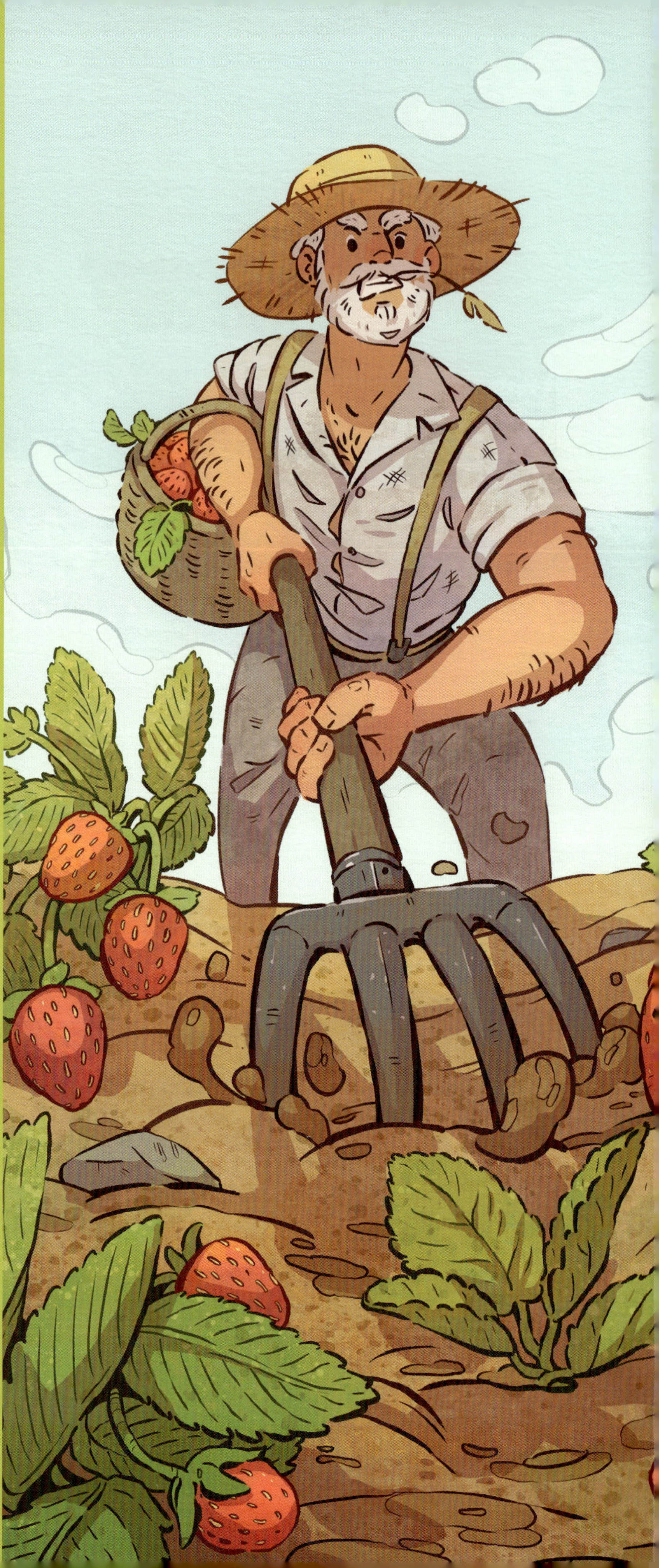

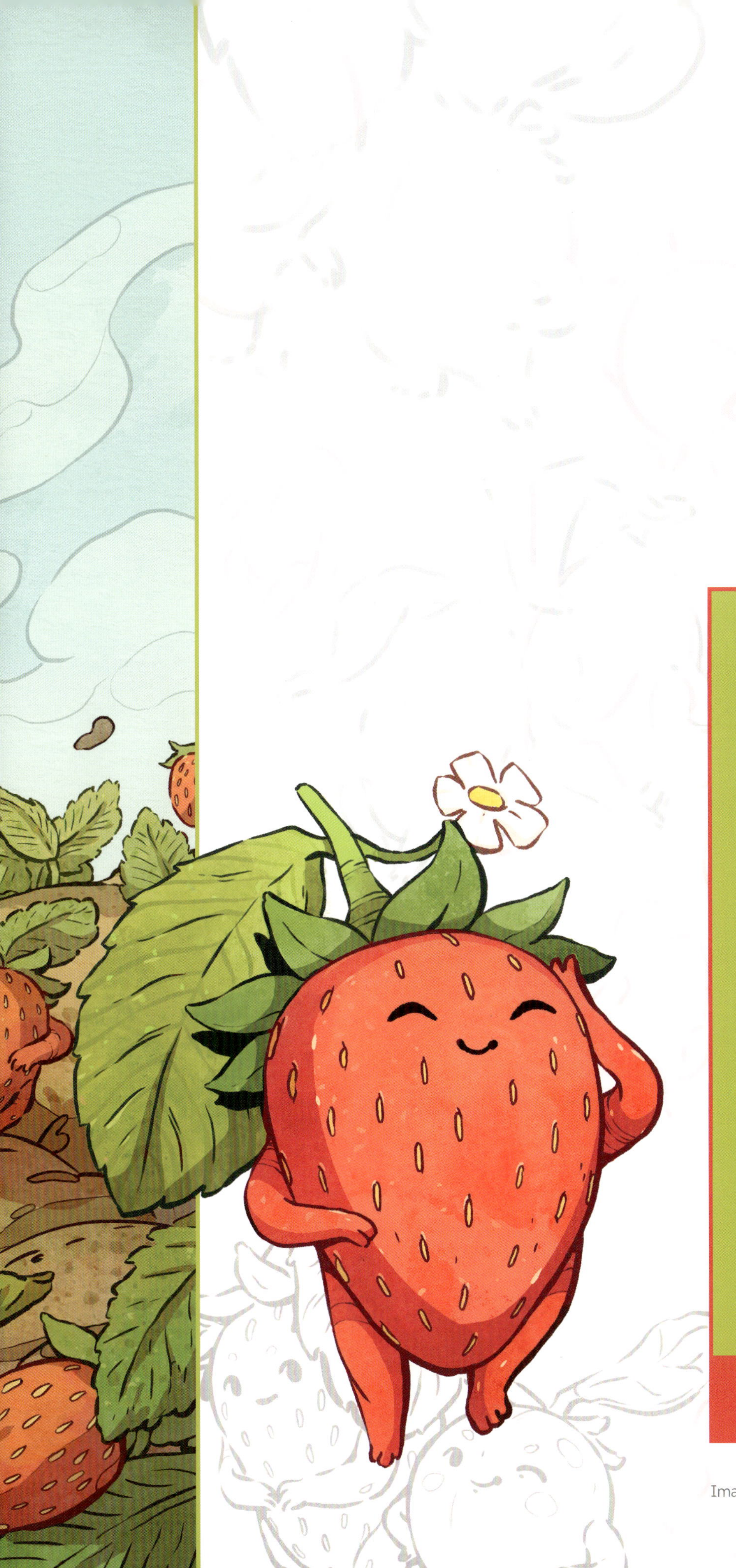

50%

of net profits donated
TO CHARITY

In 2022, 3dtotal Publishing became successful enough to make a pledge to donate **50% of its net profits to charity**. This continues to be possible due to the incredible support from all our customers, employees, and partners. At the time of printing, we have donated over $1.62 million (USD) to charity.

We focus our giving on three charitable areas: **environmental**, **humanitarian**, and **animal welfare**. We use organizations such as Effective Altruism and Founders Pledge to guide who we help within these causes. Some ways of doing good are over 100 times more effective than others, so donating this way hugely increases the impact of our contributions.

See **3dtotal.com/charity** for full details.

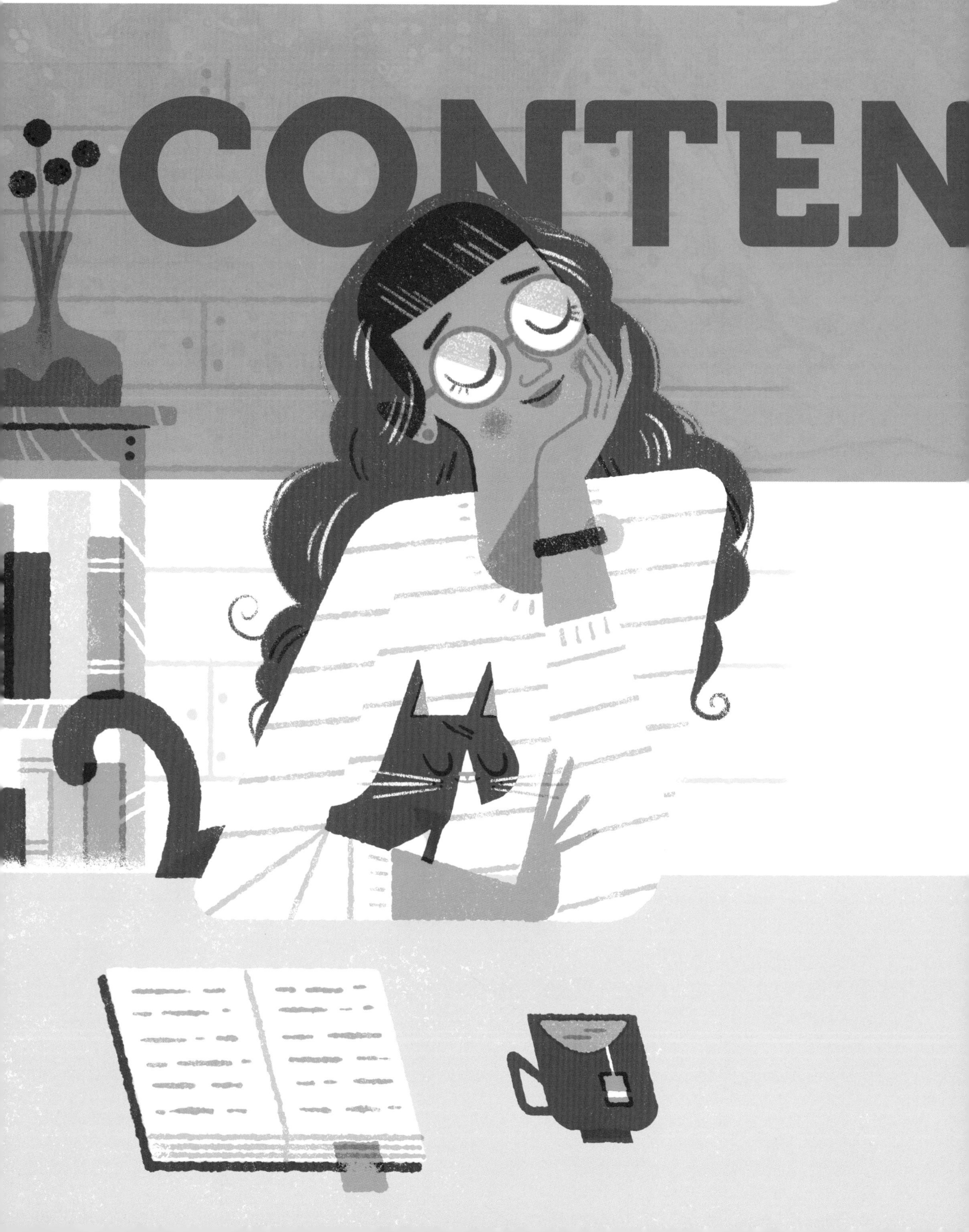

CONTEN

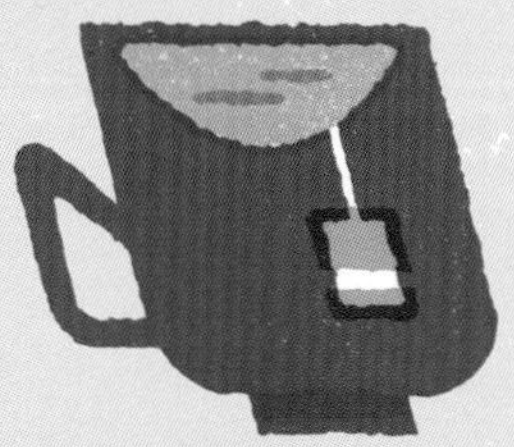

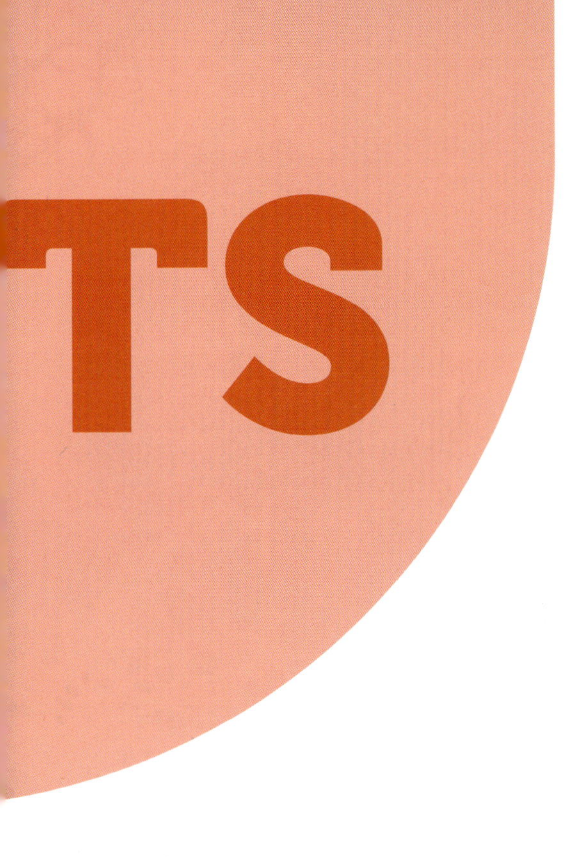

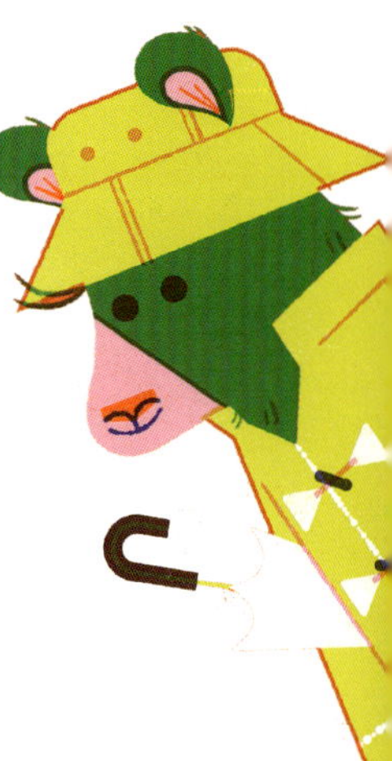

6 INTRODUCTION

160 CONTRIBUTORS

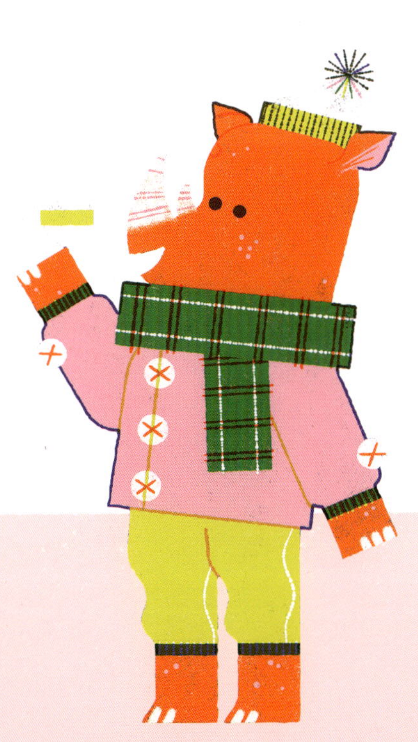

INTROD

Image © Lydia Nichols

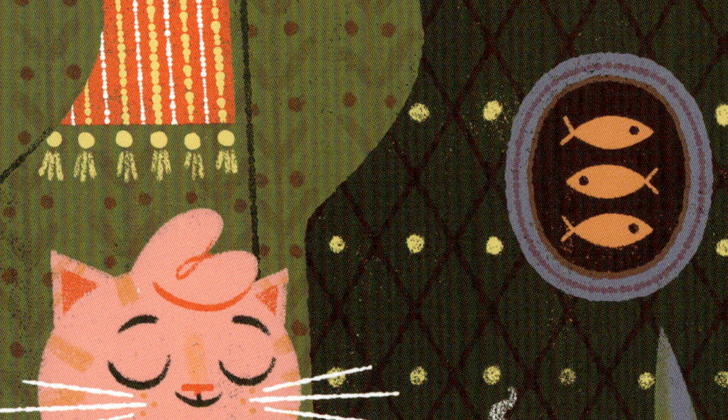

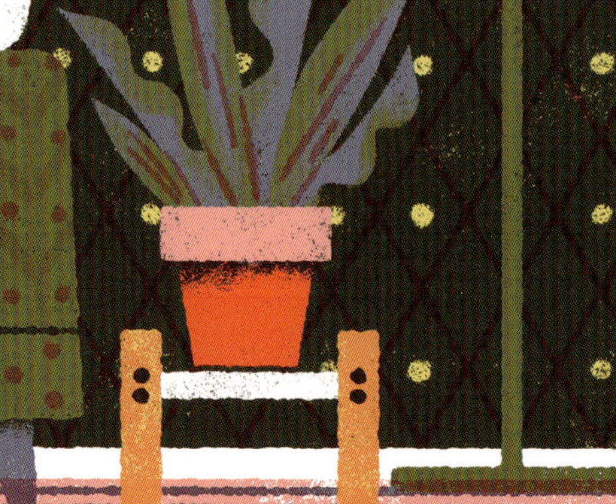

UCTION

Welcome to *Character Design Essentials*, a collection of the best tutorials from the pages of *Character Design Quarterly*. For almost a decade, *CDQ* has featured work from hundreds of professional artists, working across film, TV, video games, and beyond. With so many wonderful characters to choose from, the hardest part of putting together this book has been narrowing down the selection.

We'll start by taking a deep dive into the core disciplines that underpin any good design. From creating early sketches and understanding shape language, through to mastering colour and narrative, and on to finalizing the final design, we'll break down every aspect of creating fun, exciting, and memorable characters. We'll then bring everything together with a series of complete, in-depth tutorials, showing you every step involved along the way.

Whether you're a complete beginner or a *CDQ* veteran, the carefully curated and remixed tutorials within will be sure to inspire you to create your own fantastic characters. And who knows, maybe one day you'll feature in *Character Design Quarterly*, too!

EDITOR, SAM DRAPER

SHAPE LAN

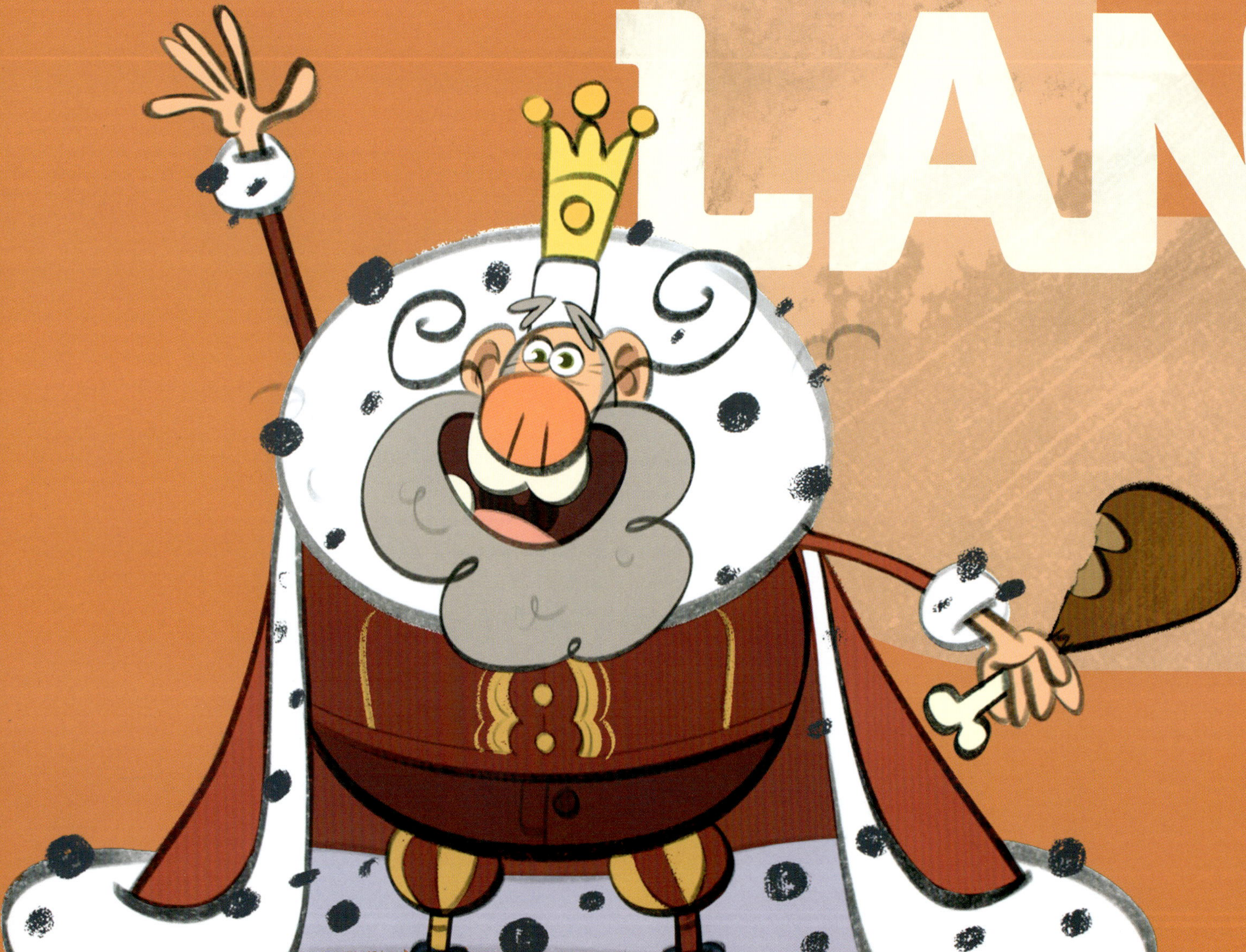

GUAGE

Speaking in shapes

TOM HÄNNI

An elaborated shape language is crucial for crafting character designs. It enables you to develop interest, tell clearer stories, and therefore develop more believable characters.

Here are some of my design methods to explain how you can improve your overall shape language and create more impactful and expressive designs.

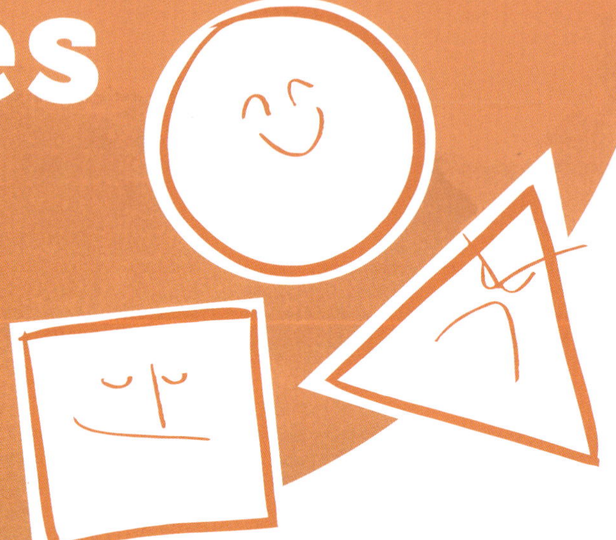

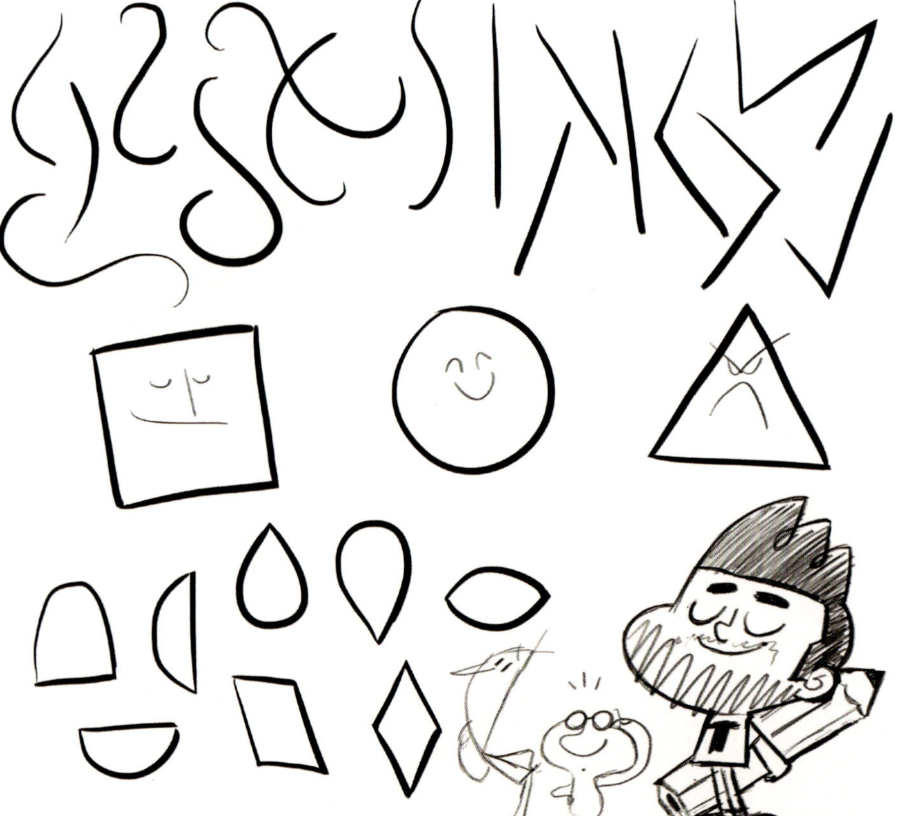

THE BASICS

Let's start with the basics of shape design: there are curves, straight lines, angular lines, the basic geometric shapes and, of course, plenty of variations in between.

To ensure a design is balanced it is crucial to use a mixture of shapes and lines. A well-balanced combination of forms builds the foundation of every good character design.

THE POWER OF IMAGINATION

Once you have really figured out who your character is going to be and what adjectives suit them best, you need to use your imagination. When you have some vague ideas in your mind, sketch them out roughly until you get closer and closer to the appearance you visualized. It's kind of like a search using your mind's eye.

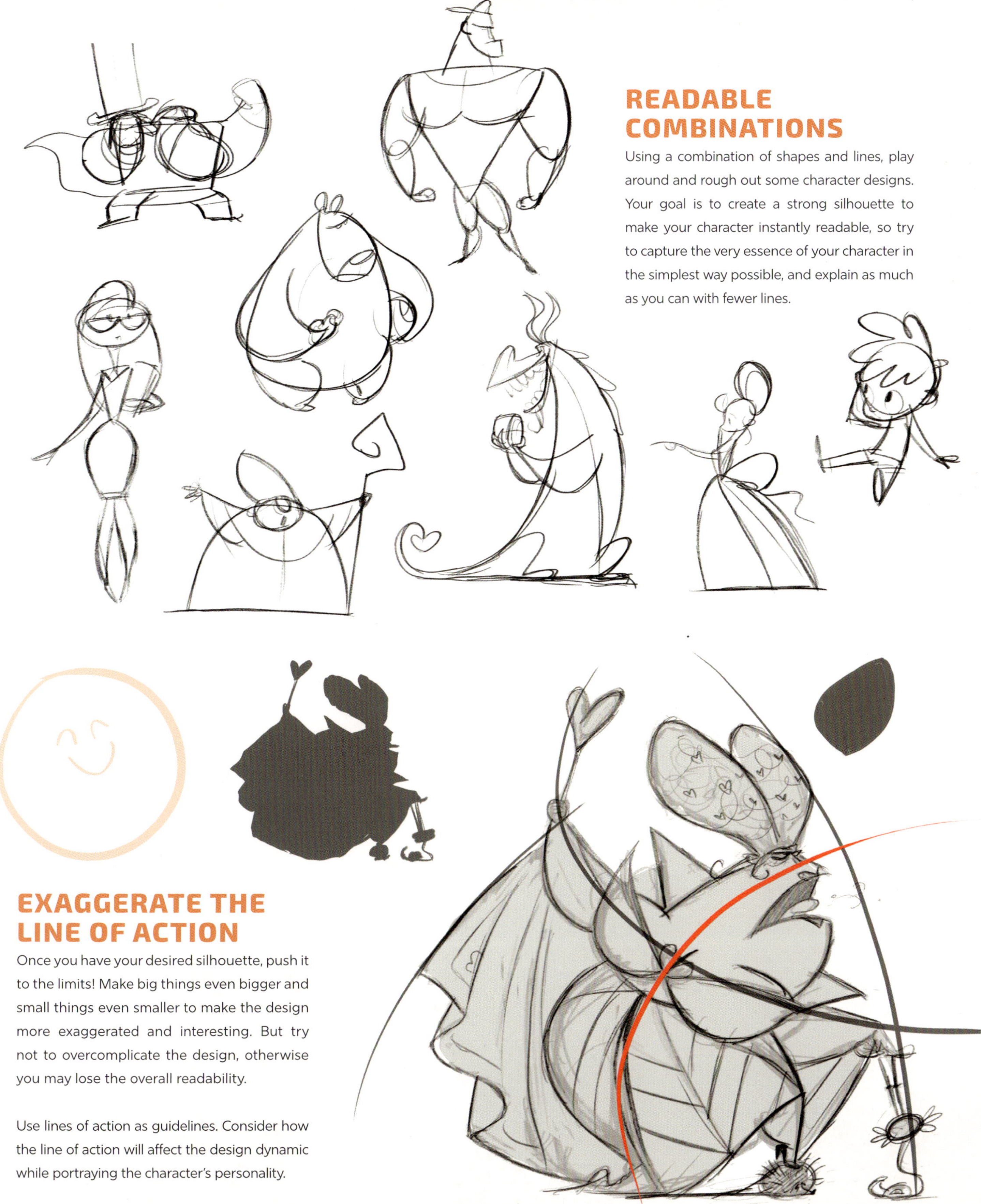

READABLE COMBINATIONS

Using a combination of shapes and lines, play around and rough out some character designs. Your goal is to create a strong silhouette to make your character instantly readable, so try to capture the very essence of your character in the simplest way possible, and explain as much as you can with fewer lines.

EXAGGERATE THE LINE OF ACTION

Once you have your desired silhouette, push it to the limits! Make big things even bigger and small things even smaller to make the design more exaggerated and interesting. But try not to overcomplicate the design, otherwise you may lose the overall readability.

Use lines of action as guidelines. Consider how the line of action will affect the design dynamic while portraying the character's personality.

THE EBB & FLOW OF LINE WORK

Pay attention to your lines and consider how they flow; you want to aim for a combination of curvy and straight lines that flow together nicely. Don't forget to break them up in some places and build in strong corners and edges to give your design more contrast and dynamism, and automatically develop more interest. Oppose vertical lines to horizontal ones, and angles to arcs, to build up further drama.

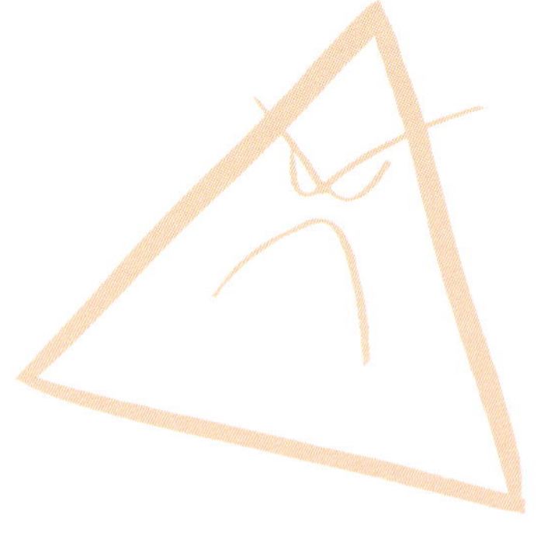

ALL ABOUT THE CONCEPT

While mastering techniques and tools is important, I would advise concentrating on your concept first. Think about adjectives that suit your character's personality and story and make sure they are clearly reflected in your design. Consider how you will tell the story and concept behind your character to the viewer. From the moment you define your character's silhouette and shape, it's all about acting and finding the best pose.

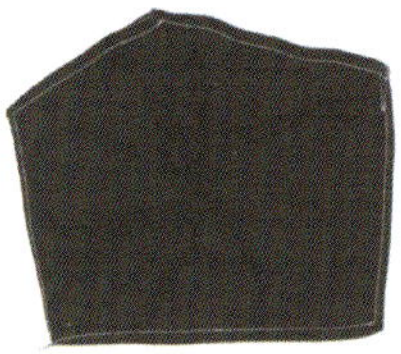

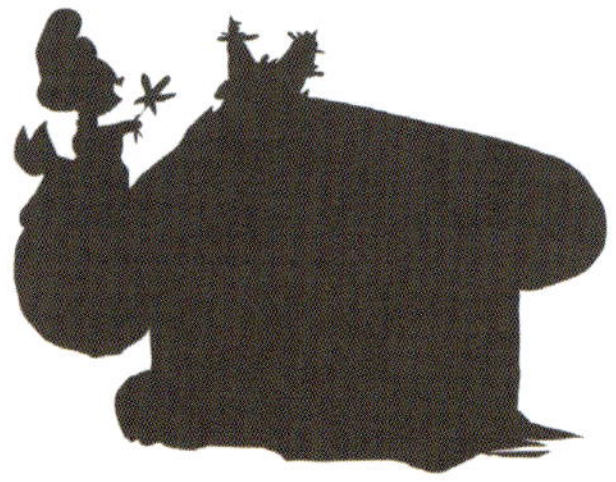

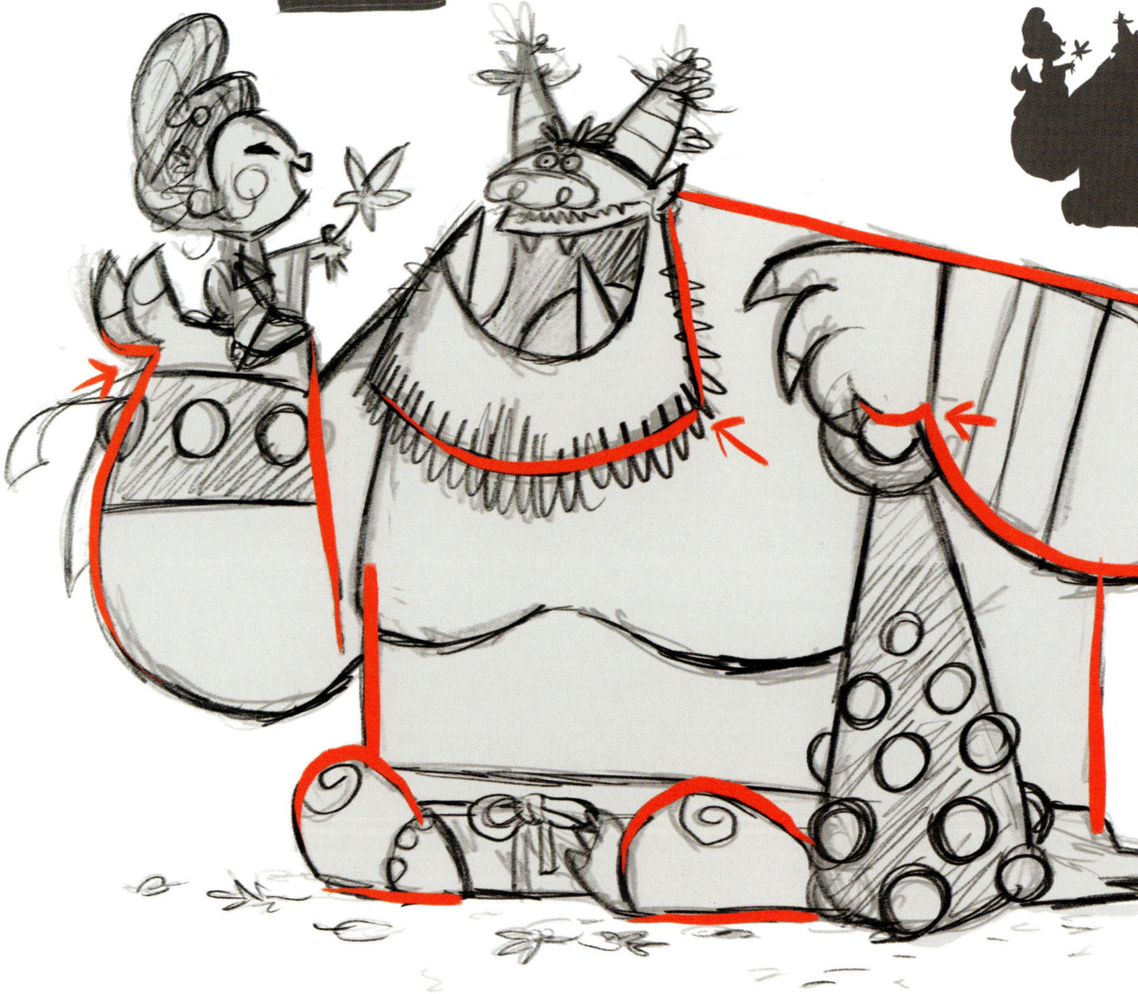

LOOSEN UP

If you're feeling a bit stuck or uninspired, a great exercise for generating fresh ideas for character designs is by doodling quick, loose shapes, then bringing the forms to life with the addition of a few basic features. Don't overthink – simply draw whatever comes into your head when you see the shape. You might create new faces, creatures, or objects – your imagination is the limit.

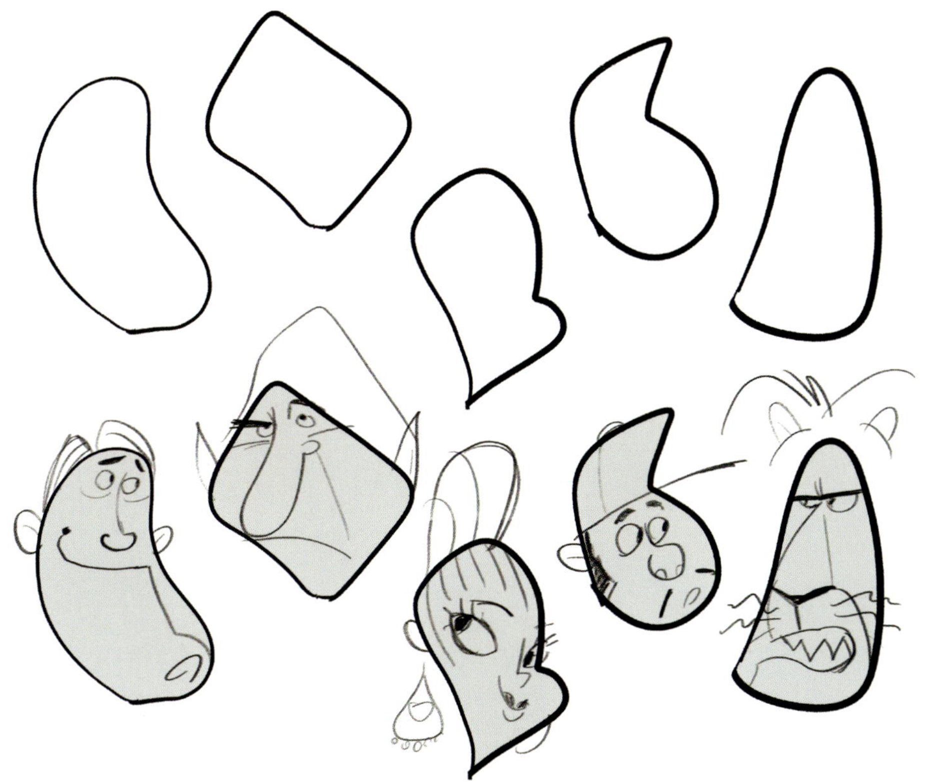

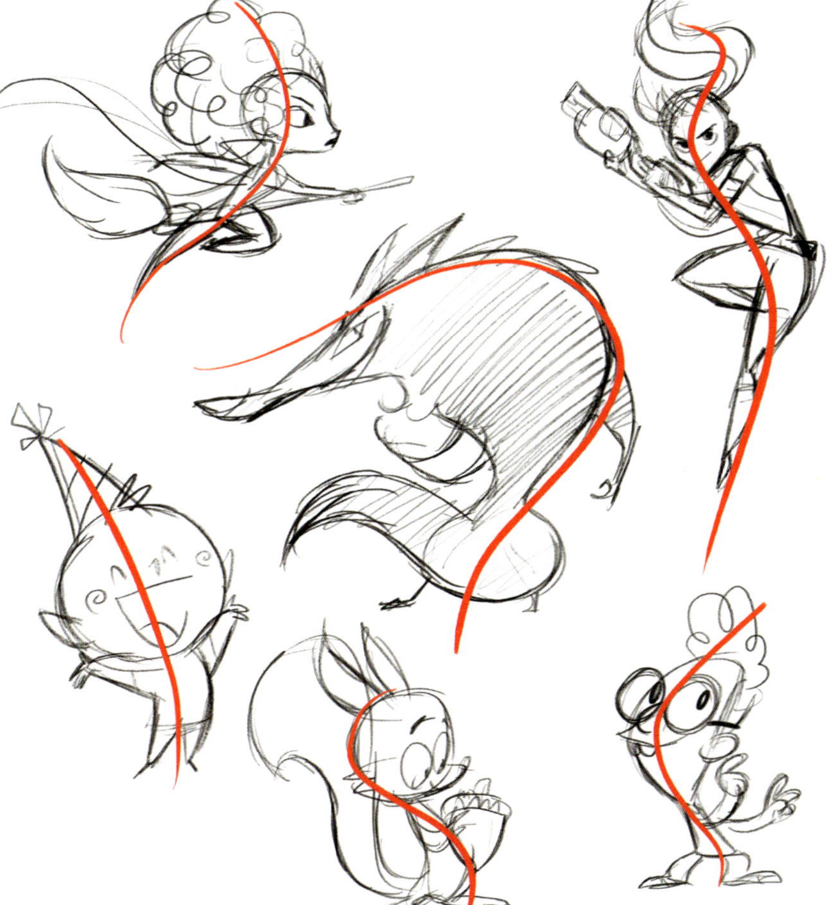

The same technique works with lines of action. Loosely draw several dynamic curves and use them as your lines of action to build and create effective poses for your characters. Again, it will give you new ways to present and shape your designs.

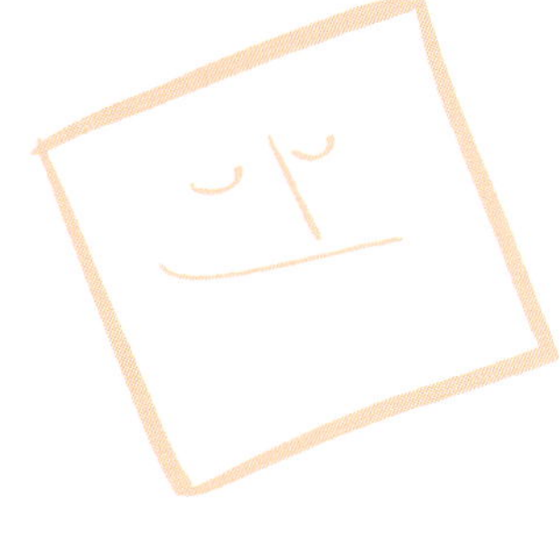

'Don't overthink – simply draw whatever comes into your head'

Bat to basics

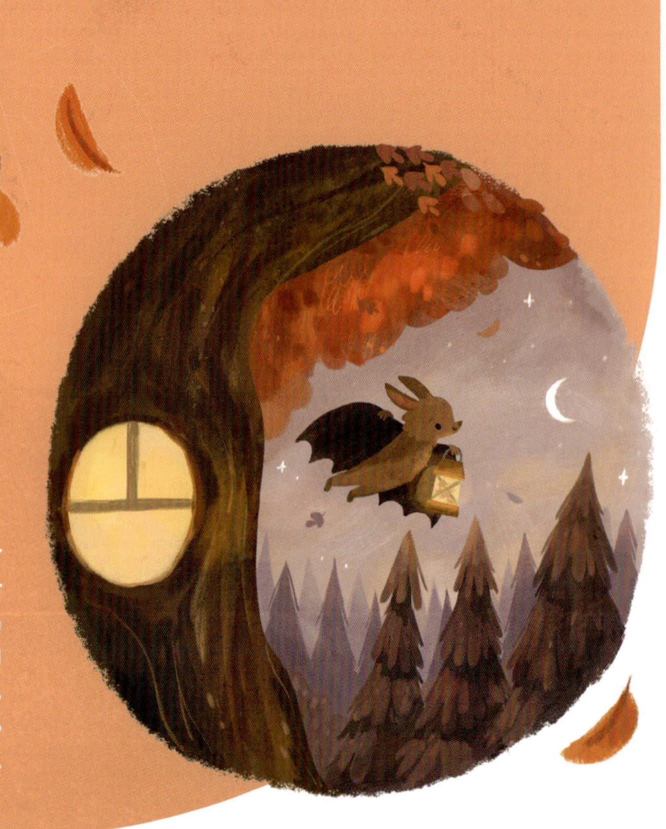

RAAHAT KADUJI

There's so much fun to be had in imagining and designing a character for children to enjoy. Let's take a closer look at how I designed the character Bat from my debut children's book, *I'm Not Scary*. I'll walk you through the process, starting simply, introducing emotion and personality, and experimenting with colour to help convey the character's narrative. I usually begin with pencil sketches in my sketchbook before moving to Photoshop for further design development and the final digital illustration.

SIMPLE SHAPES

For a solid foundation, start with basic shapes. These can be transformed into anything, but at their core they are easy for children to recognize. Think which shape best represents your character. Are they smooth and gentle like a circle, or are they pointy and sharp like a triangle? My character Bat is gentle and kind, so he's rounded in shape.

'For a solid foundation, start with basic shapes'

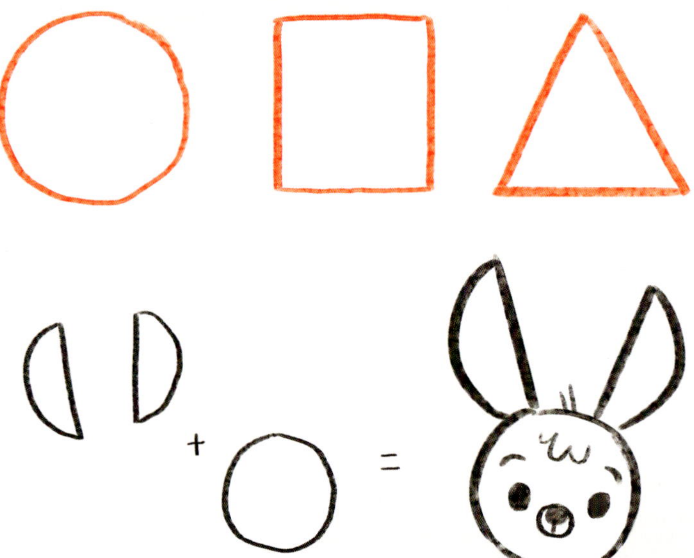

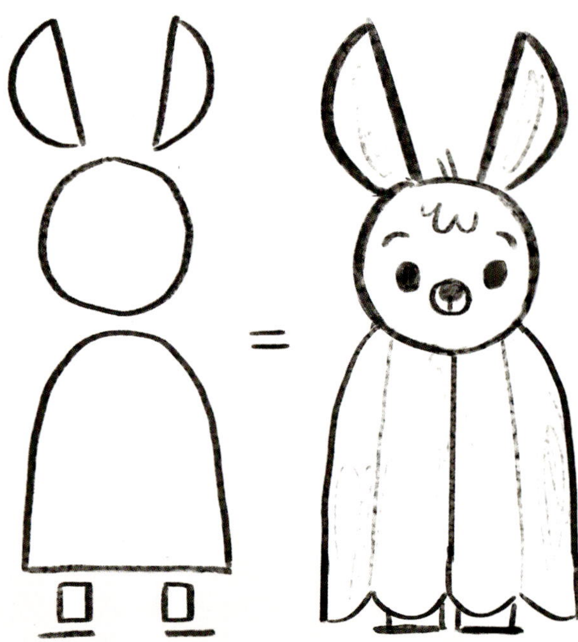

CHILD-LIKE PROPORTIONS

Characters don't need to be realistic. Exaggerate or simplify their proportions to make them more playful. A big head and shorter limbs will make your character appear younger and more familiar to an audience of children. You can apply this technique to both human and animal characters.

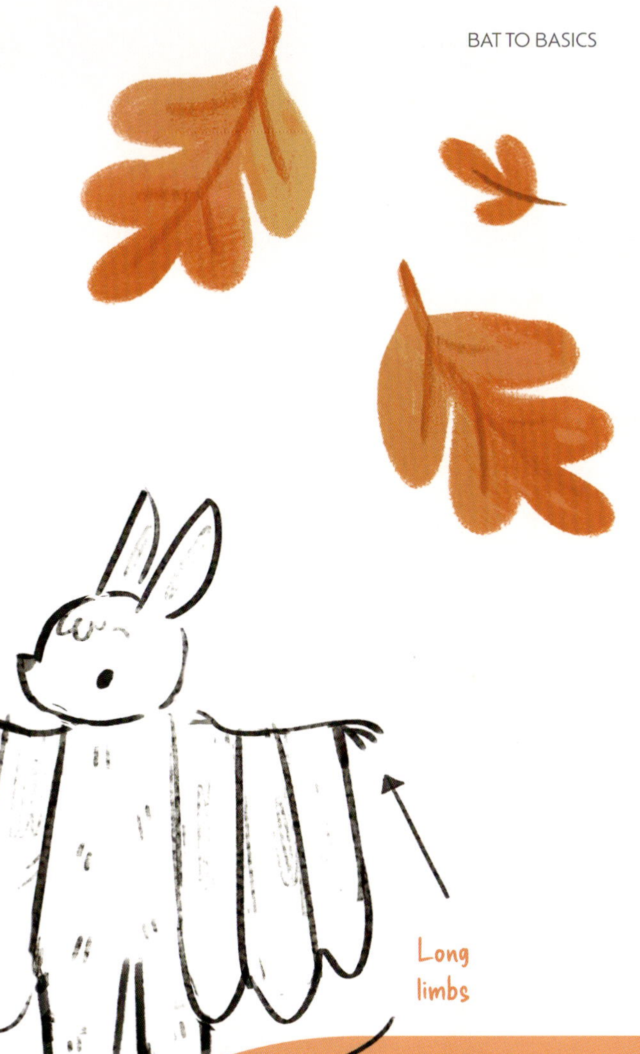

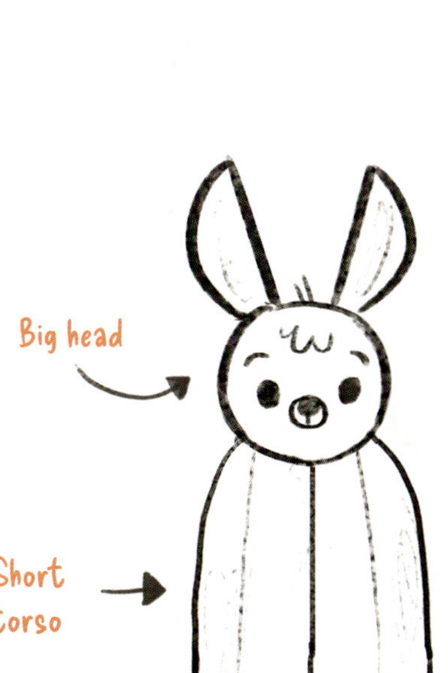

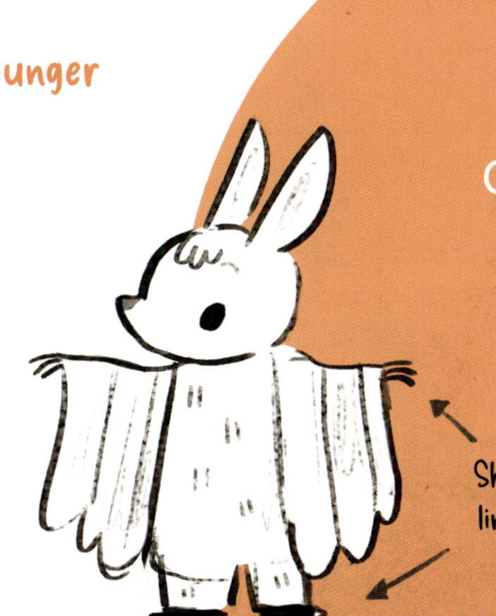

> 'Characters don't need to be realistic'

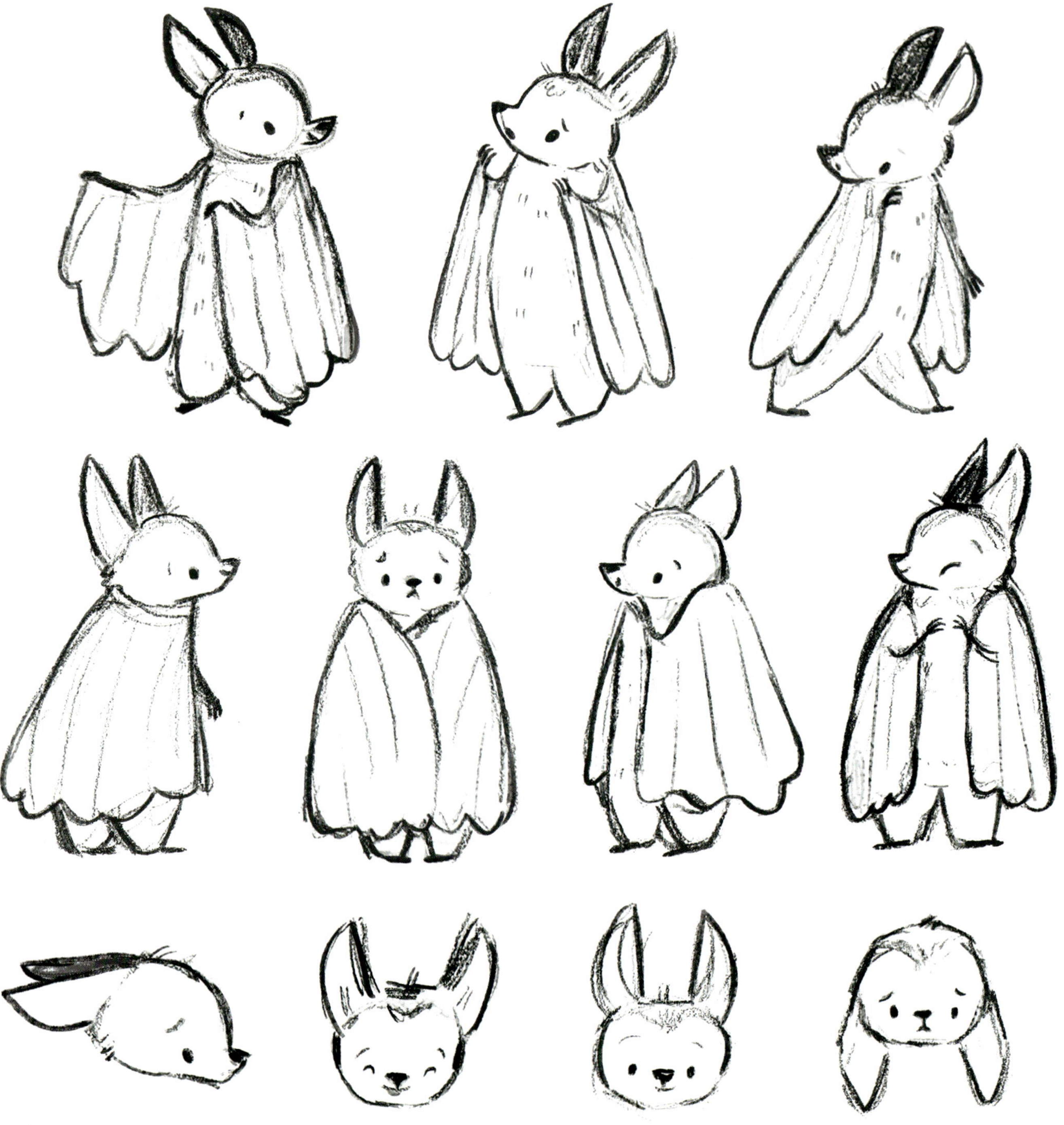

EXPRESSIVENESS

Begin to explore different facial expressions and poses to introduce feeling. It's important to explore a whole range of emotions to establish your character's nature. These are sketches of Bat from my sketchbook. Notice how expressions make him appear more animated and alive as his shape continues to evolve.

PROPS & PERSONALITY

Become familiar with your character's narrative and really dig into who they are. Consider their likes and dislikes, their hobbies and interests, and where they live. Think about items, clothing, or possessions that you might see them with. Bat lives in a forest and enjoys baking, so I've sketched some baked goods, berries, and a lantern that he carries to see at night.

'Become familiar with your character's narrative and really dig into who they are'

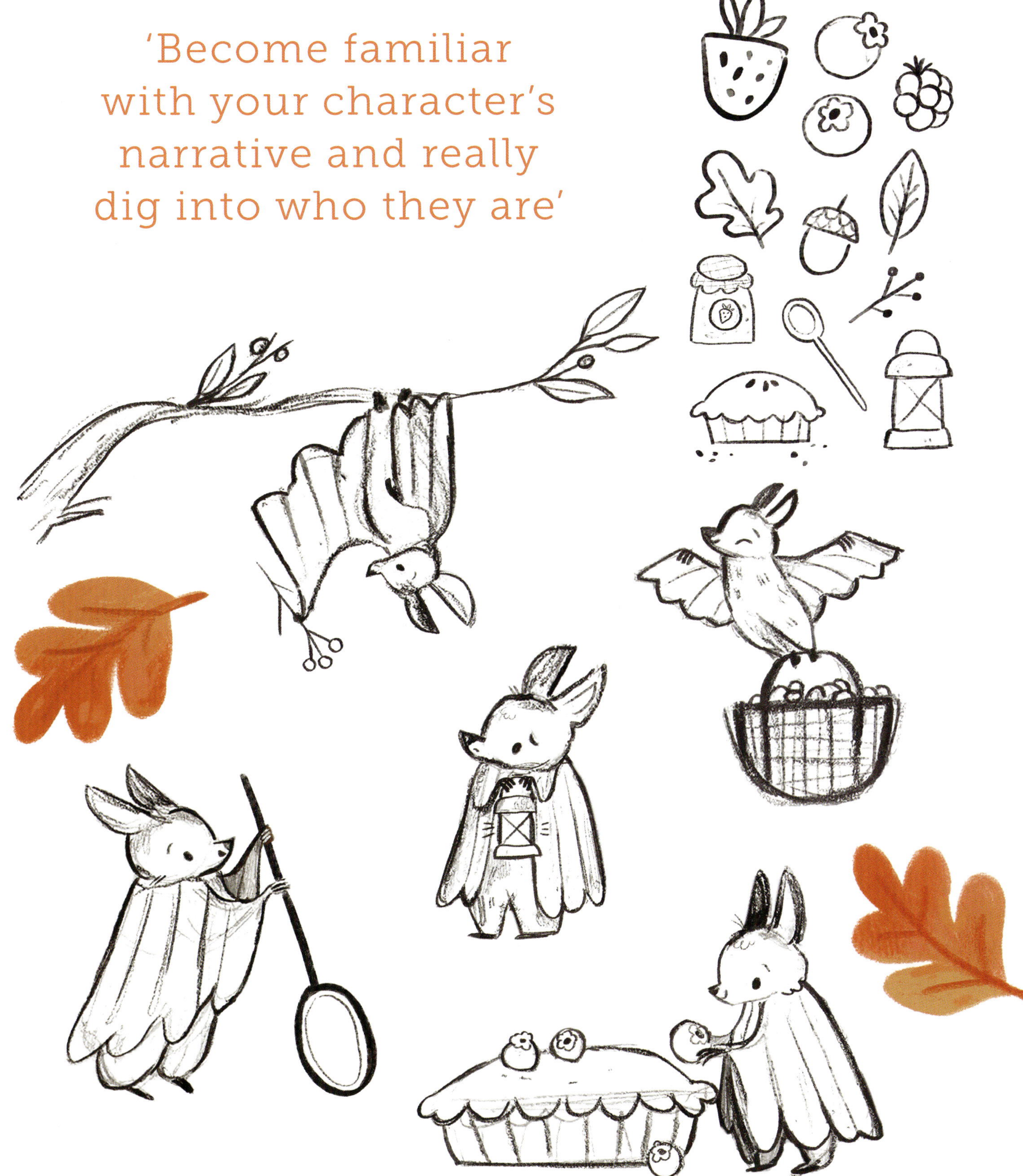

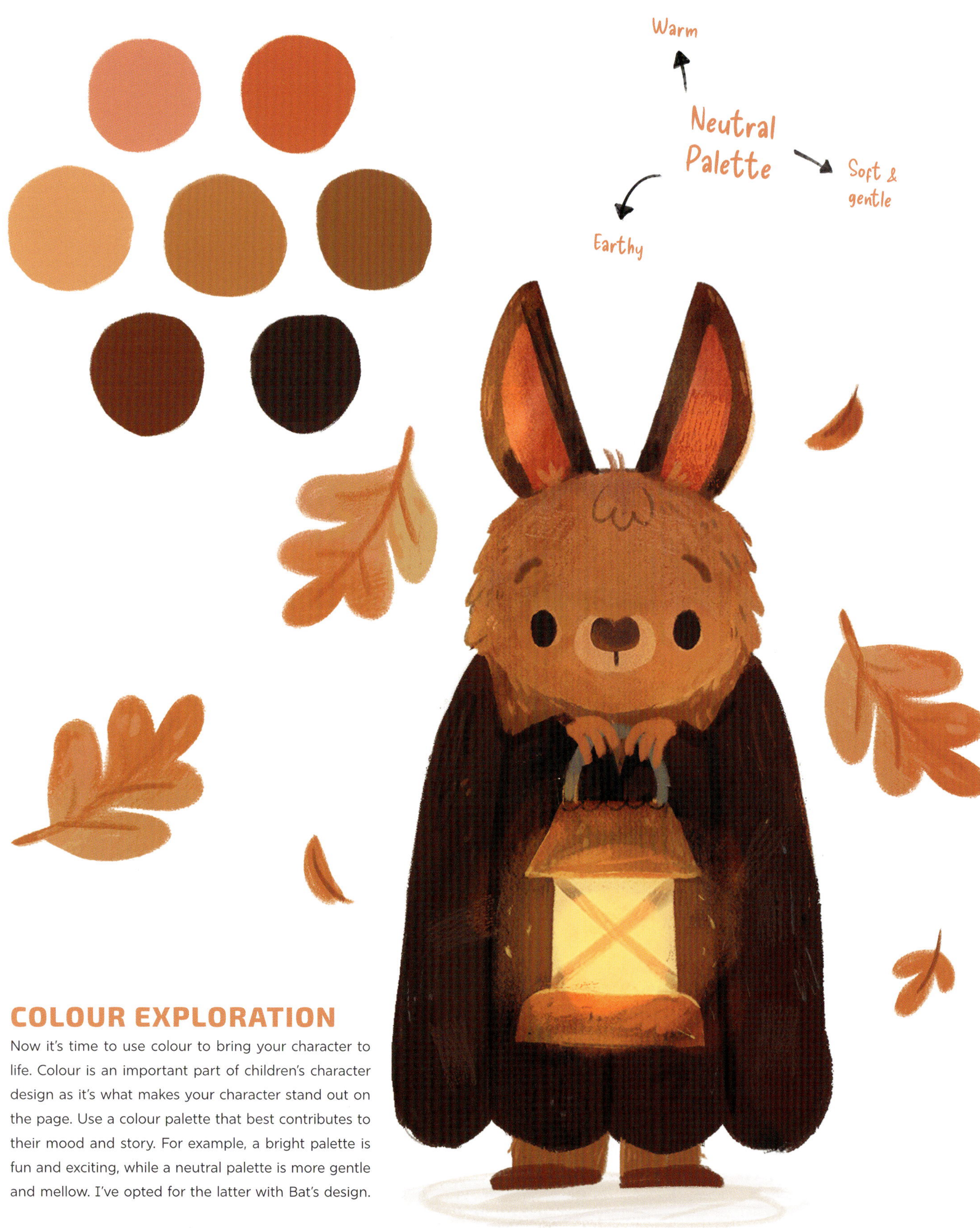

COLOUR EXPLORATION

Now it's time to use colour to bring your character to life. Colour is an important part of children's character design as it's what makes your character stand out on the page. Use a colour palette that best contributes to their mood and story. For example, a bright palette is fun and exciting, while a neutral palette is more gentle and mellow. I've opted for the latter with Bat's design.

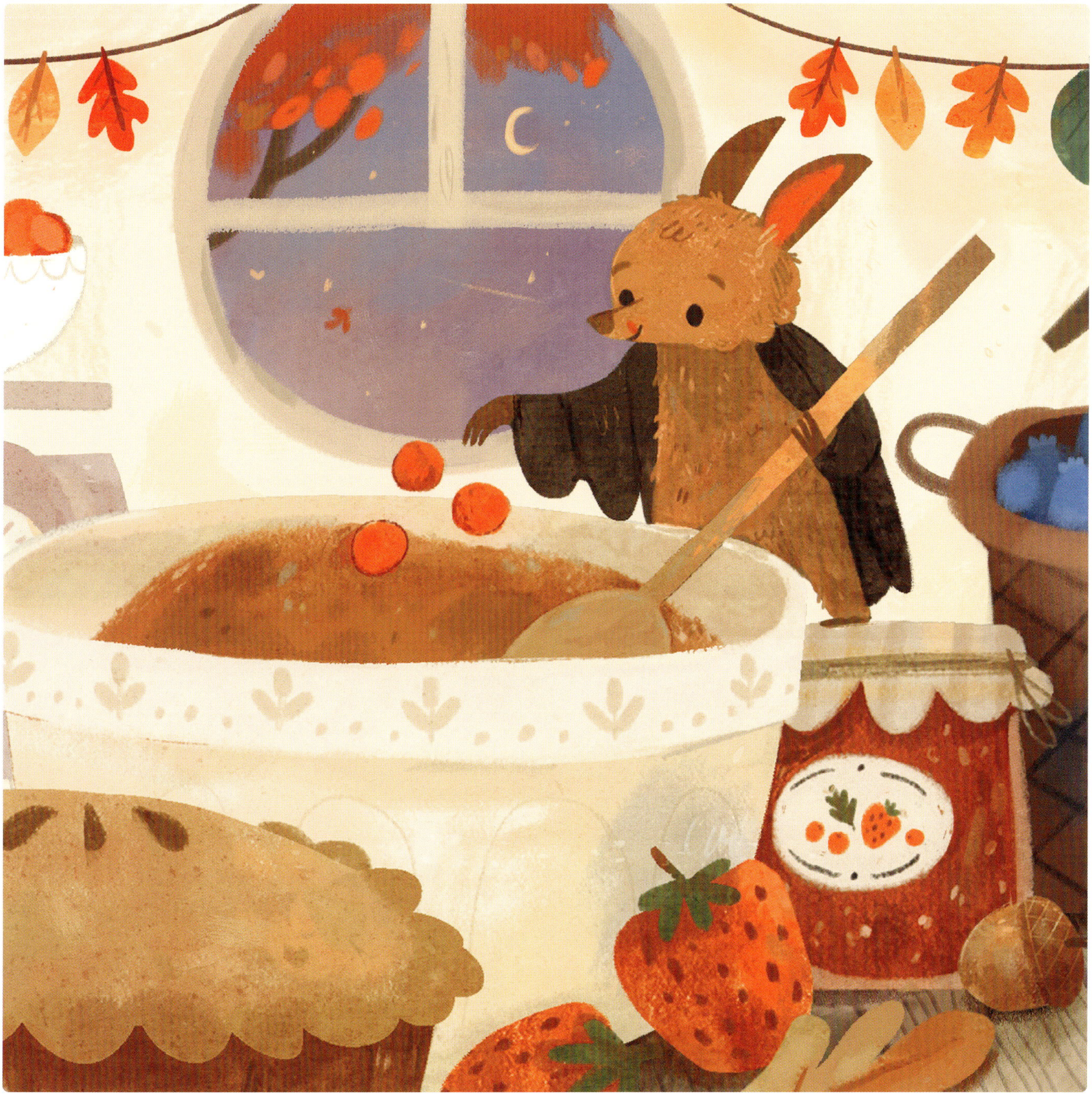

BRING IT ALL TOGETHER

Once you've got to know your character, their personality, and their appearance, you can go one step further. Drop them into a scene and show them interacting with their world. You can include some possessions or have them engaging in their favourite hobby to truly bring them to life.

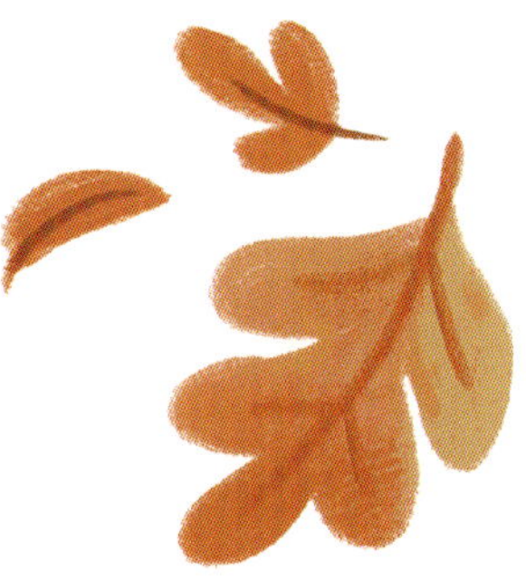

Splendorous shapes

MELANIE PEÑALOZA TIKHONOVA

Every aspect of a character's design works together to create a unique personality. In this article, I will talk about how using specific shapes can help to tell a character's story. We will create three characters with variations for each one, to see how different shapes influence their design. I will be using a paper cut-out method first, and then move to a digital format. Let's get started.

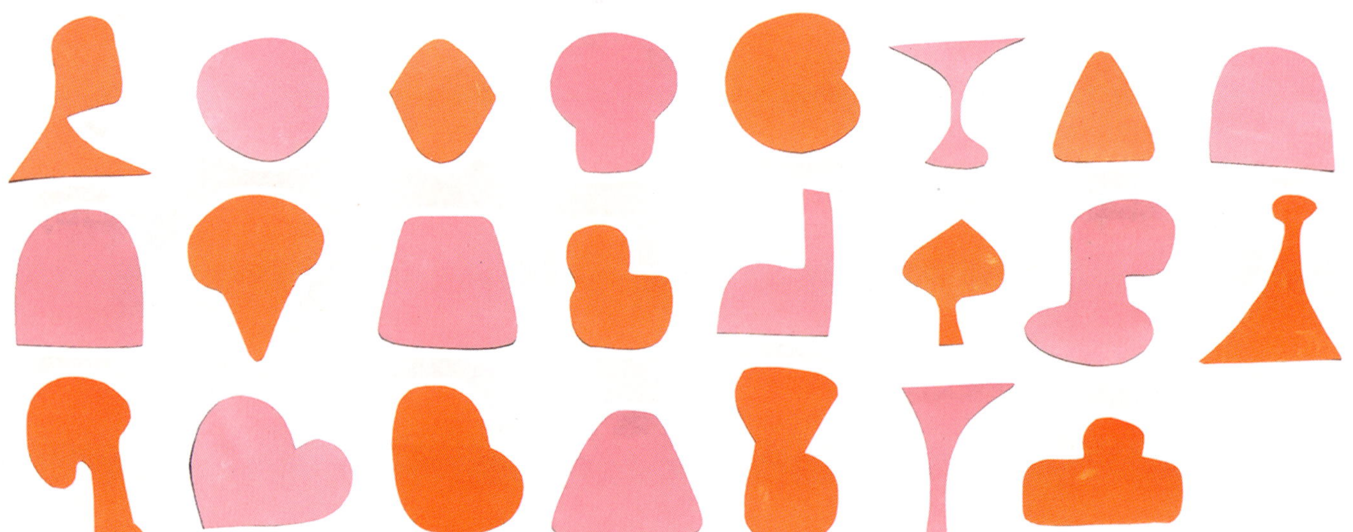

PREP ON PAPER

Start by grabbing paper and drawing all kinds of random shapes – anything you can imagine. Cut out the shapes and paste them onto a separate piece of paper, take a picture, and bring them into a graphics editor, such as Photoshop or Procreate.

A similar method to the paper cut-out technique used in this article is the silhouette method. You can begin creating characters by blocking out body types with a single fill, then lowering the opacity to sketch on top of them.

SHAPE THEIR PERSONALITY

Think about your characters' personalities and build a base from the shapes you have. In general, circles feel friendly and approachable, squares feel sturdy and grounded, and triangles feel energetic and dangerous. When mixed together, they can create more complex personalities. Add more information to your base shapes, such as suggestions of costumes and limbs. Explore and see what you can come up with – there are no wrong answers at this early stage.

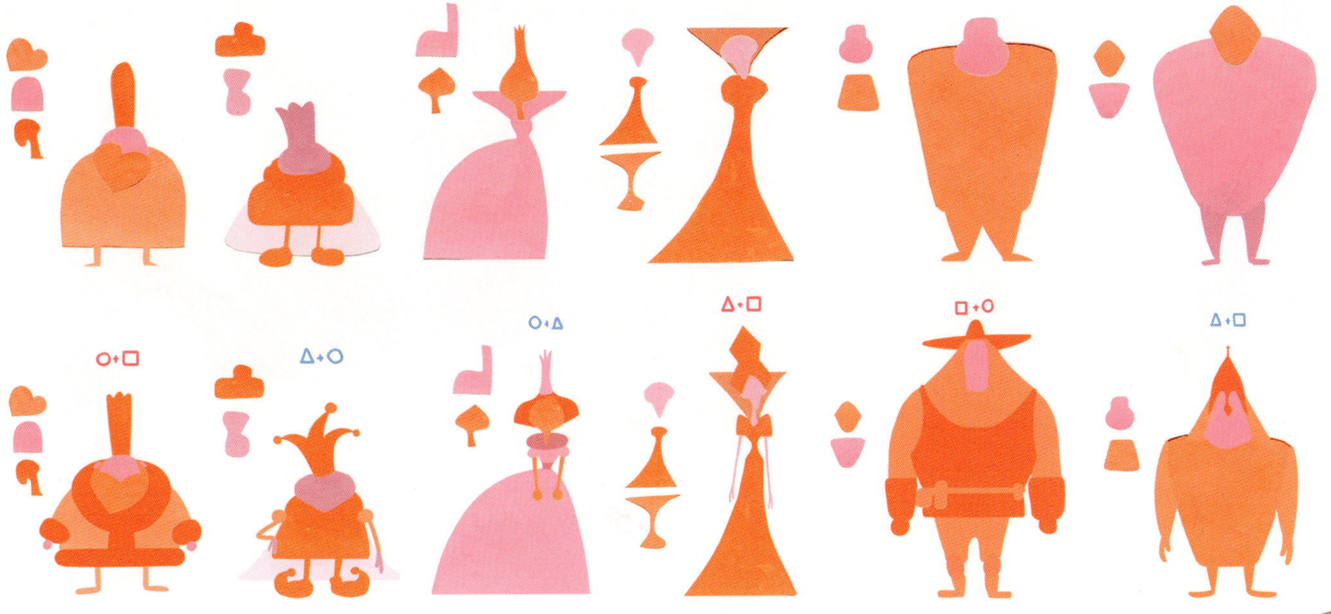

START SKETCHING

Use your base shapes as a guide and begin to sketch out your characters while thinking about their personality. Change their pose and proportions, and exaggerate shapes as much as you like. You can also adjust the major shapes used if you want to convey a different personality. Once you are happy with your designs, it's time to start adding line and colour to your characters.

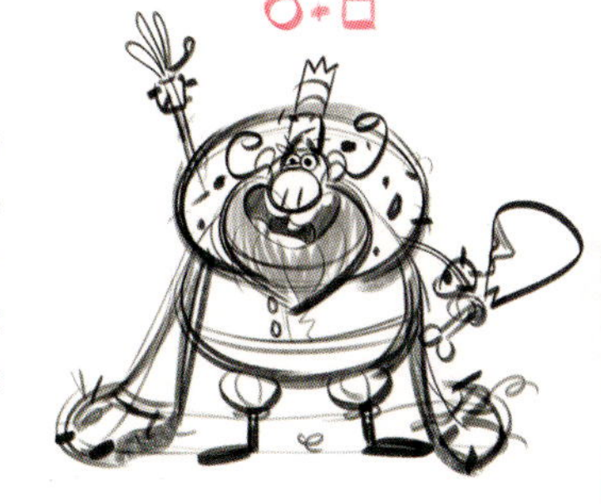

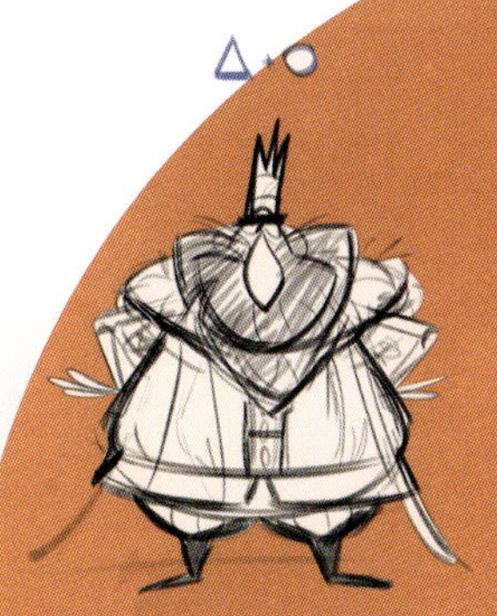

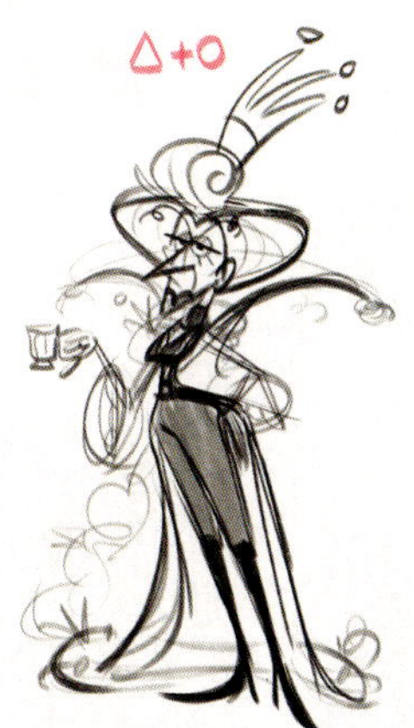

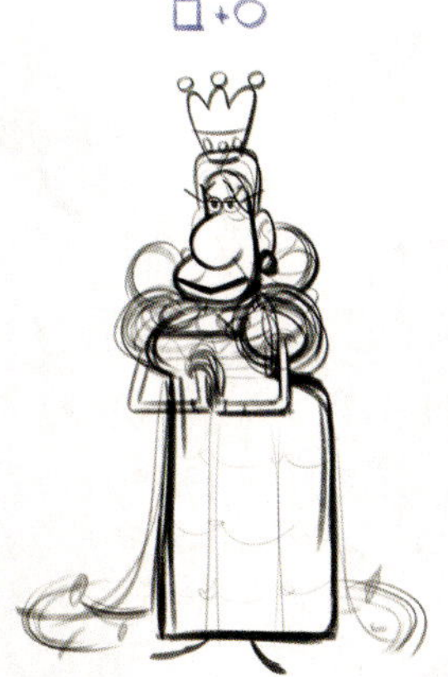

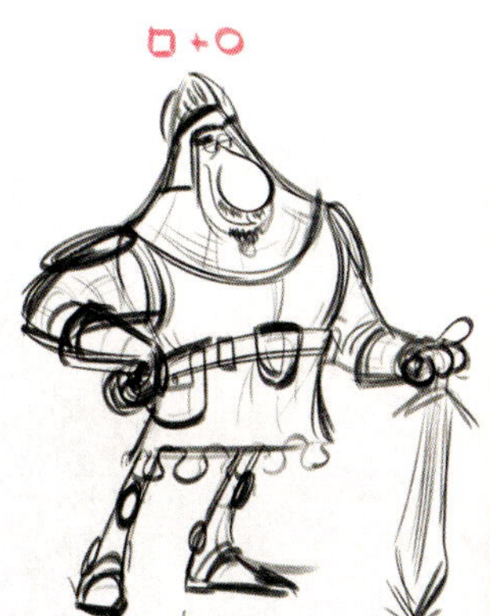

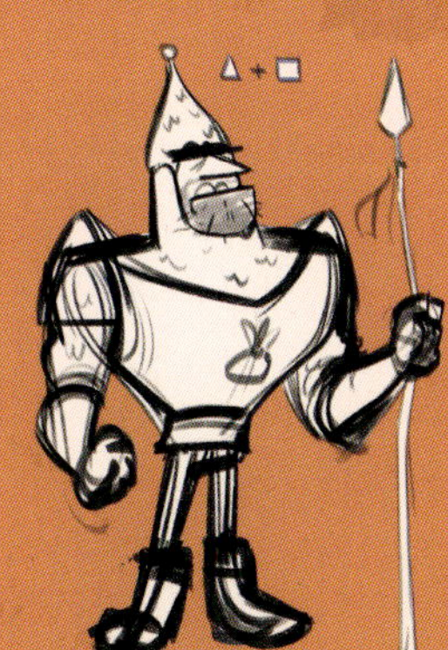

The King

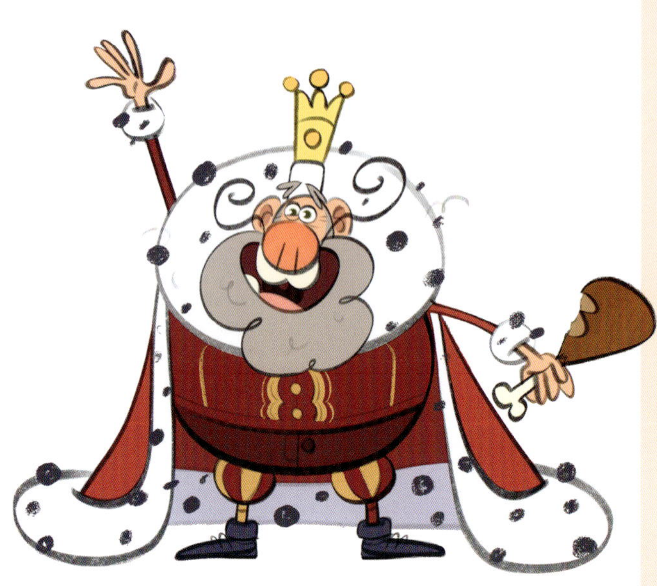

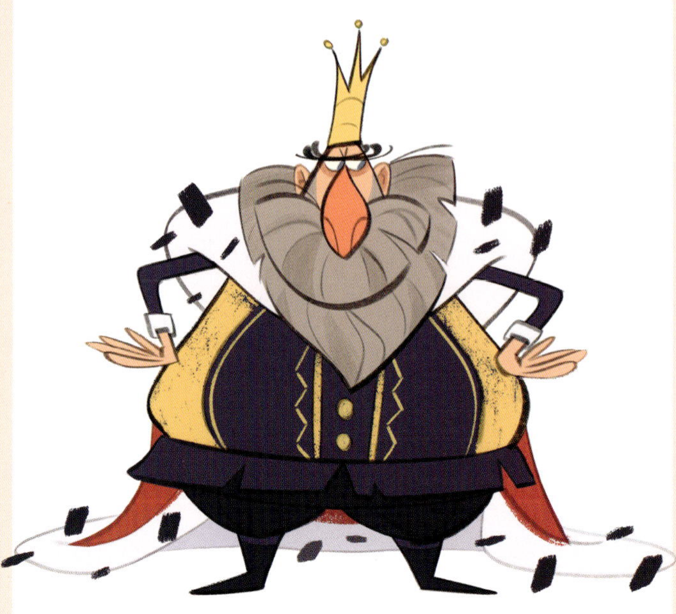

In this design, the triangular shapes give the king a more devious look, while the circular shapes soften his character, making him come across as a little inept.

The Queen

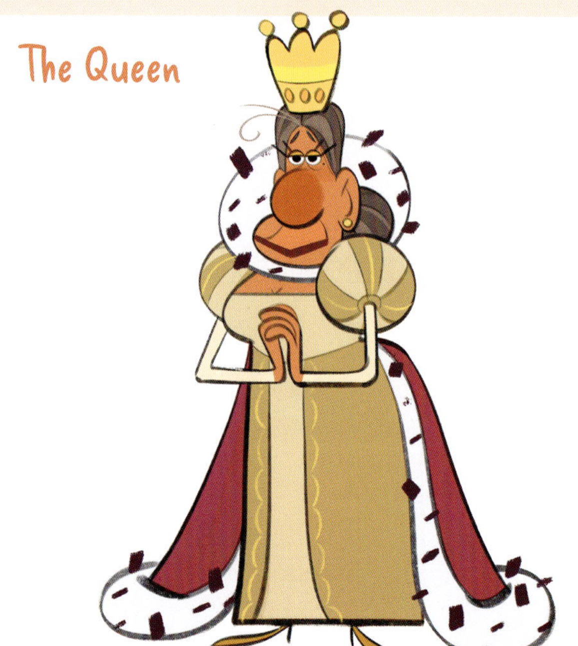

This queen uses rectangular and circular shapes to demonstrate her motherly and grounded nature. The rectangular design conveys stability and the circles radiate warmth.

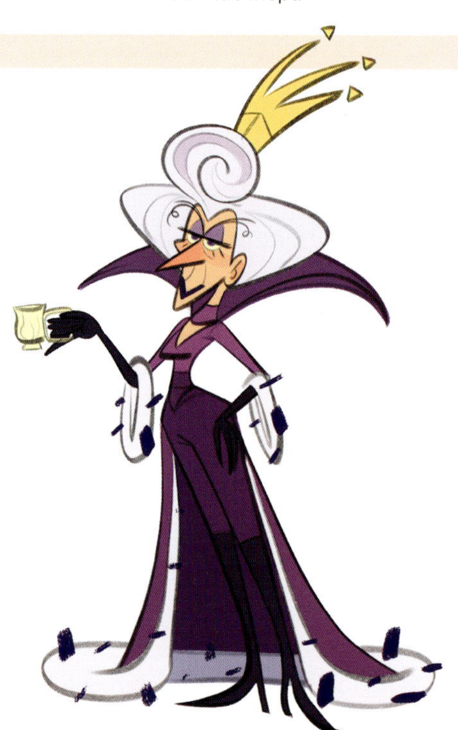

By focusing on triangular shapes, this version of the queen feels dangerous and sly. There are still some circular shapes here, to prevent the design from coming across as too evil and unlikeable.

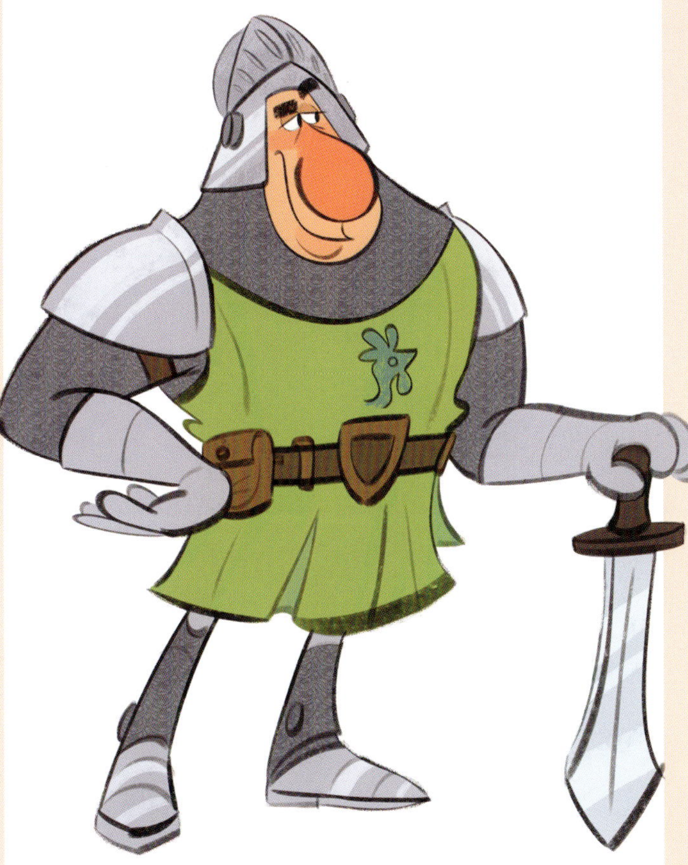

For the knight, I've used square and circle shapes, with the emphasis on the squares. This is to show his strong and sturdy side, with the circular elements added to soften the design, making him seem friendly.

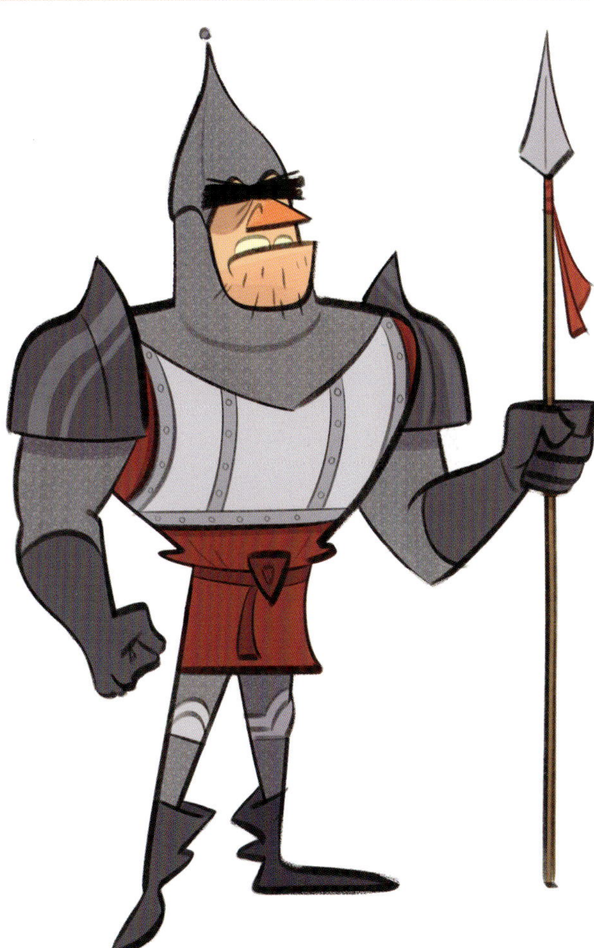

Triangles again add an unpredictable and dangerous element to a design. This guard still has square shapes at his core for stability and strength, but the triangles create a less friendly overall look than the circular knight.

INSPIRATION IS EVERYWHERE

A great way to create your characters is by observing life. Sketch in the café, draw at the zoo – look around your surroundings for shapes and objects you can turn into characters. Try new mediums, carry around a mini sketchbook, and just have fun!

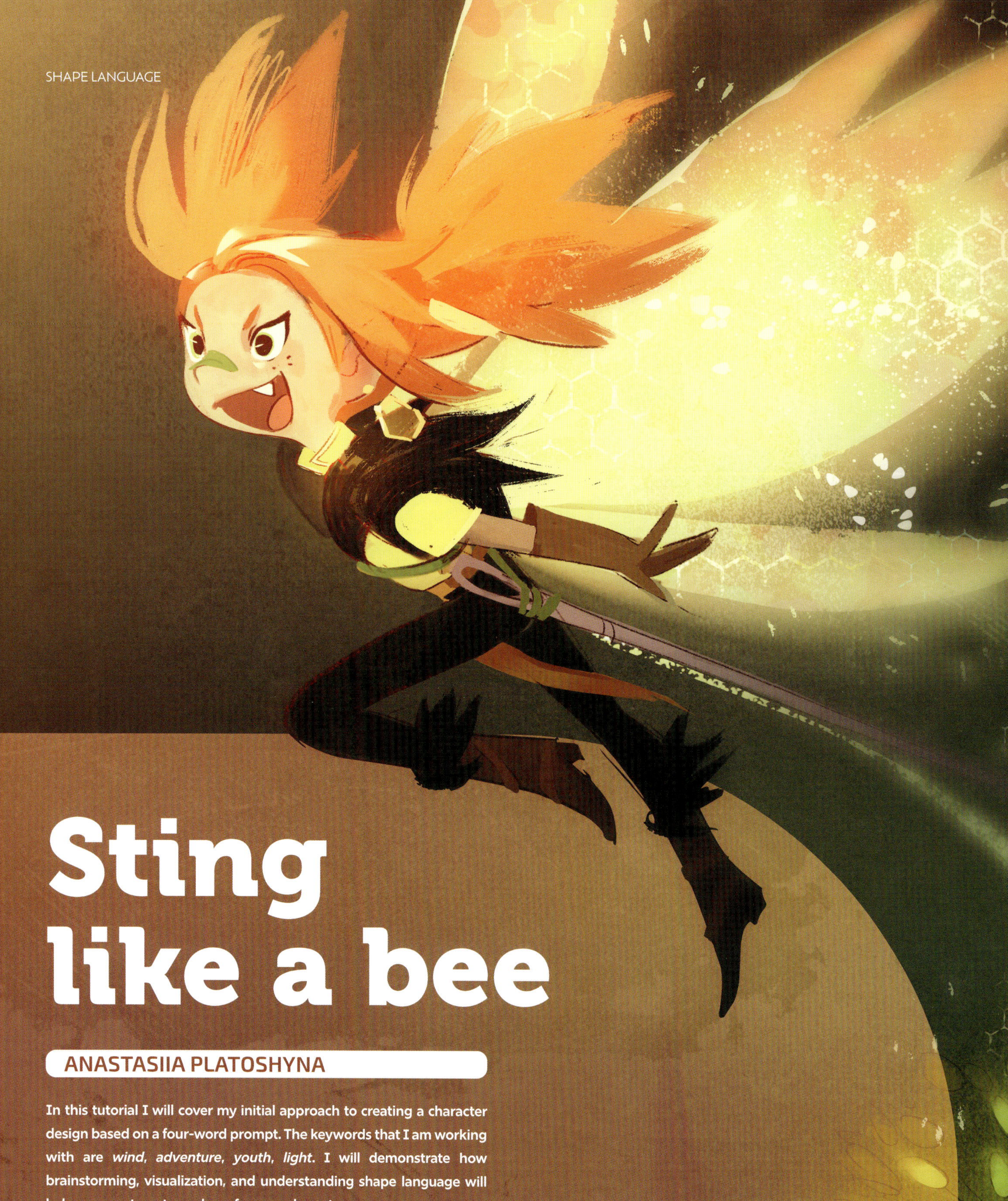

Sting like a bee

ANASTASIIA PLATOSHYNA

In this tutorial I will cover my initial approach to creating a character design based on a four-word prompt. The keywords that I am working with are *wind*, *adventure*, *youth*, *light*. I will demonstrate how brainstorming, visualization, and understanding shape language will help you create a strong base for your character.

BRAINSTORMING

Start by breaking down the prompt you're working from. I use sticky notes because they make it very easy to quickly cycle through my ideas and any associations that come to mind when looking at each of the four words. There are no wrong answers or bad choices – it can be anything that pops into your head. Once you put your associations and abstract thoughts onto paper, you will start noticing some interesting combinations.

Next, narrow these ideas down to those that appeal the most. There are so many variations now – where to start?

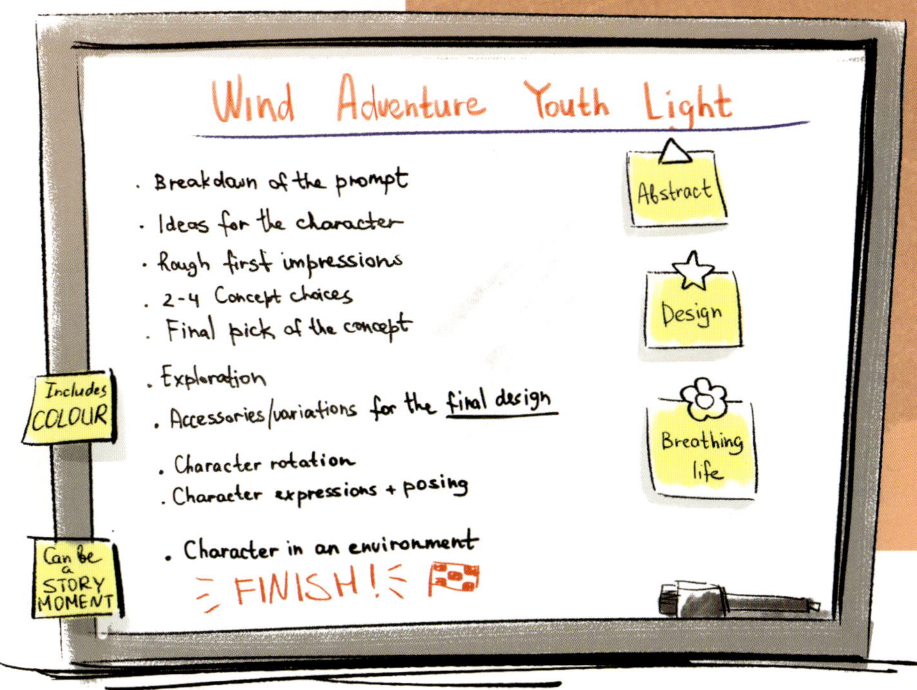

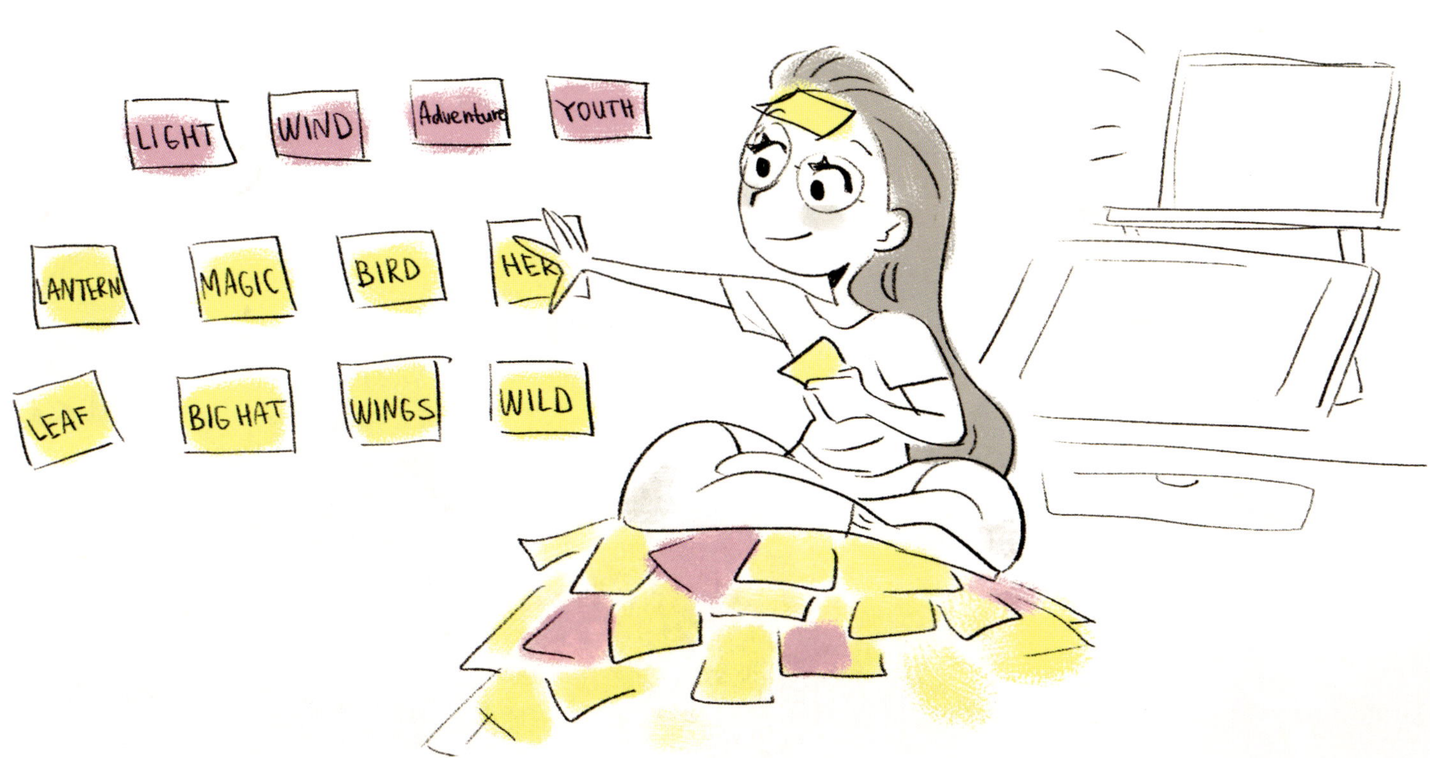

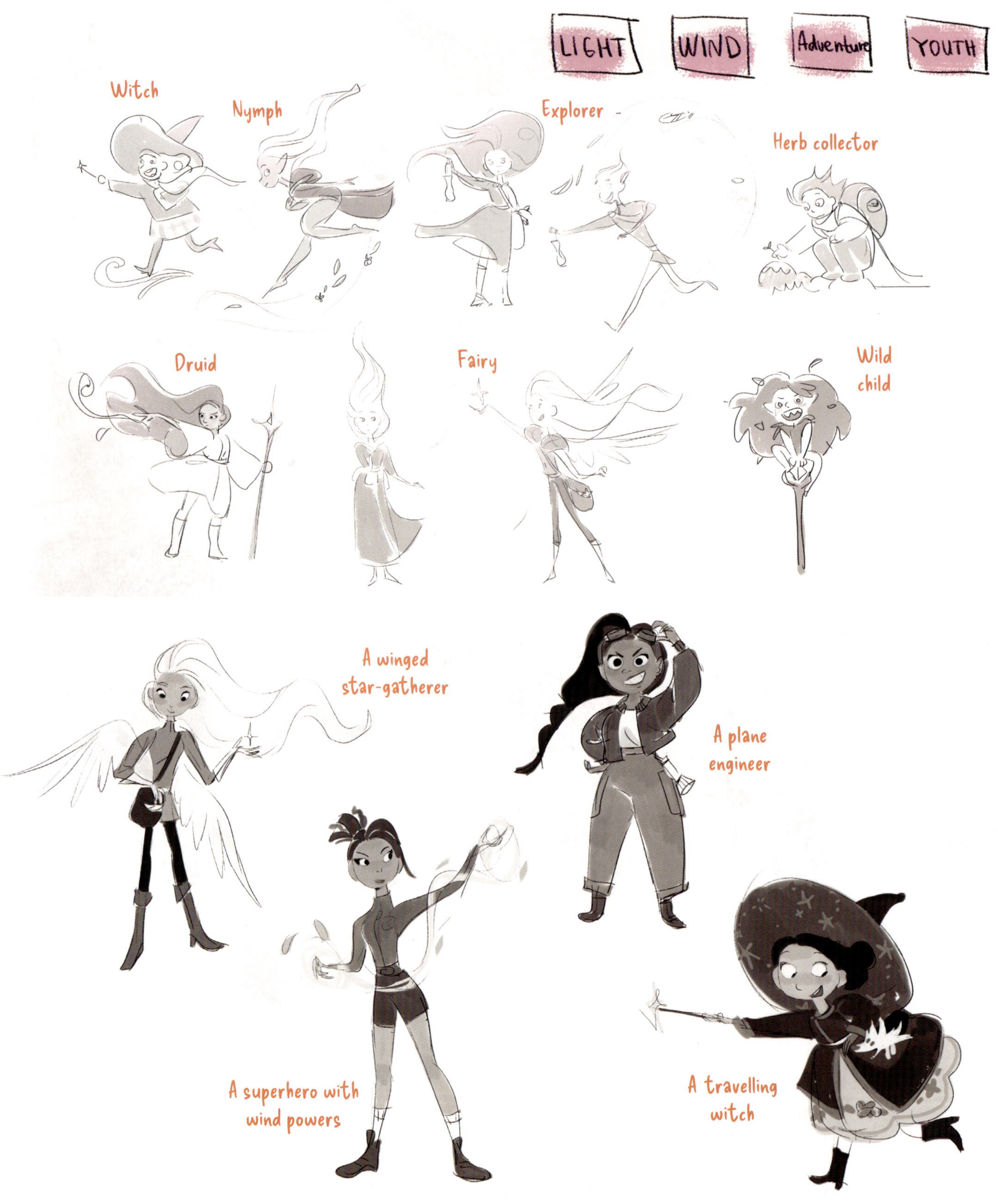
LIGHT
WIND
Adventure
YOUTH
Witch
Nymph
Explorer
Herb collector
Druid
Fairy
Wild child
A winged star-gatherer
A plane engineer
A superhero with wind powers
A travelling witch

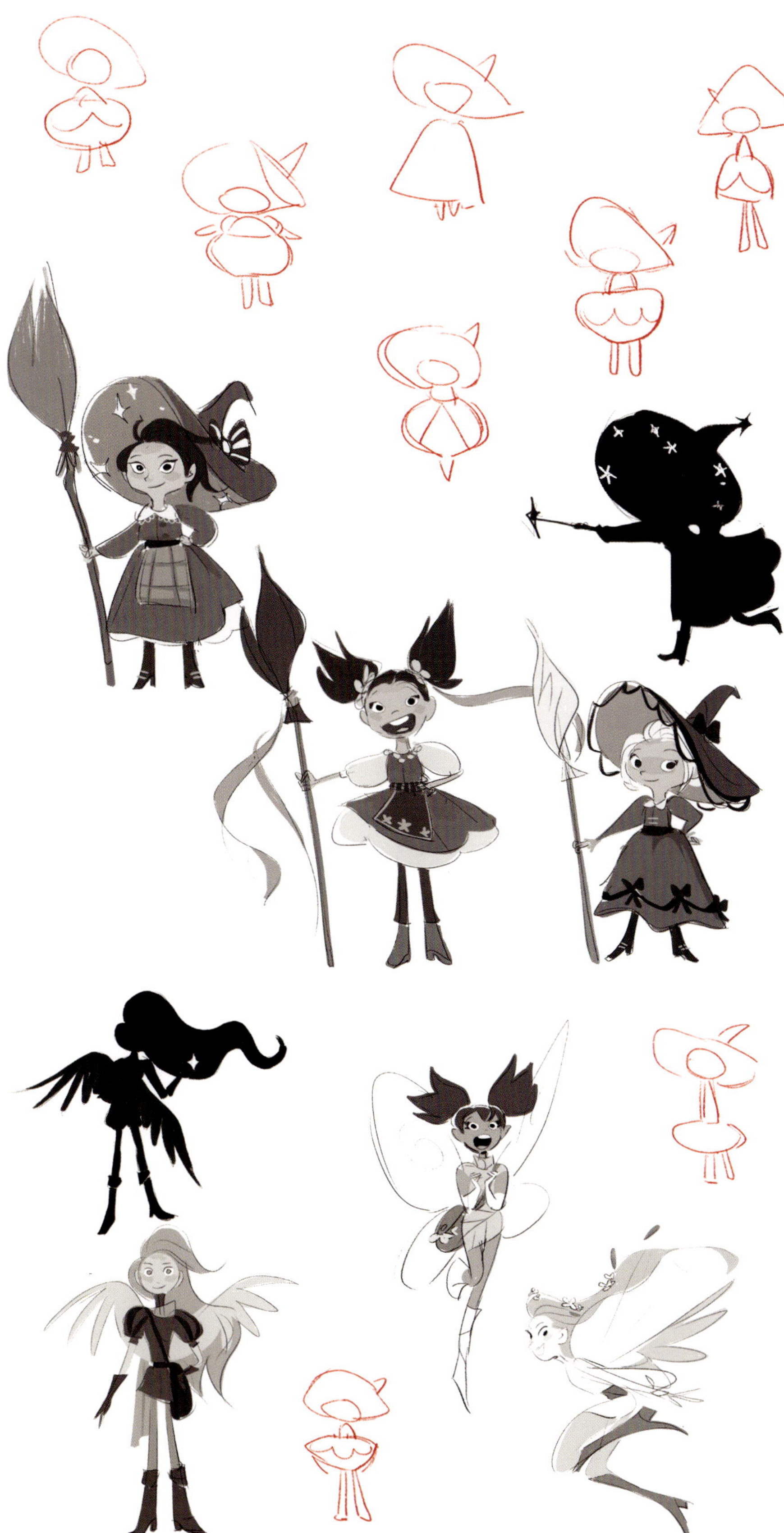

VISUALIZATION

It's time to start turning ideas into drawings. Your first explorations should evoke an immediate association with the prompt. I start sketching out the ideas that I came up with during the brainstorm session. The key is to keep the prompt in mind and stay true to the spirit of the assignment. All four elements should be present, even if you want to make one or two the focus and have the rest be supporting elements or items. Keep your sketches quick and loose and don't get too attached to any of the gestures just yet.

TAKING A CLOSER LOOK

To make it easier to pick one idea, sketch your options in an exploratory way. By dabbling in each concept you can get a clearer idea of which direction you want to take.

I pick two concepts to develop further based on how much potential I think they have. I choose the winged star-gatherer and the witch because they feel the most fun to me. Both explorations combine all four prompt words perfectly. I develop each further and find an interpretation of the winged character that draws me in. I decide to proceed with a fairy concept.

> 'Keep the prompt in mind and stay true to the spirit of the assignment'

SILHOUETTE & SHAPE LANGUAGE

Next, we need to think of a strong silhouette and how to visually balance all of the character's elements and features. You do not have to start with complex shapes right away – you can use simple circles, squares, or triangles as the basic building blocks.

Readability is essential for a successful design, so the silhouette of your character needs to be clear. It should tell you something about their personality. Think about who they might be. If they are friendly, use rounder shapes; if they are more edgy or even villainous, sharp shapes like triangles will help communicate that type of personality.

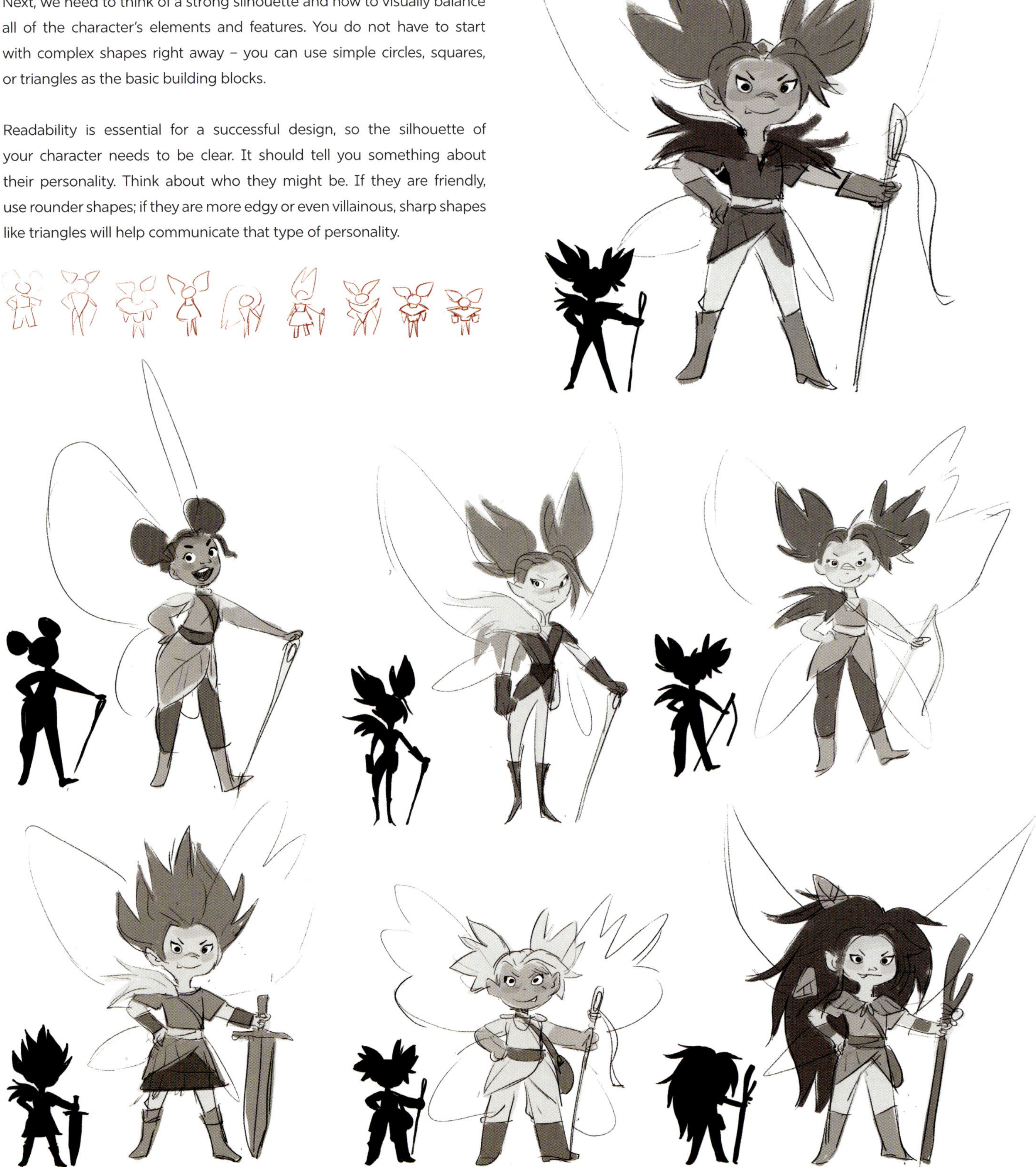

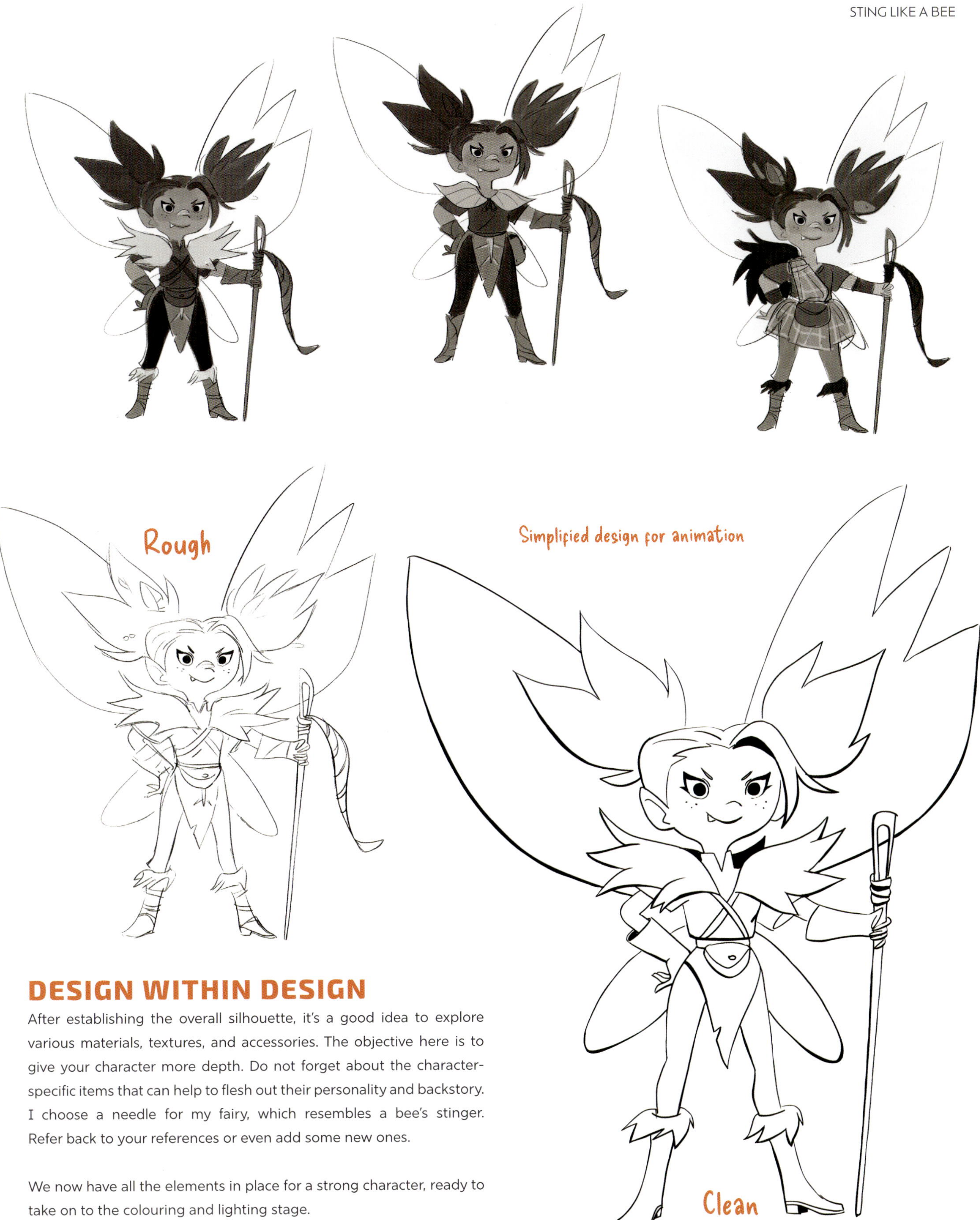

DESIGN WITHIN DESIGN

After establishing the overall silhouette, it's a good idea to explore various materials, textures, and accessories. The objective here is to give your character more depth. Do not forget about the character-specific items that can help to flesh out their personality and backstory. I choose a needle for my fairy, which resembles a bee's stinger. Refer back to your references or even add some new ones.

We now have all the elements in place for a strong character, ready to take on to the colouring and lighting stage.

Final image © Anastasiia Platoshyna

NARRA

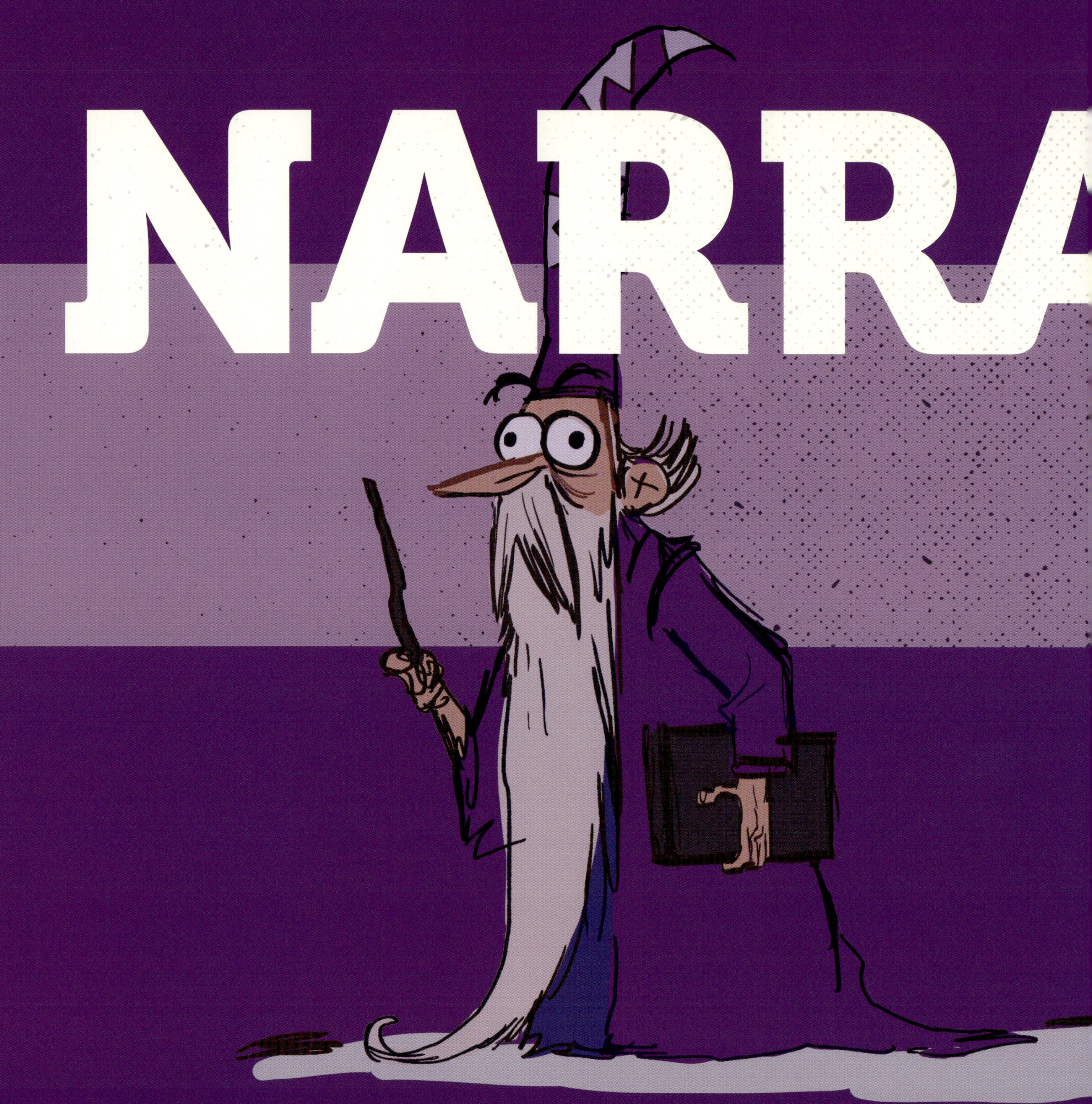

ATIVE

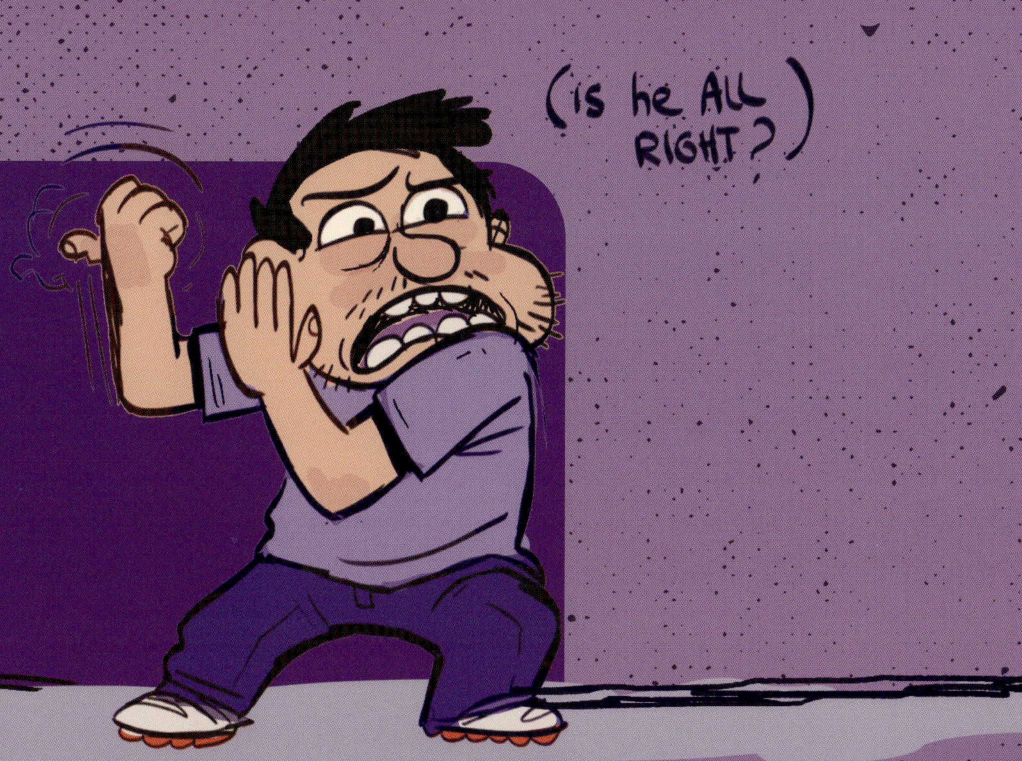

Image © Alex Relloso

Characters with a story to tell

ALEX RELLOSO

Characters are always part of a larger story, intended to be the main ingredients in the plots of movies, books, comics, games, and more. This is why I love approaching character design by thinking of the story first – infusing a narrative into my characters so they embody it.

I have worked as both a storyboard artist and a character designer. As a storyboard artist, you are often asked to come up with gags and funny situations for a character, or to imagine interesting aspects of their daily life to improve a story. There's no doubt these exercises have helped me to create more complete characters.

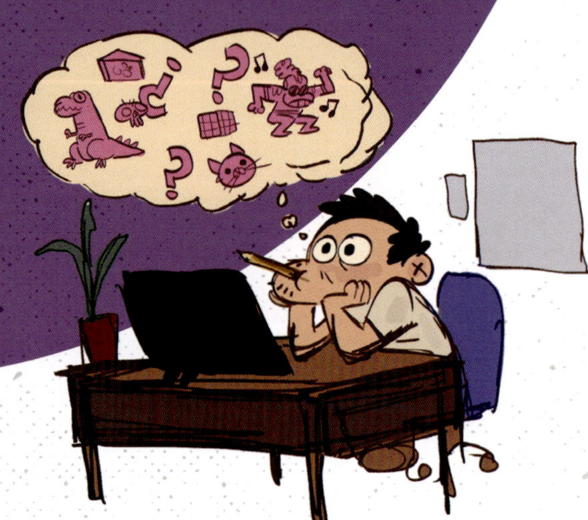

LET'S MAKE A WIZARD!

So, let's say we want to design a wizard. Instead of just doodling him standing up, holding a wand, or in another cliché pose (like throwing a spell), let's go deeper and find out who he really is. What does he eat for breakfast? What kind of music does he listen to? Whatever you decide, go beyond cliché and give your character true personality.

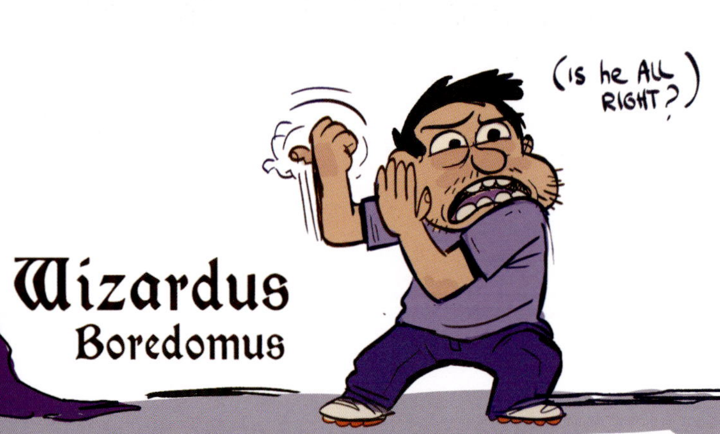

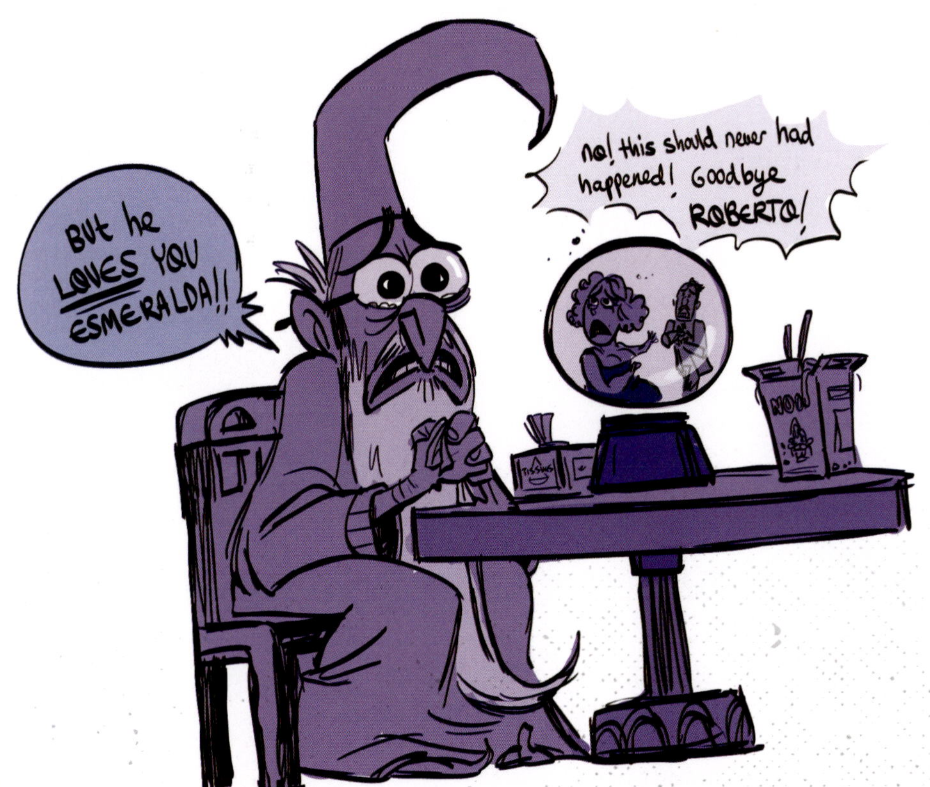

GET INSIDE THEIR HEAD

Ask yourself questions about your character. What is their secret hobby? What do they do at the weekend? Do they have any pets? Maybe this wizard is a fan of soap operas! If you are developing a character from scratch, this method can be super fun and you'll learn a lot about who you are trying to create. I've also seen this process work well with projects in which characters have already been defined, in terms of psychology and personality.

'Research your subject everywhere you can, digging into books and mining the internet'

HIT THE BOOKS

Research your subject everywhere you can, digging into books and mining the internet. You'll find many amazing stories and anecdotes that will spark original ideas for your design. Go outside and look around. Maybe you'll bump into people or situations that will inspire you – maybe the guy waiting at the bus stop looks exactly like the sorcerer you're trying to design?

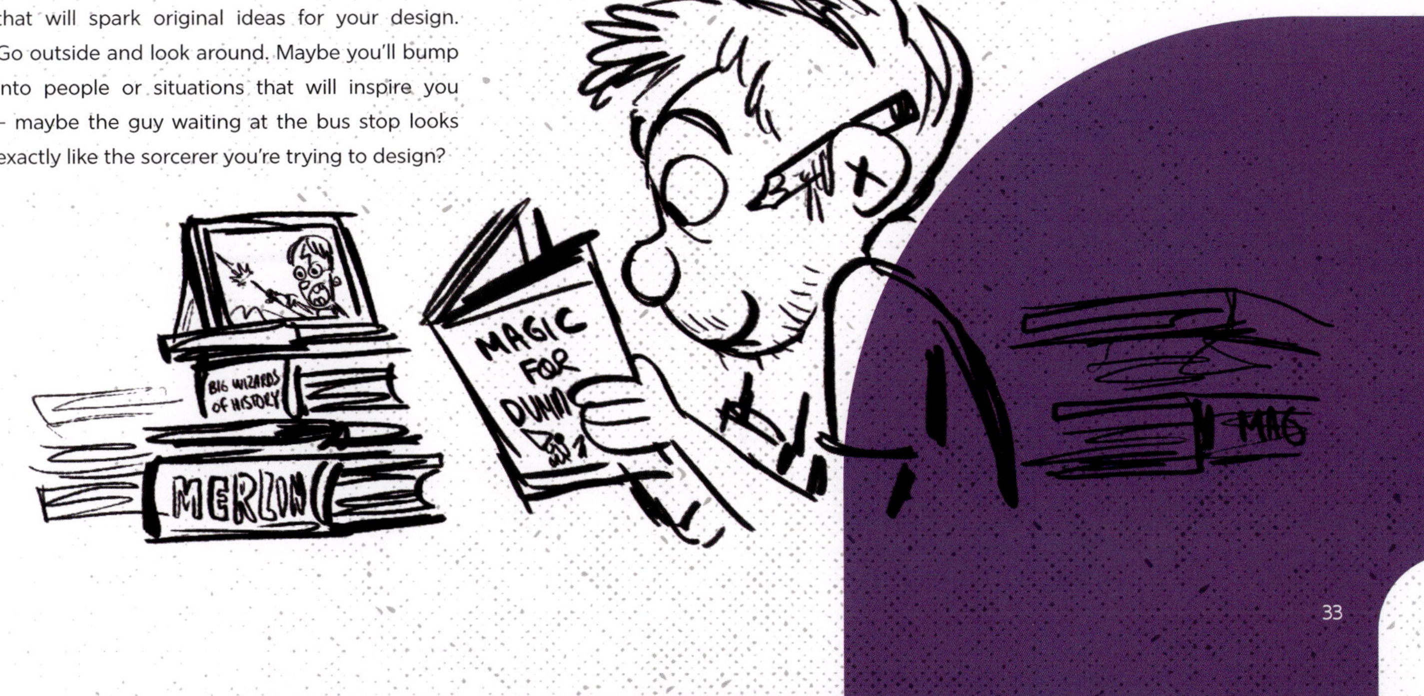

RETHINK THE CLICHÉ

Use clichés as a base to come up with original ideas. Let's start with 'wizard' clichés. Traditionally, they brew potions, can travel on a broom, and wear tall hats. How can we innovate within each of these ideas to get to know more about our character?

The more we question how our characters behave, and challenge our traditional idea of who they are, the more we can push their attitudes in original and exciting directions. There are no incorrect questions to ask – everything helps us get closer to the ideal version of the character we are building.

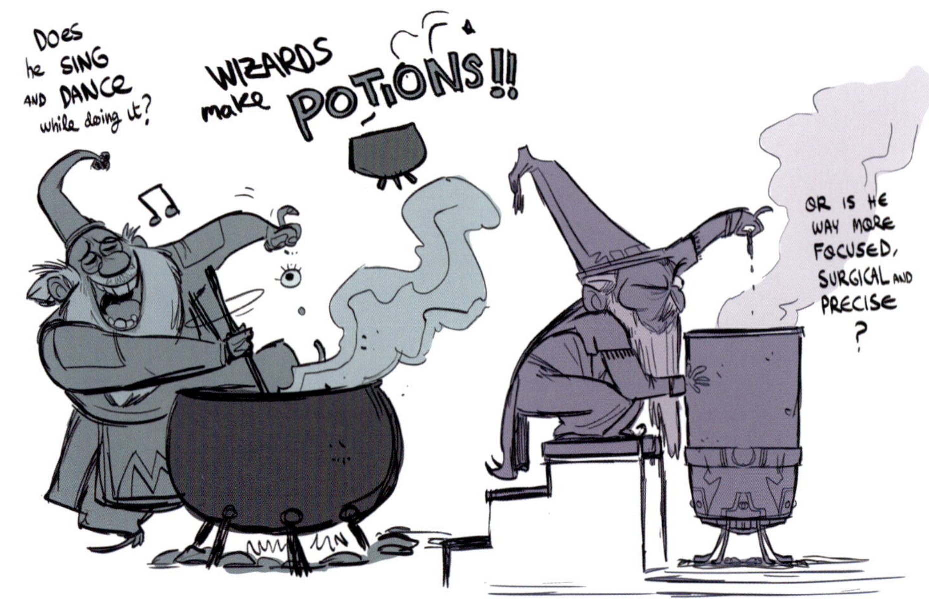

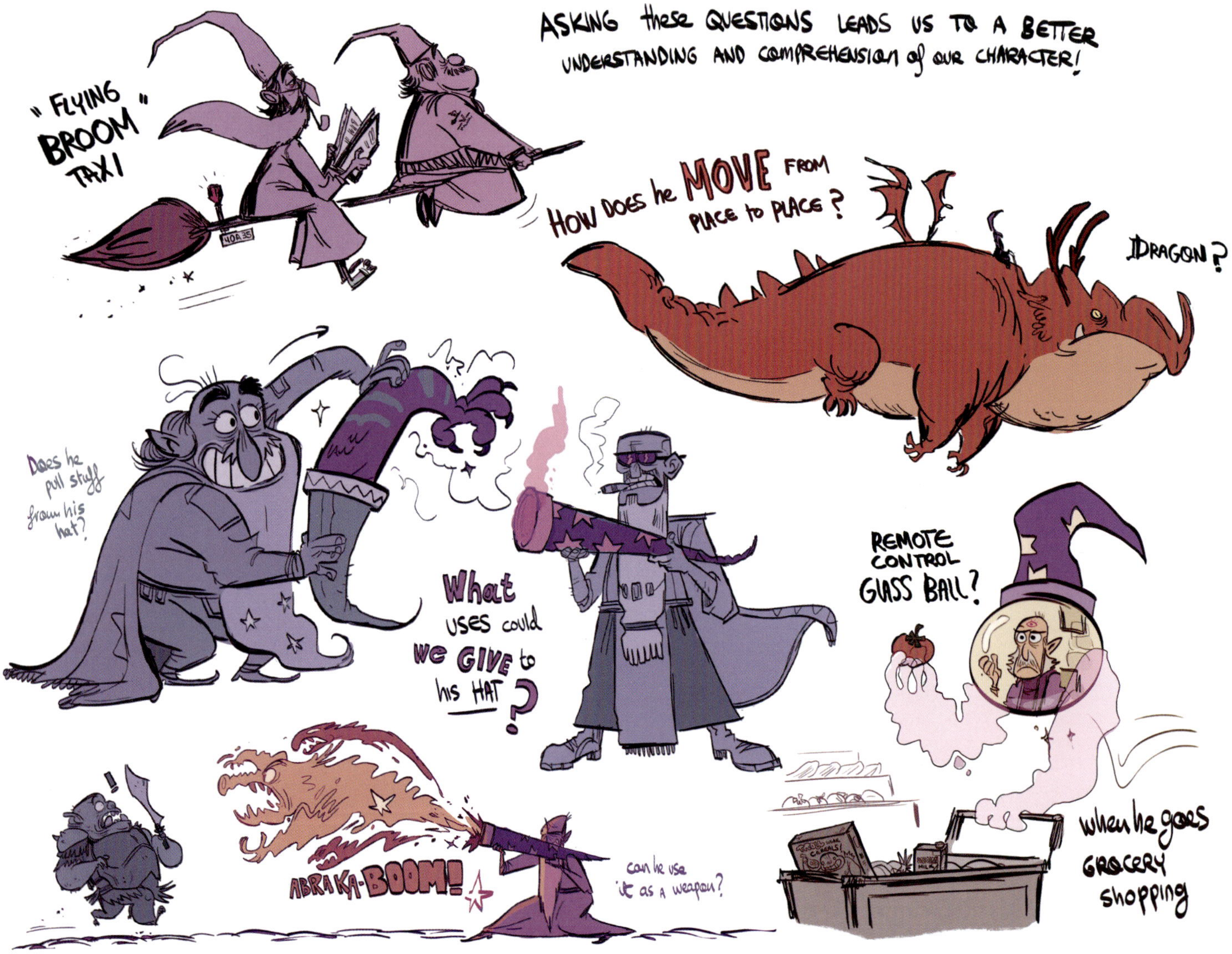

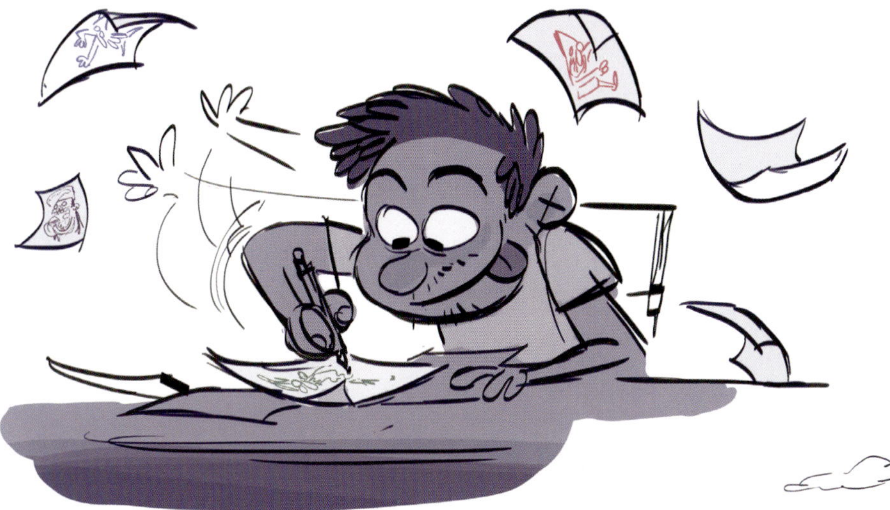

ALWAYS BE SKETCHING

Always carry a sketchbook with you, in order to quickly put down any random thoughts and ideas you might find. Don't worry about your sketches being too 'clean' either. I fill the pages of my notebook with scribbled doodles, random thoughts, annotations, and variations. There will be time to clean up later – the important part is to find cool ideas wherever you can!

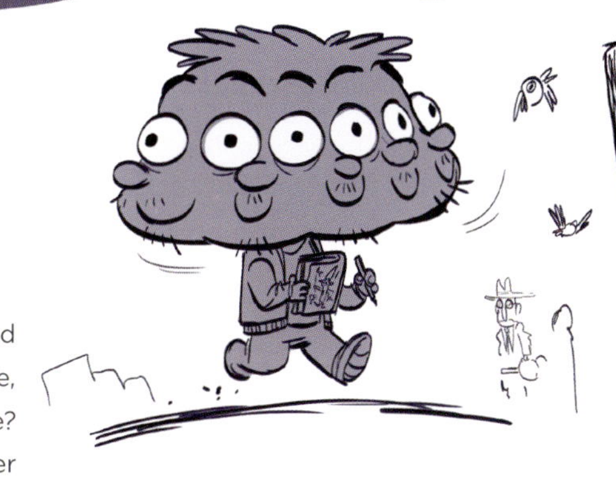

NARRATIVE MOMENTS

Building a specific story moment will lead you to new discoveries. For example, what if the wizard sets up a poker game? Drawing a narrative scene will spark other ideas, which in turn will lead to even more ideas! Be careful, this process can become overwhelming if you let it. Don't get stuck in a never-ending loop of finding new things to draw. At some point, it's good to stop, breathe, and evaluate what you've created. With time, you'll get better at asking more interesting and on-point questions, which will help you come up with a wide range of funny ideas and moments for your character that reinforce the perception of them as 'alive'.

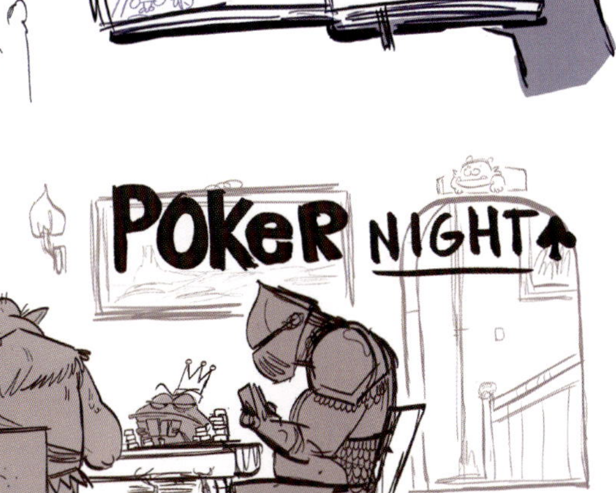

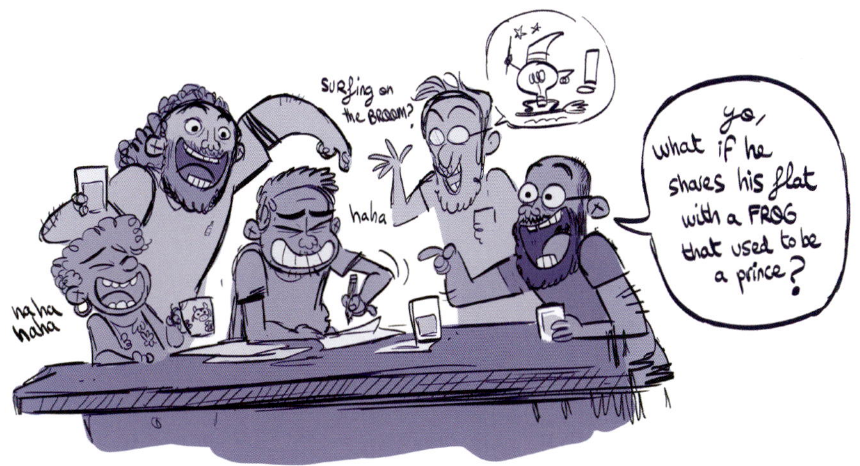

THAT'S WHAT FRIENDS ARE FOR

Many of the best ideas come from chatting about different iterations and hearing your friends say, 'Oooh, that's cool – and what if ... ?' Overall, try to have fun while creating your characters – I always do! I hope you have fun too, and find some cool stories and characters along the way.

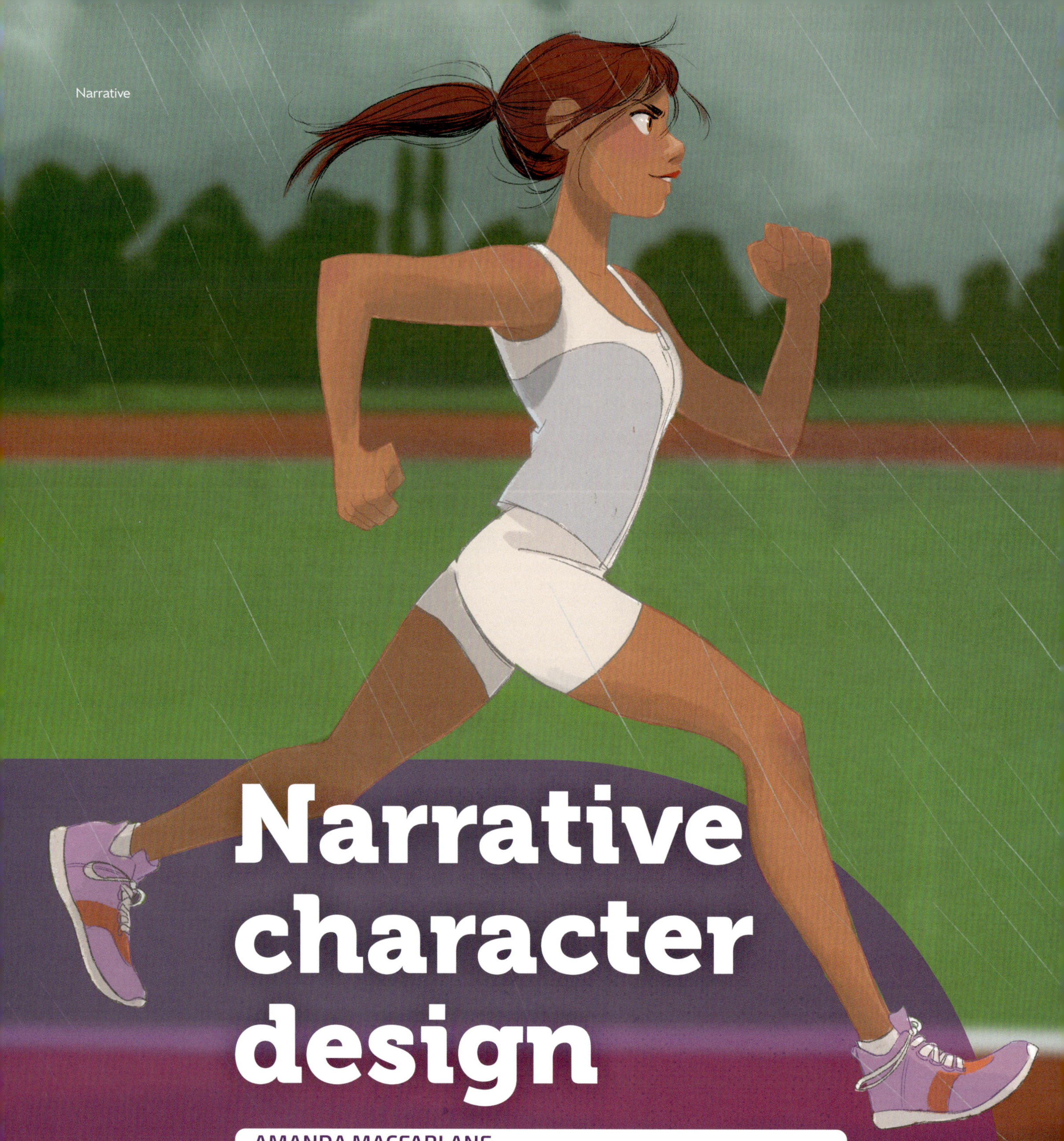

Narrative character design

AMANDA MACFARLANE

In this tutorial I will explain how a narrative brief can guide character development, helping you define your character and bring them to life. Even when following a brief, designing a character will take you on an exciting journey, in pursuit of imagination.

THE NARRATIVE

It's not easy coming second ... all ... the ... time. This character trains and trains running around and around the track day and night, breaking personal bests in the sun and wiping hair from her face in the rain. Each morning she's in the gym, protein shake in hand, quinoa salad in her bag. And each podium she's still in silver, forever looking up to gold. Next time, she thinks, I'll get you.

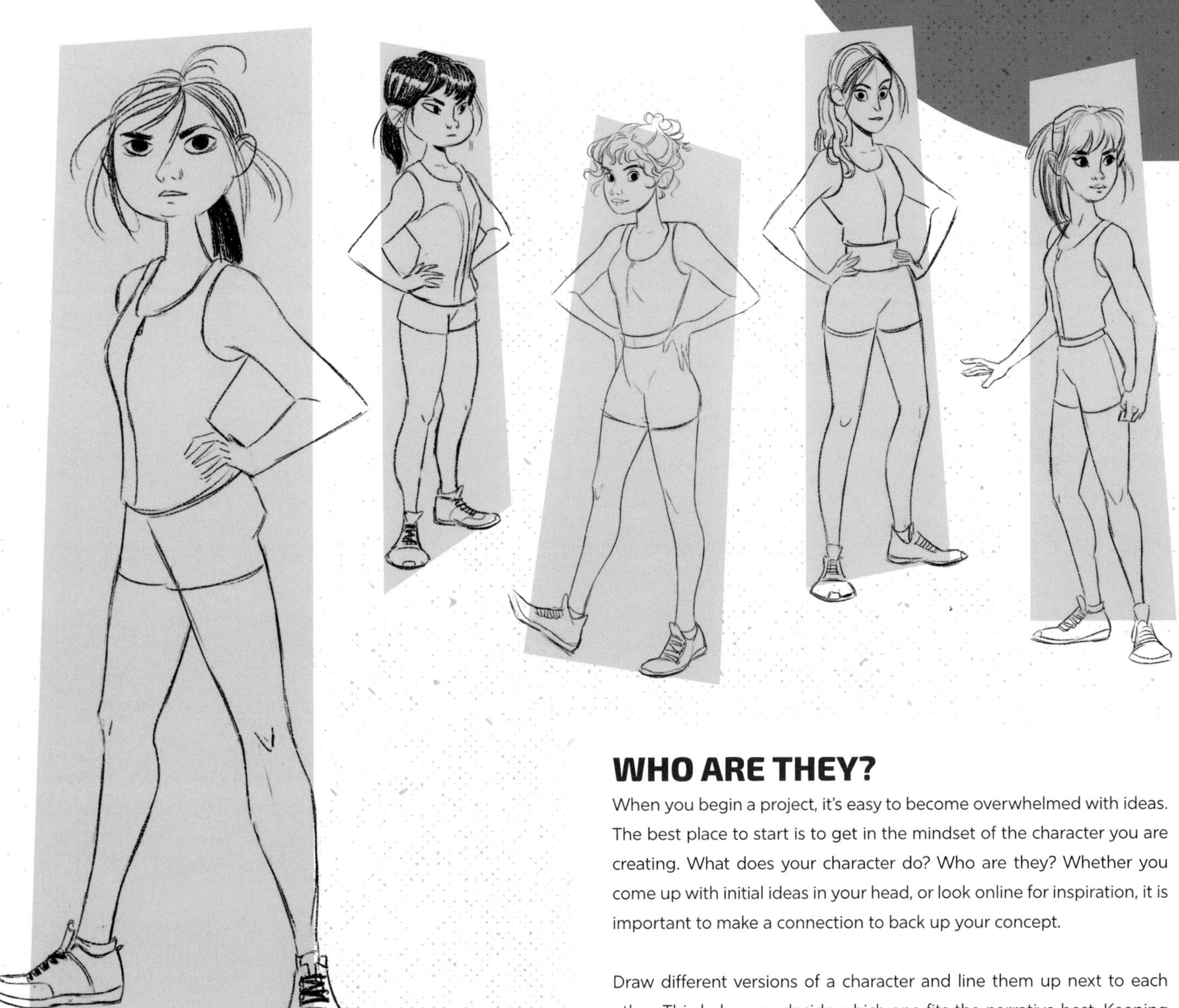

WHO ARE THEY?

When you begin a project, it's easy to become overwhelmed with ideas. The best place to start is to get in the mindset of the character you are creating. What does your character do? Who are they? Whether you come up with initial ideas in your head, or look online for inspiration, it is important to make a connection to back up your concept.

Draw different versions of a character and line them up next to each other. This helps you decide which one fits the narrative best. Keeping the original narrative in mind, I want my character to show a look of determination to convey her driven spirit and ambition to win.

STYLE & PRACTICALITIES

Create thumbnails of your chosen character and think about styles that are not only fun to look at, but practical for them. As a runner, I deduce that my character is likely to have her hair tied back out of her face so that she doesn't need to keep pushing her hair back while on the move. Her hair needs to be a little bit flat from sweating and a little dishevelled from running – this is a runner who cares more about beating her score and being the best than about what her hair looks like.

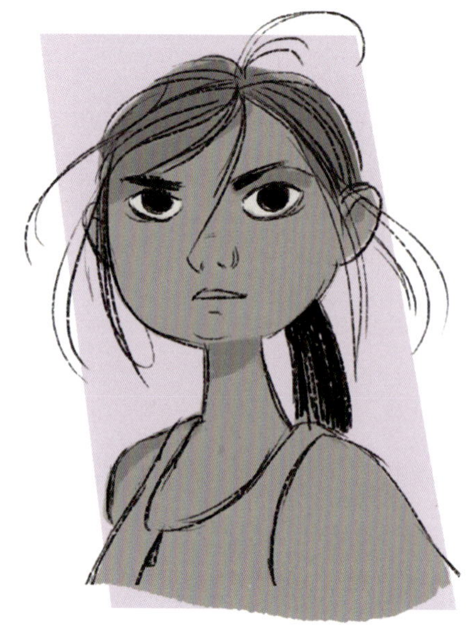

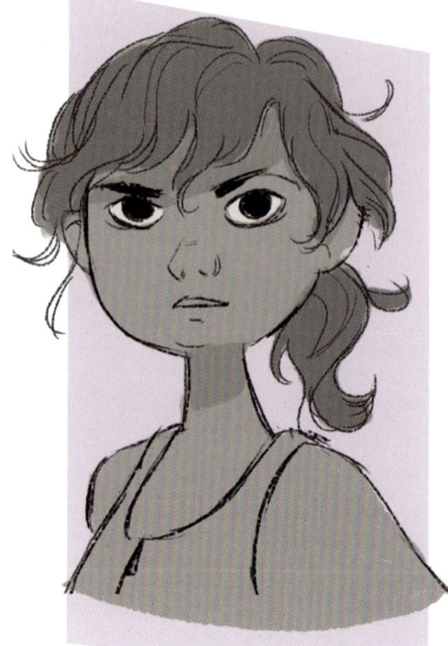

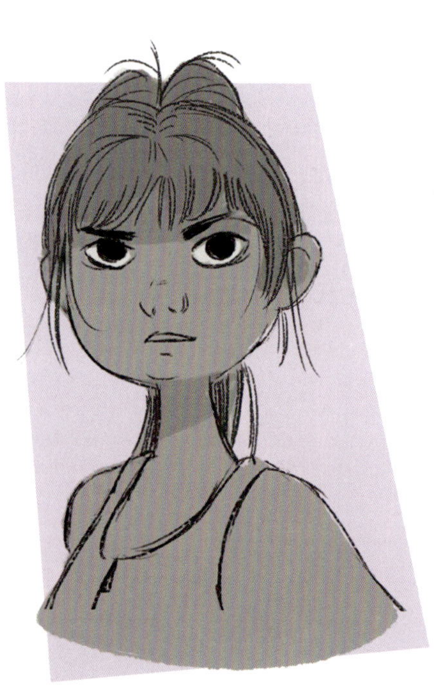

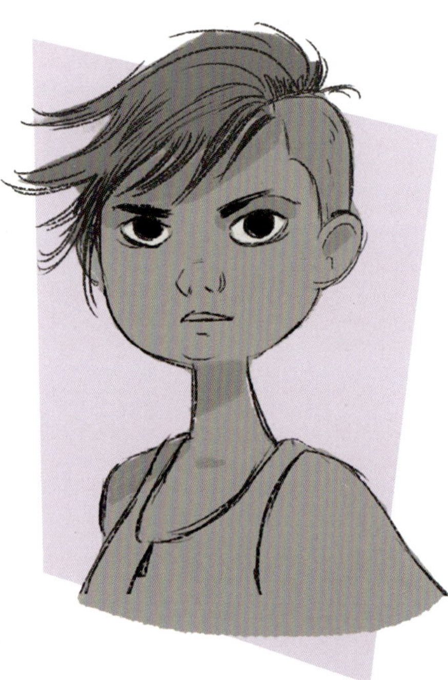

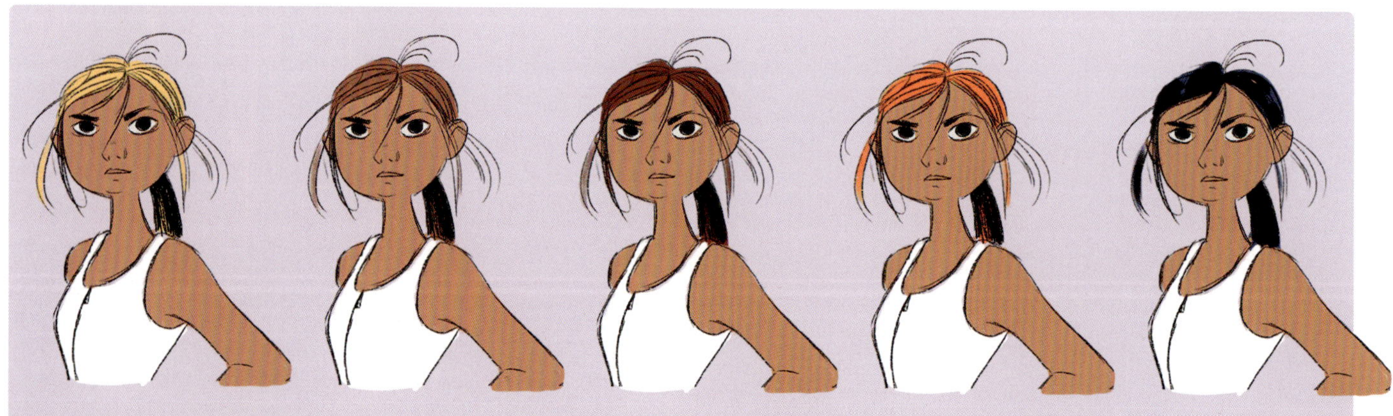

PUT YOURSELF IN THEIR SHOES

When you are faced with wardrobe decisions, it's the perfect opportunity for you to get into the mindset of your character. Imagine what it's like to be them. Relating to your character helps you decide the outcome of how they dress and how they style their hair. Doing this allows them to become more relatable to an audience.

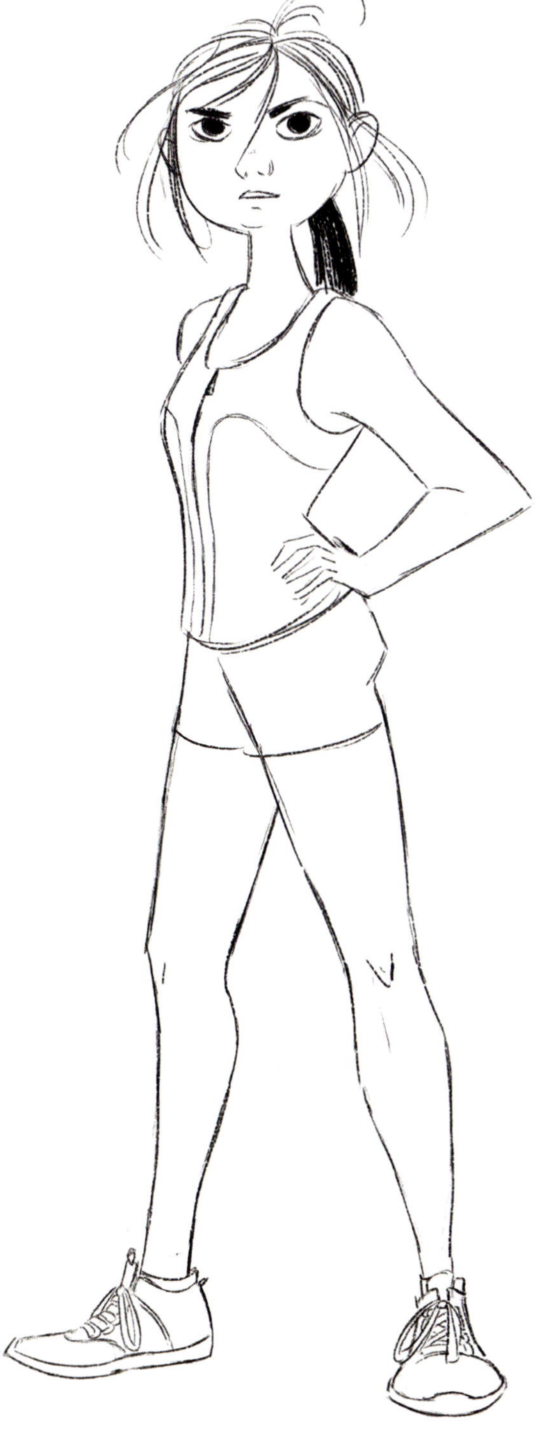

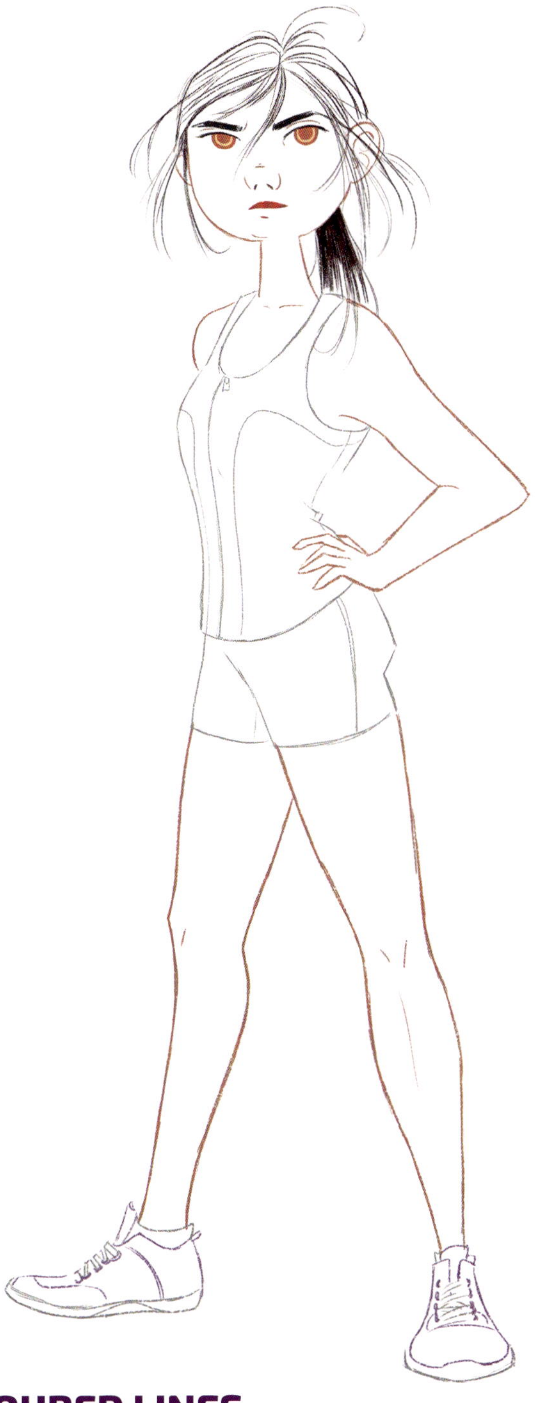

COLOURED LINES

Once you have decided on the overall pose and style of your character, convert the line art into coloured lines. Drawing a coloured outline provides a base for your rendering and creates a more professional outcome. Choose colours that are a few shades darker than the colour you will be filling the subject with. If you're working on character designs for a movie, this step will help the 3D modeller in the next phase of design.

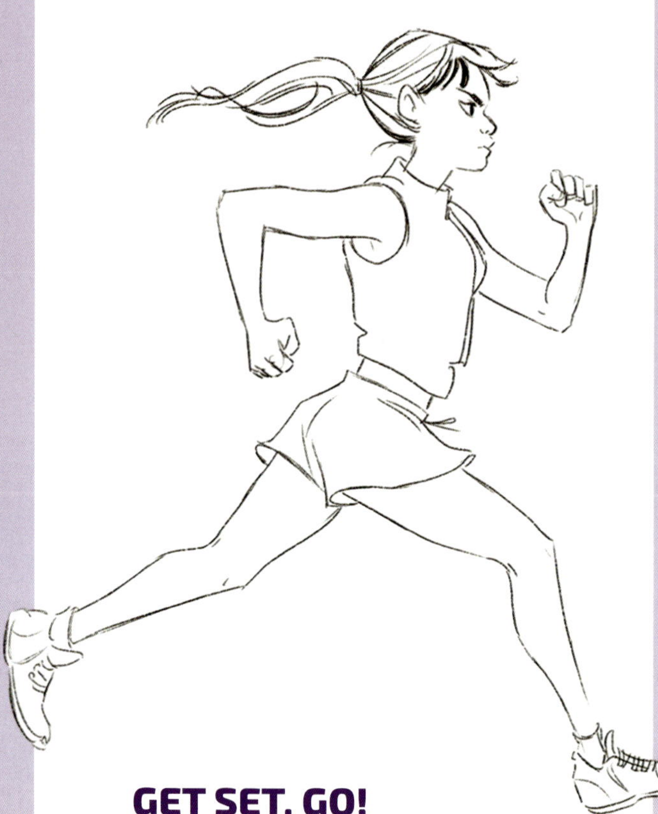

> 'Draw your character from different angles and consider how they will look in action'

GET SET, GO!

Briefs often require you to create a turnaround of a character, so it's good practice to draw your character from different angles and consider how they will look in action. Considering the line of action is important when creating an action shot. It helps you keep focus and makes your character have a natural flow.

When you are drawing a runner, you have to keep in mind the runner's form. A more seasoned runner will have better posture while running, their eyes straight ahead, and have a straight diaphragm. Runners also usually have clothes that are aerodynamic and cling to the body. Use reference material to guide the placement of the feet and bends in the joints – the character's anatomy will also need to be prepared for impact.

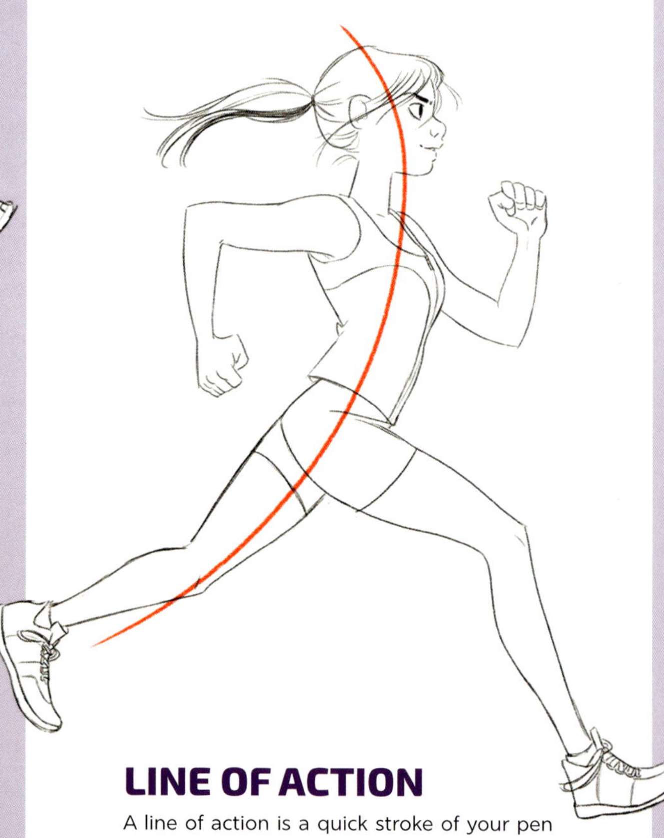

LINE OF ACTION

A line of action is a quick stroke of your pen or pencil that will direct your character's body. Every living thing has a line of action. It is a great tool to use while sketching from life quickly, and will help you construct both the frame and detail of a character.

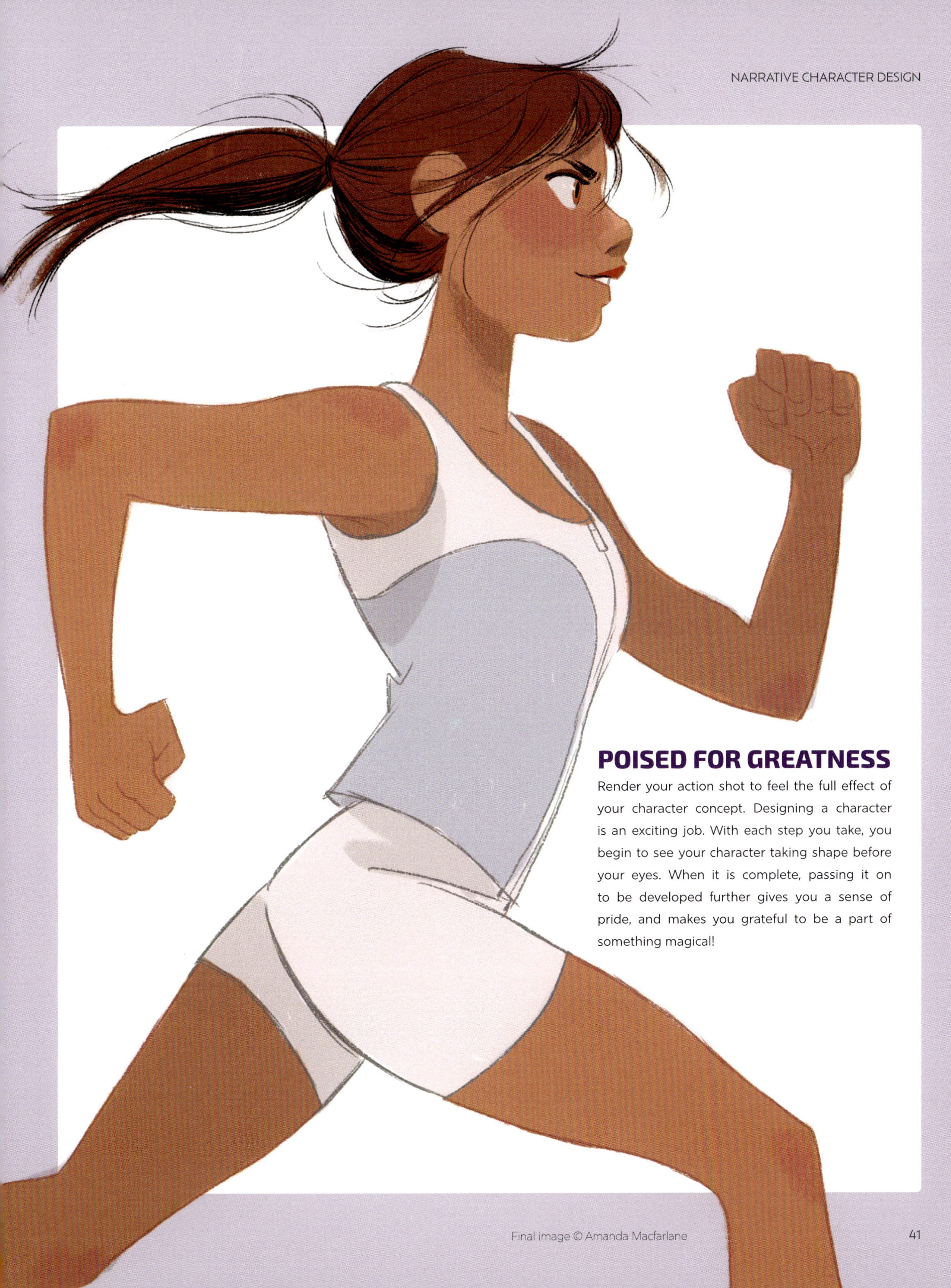

POISED FOR GREATNESS

Render your action shot to feel the full effect of your character concept. Designing a character is an exciting job. With each step you take, you begin to see your character taking shape before your eyes. When it is complete, passing it on to be developed further gives you a sense of pride, and makes you grateful to be a part of something magical!

Final image © Amanda Macfarlane

Atmospheric conditions

RAQUEL VILLANUEVA

As artists we are constantly telling stories. Sometimes these are simple, providing essential information such as the colours our character likes to wear, or insights into their personality or attitude. But when we want to go further, we can push it more and create a whole backstory for them. In this tutorial, I will show you my process: from finding an idea and developing it to executing a full composition that tells a story of the character.

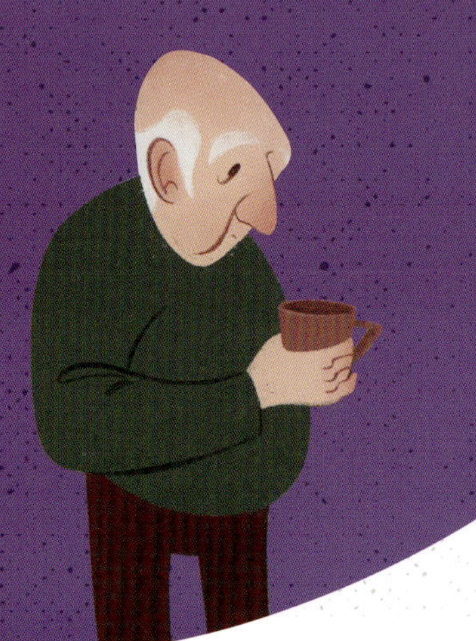

A FRESH IDEA

When you want to create something new, you can sometimes feel overwhelmed by the endless possibilities. To avoid this, I try to start with a very simple idea, then play around with it and push it in different directions. In this case, I want to work with the feeling of nostalgia – that bittersweet feeling that we have all experienced at some point in our lives. Nostalgia is often associated with the past – it makes us feel both happy and sad. How can we translate this into an image? It's helpful to begin by thinking about things that make us feel this way. I know I want a scene that depicts real life, during those early or late hours of the day that have a quiet and calming atmosphere.

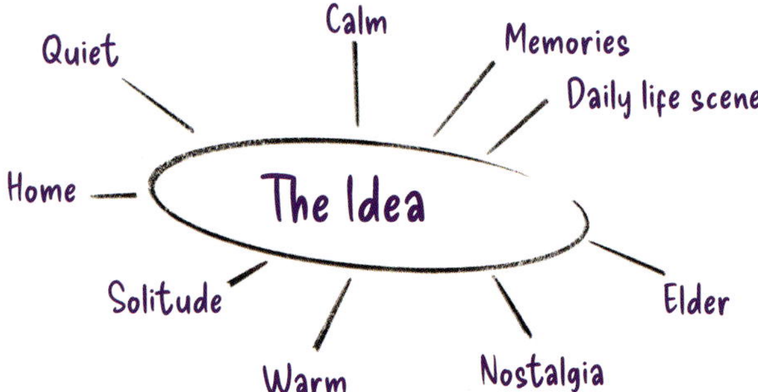

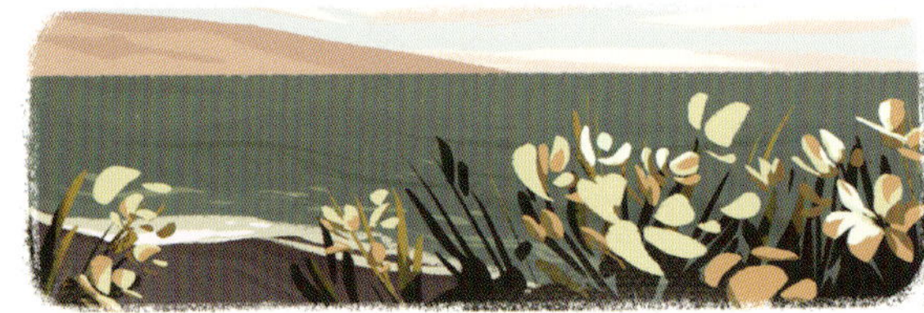

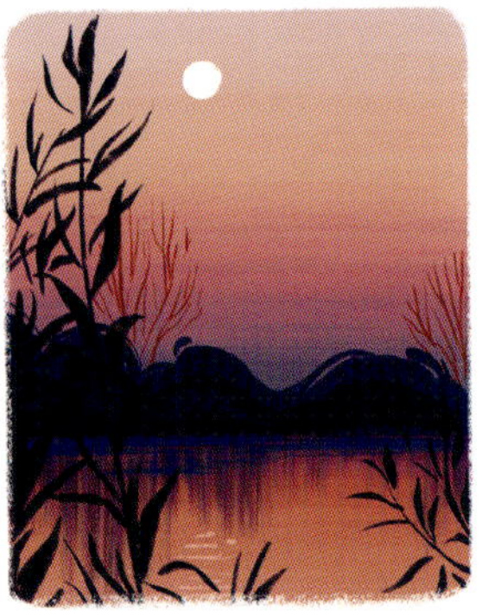

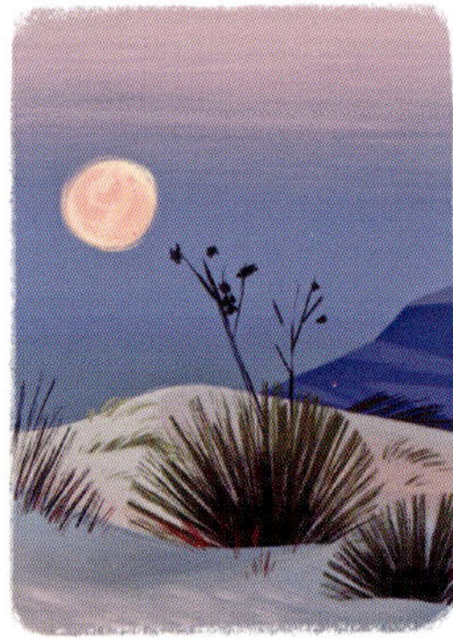

WARM-UP

Little landscapes are one of my favourite things to paint when I want to get my creative juices flowing. I keep them very simple and graphic, but they help inspire me and get me into 'work mode'. Warm-ups can also be a great time to experiment with colour palettes.

MEETING OUR CHARACTER

Once you have the initial ideas, you can start to build the main character of the story. I opt for an older person because they are full of life experiences, which is useful when creating a backstory. Make some sketches to find an interesting design that could work with the story. At this point, keep it loose and simple.

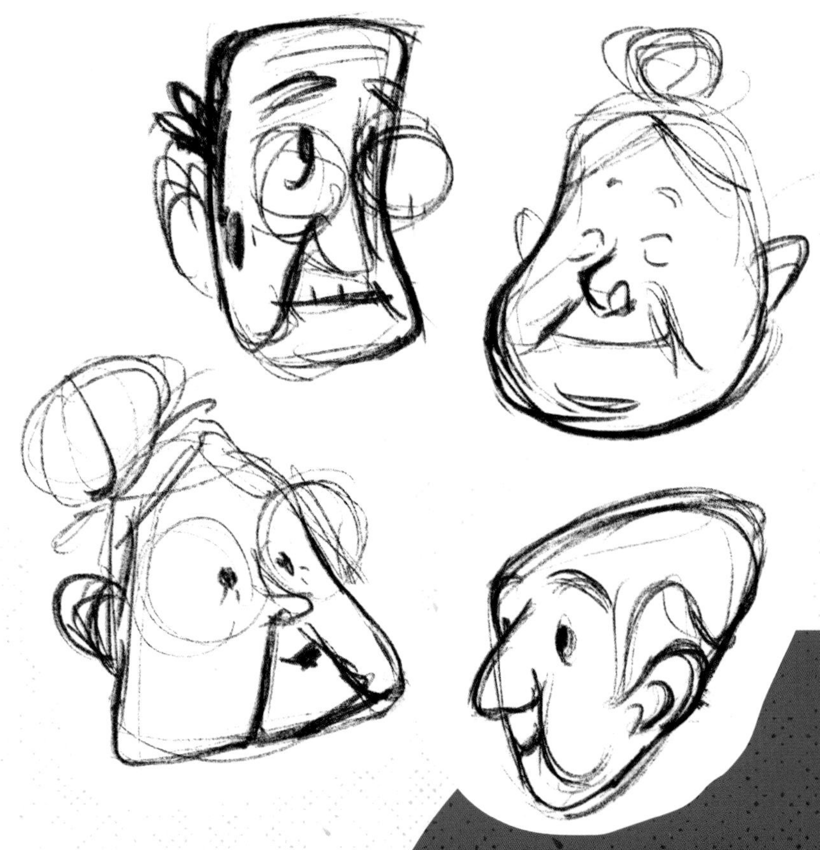

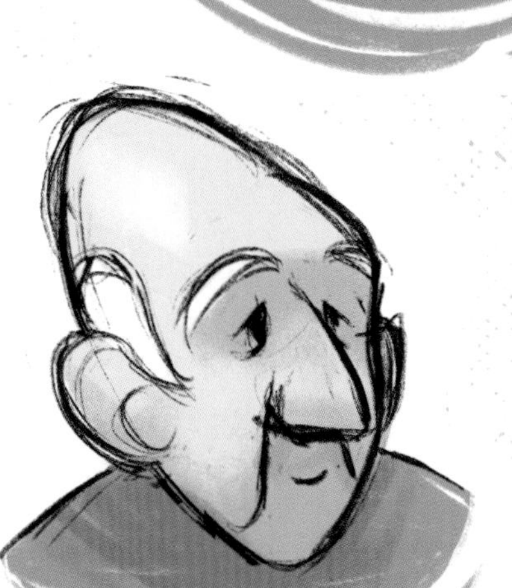

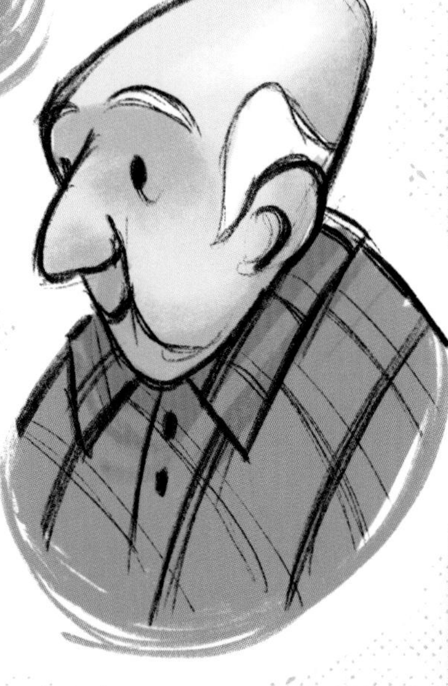

GETTING TO KNOW YOU

After exploring some options, I decide on this particular elderly gentleman. He evokes a warm feeling, like a grandpa who would hug you and tell you stories. He has a simple silhouette and shapes, and not too much detail, which will work well as I want to create a busy background. He'll be wearing some pyjamas or cosy leisure wear to make him look more relaxed.

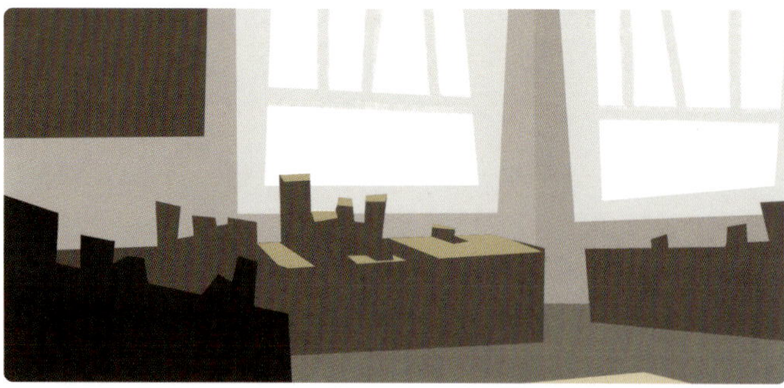

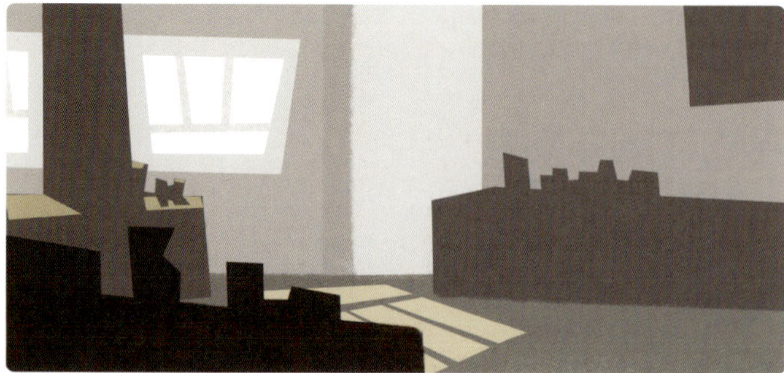

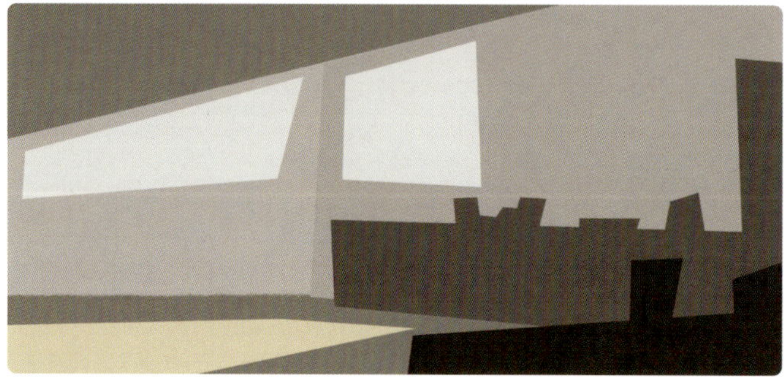

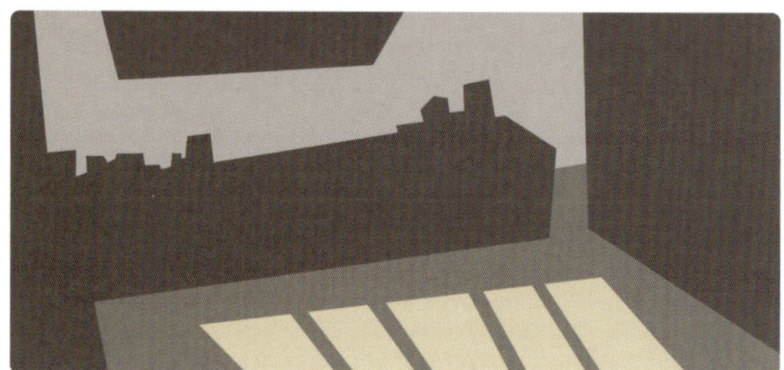

SETTING THE SCENE

To begin the background design process, first create quick sketches to see which compositions work better. It's important to push yourself, to test out different approaches and move away from your initial ideas – this will help give variation to your design. The final thumbnail has a simple composition, where the character can begin his day on a quiet morning and become lost in thought.

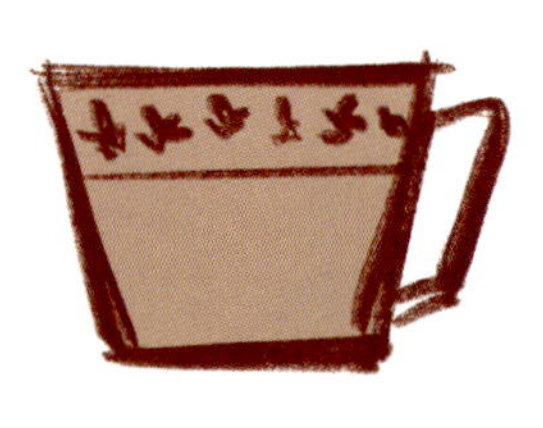

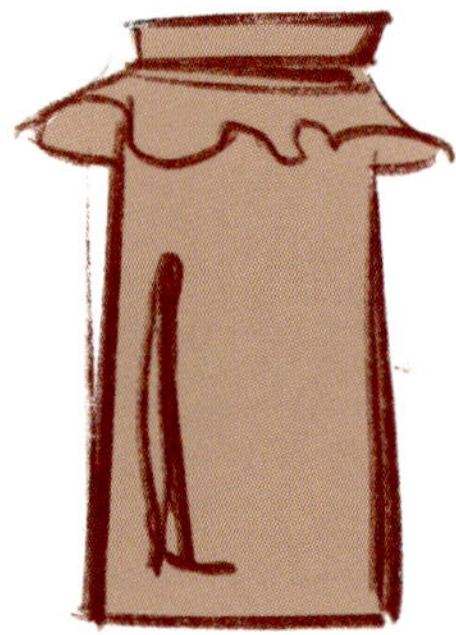

DELVING INTO THE PAST

You might have come across the common misconception that using a reference is cheating – this could not be more wrong. Looking for a reference and using it is as important as the execution of the painting itself. Take your time to look for inspiration. For this piece, I research old, rustic kitchens, which helps me figure out what would look good and help portray the mood. I search for old houses, vintage objects, and images that maybe don't have a lot in common with the concept, but have a similar feel or colours that could be carried over.

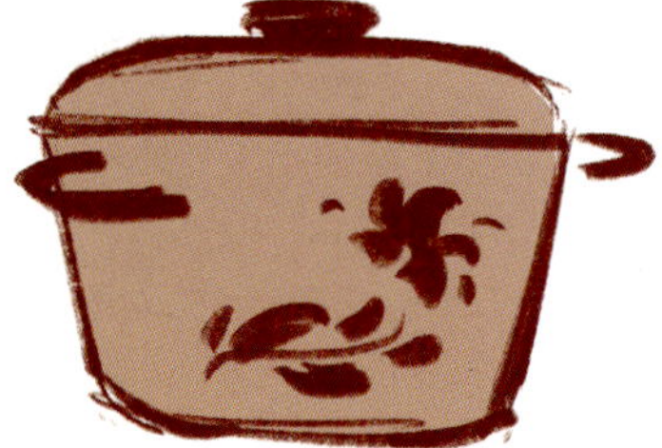

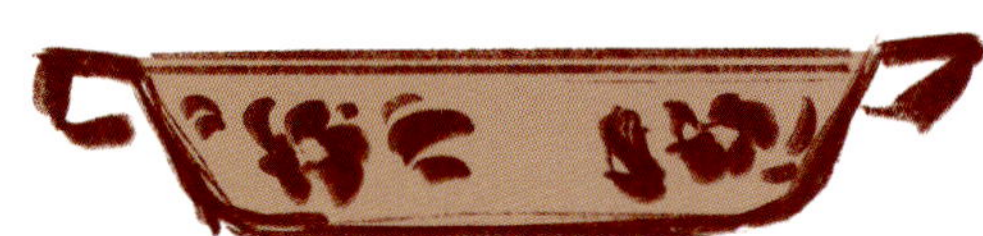

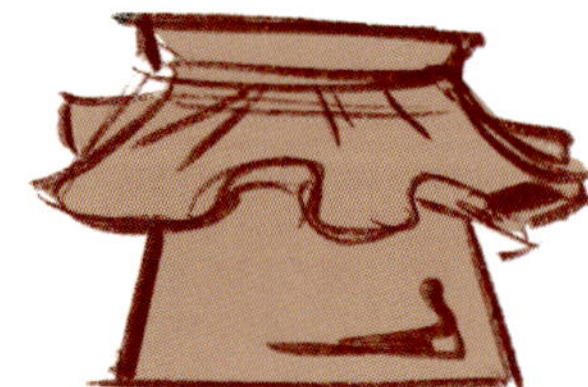

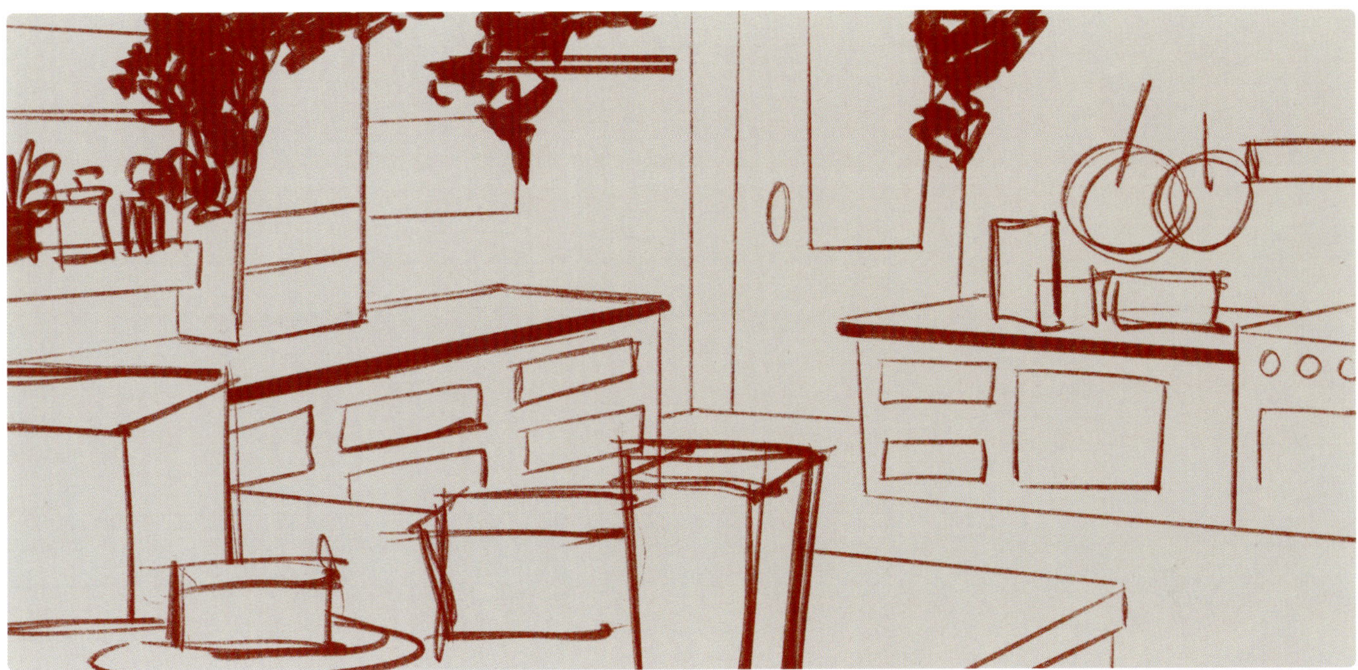

SKETCHING THE DETAILS

Now we can begin taking our sketches to the next step. Go back to the chosen thumbnail and clean it up by sketching over the details you want to define – in this case, the elements for the kitchen. Taking information learned from the research, I play around with different ideas for the countertops, stoves, and other accessories. At this point you can also adjust the composition if you feel it's needed.

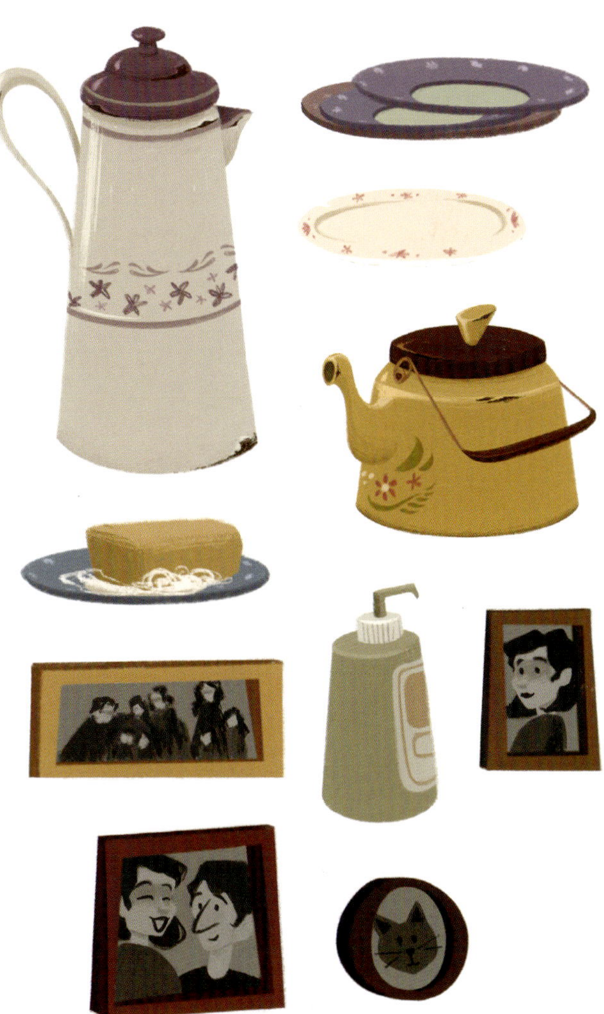

KITCHEN CLUTTER

After the research stage, I have many ideas on how to fill the interior. To help build the personality of our character, I want to fill the space with kitchen tools and gadgets. This will help it feel much like our own grandparents' kitchens, where it might be a little messy, but not too cluttered and chaotic – just full of the things they have collected over the years. I add old-fashioned tools and stylize their shapes to make them easy to read. I also make them age-worn to help emphasize the storytelling element of our image. I add some smaller details too, such as framed pictures showing our grandpa character when he was younger. This gives more interest to the visual storytelling we are establishing in the piece, and the viewers are invited to make their own conclusions about who the people in the frames are.

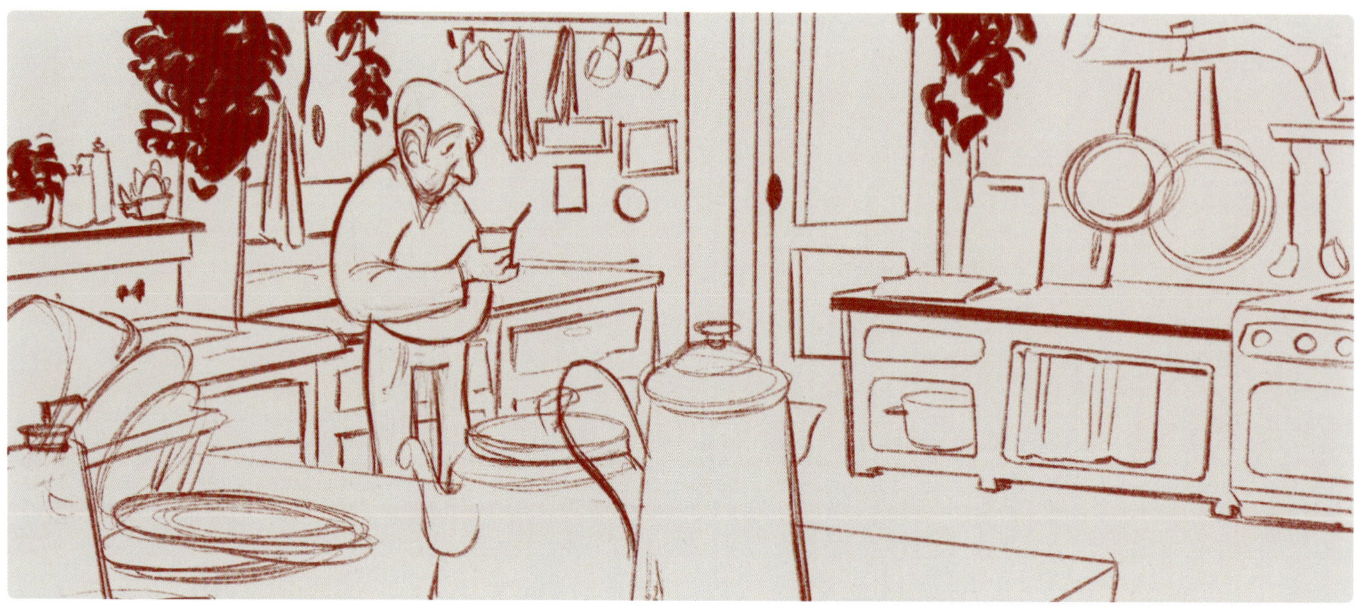

COSY KITCHEN

Now it's time to clean up the space and introduce our character. I pose the character with his back against the window – this combined with the light leading into the interior will help the viewer focus on what's going on inside the room. The elderly man's thoughtful gaze into his mug will make the viewer wonder what he's thinking, evoking that feeling of nostalgia I'm aiming for. It's these subtle choices that can help to tell a story – elements that will help the viewer understand the character's mood and make them want to know more.

LIGHT & DARK

Usually I jump straight into colouring the character, but since this is a larger piece, I would like to check the values first. Values are a helpful guide when moving on to colour as they help establish how light or dark areas of your image will be. It's a good idea to make a rough pass to define the values of all of the elements within the composition – this helps you see if there is enough contrast in the piece to make it easily readable for your viewer.

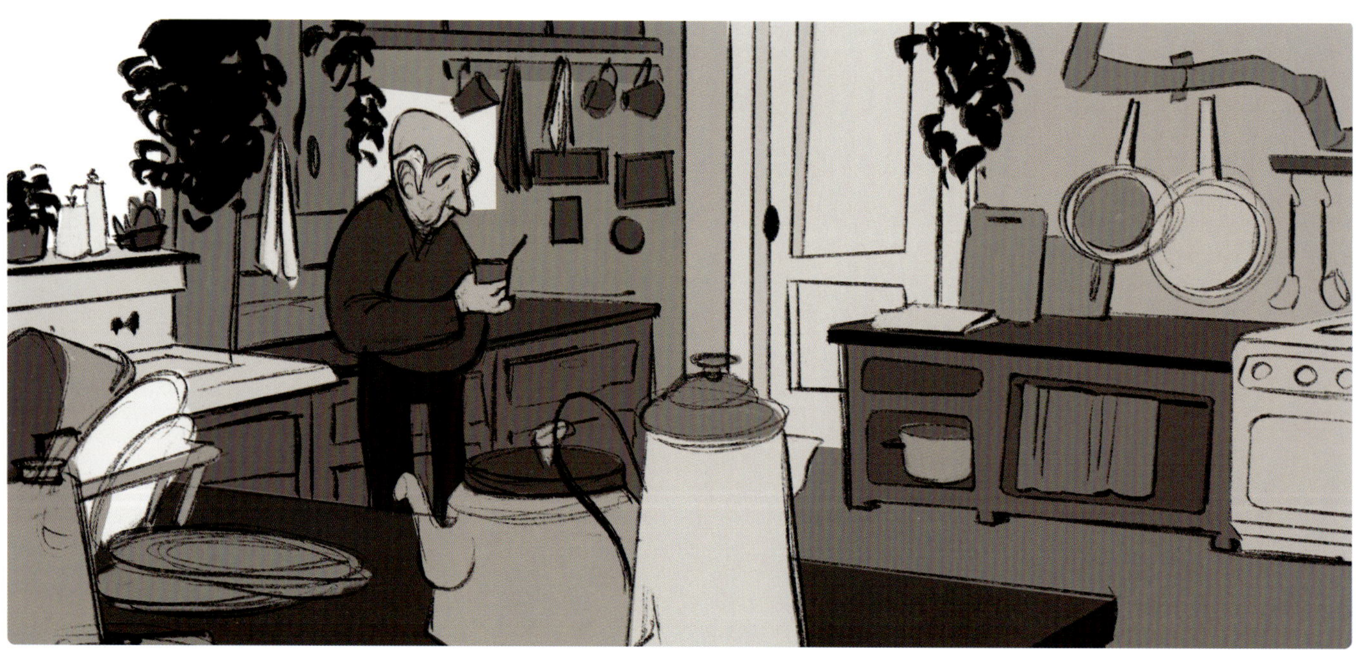

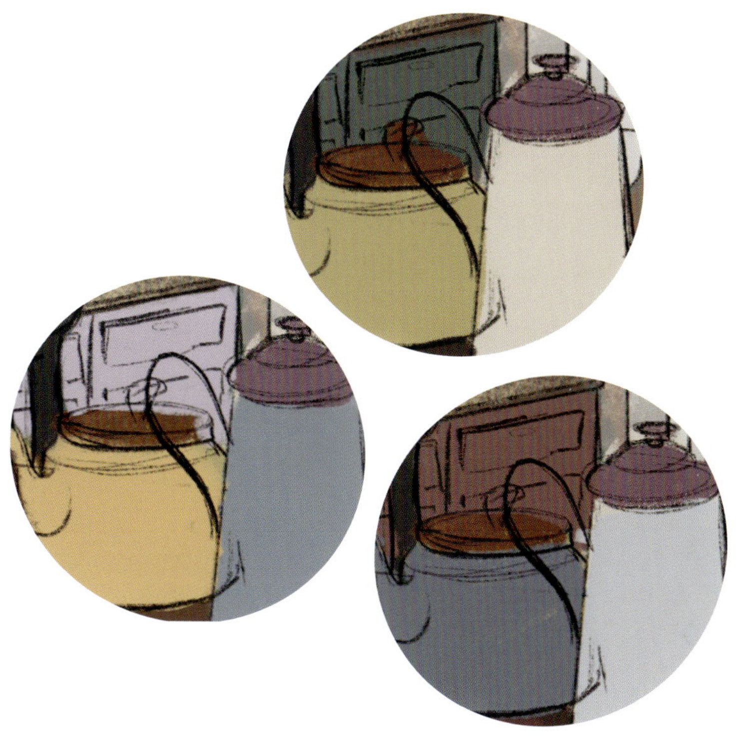

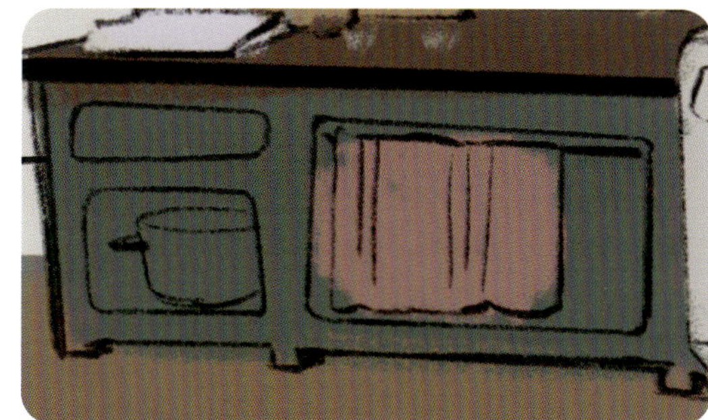

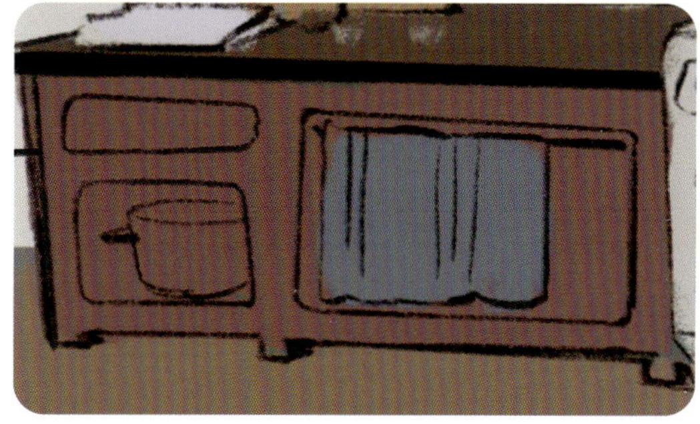

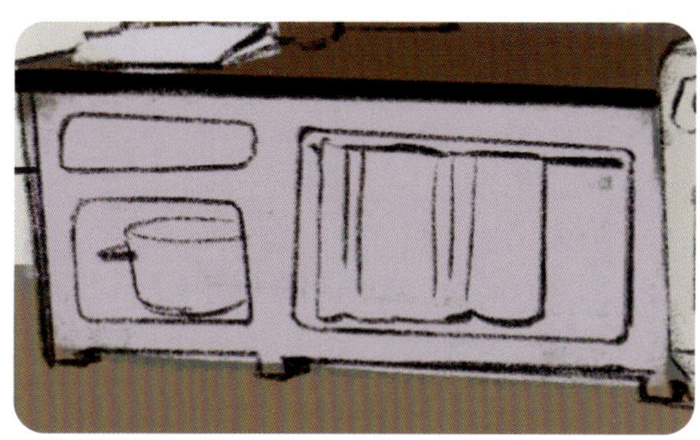

ADDING WARMTH

Now comes my favourite part – adding colour. At this point it's best to explore and test different colour palettes; much like with the sketching step, it's good not to stick with the obvious or initial choice. Colour is a strong tool to communicate and generate sensation from your viewer, so think about what you want to convey with your colour choices. For this piece, choose warm colours to create a homely vibe.

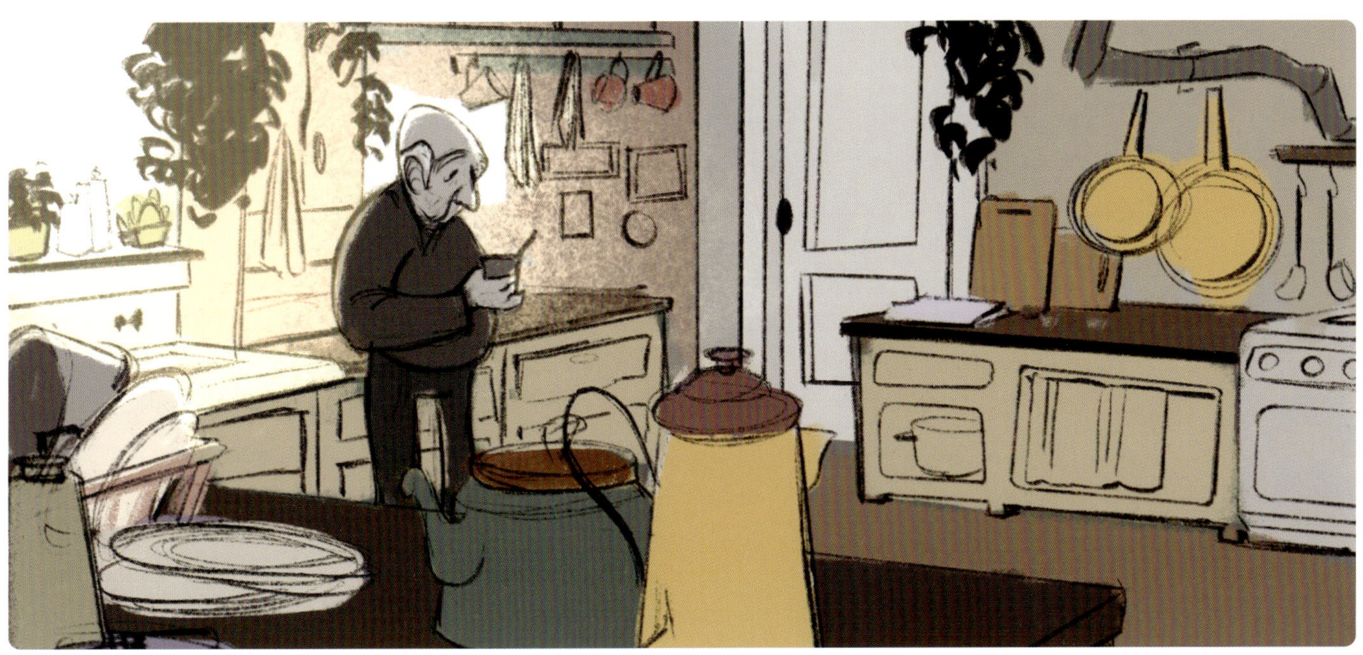

A SPLASH OF COLOUR

Once you've selected a colour scheme that works, you can block in the base colours of everything within the composition. Group the elements in different layers so they are easier to work on – this is especially helpful later on when adding texture and lighting.

I separate my composition into four layers: foreground, props, character, and background. I tend not to need more than that. Try not to go overboard separating every item on a single layer, as that can get annoying and messy when you work on later steps.

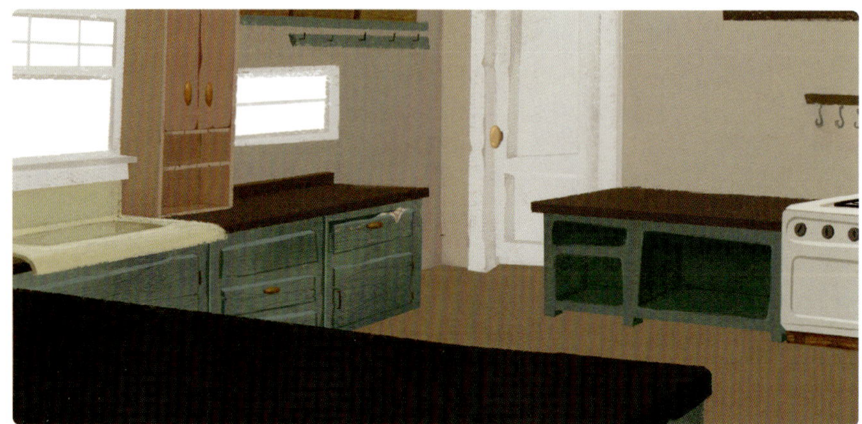

'Block in the base colours of everything within the composition'

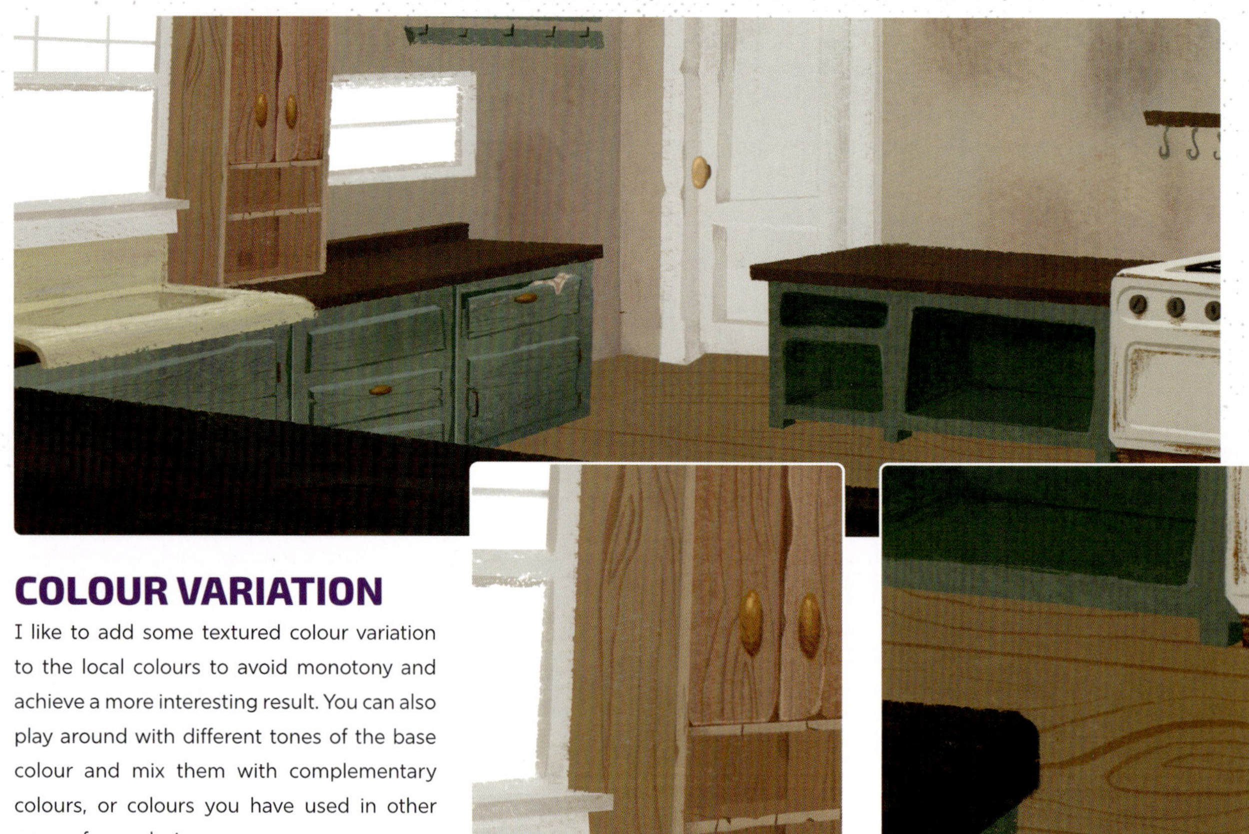

COLOUR VARIATION

I like to add some textured colour variation to the local colours to avoid monotony and achieve a more interesting result. You can also play around with different tones of the base colour and mix them with complementary colours, or colours you have used in other areas of your design.

HOME-MADE

I prefer my work to feel expressive and stray away from the more digital look, so I like to use a lot of textures when I'm painting. I pay special attention to the edges of the shapes, making sure they don't have perfectly defined lines. This makes them look like they've been drawn in chalk or gouache. Another way to create this look is to avoid smoother airbrush tools and instead go for chunkier, gritty ones to give a more organic texture.

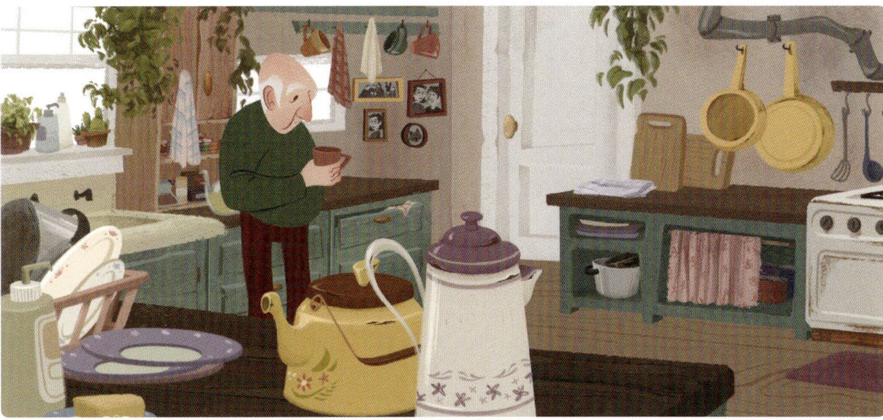

RISE & SHINE

Shading can change the mood and set the atmosphere of the whole painting. I have set this scene in the morning, so I add a strong light source from the rising sun coming through the open windows. You can emphasize strong light by adding rim light on the objects in the foreground – this makes them stand out from the shadows and creates interesting lines around the silhouettes of the kitchen gadgets.

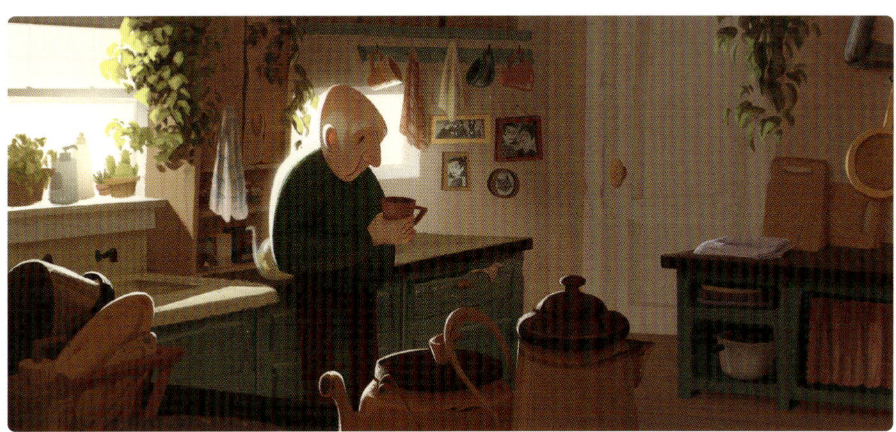

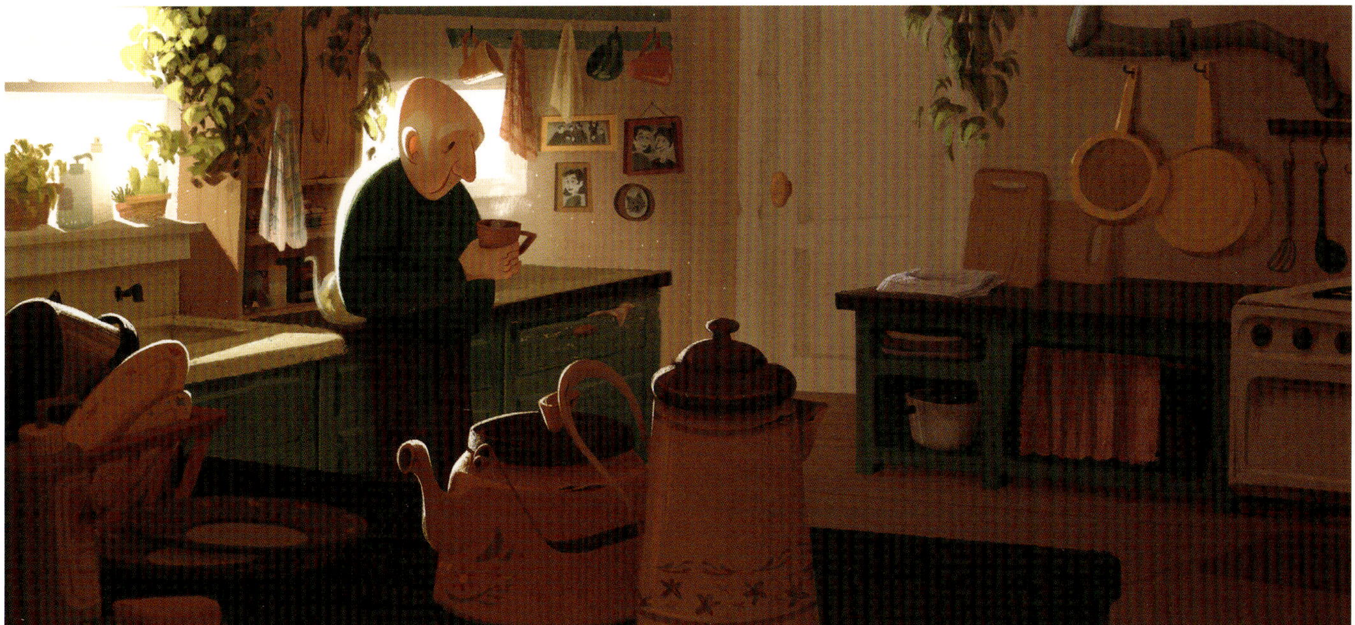

EARLY BIRD

Finally, it's time to add some subtle details to pull the piece together. To accentuate the nostalgic atmosphere I want to portray, I add a little extra texture to help the image feel cinematic. I also add floating dust around the light source to make the scene feel more alive. As a final touch I adjust the contrast and darken the corners to add depth – and it's done!

Final image © Raquel Villanueva

LINE OF ACTION

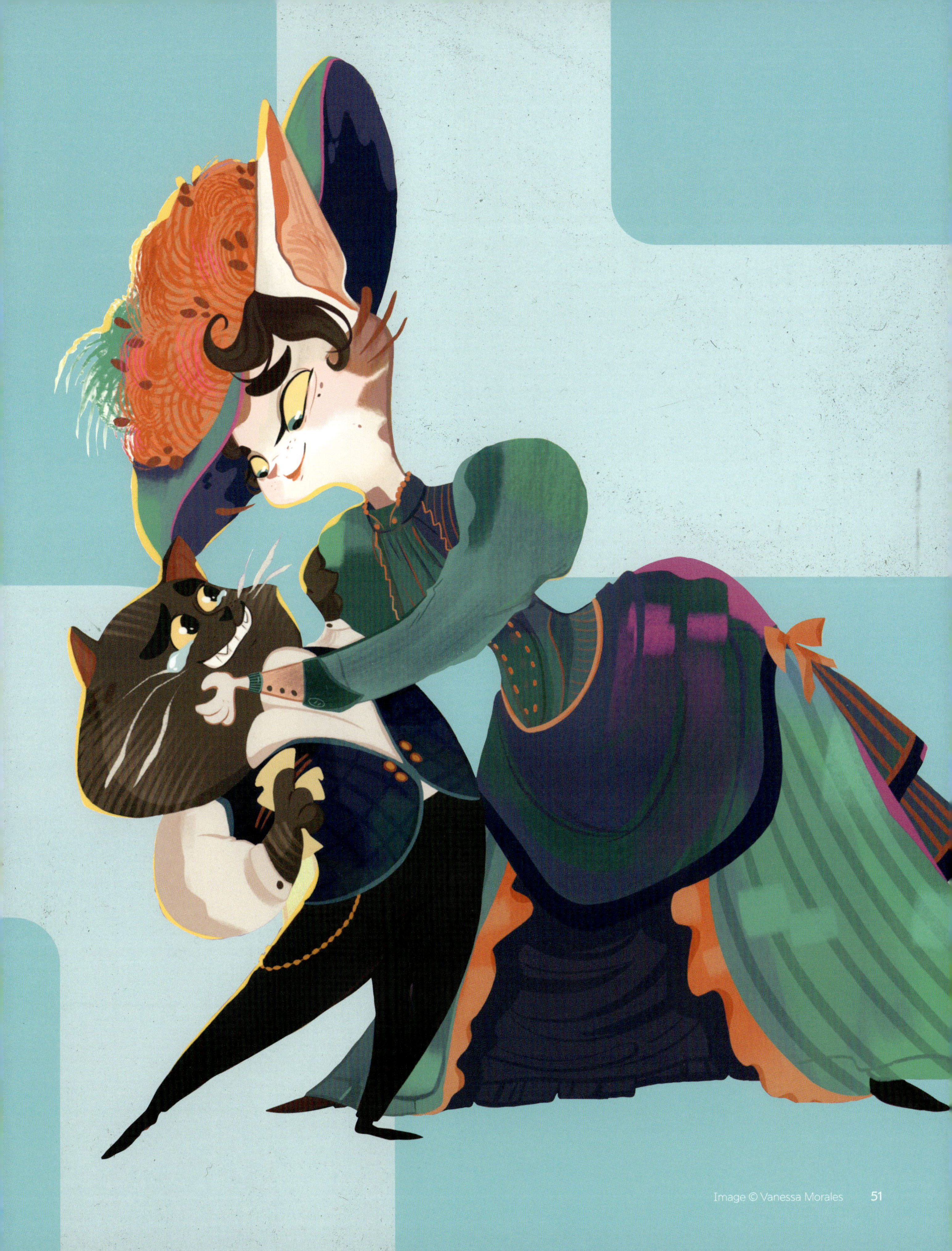

Image © Vanessa Morales

A motion masterclass

JOAKIM RIEDINGER

Our whole universe is in constant motion – flowers grow, trees sway, people walk, and everything is always evolving. Movement is at the centre of our lives, but how do you express this energy in your work? Let's look at a few principles that will help to translate force into movement in drawings.

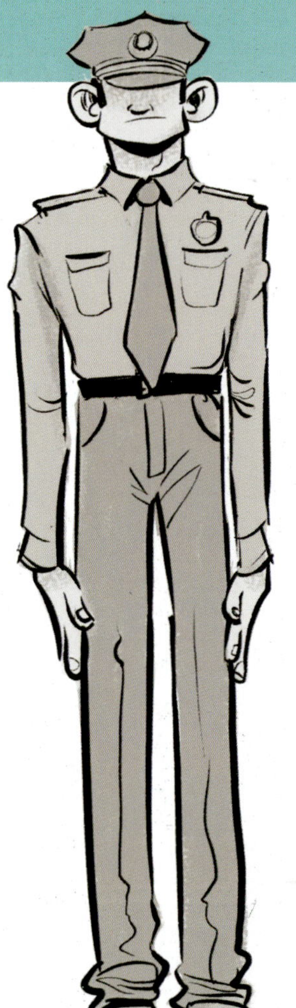

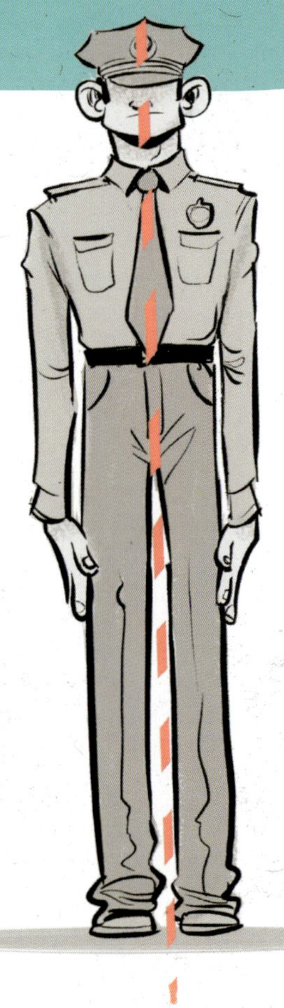

DRAW SMALL, QUICK THUMBNAILS FIRST

Drawing small thumbnails allows you to think about the overall design, silhouettes, and action lines, rather than focusing on small details. It's also much faster to generate a lot of ideas when they are done in a few seconds.

STARTING STATIC

To create the illusion of movement and motion in your drawing, you need to avoid symmetrical poses. They tend to make a drawing seem unnatural and stiff – unless, of course, you want to convey that someone is firm and strict, like this police officer.

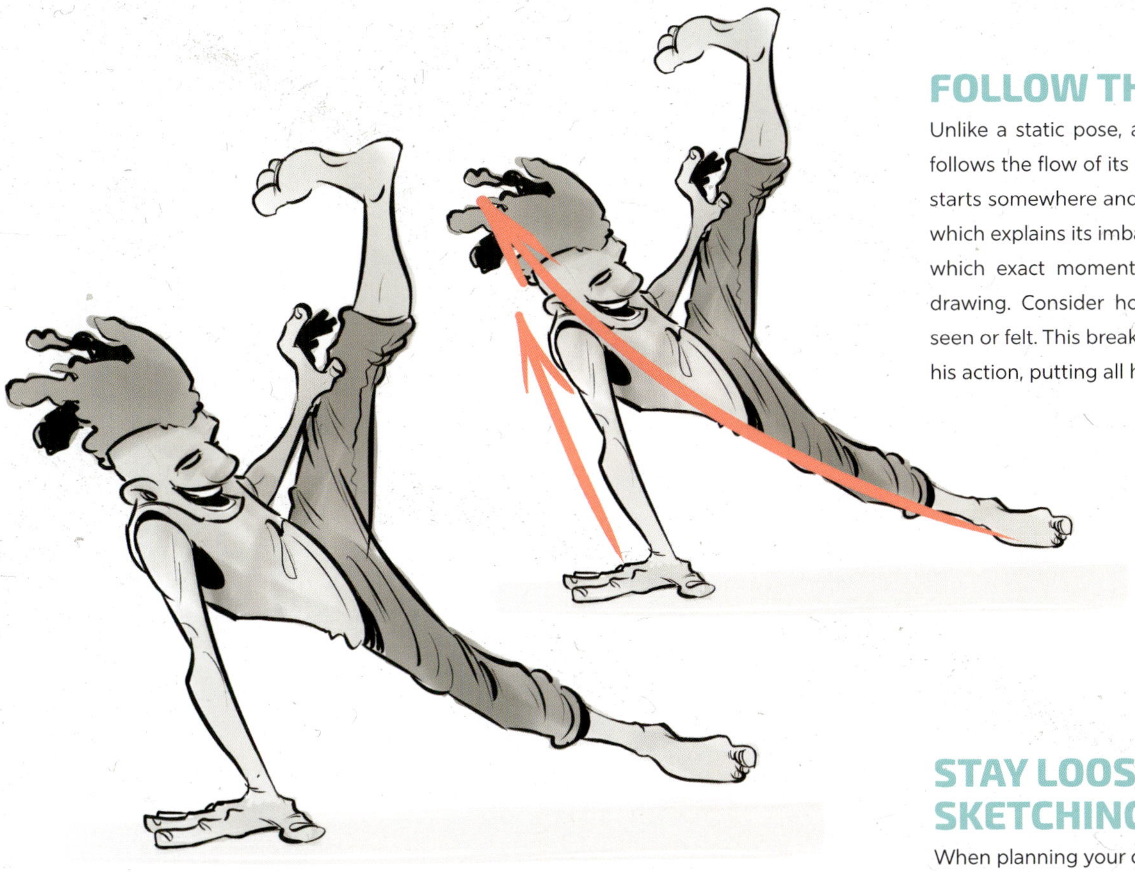

FOLLOW THE FLOW

Unlike a static pose, a dynamic pose always follows the flow of its movements. The action starts somewhere and ends somewhere else, which explains its imbalance. It helps to know which exact moment of an action you are drawing. Consider how much force can be seen or felt. This breakdancer is at the apex of his action, putting all his weight on one arm.

STAY LOOSE IN THE SKETCHING STAGE

When planning your design, stay relaxed and try to draw quickly – energy will naturally flow from you.

THE EXTENSION IS THE MOTION

To generate maximum force, a muscle chain must reach an extension, which is why all limbs line up and follow a line of action. It helps to include this physical principle in your drawings to show a sense of weight. This bull is heading in one clear direction, and his whole body and movement mirrors that.

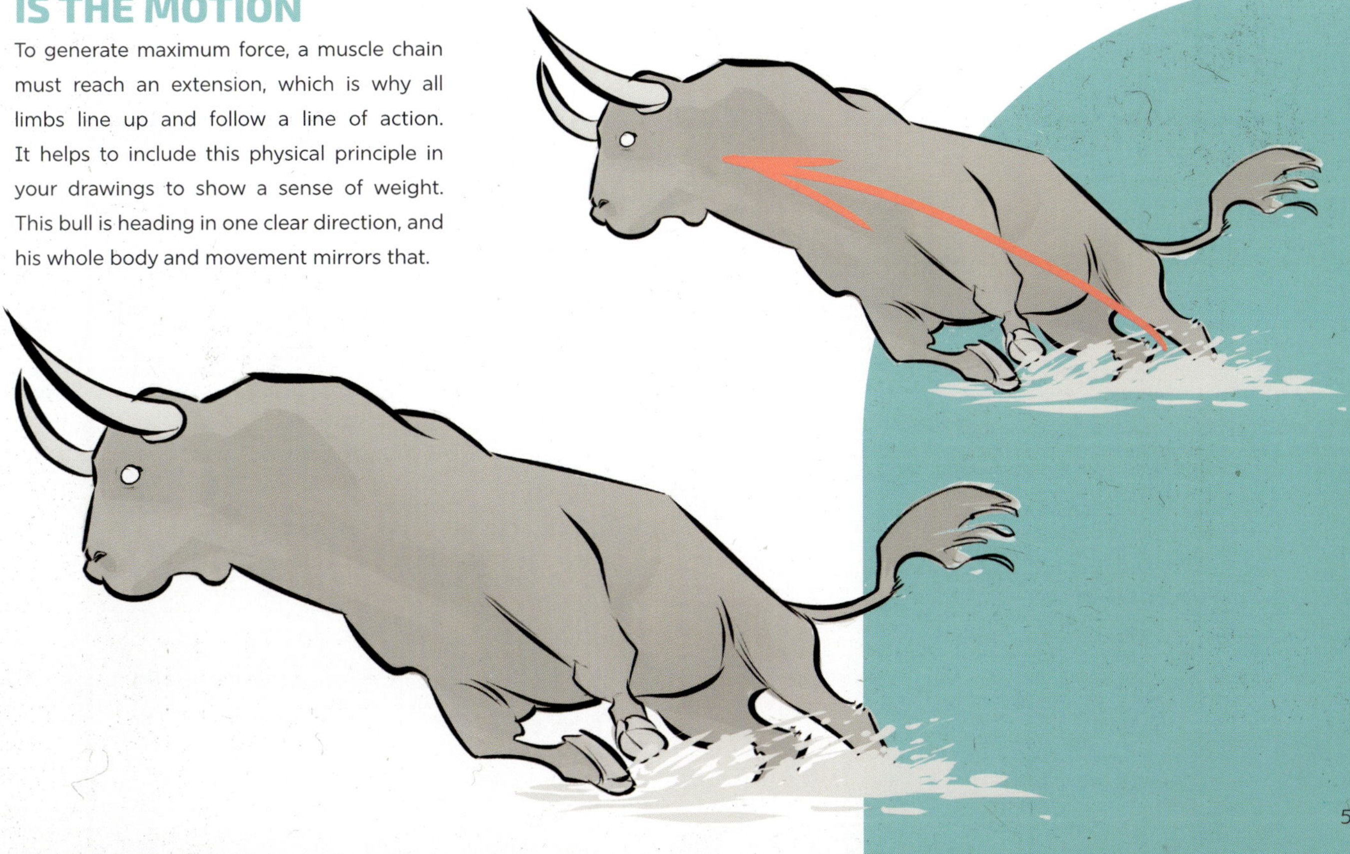

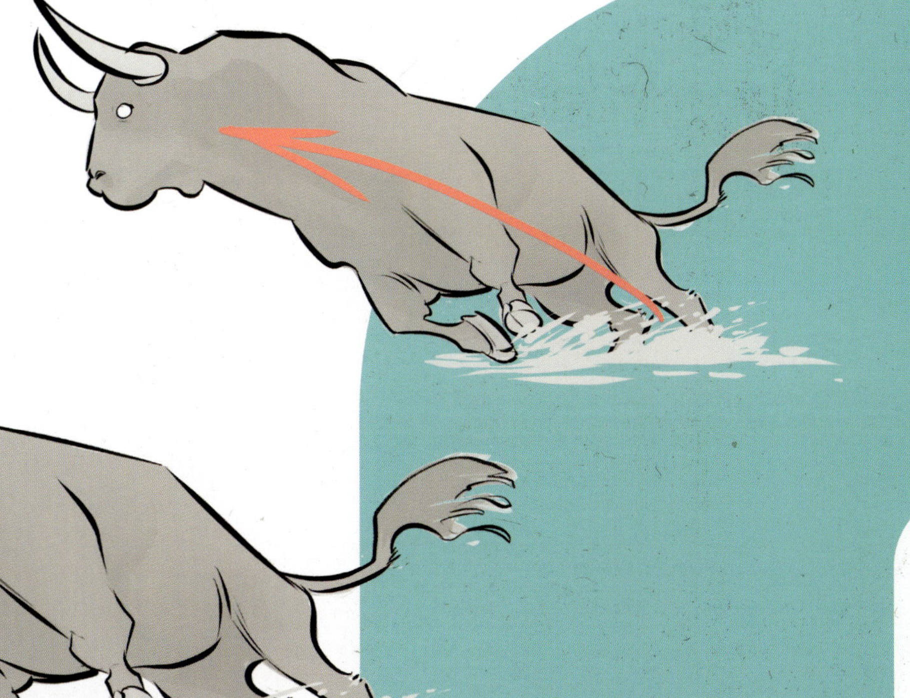

> 'When a force is applied to an object or a character, an opposite reaction must also be apparent – action means reaction'

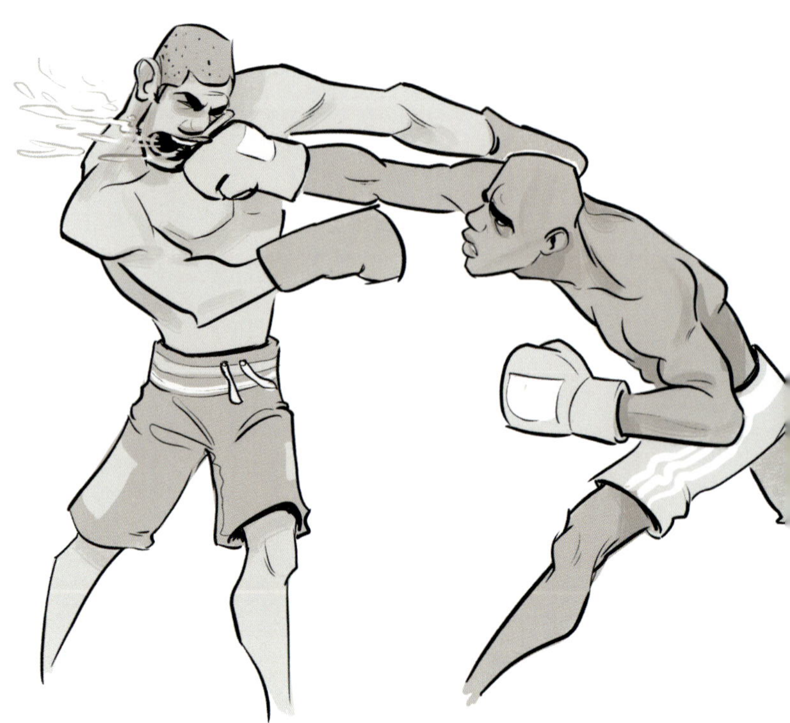

ACTION & REACTION

When a force is applied to an object or a character, an opposite reaction must also be apparent – action means reaction. This principle makes the two parts more related to each other. Look how the force of one boxer has an extreme impact on the face of the other boxer, and his line of action. In the other example, the hug of two friends looks almost magnetic. Use this principle to emphasize your characters' situations.

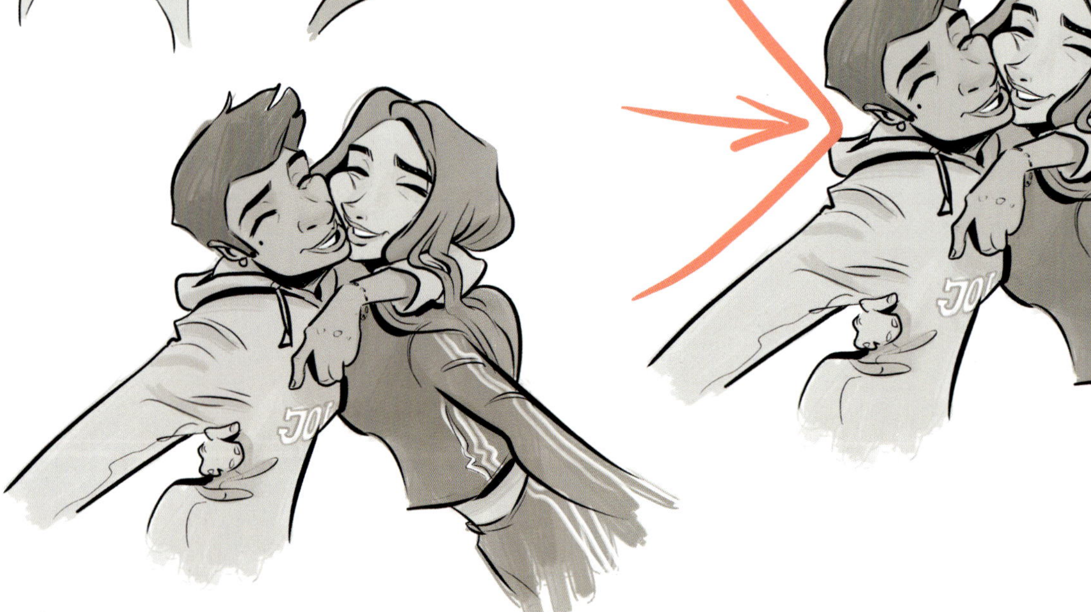

LAYER & INCREASE ACTION LINES

To make a gesture appear more textured and interesting, try to introduce a multitude of patterns that align with a consistent overall direction. Look at the contours of this dancer's pose – not only does her dress show curvy movement, her body does, too. This multiplicity of curvy lines will enhance the sense of rhythm and fluidity in the action lines, and adds a certain grace and elegance to your character.

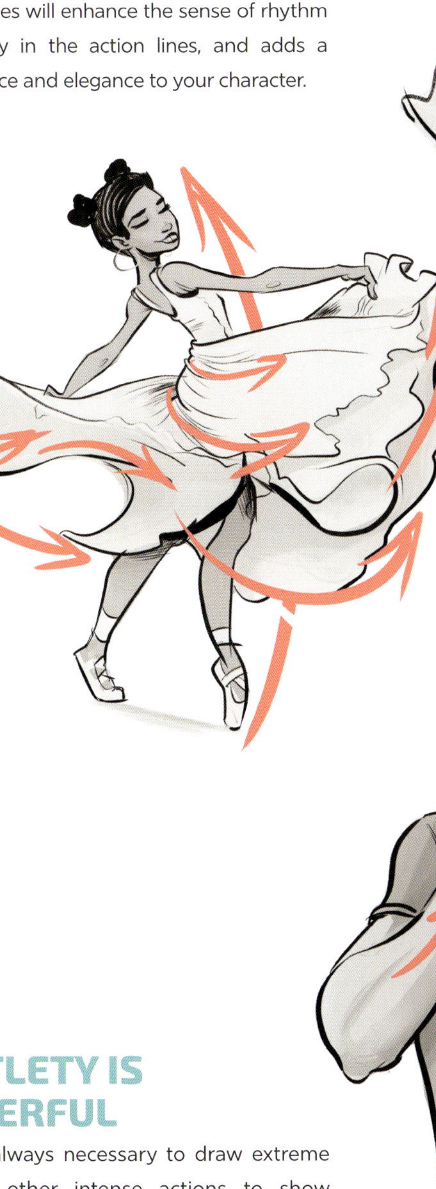

SUBTLETY IS POWERFUL

It is not always necessary to draw extreme fights or other intense actions to show dynamism. Emotion flowing through the body can also be expressed in subtle ways. In this case, the body of the man is still, his arms are close to his body, and his eyebrows are pointing upwards – the emotion is subtle, but no less effectively conveyed.

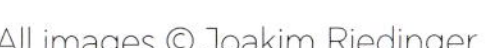

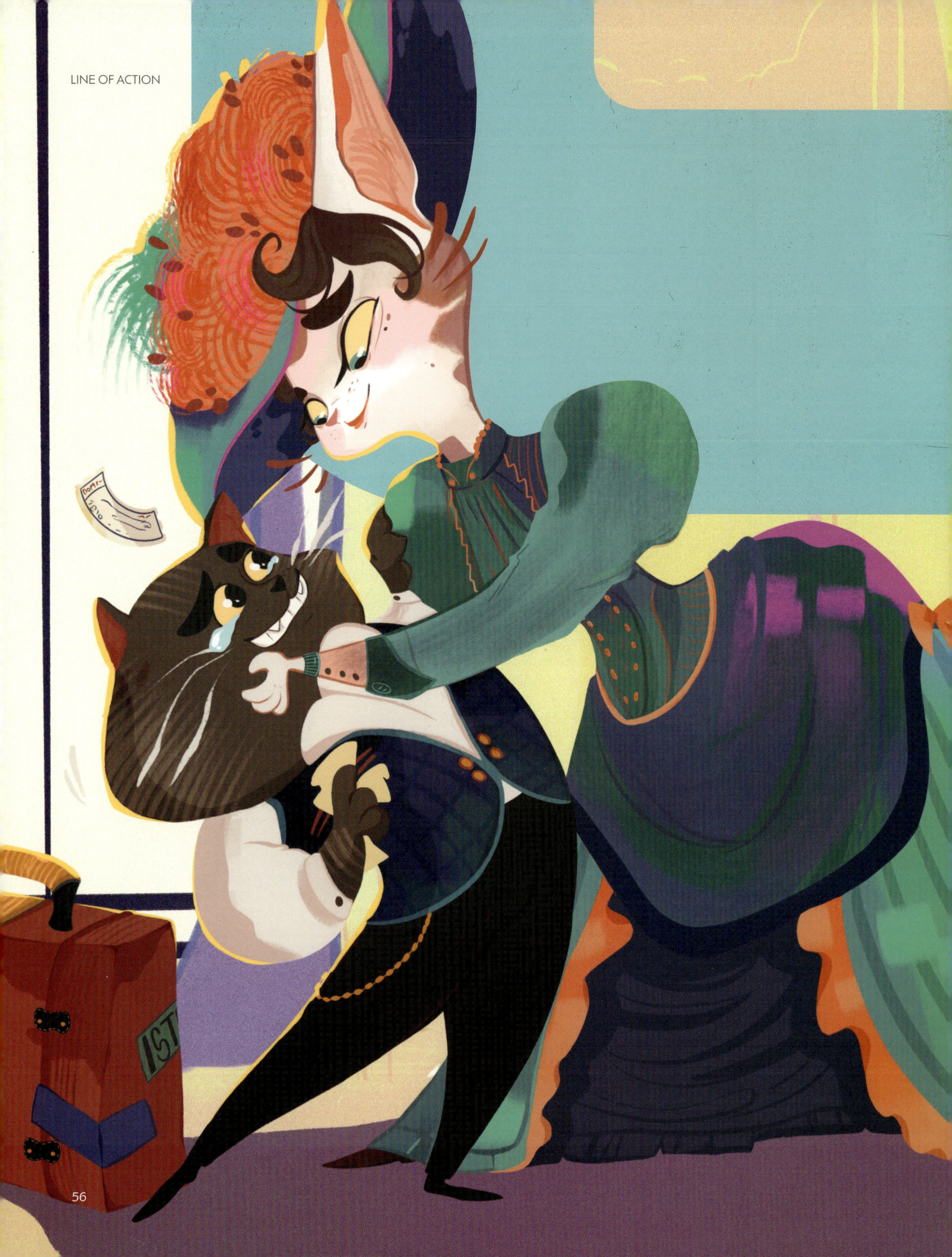

An emotional reunion

VANESSA MORALES

Over the course of this tutorial I will demonstrate how I develop a character-driven scene depicting an emotional meeting. I'll design a pair of anthropomorphic cats from the Victorian era, whose palpable connection is enriched by the design considerations behind their creation. Through the design process, the characters' backstory, shape language, expression, and interaction must be interrogated and perfected in order to bring them to life!

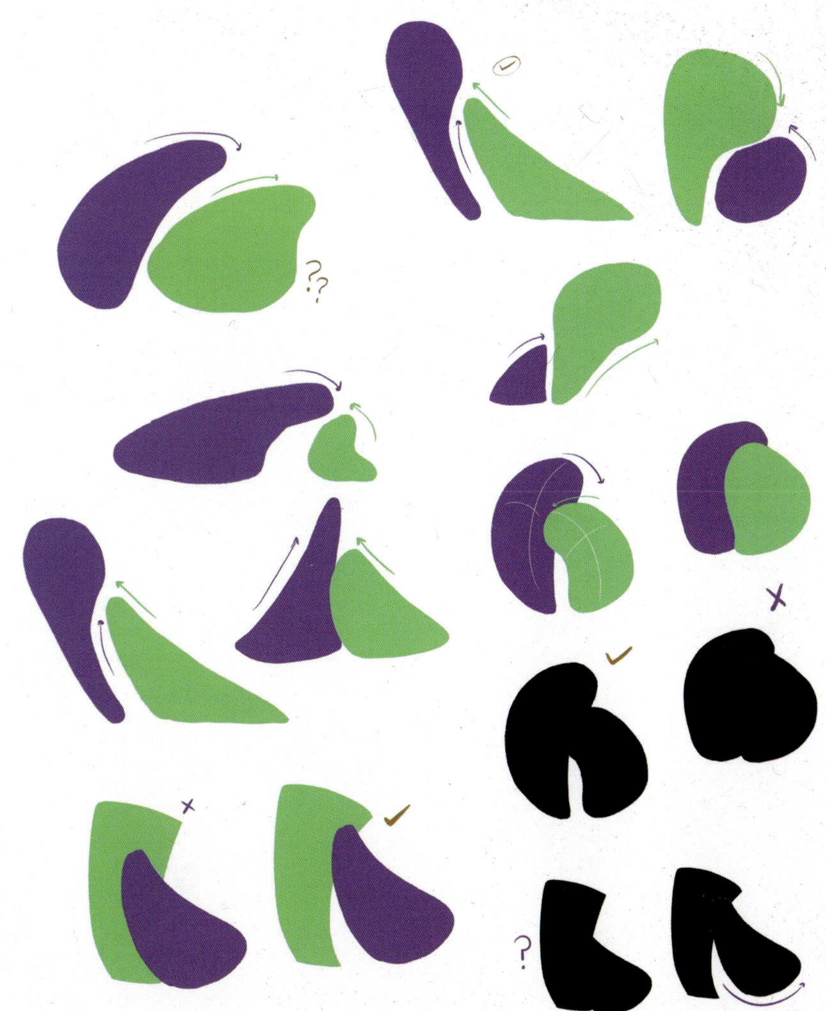

FEELING THROUGH SHAPES

One of the easiest ways to figure out if your characters work together is the use of shapes. If a shape is recognizable and readable then so is your character, and you can start to develop interactions through basic outlines of shapes. I opt for a contrast in the sizes of the characters, and sketch different shapes side by side to see how they work together. Consider how your characters will interact in the scene. Drawing simple, solid but interesting shapes such as these can help you decide on shape and size.

GESTURE & ACTION LINES

To depict readable emotions, gestures and expressions must be exaggerated. And when designing an interaction between two characters it is important to find the right composition to display the emotional connection between them. Spend some time exploring different pose dynamics. By varying the positions, the mood can change completely. If the characters are interacting with one another, their individual lines of action need to be in sync in order to harmonize their dynamic as a group.

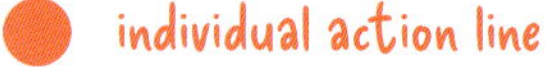

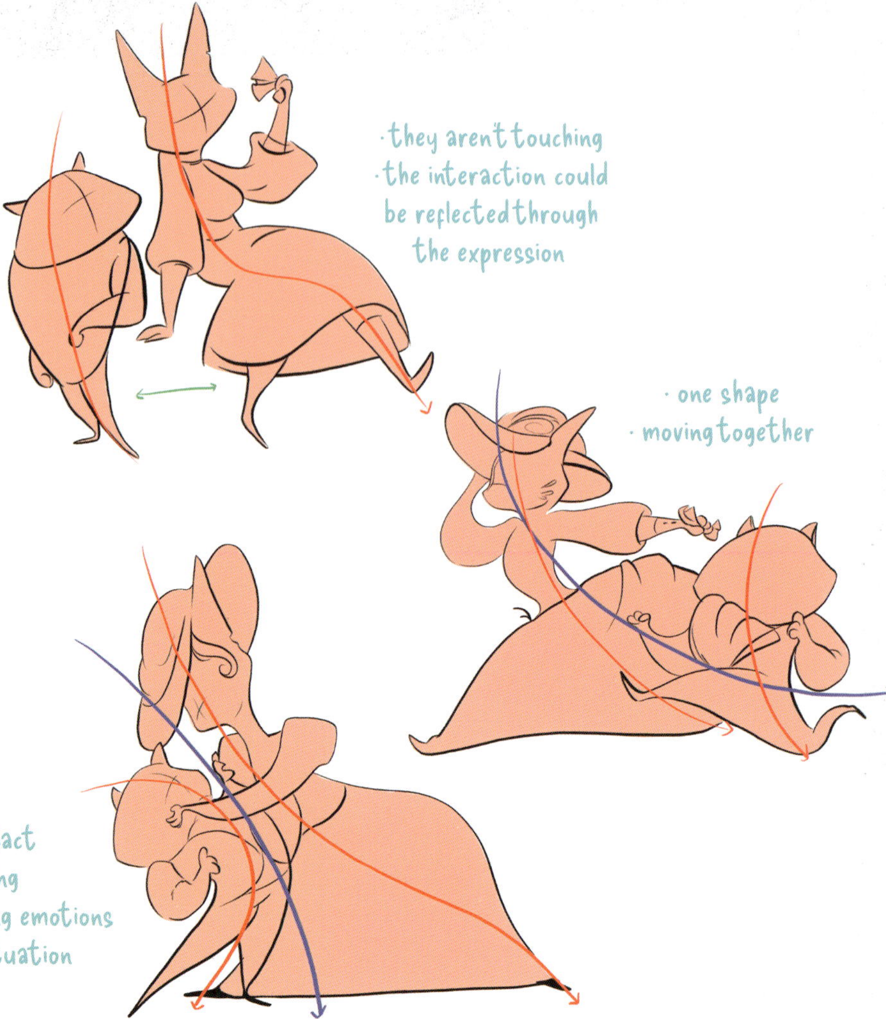

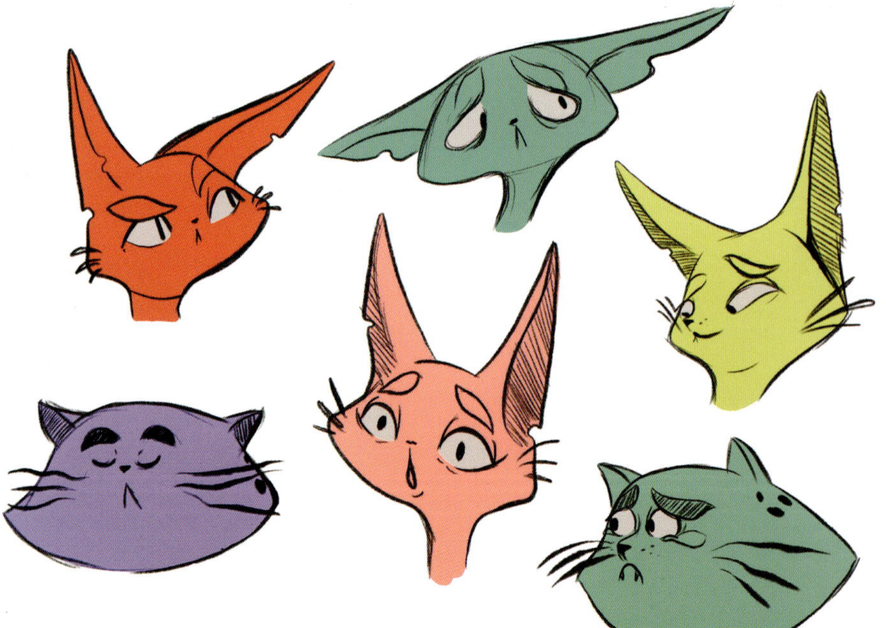

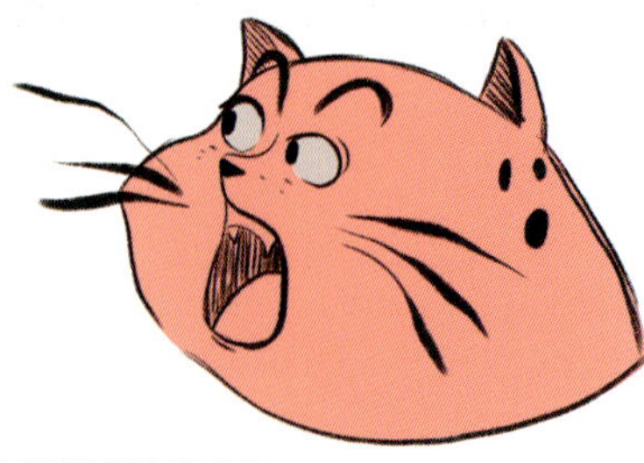

EXPRESSION

Try to understand the emotions of the characters to decipher their subsequent expressions and reactions to certain situations. A greater understanding of the characters' emotions and personalities makes them more relatable to the viewer. I find making duplications of the face and changing the expression is a useful exercise when trying to convey emotional connections.

SHAPE & SILHOUETTE

Now it's time to create the silhouette. Focus on a few interesting poses and consider whether they are recognizable in silhouette form and if the emotion is still readable. Sketch basic shapes following previous shape exploration and create the characters' silhouettes around this structure. Take account of clothes and any accessories the character may have as these will also affect the final silhouette. Sketch the silhouettes of the individual characters at the same time to make sure you are maintaining the connection between the two characters.

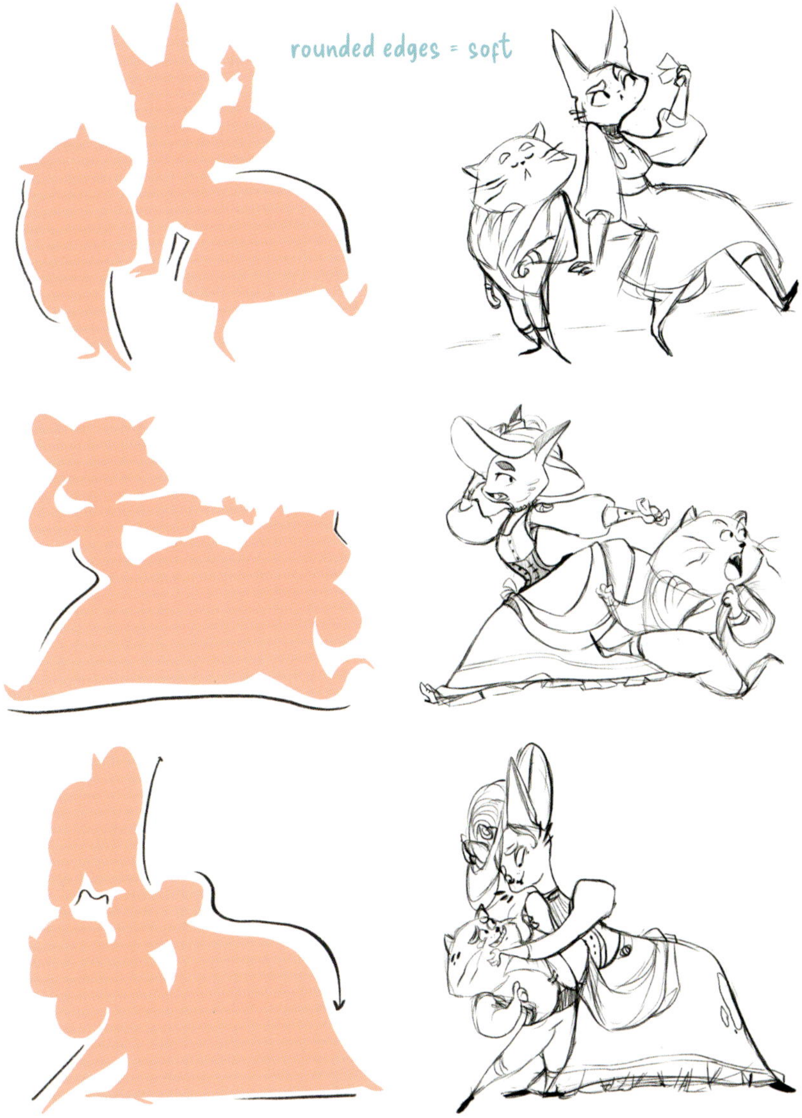

COMMUNICATING THROUGH COLOUR

This is one of my favourite parts of the character and world-building process – using colour to reinforce concepts and emotions. A colour palette can make a design feel weak if used incorrectly, so it's important to create a scheme that is easy to use and read. Communicating through colour is a crucial skill for designers – sticking to a palette of three to five colours helps keep designs clean and clear.

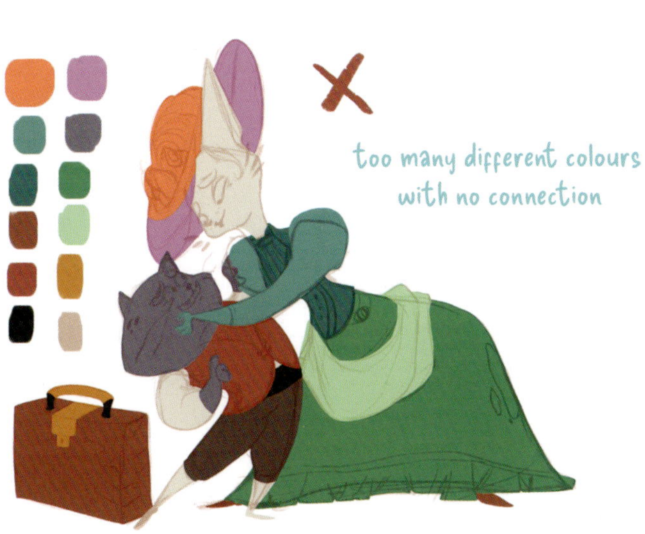

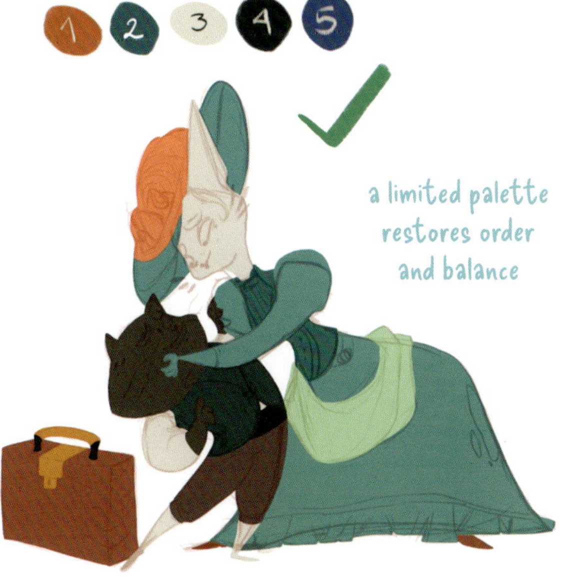

CHOOSING YOUR COLOURS

The colour palette needs to tell the story of the character as well as supporting the emotions that are being portrayed. While saturated colours are joyful, less-saturated colours can show sadness; a bright palette can make a character look young, and a neutral or dark palette can make them appear serious. Play around with saturation, hues, and brightness to develop a palette of colours that keeps the characters connected. I often use four analogues and one complementary colour to provide an accent.

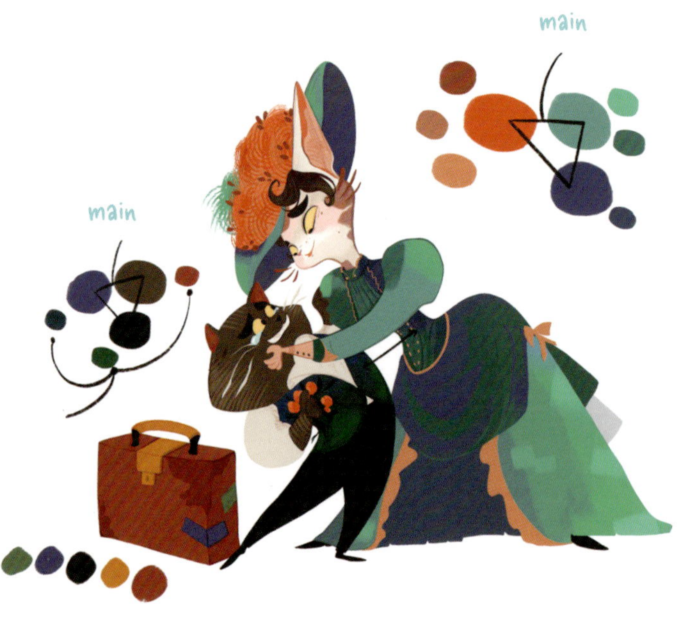

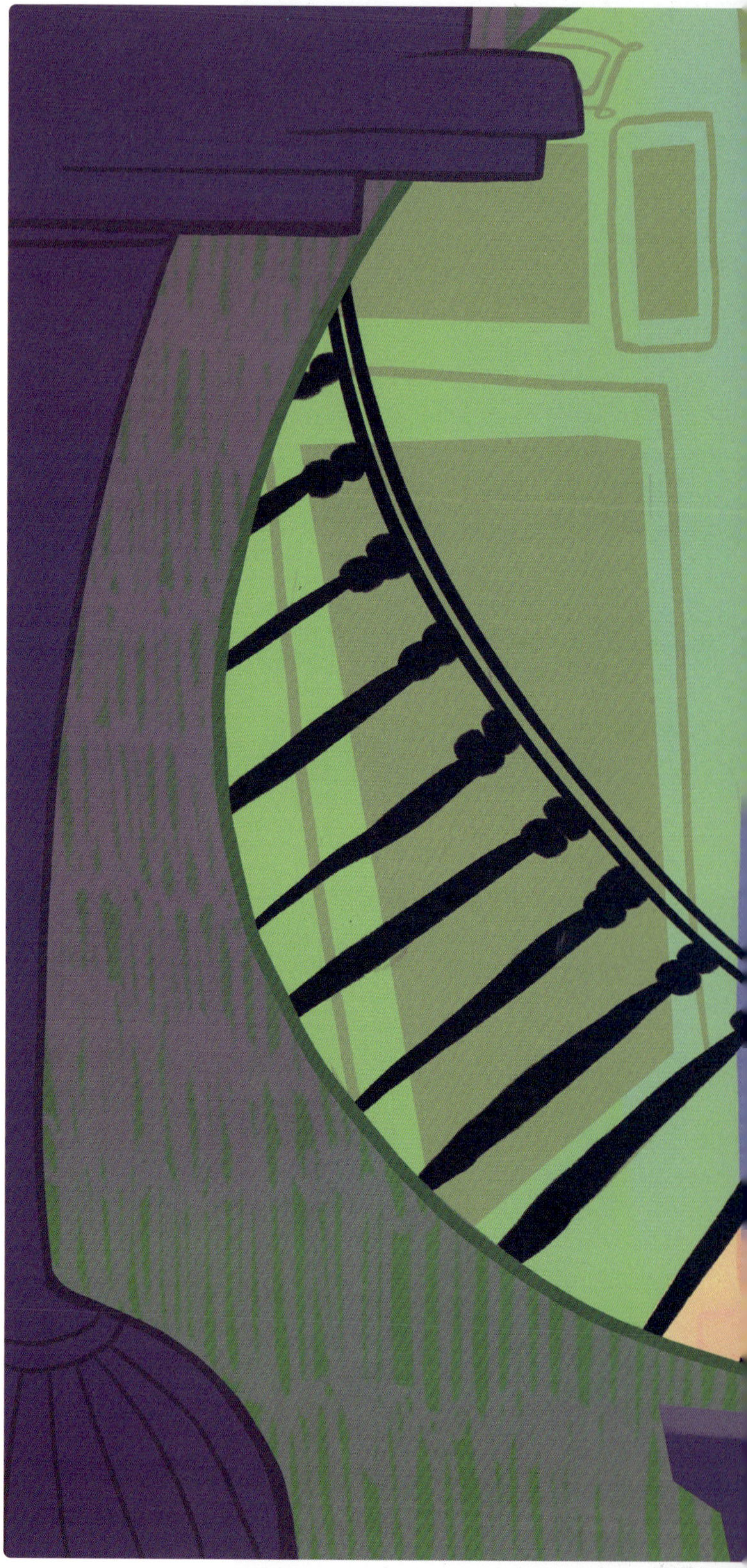

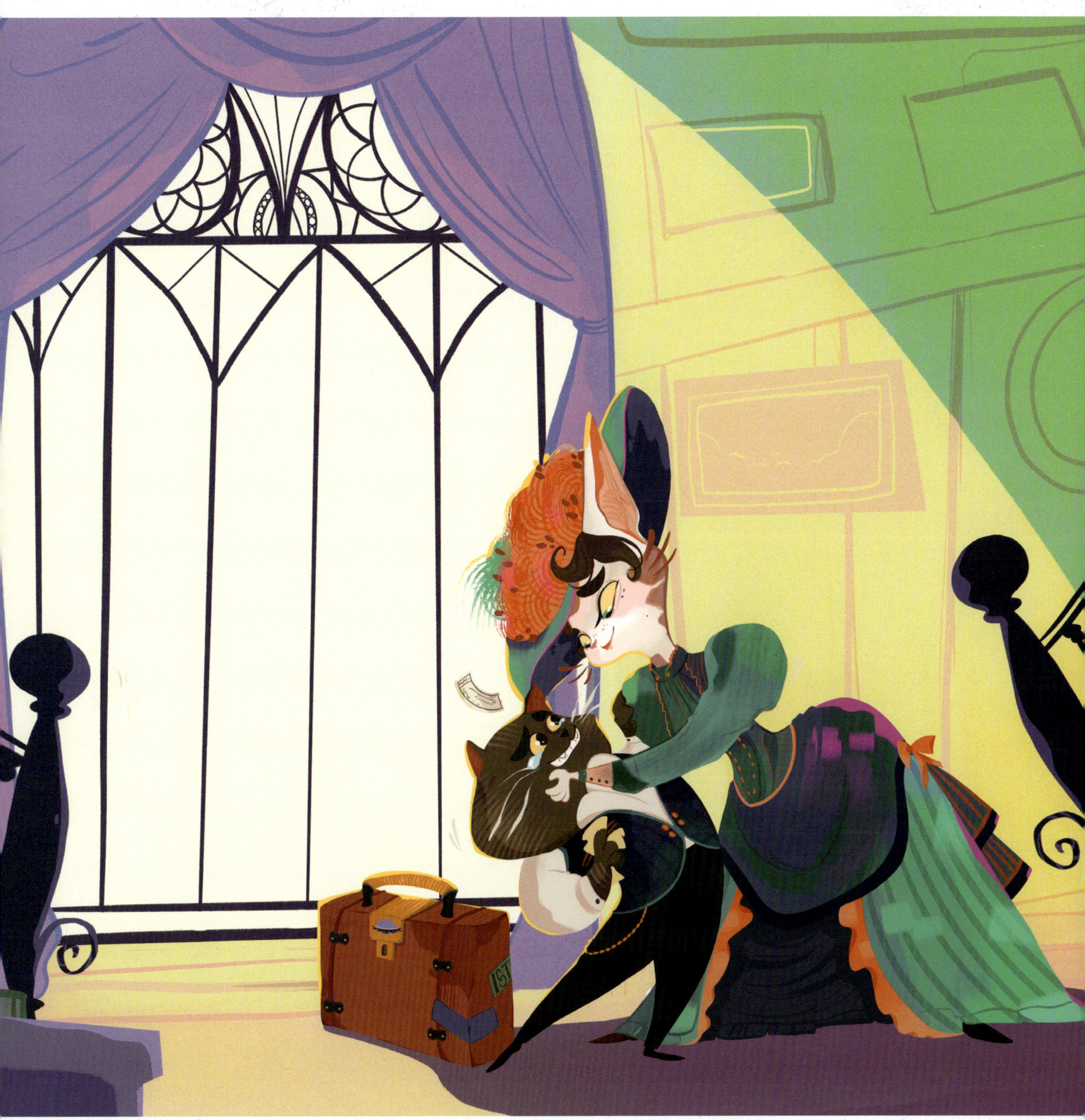

Final image © Vanessa Morales

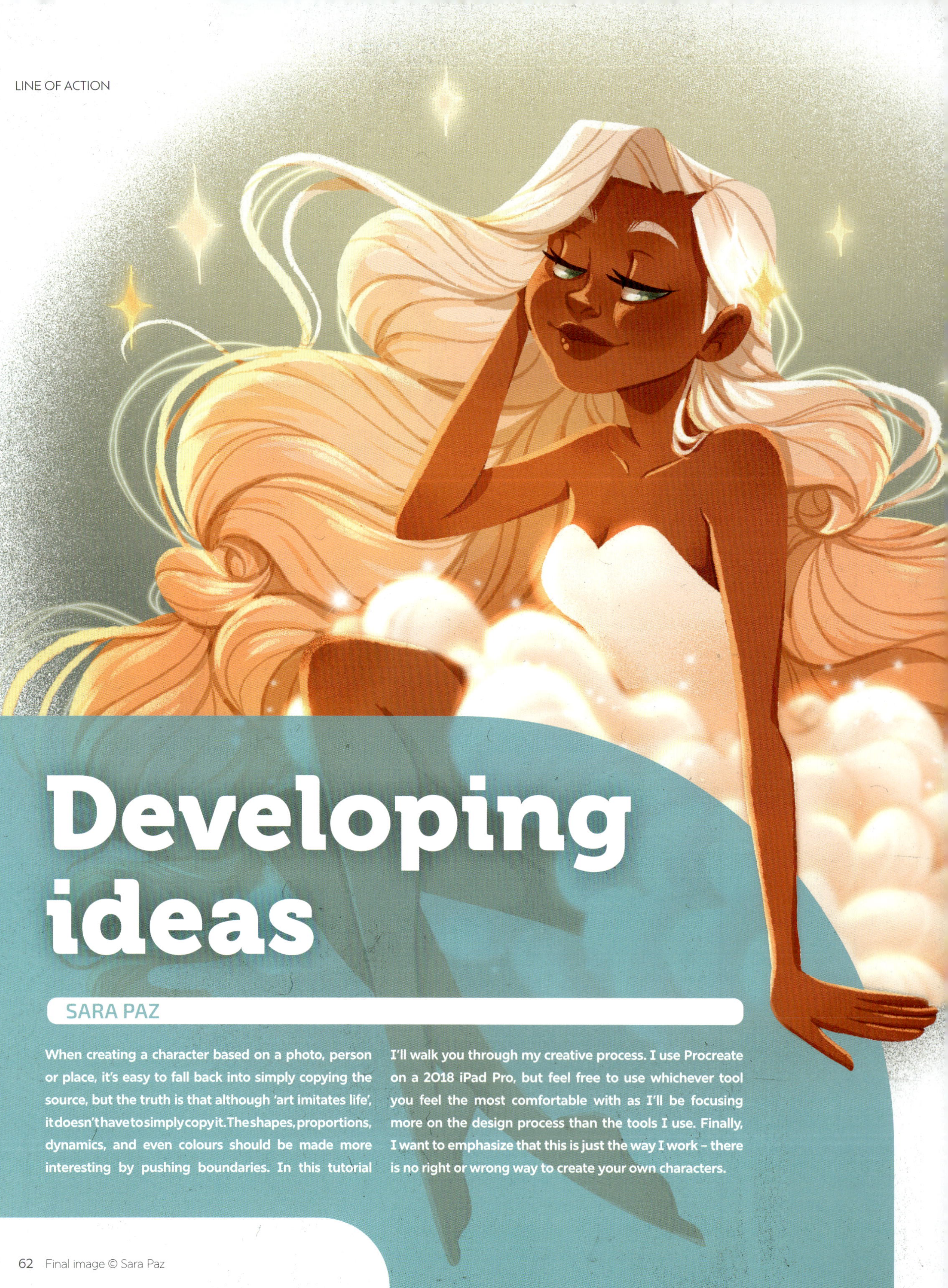

Developing ideas

SARA PAZ

When creating a character based on a photo, person or place, it's easy to fall back into simply copying the source, but the truth is that although 'art imitates life', it doesn't have to simply copy it. The shapes, proportions, dynamics, and even colours should be made more interesting by pushing boundaries. In this tutorial I'll walk you through my creative process. I use Procreate on a 2018 iPad Pro, but feel free to use whichever tool you feel the most comfortable with as I'll be focusing more on the design process than the tools I use. Finally, I want to emphasize that this is just the way I work – there is no right or wrong way to create your own characters.

 Final image © Sara Paz

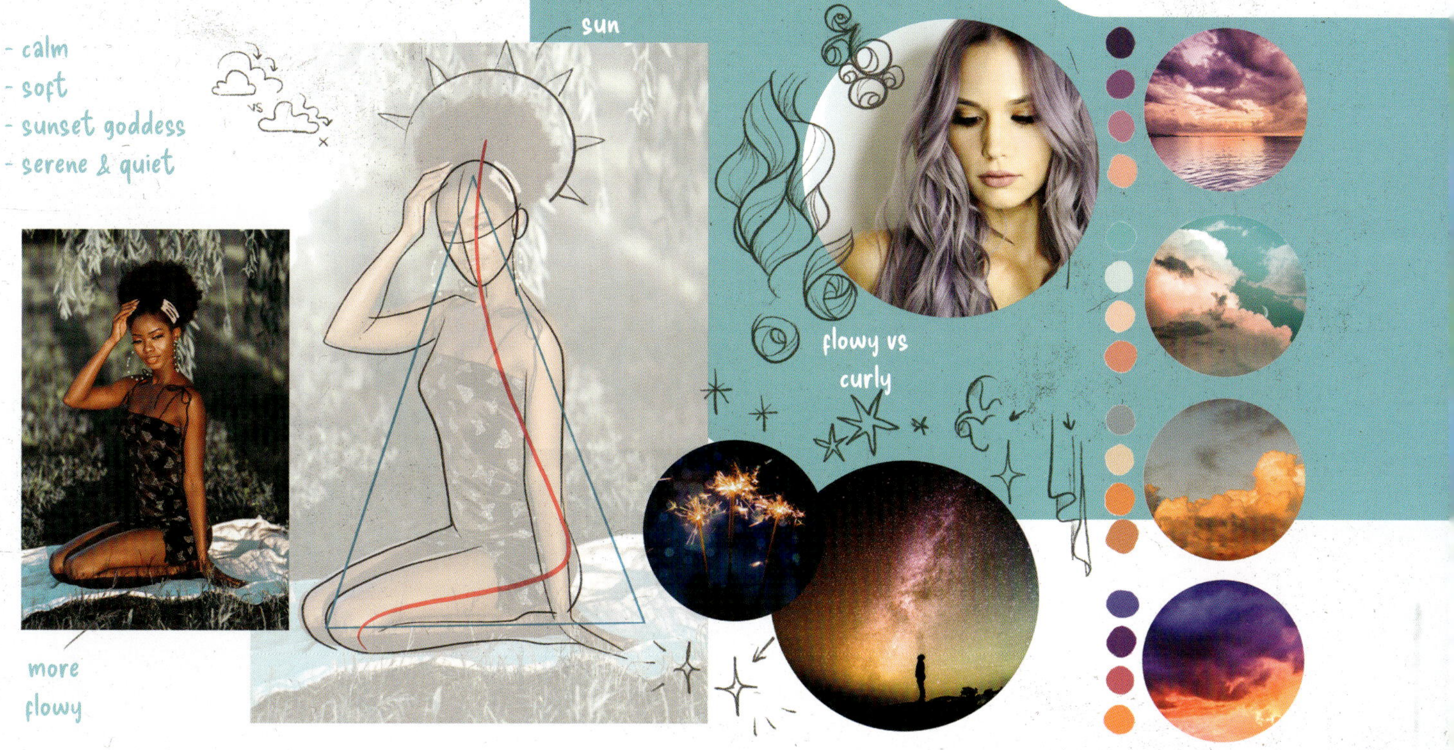

- calm
- soft
- sunset goddess
- serene & quiet

sun

more flowy

flowy vs curly

FINDING YOUR FOUNDATION

Choose an image that has the pose or shape you'd like to give your character and loosely sketch over it. Remember, the picture needs to spark your imagination – just being a pretty image won't be enough. Drawing this initial shape will make it easier to envision what it can become and where you can improve its structure throughout the process.

From this basic shape we can now start to build a character. Ask yourself, who are they? What sort of mood are they in? Where are they? What's their personality? Add photos, doodles, and notes that'll help you remember what you envision, and create a mood board from these ideas.

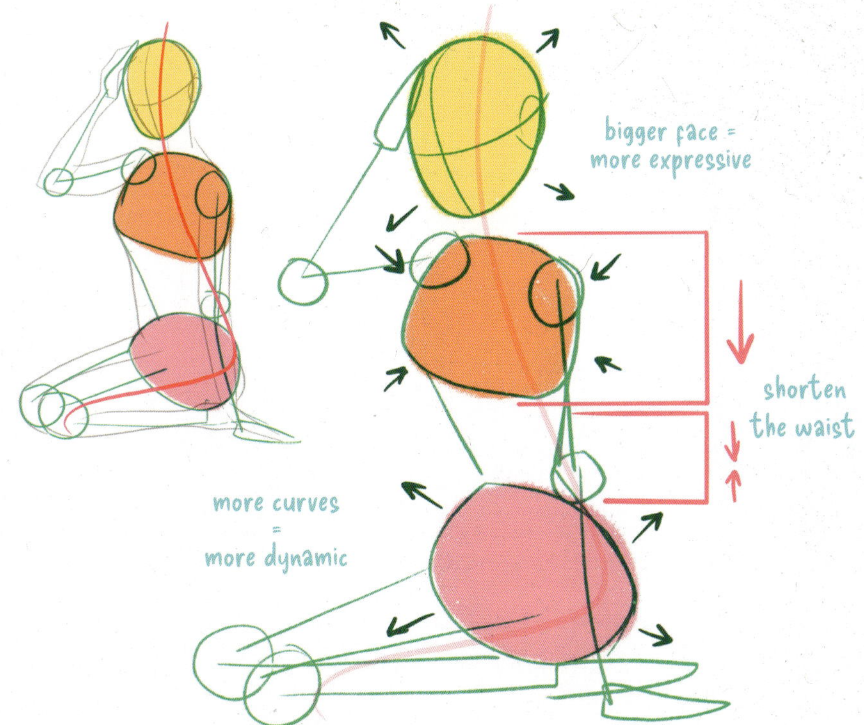

DECONSTRUCTING PROPORTIONS

On top of your loose figure, draw the main structural shapes that form the body: head, chest, hips, and joints. Now comes the fun part – we're going to play with these proportions! Sticking with the original 'perfect' look of a real image can lead to a dull, uninspired final illustration. Pushing and pulling these shapes can help make your drawing more visually interesting and dynamic. There are no rules with how far you can stretch the shapes, but for this exercise I slightly enlarge the head and make the torso and chest smaller, more in line with the shape of the hips, which I also enlarge.

THE LINE OF ACTION

Now let's play with line of action. Currently, our character has a static, almost perfectly inverted 'L' shape. Her shape is fairly stable and balanced – we want to try to maintain this while still making the design more dynamic and fun. To do this, we want to exaggerate the line of action, making it more curved by tilting the head, chest, waist, and hips, gradually changing the 'L' shape into more of an 'S.' Don't be afraid to push for unrealistic proportions – this is art, not anatomy drawing, and even the most extreme real poses will look that extra bit better when stretched a little further.

THROWING SHAPES

Avoid tangents and confusing shapes by shifting the positions of the legs or arms in order to make the shape clearer and give it a little extra 'oomph'. Don't be afraid to push shapes harder than you might think – that's where fun ideas are born. In this example, changing the position of the legs made the design more dynamic while maintaining the balance and feel of the composition.

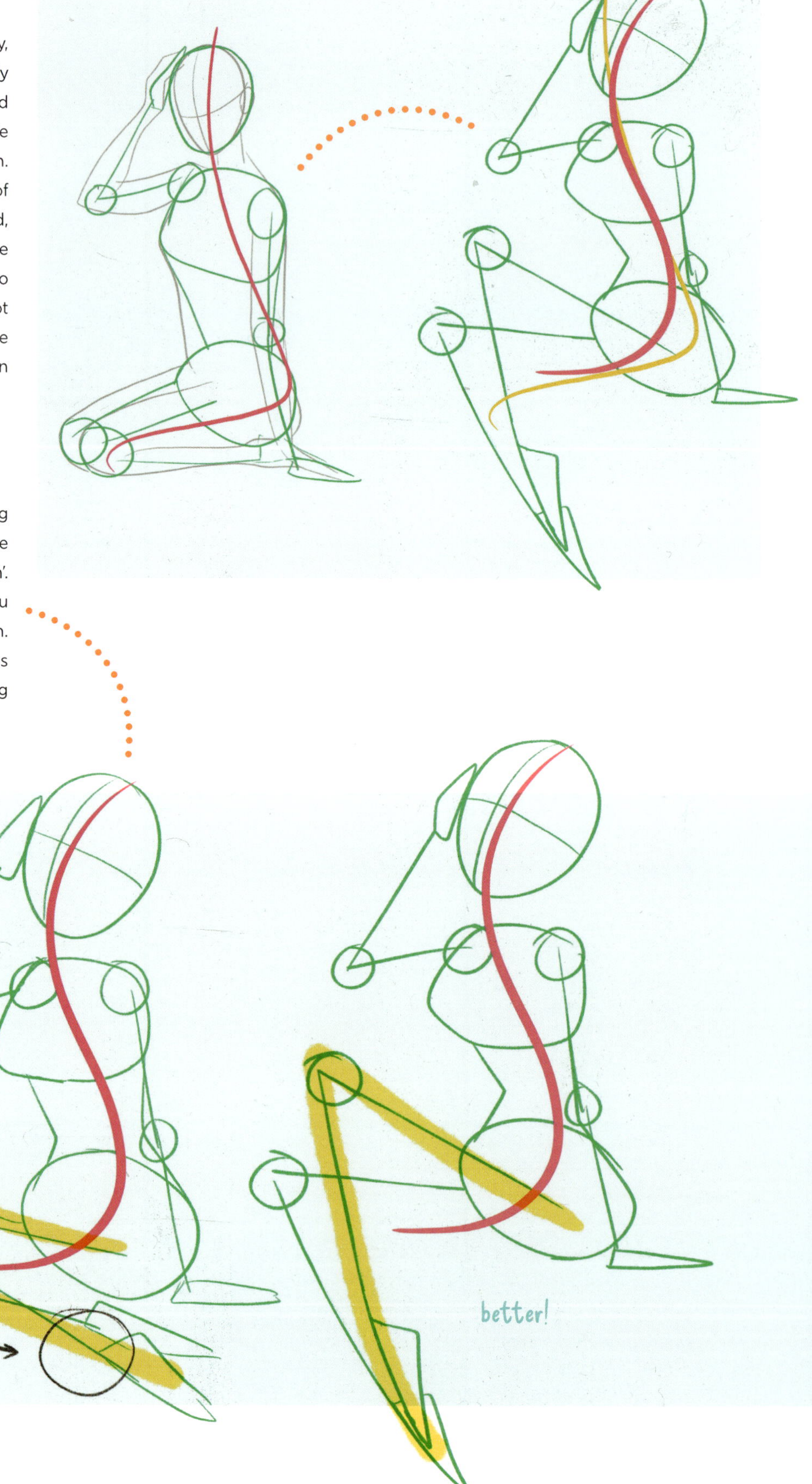

ADDING DETAIL

Now let's fill in the gaps in the structure, the 'muscles' that connect the shapes and define the silhouette. Roughly sketch the overall shape and try contrasting straight lines with curved ones to convey more dynamism in your figure. Focus on this while experimenting.

By now you should already know who your character is, so it's time to draw their emotions. I start by drawing loose shapes to get a better grasp of where everything goes and then redrawing as needed to perfect them. Take your time with this step – choosing the right emotion is key for an eye-catching character.

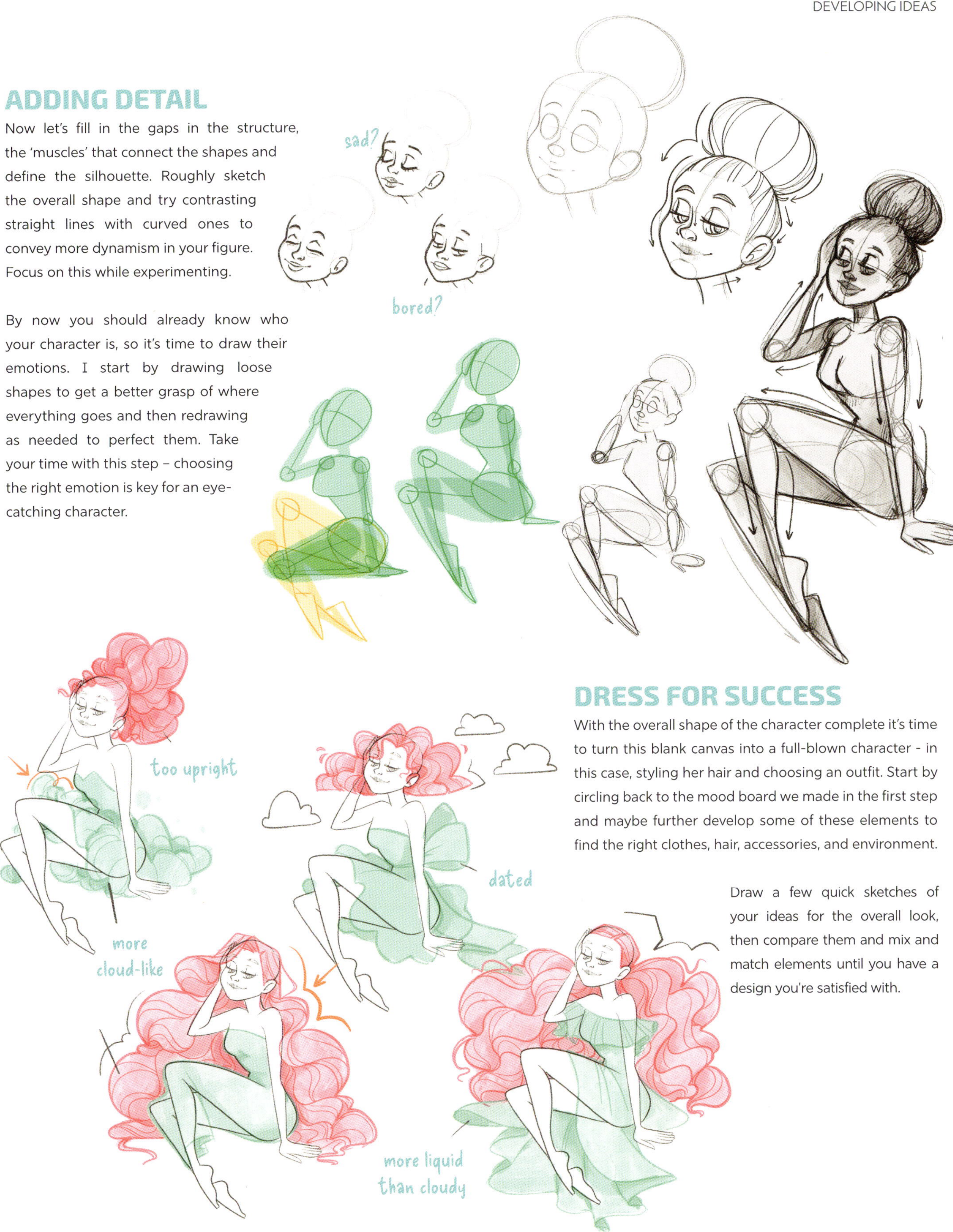

DRESS FOR SUCCESS

With the overall shape of the character complete it's time to turn this blank canvas into a full-blown character - in this case, styling her hair and choosing an outfit. Start by circling back to the mood board we made in the first step and maybe further develop some of these elements to find the right clothes, hair, accessories, and environment.

Draw a few quick sketches of your ideas for the overall look, then compare them and mix and match elements until you have a design you're satisfied with.

READY, SET, COLOUR!

Start from the bottom and build the layers up from there – hair, skin, and finally clothes and details. Lock your line art as the top layer and set it to Multiply at 30% opacity as a guide. It's good to already have an idea of the texture and details of each element before you start creating them – are they hard or soft, defined or fuzzy? Do you want a more realistic look or a more graphic stroke? I tend to start with a precise, textured feel – my favourite brush is Dry Ink. Colour all the areas of the base layers one by one until the character is complete.

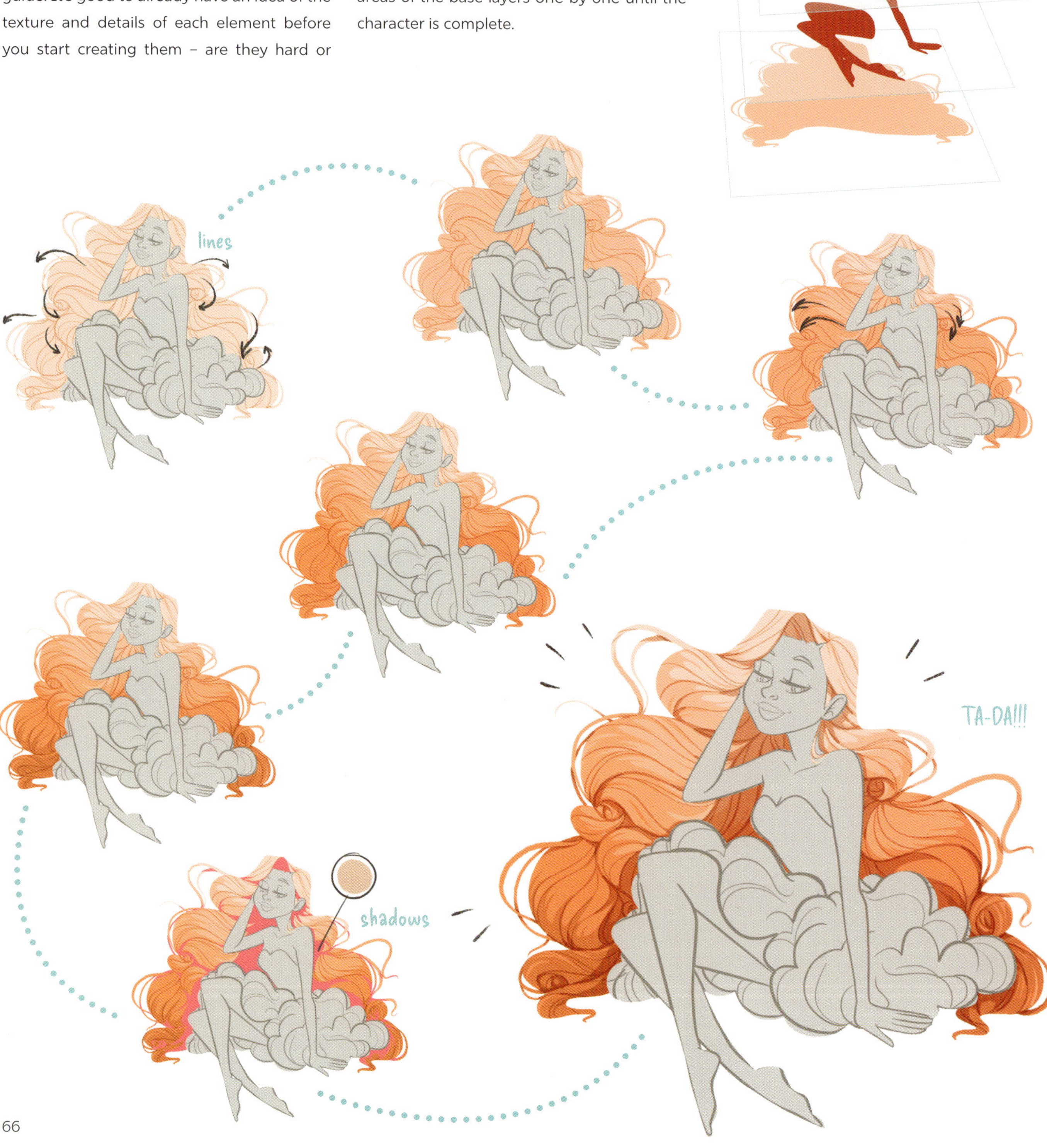

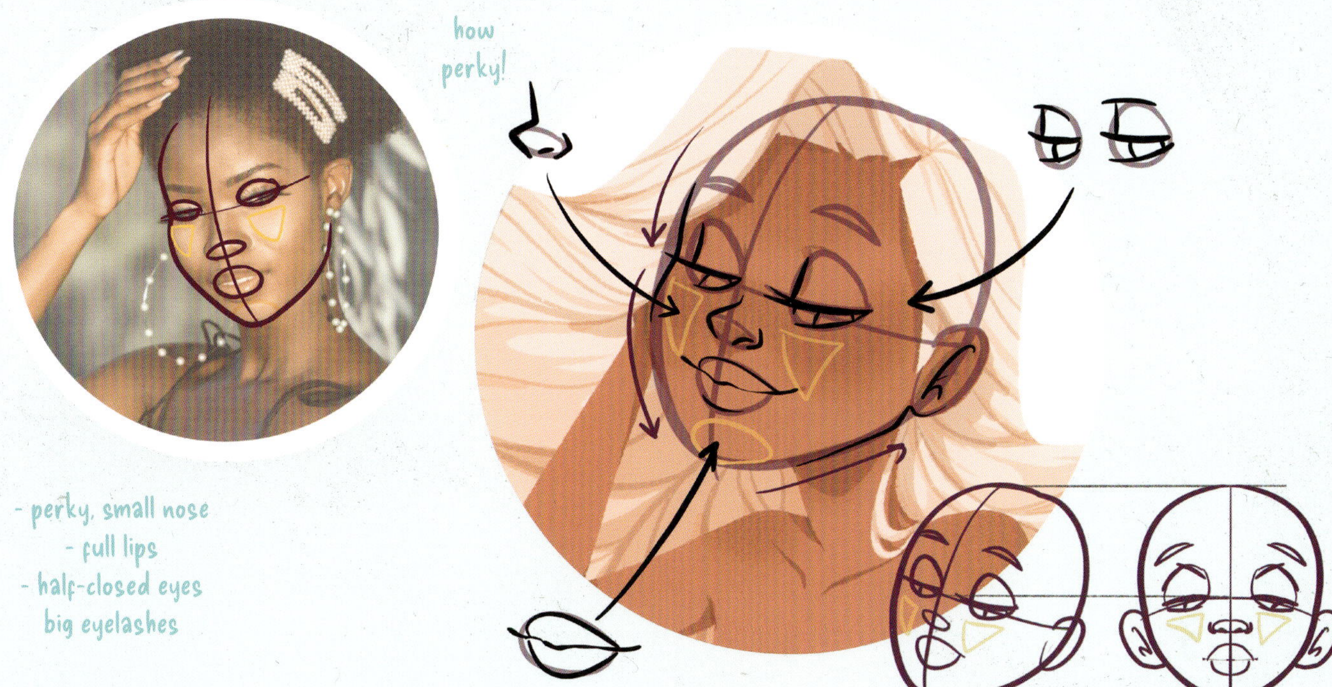

READY FOR YOUR CLOSE-UP

Right, let's make your character's expression really shine! Take another look at the photo you're using for inspiration and break down the individual geometric shapes that define the nose, eyes, lips, and other elements of the face. Work with each shape separately, like we did with the body, and don't be afraid to exaggerate the lines to make the features that much more interesting. Remember to focus on the emotion you are trying to express – something as small as a twinkle in an eye can add so much life to a character. Consider where to place each element carefully and use colour to your advantage to help the emotion shine through.

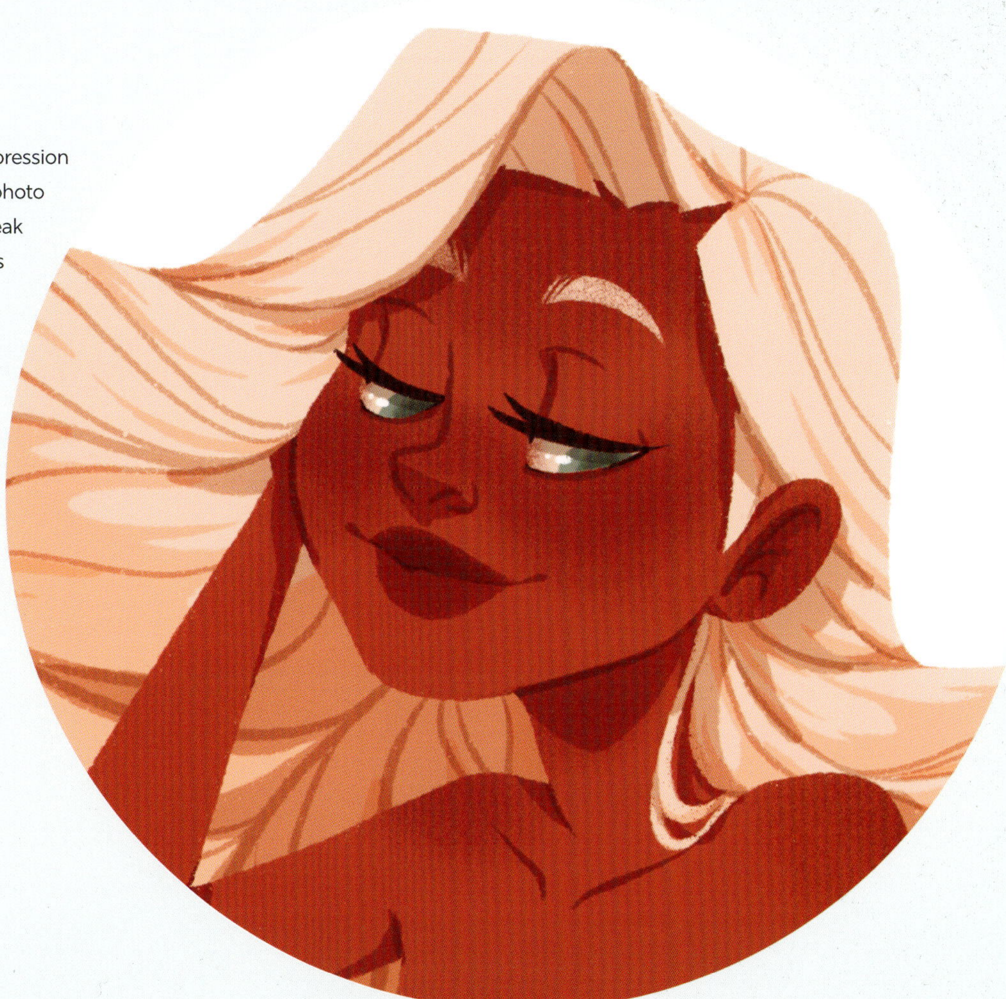

DRESS TO IMPRESS

You can choose to dress your character in a similar way to your original photo or follow your own concept, as I've done with my design. Either way, paying attention to the fabric you're trying to recreate is key! Again, don't be afraid to exaggerate elements of the design – maybe a flowing dress can be painted like a waterfall, adding lots of shine and a little motion blur. I want my character's dress to look like a cloud, so adding diffuse light and blur help to really sell this idea.

BACKGROUND CHECK

A striking background can bring a whole scene alive or completely mute the focal point. Finding a balance between interesting and distracting can be tough! If you're recreating an image then mimicking the background can be an interesting option, but if you find it draws the viewer's eyes from the main character then try adding blur or adjusting the contrast.

Creating a romanticized version of the original background that more clearly serves to highlight your character can also be a good option. Even a plain colour with some added little details will also work. Remember, you want the whole picture to be clear, harmonious, and balanced. Experiment until the background looks interesting, but not overwhelming.

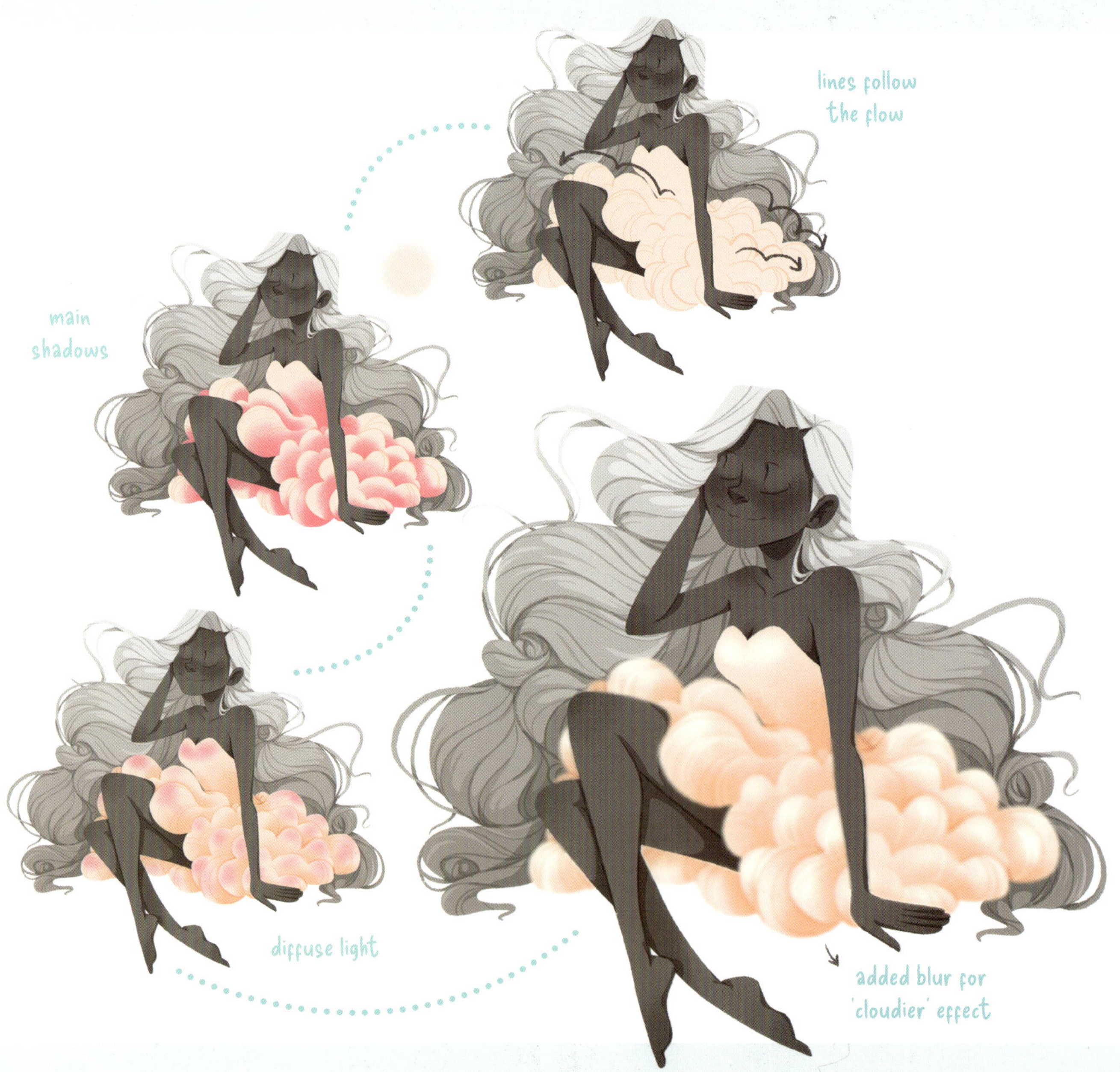

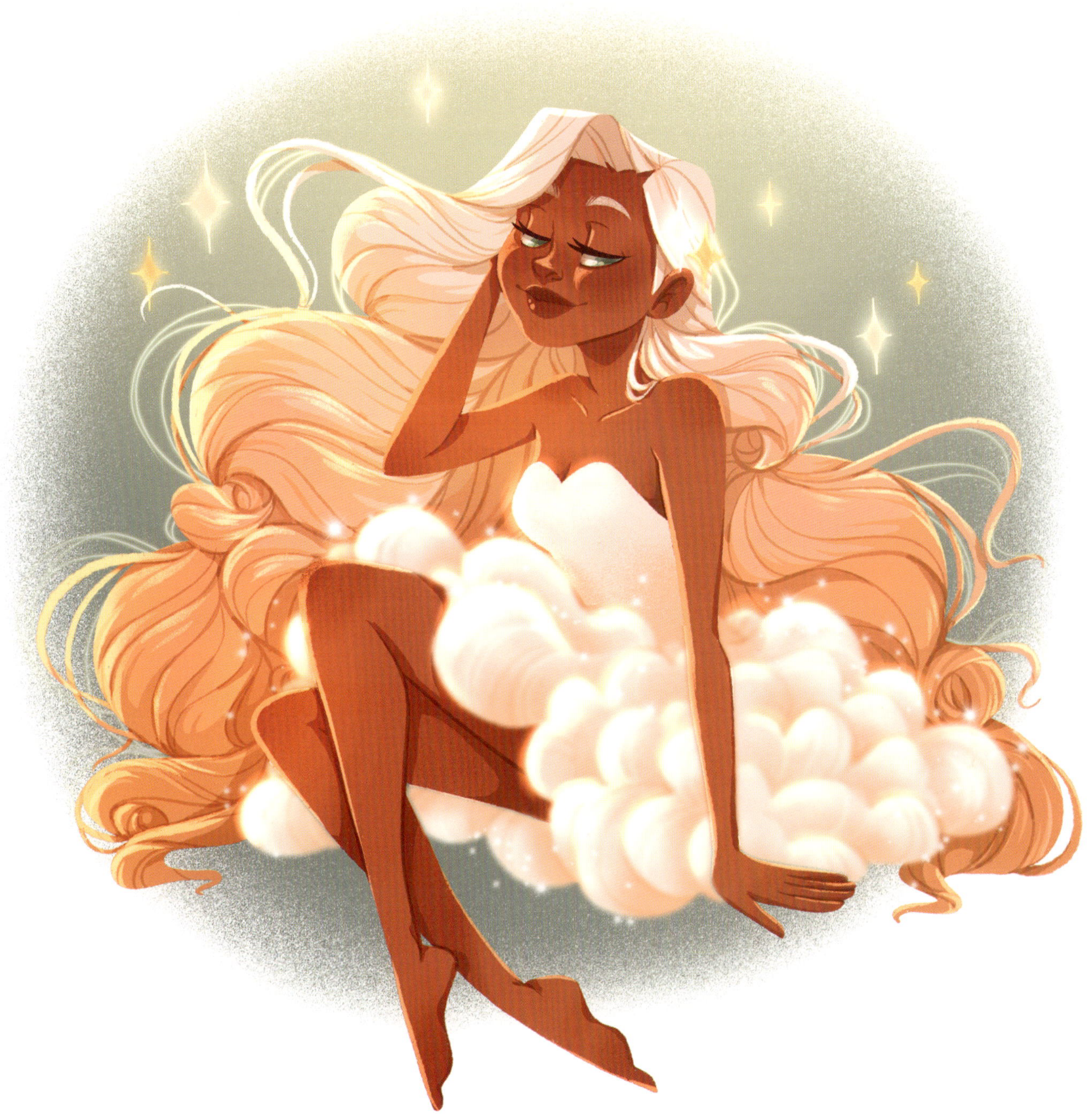

THE FINAL GLOW-UP

With the design almost complete, let's go back to the original inspiration one last time and really look at it. Are you still missing something that would make your concept come alive? Small details can make a big difference, like loose strands of hair, a bit of extra texture, or added glow. Playing with hues and contrast can also make an image more striking and using a little motion blur can bring an image to life. And with that, we're done! I hope you had as much fun as I did putting this image together.

Final image © Sara Paz

LIGHTI

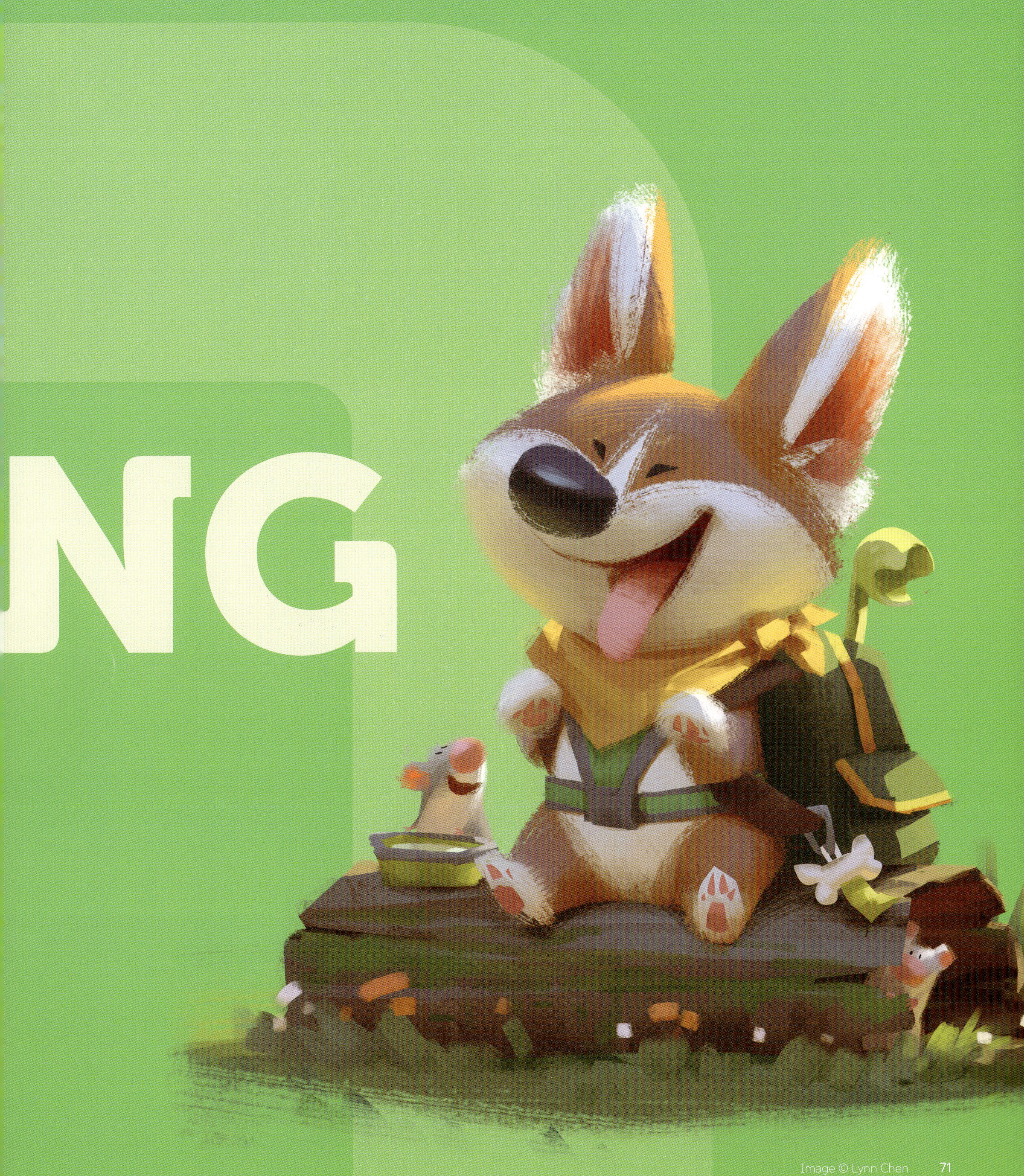

Image © Lynn Chen

Lighten up!

LYNN CHEN

The use of light is invaluable when telling a story in your designs. It's important to know how to design lighting scenarios and use colour temperature, pushing warm and cool light to enhance the overall mood of your image. I will show you how to set up simplified lighting structures with key light, ambient light, and bounce light, to help you start sculpting forms. I've used Photoshop, but the same techniques can be applied to any software.

spine direction (action line)
connections
joints/ skeleton

INSIDE/OUTSIDE

When creating illustrations, a solid base for your design goes a long way, so it's necessary to learn and analyse your subject's anatomical structure first. Even stylized characters benefit from this – it helps the design look more believable, especially if the character needs to be animated. One of the easiest ways to achieve this is to use the 'inside/outside' method. To do this, you need to simplify the 'inside' by imagining the skeleton within the body and locating the spine – this is your 'line of action'. Then sketch the 'outside' forms to create dynamic gestures. Once you have established this basis you can refine the sketch, but at this stage still keep it loose.

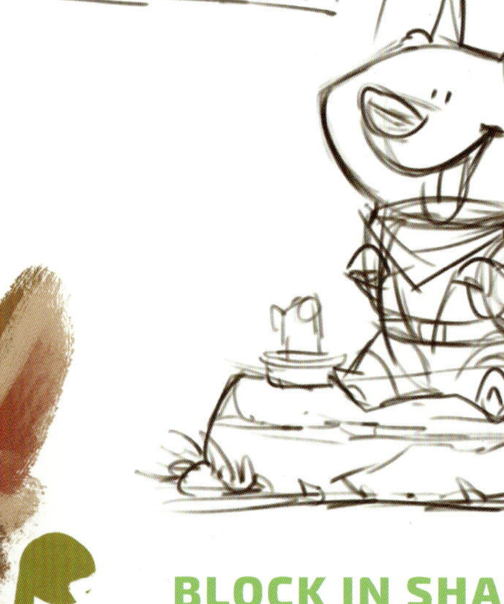

BLOCK IN SHAPES

In this image, I use neutral colours to block in the shapes, with each colour on its own layer. I add in some details and secondary characters to create a story and make the image more interesting. Remember, when choosing to add details, that they should complement the main character and not be too distracting. Keep flipping the canvas back and forth to check the balance of your design.

LIGHTING PLANNING

Before you start painting, it's a good idea to plan out your lighting set-up. Break down each light source and assign them a warm or cool colour. For example, in this particular design the sunlight and bounce light are warm and the fill light is cool. Try designing lighting with different temperatures coming from opposite directions – this will create volume and make the image appear three-dimensional. There are other things to consider, such as overcast lighting where the colours are mostly neutral, but even then you can paint in subtle colour variations so that the colours appear rich rather than plain grey.

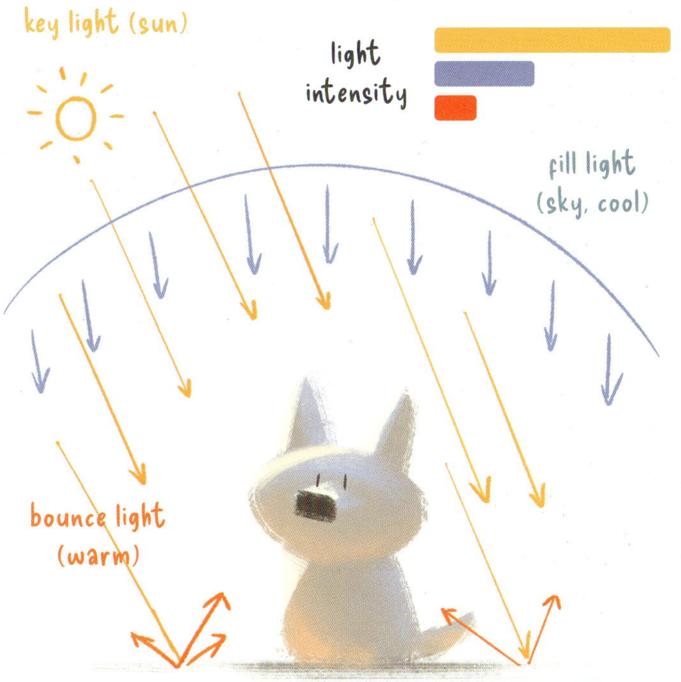

COLOUR PROOFING

Painting light directly (without referring to a black-and-white thumbnail) can be difficult, as the values (light and dark) can get lost during the painting process. To avoid this, it's crucial to use greyscale mode to check your values throughout the process. This can be easily done by 'colour proofing' within Photoshop. Go to Menu > View > Proof Setup > Custom. Then, under 'Device to Simulate,' choose 'Black & White' and click OK. Now you can toggle between normal and greyscale colour proofing by pressing CMD + Y (CTRL + Y on PC).

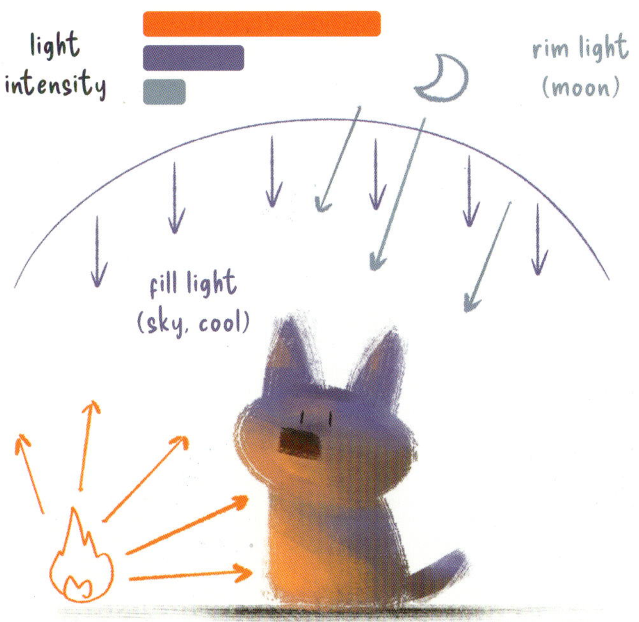

'Try designing lighting with different temperatures coming from opposite directions - this will create volume'

SCULPTING WITH LIGHT

Building on the base colours, start painting in one light at a time. The blue light comes from the sky, so all the surfaces facing upwards will be affected by this light. To achieve this effect you can shift the local colour towards a brighter, cooler colour and apply it on all these surfaces, giving the appearance of being lit from above. Then move on to the secondary light source, and so on. This way, we can focus on the forms and have fun 'sculpting' the character.

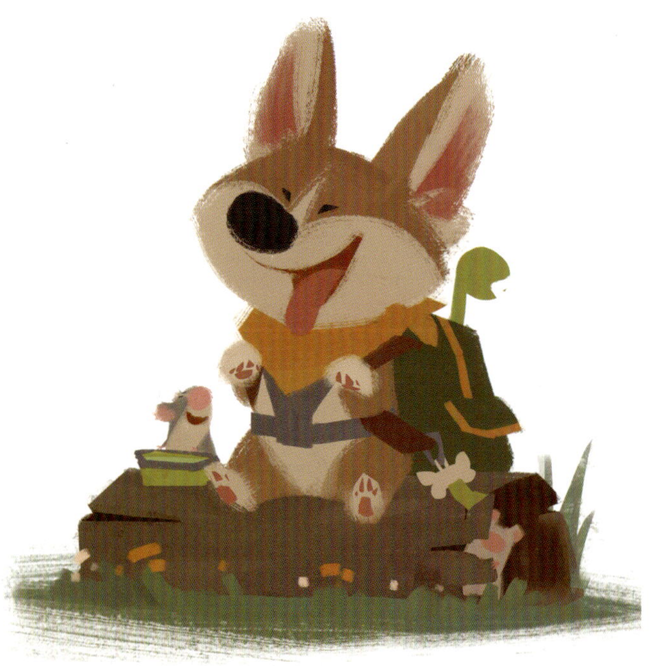

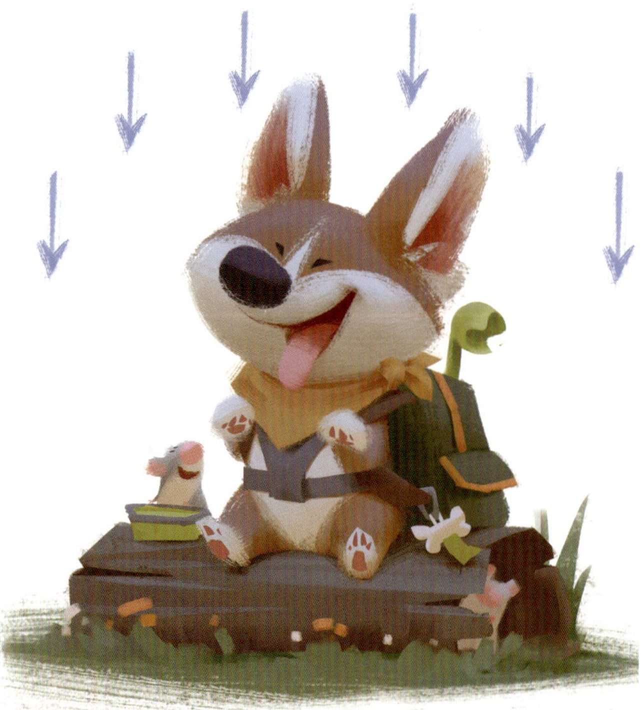

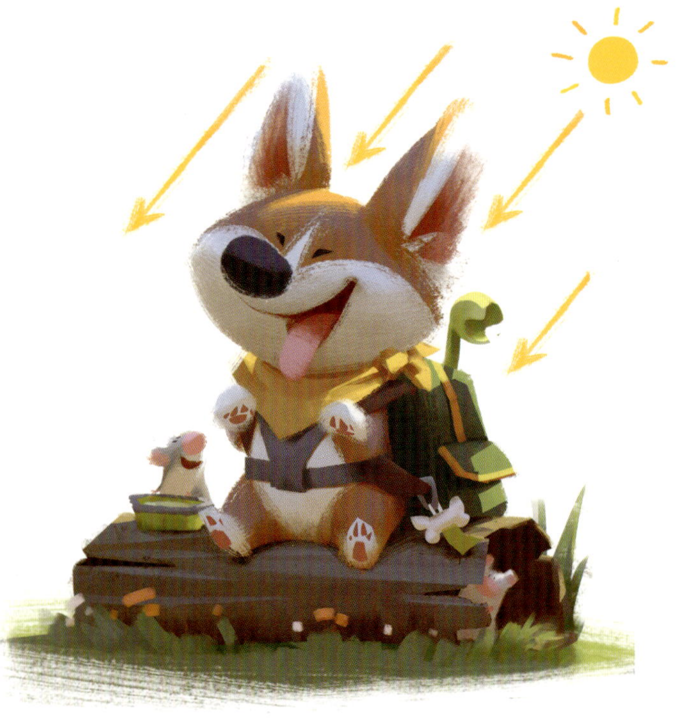

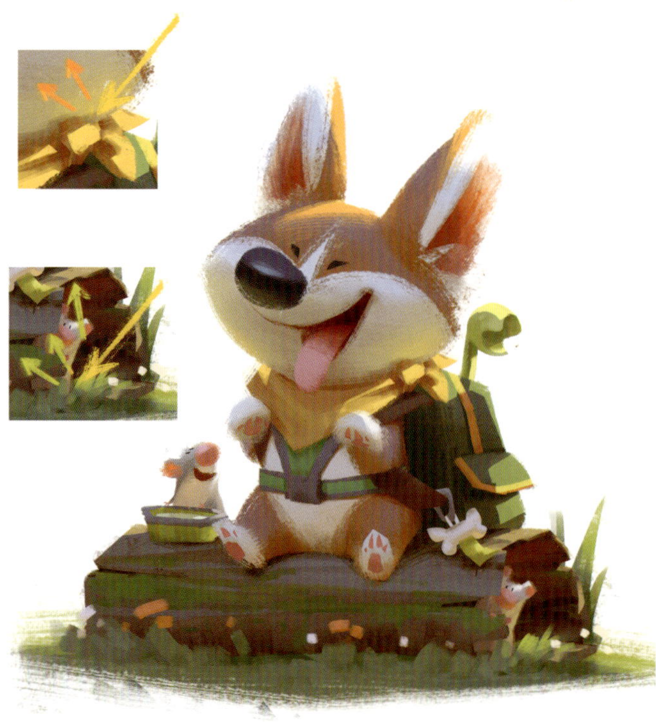

STAY BALANCED

When it comes to adding a background to your image, be aware of maintaining good contrast between busy and less-detailed areas. In this case I have blurred the background so the eye is drawn to the character. Try to avoid having very detailed backgrounds, as your character may get lost in the scene. Adding some simple details, such as a blade of grass peeking out from behind a log, will help establish the environment without going overboard.

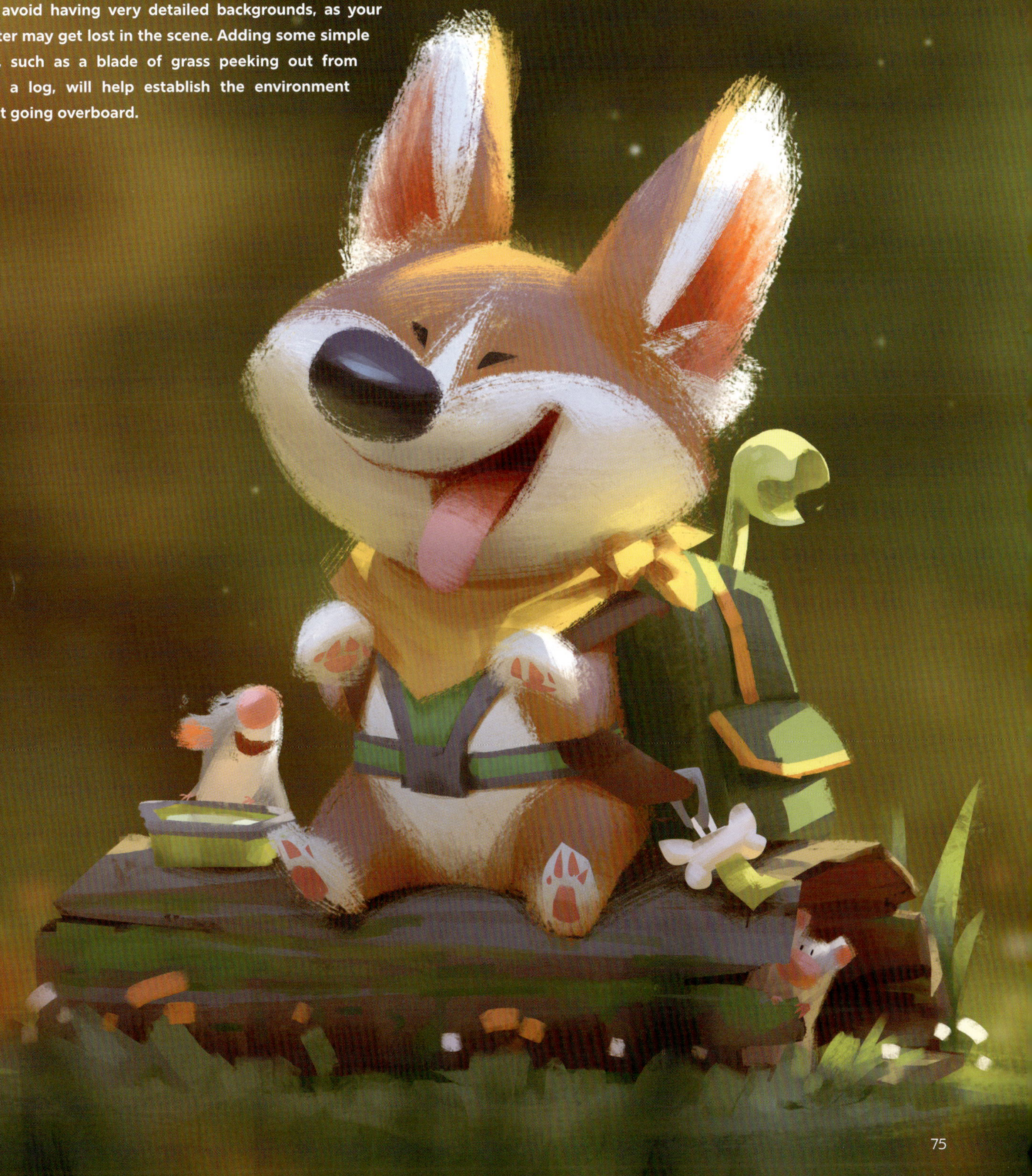

PUSH COLOUR TEMPERATURE

When selecting colours to represent warm and cool light, try using a LAB colour picker instead of HSB. Visually, it is a more straightforward way of selecting warmer and cooler colours. As long as each colour has a similar amount of colour shift, the light will look consistent across the image. In Photoshop, the panel shown appears when you select the foreground colour – I also have a shortcut set up for this panel for easy access when painting. Give it a try!

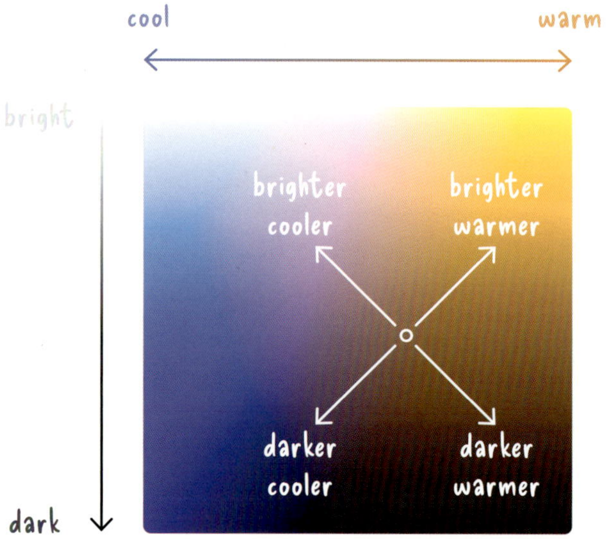

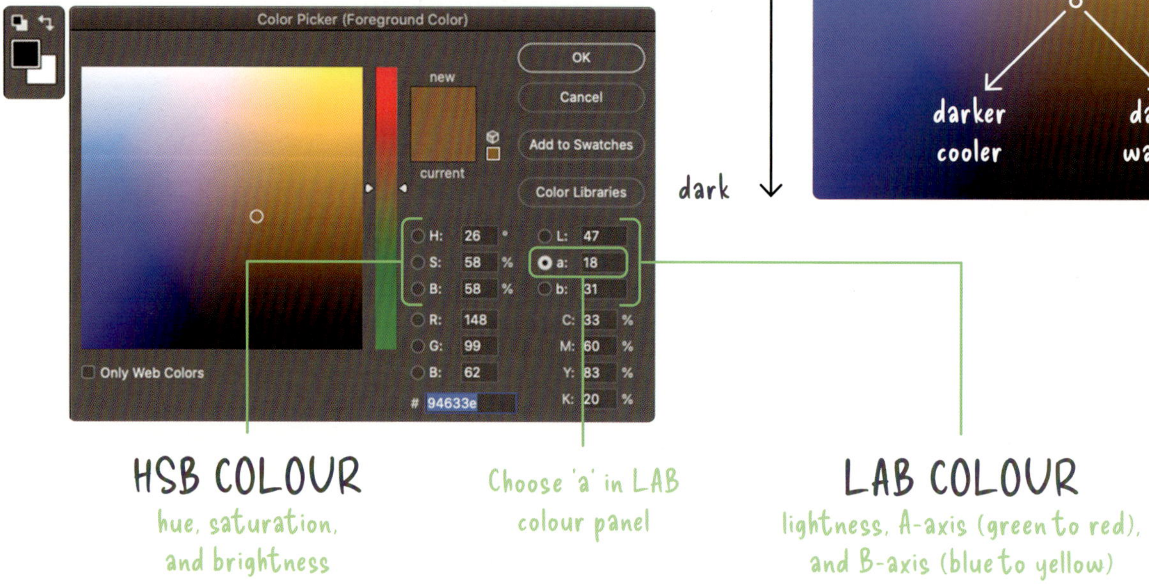

cool
warm
bright
brighter cooler
brighter warmer
darker cooler
darker warmer
dark

Color Picker (Foreground Color)
OK
Cancel
Add to Swatches
Color Libraries
new
current
H: 26 °
S: 58 %
B: 58 %
R: 148
G: 99
B: 62
L: 47
a: 18
b: 31
C: 33 %
M: 60 %
Y: 83 %
K: 20 %
94633e
Only Web Colors

HSB COLOUR
hue, saturation, and brightness

Choose 'a' in LAB colour panel

LAB COLOUR
lightness, A-axis (green to red), and B-axis (blue to yellow)

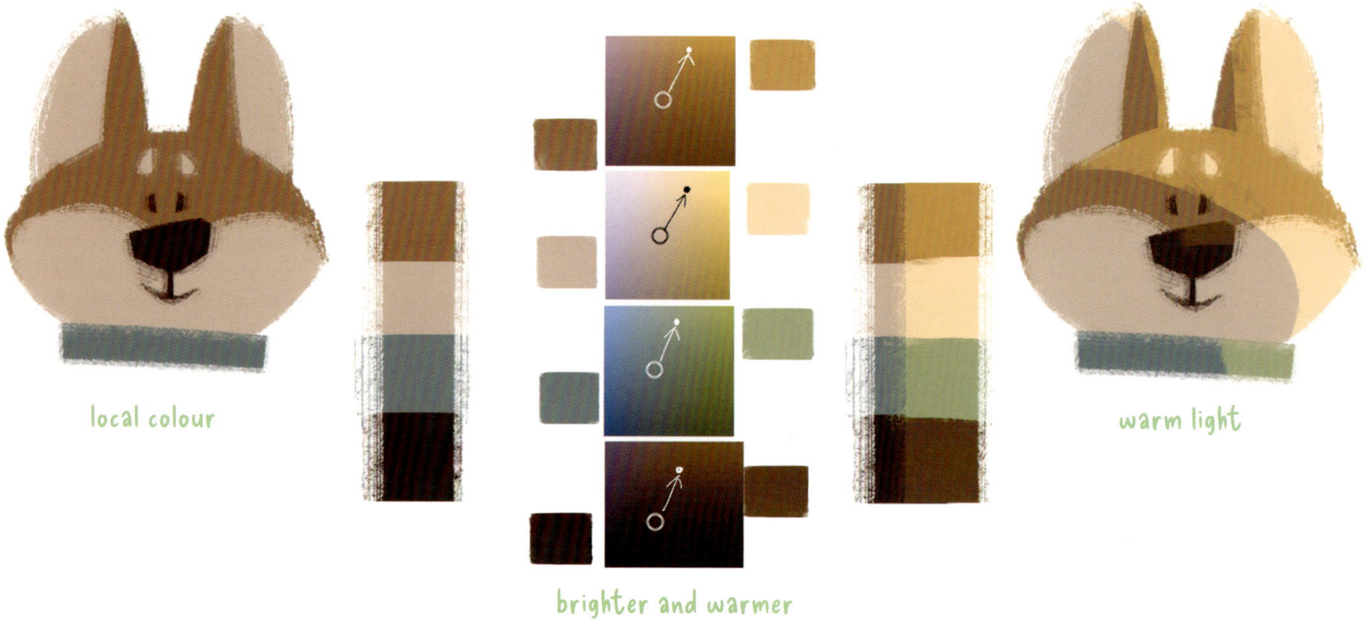

local colour

brighter and warmer

warm light

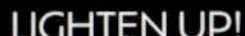

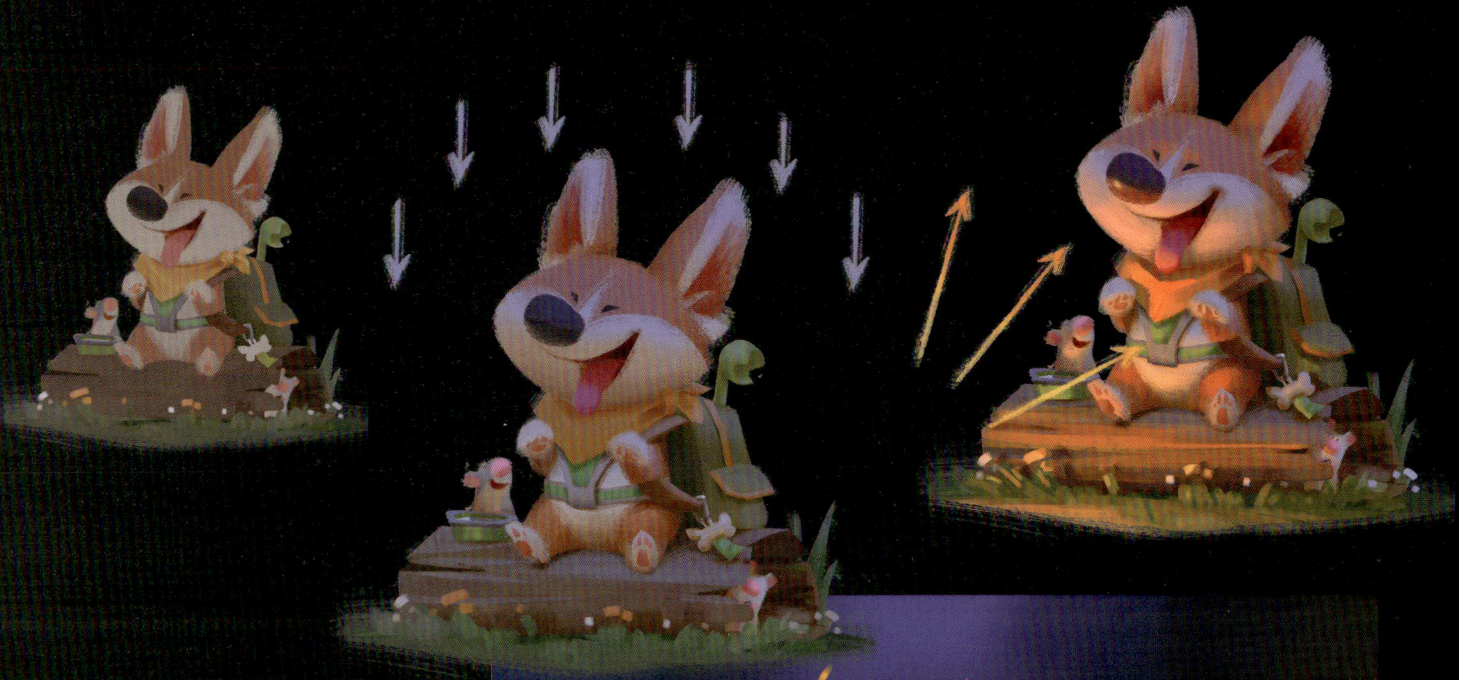

NIGHT TIME

I can now create a 'night time' version of the image. It can be useful to experiment with light plans when you are undecided on colour variations for your final design. In order to make this version, we need to adjust the base colour and paint in ambient shadows, with a cool skylight contrasting the warm 'day time' version. The warmth within this design instead comes from the campfire. Compared to the sunlight, the campfire has a smaller cast, and therefore the light diminishes as the forms get further away from the light source. To increase this effect, make sure the areas closest to the light are brighter than those further away.

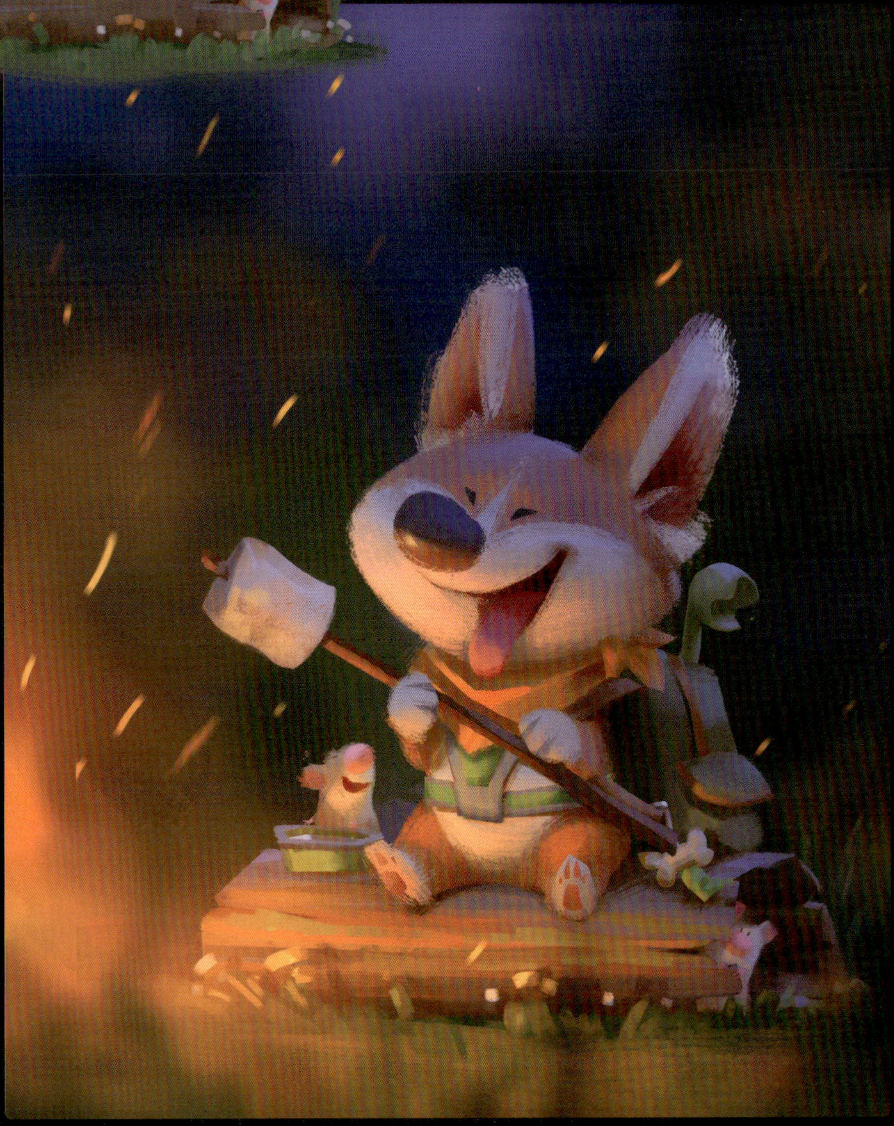

Setting the mood

AURÉLIE LISE-ANNE

This tutorial will explain how to change the emotions of a character and narrative mood simply by adjusting lighting. I will use a fairly simple character, keeping its pose the same throughout the different examples to show that lighting goes a very long way to convey a mood and tell a story. This specific tutorial was made in Photoshop, but the same method will work in Procreate. In general, the layer modes in this tutorial are Multiply for shadows, Overlay for main lights, and Normal for ambient and bounce.

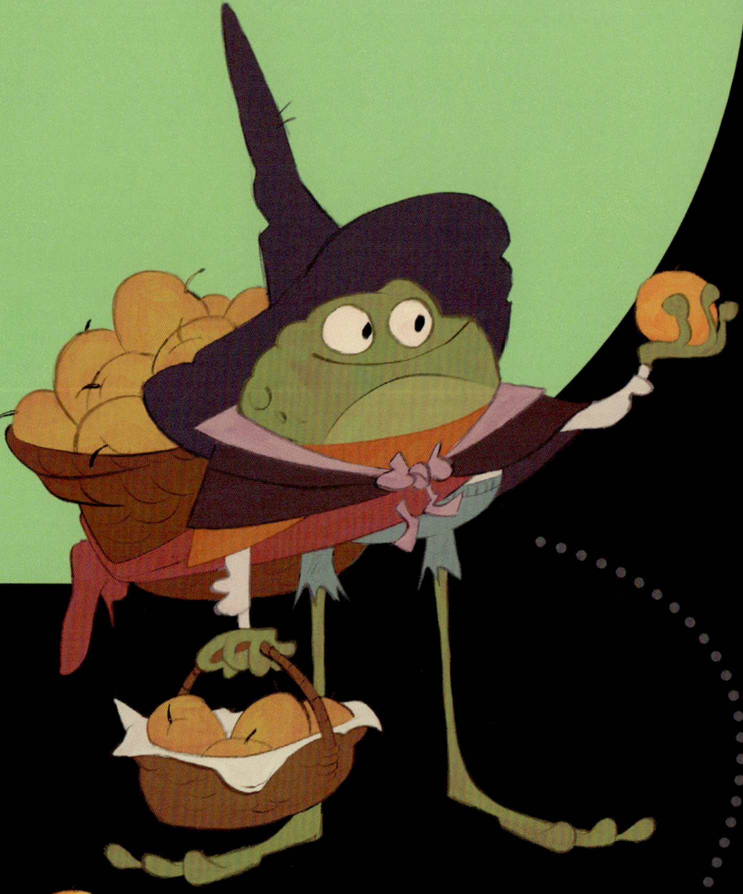

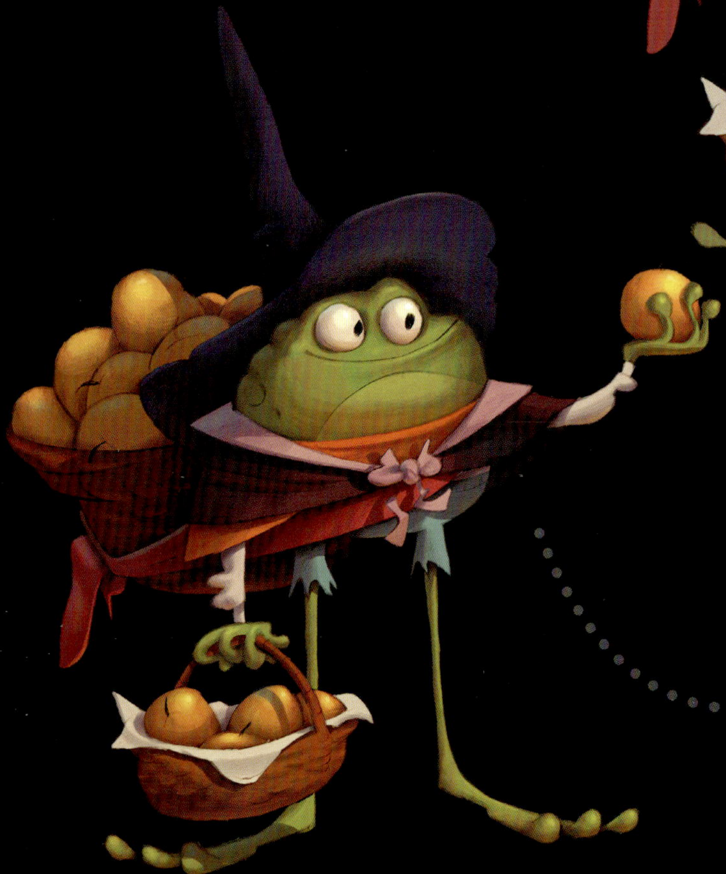

START WITH FLAT COLOURS

When painting multiple lighting set-ups of the same character, paint the flat local colours first. Then, on top of these, paint the lighting using Adjustment layers. That way the lighting will always be easy to change.

SUNNY SIDE UP

Use hard shadows and warm, saturated light to create a sunny look. Add a warm bounce light to the downward-facing shadow parts and a cold light on the upward-facing sections. This is the ambient light that – in this case – is coming from the blue sky above.

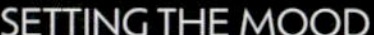

> 'Keep in mind their backstory and intentions'

MORE THAN A FEELING

When lighting your character, keep in mind their backstory and intentions. In this step, the expression of the character has been changed without changing the lighting. Notice how the story is much less clear than in the next step, where the lighting has been adapted to suit the story.

QUICK SHADING TIP

Keep the flat colours from the first step on different layers, so you can quickly select separate areas for shading. To select a certain area, click on the layer thumbnail of your desired area while holding Ctrl (Windows) or Cmd (Mac).

SHROUNDED IN DARKNESS

Put the main light behind or next to your character to put its face in shadow. Make it a cold light for a dark and menacing mood. When a big part of your character is in shadow, use bounce and ambient light to avoid losing any shapes in the shadows.

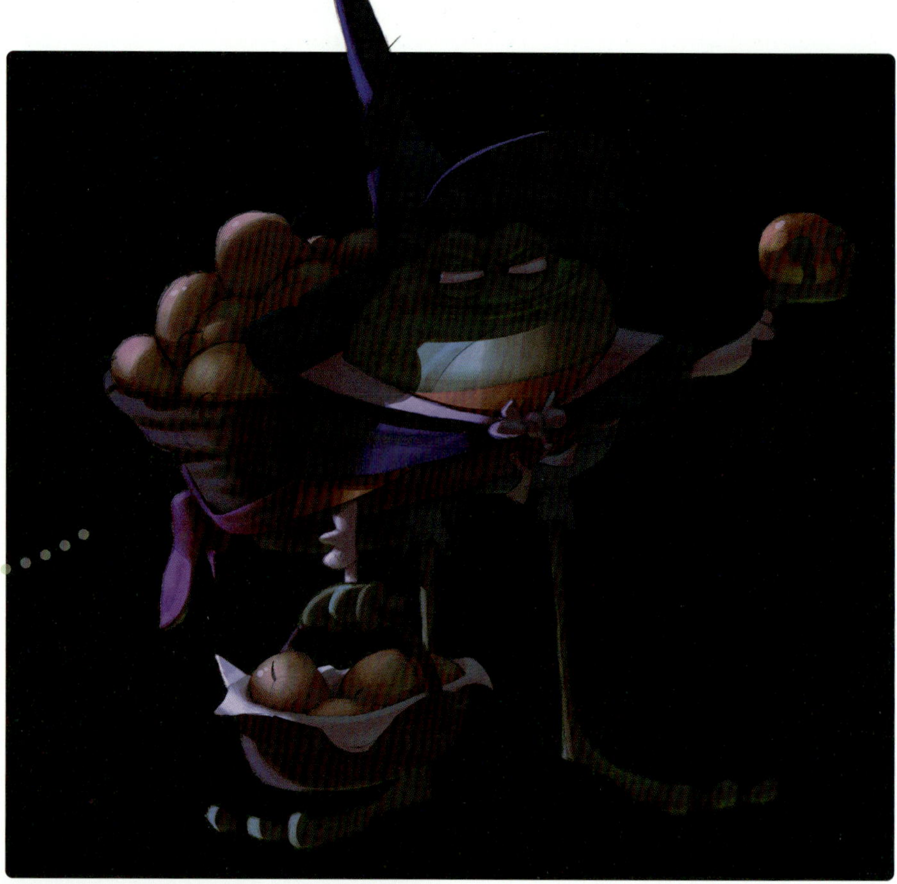

MYSTERIOUS MOODS

Paint soft shadows to diffuse the lighting. If your main light is cold, use a warm ambient light to create a nice contrast, and vice versa for a warm light. If you lose the silhouette of your character in shadow, you can add a rim light to bring it back.

KEEPING TRACK OF COLOUR

It can be annoying having to switch between colours every time you switch between different Adjustment layers – you probably have one for each different light and shadow. Mask your Adjustment layer and paint only in the mask. That way, you always have the right colour for each light or shadow and you only have to switch between black and white. Also, you won't have to keep switching from brush to eraser!

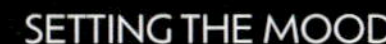

'Be careful not to saturate your shadows as this can introduce too much colour into your drawing'

SAD IN THE SHADOWS

Use a white light as the main light source to desaturate your drawing altogether. Be careful not to saturate your shadows as this can introduce too much colour into your drawing. However, if you want to add some more colour, try to have cold tones as the majority.

LIGHT THE WAY

Have fun experimenting with several different lighting situations. For example, try making the main light source a part of your character, or change the light to a very strong, saturated colour and see what happens.

Lighting for narrative

JOHN LOREN

When lighting a character, the two questions I like to focus on are 'What setting does the character occupy?' and 'What do we want to say about the character's narrative?' In this chapter, I will encourage you to think about light as a tool to help set the appropriate mood and guide the viewer's eye, showcasing five different types of lighting and their varying effects. Lighting will also determine the values and colour information in your character design.

START WITH A SKETCH

Start by developing the sketch and flat base colours of the character without worrying about the lighting. The sketch should be a fast way to explore and build the character; the lines will not carry through to the final design so they do not need to be perfectly clean. You can see that before adding lighting, the character is very flat. So, the pirate spies treasure on an island, but what is his story at this point in time? We can partially answer this question through the lighting scenarios.

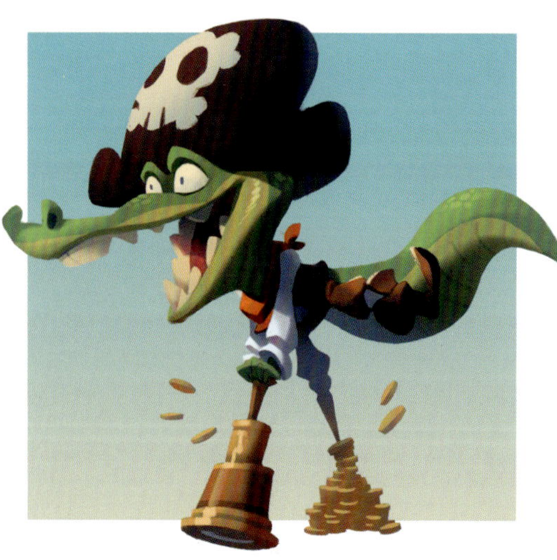

DAYLIGHT

Even in a typical daylight setting, colour is used to separate light and shadows. In this case, the tones of the shadows are a little cooler than the areas hit by warmer daylight. By carefully choosing where to create areas of contrast, lighting can be used to call attention to the important parts of the character, such as the face. For example, the very low-contrast peg-leg allows the high-contrast face to remain the centre of attention. The character is outdoors, and the daylight gives him an approachable, energetic feel.

DIM LIGHT

In a dimly lit environment, rim lighting (light that highlights the edges of the character) can be a good way to keep a character visible. Do not apply a rim light too evenly, though, as you may flatten the design. Here, the face is only slightly lighter than the rest of the body, but it is enough to highlight it without losing the overall impact of the low light. The darkness adds a mischievous feel; maybe he doesn't want to be seen.

DRAMATIC LIGHT

We do not often see characters lit from below, so this form of lighting can help to create a strange or dramatic mood. Think about holding a torch under your chin to create an instantly spooky face! Another way to immerse a character in their environment is to let the ambient light spill over their silhouette, such as the green haze shown here. This adds additional clues to where the character is situated.

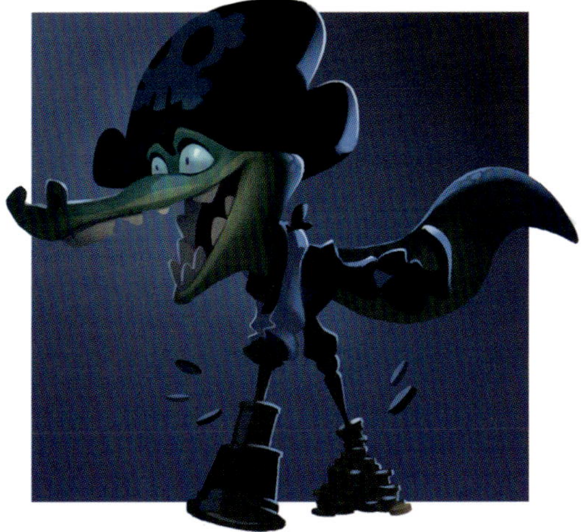

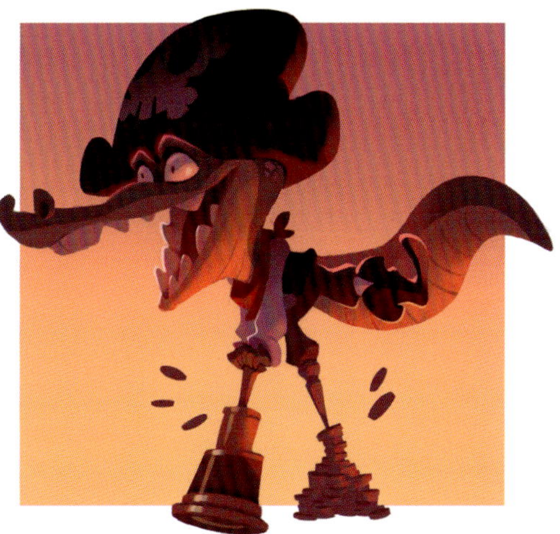

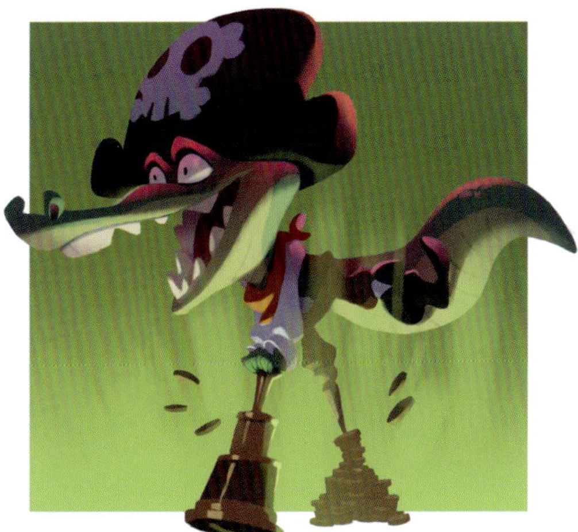

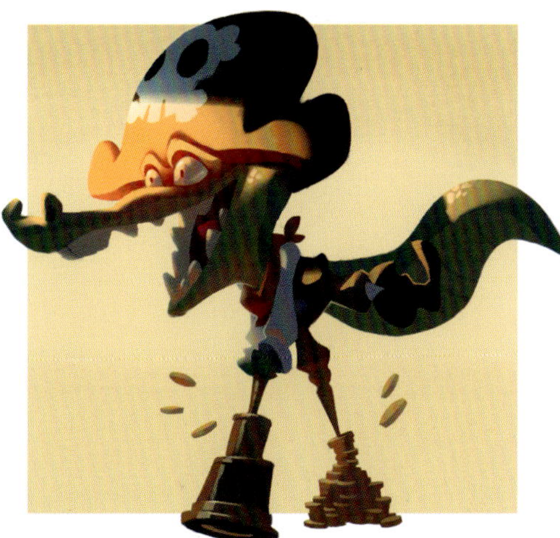

SHADOW

Casting shadows across a character can help to believably integrate it with other objects in the environment. In addition to incorporating shadows from the character's surroundings, think about the shadows the character casts on itself that will help to give convincing volume. For example, this character's tail shows a shadow cast by the hat. He could be hiding in partial shade, or overshadowed by other, larger characters.

RICH SETTING

This character's skin is normally green, but a richly coloured setting such as a sunset can override that. Here, the green scales become a shade of red. Do not worry about keeping a character's colours consistent; instead, prioritize keeping the character consistent with the lighting conditions. Even the normally white eyes and teeth reflect the lighting. The implied sunset creates a feeling of optimism that is almost romantic.

COLOUR

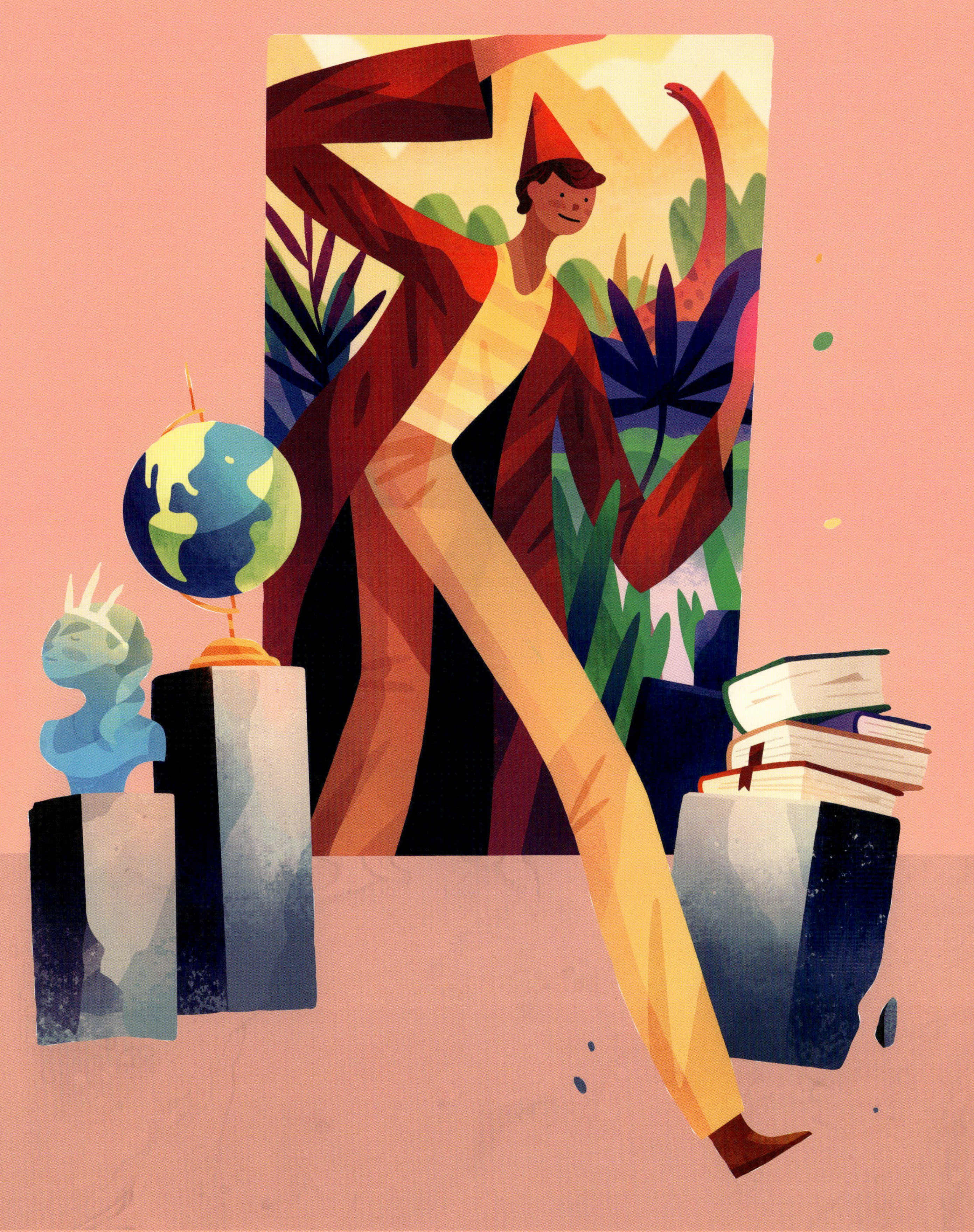

Image © Jarom Vogel

Adventures with colour

LYDIA NICHOLS

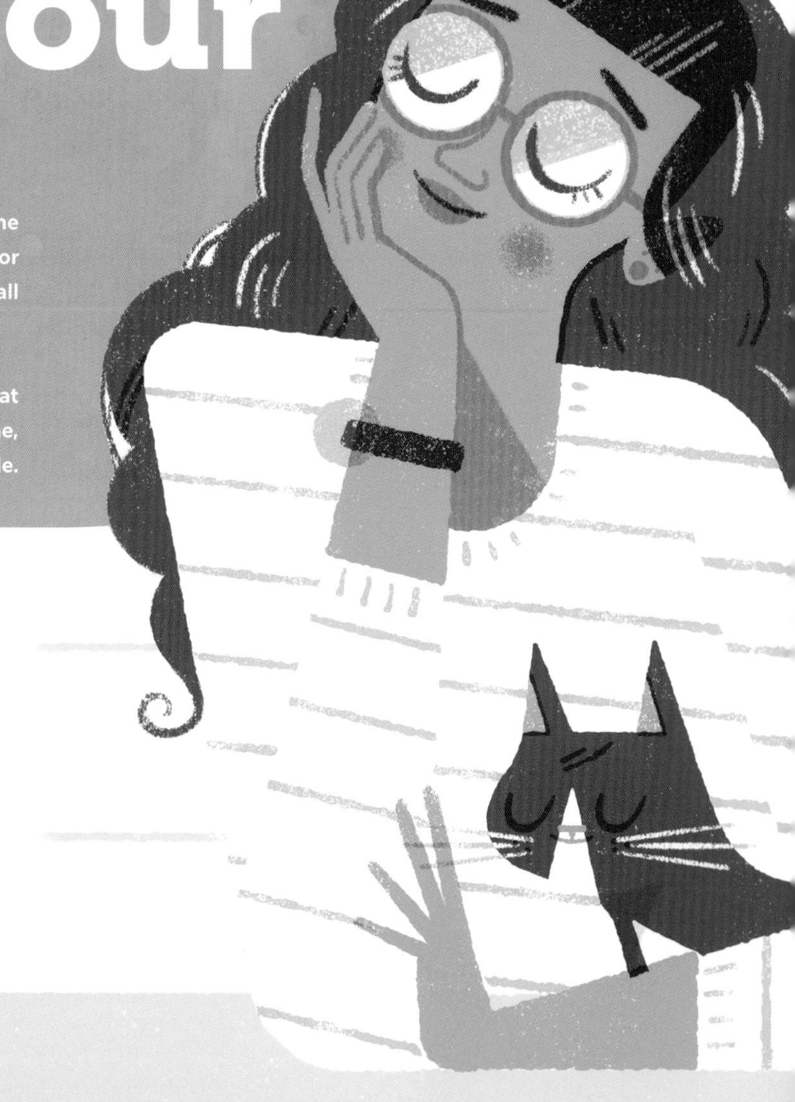

Colour is about more than, well, colour. Ten people could use the same colours and produce wildly different effects. Use of major design tools, such as negative space, contrast, and lighting, will all profoundly change the perception of colour.

My approach to colour is motivated by two things: a fear so great that I prefer not to use more than three or four colours at a time, and a love of puzzling out an image with as few colours as possible.

JUST TWO COLOURS

This image was created using two colours, each at 100% and 30% opacity. Keeping the palette limited allows more play with patterning and negative space, without feeling too visually overwhelming or dense. Overlays create secondary colours that add depth and lend a printmaking feel to the piece. The final effect of the colour and its application reflects the thoughtful yet playful mood of the character. You don't need to resort to 'realistic' colours to convey real emotions or feelings.

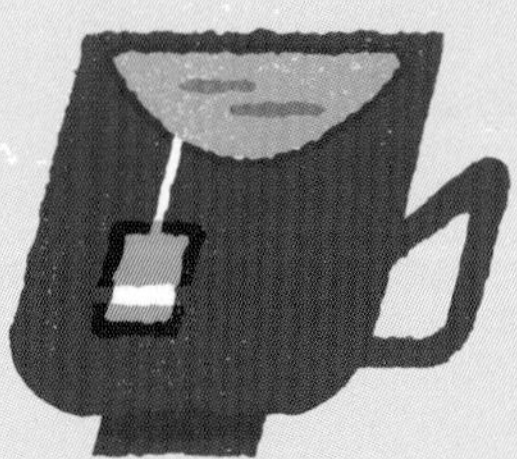

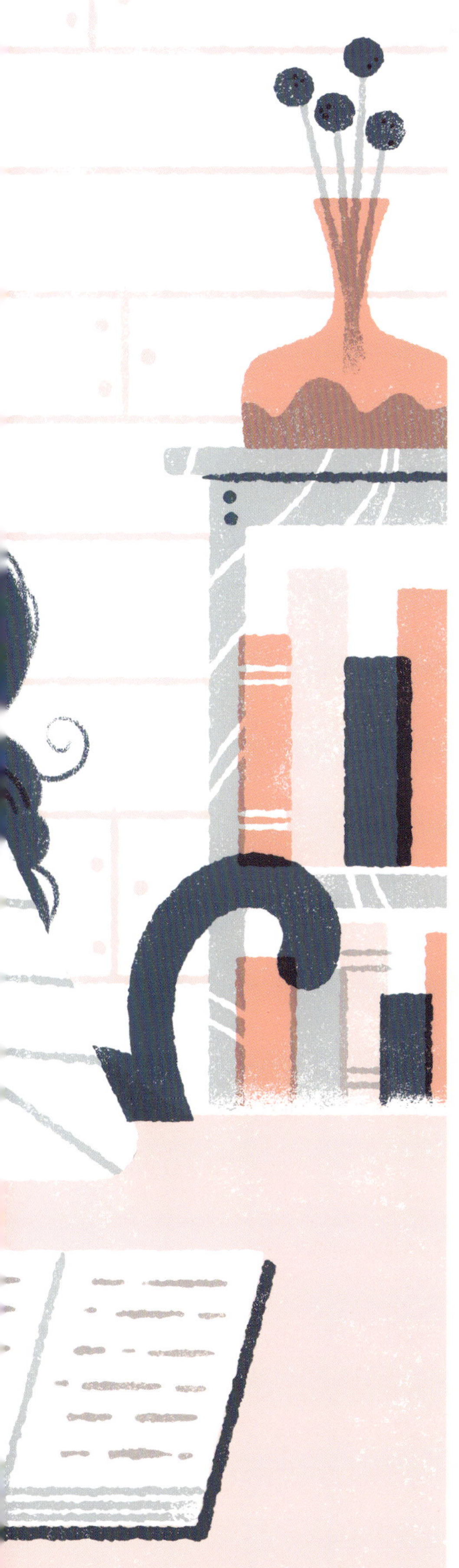

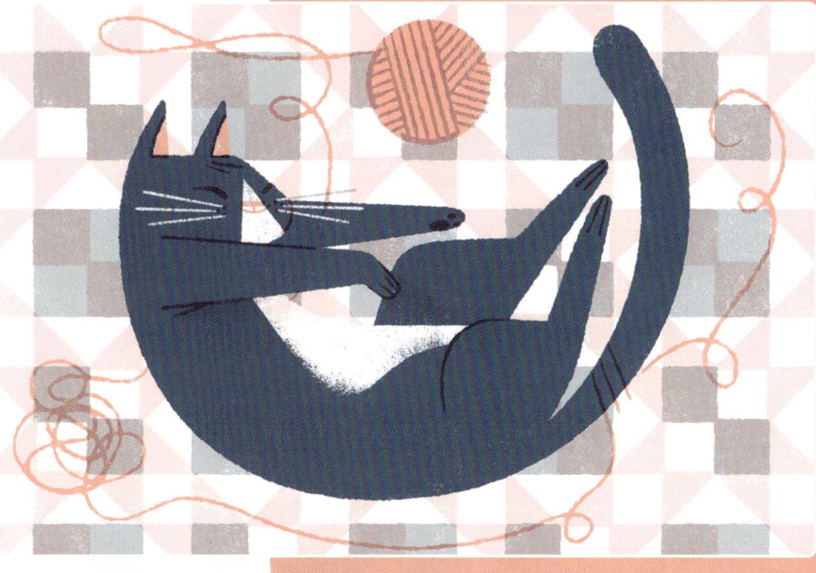

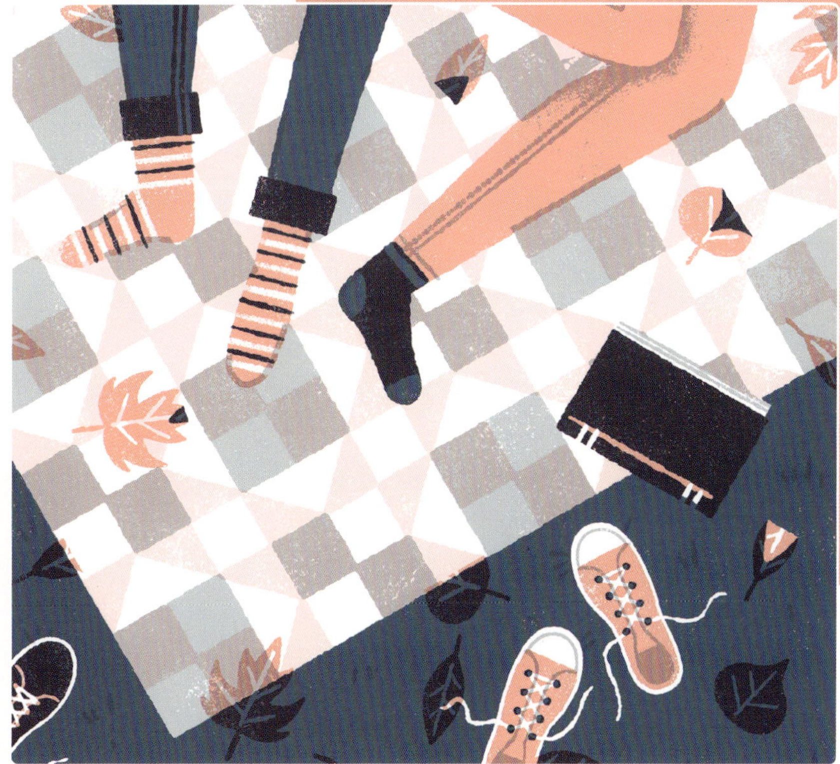

CAPTURING THE TONE

These two designs are from the same series as the first; they continue with the same palette, but with slightly different applications. Both of these images are denser than the first, with less use of negative space. In the 'cat with wool' image, the darkest colour is used to make the subject pop, whereas the legs image uses the darkest colour to frame and accentuate the subject. Like the first image, the tone of these two is quite whimsical, but each image captures a slightly different feeling despite using the same colours.

PLAYFUL COLOUR

At its core, this image has a fairly basic primary palette: red, yellow, and blue, with the addition of pink and green. The specific shades of those colours are fairly muted, but overall there isn't anything too complicated about this five-colour palette. However, by overlaying colours and playing up the darker tones, this limited palette can be used to create a playful yet moody scene. Secondary colours and texture create depth in an otherwise fairly simple image.

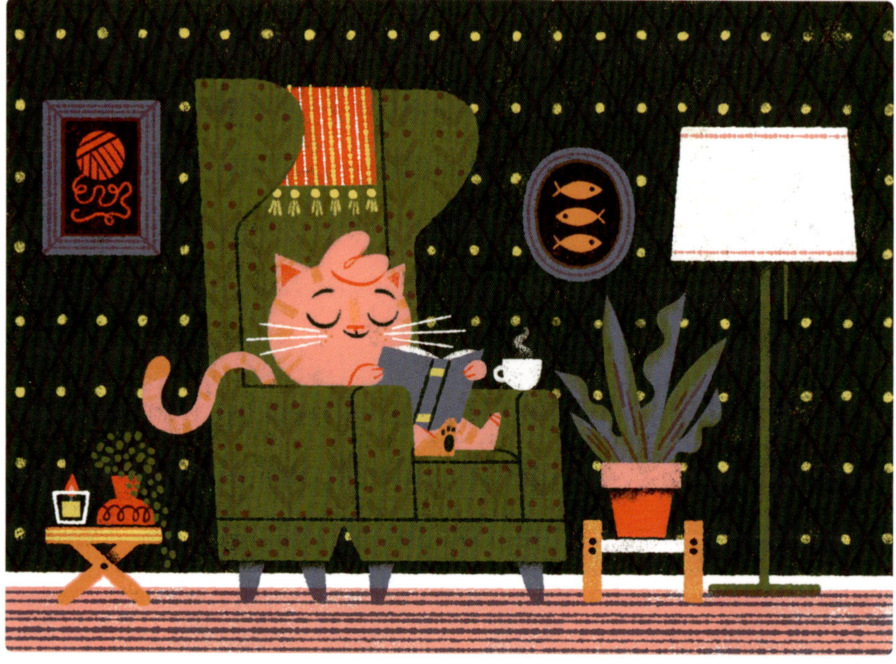

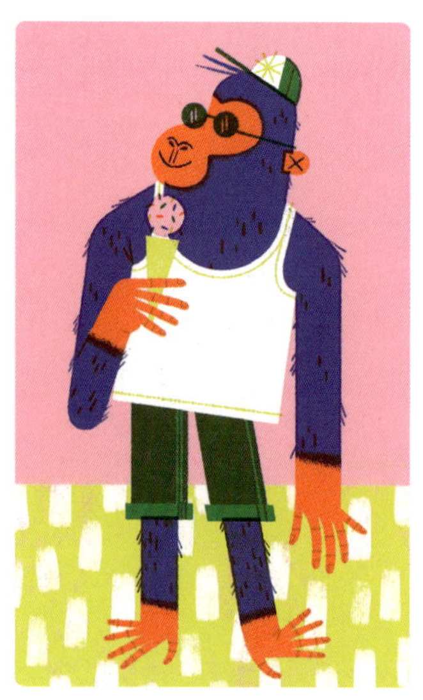

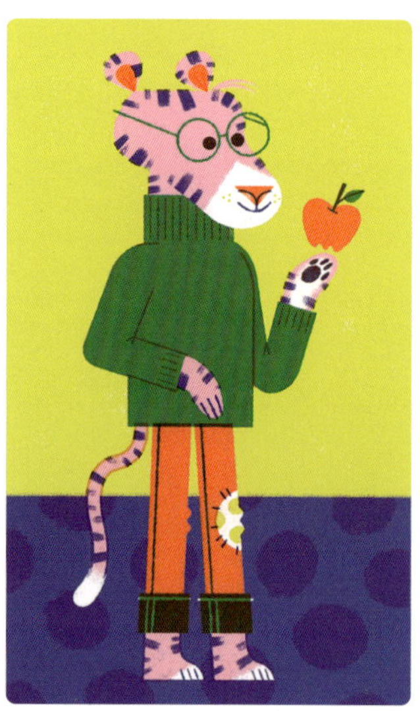

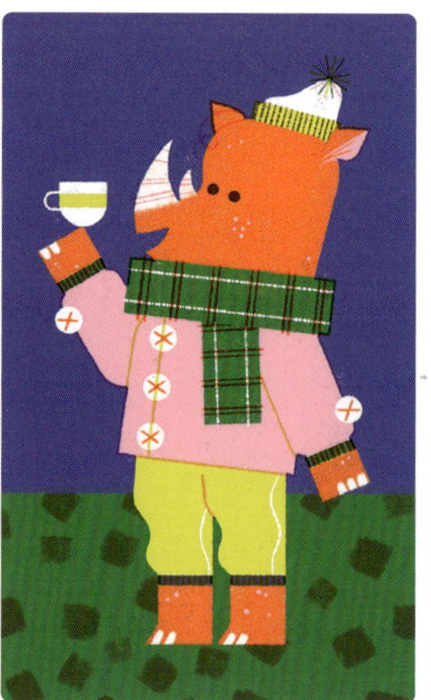

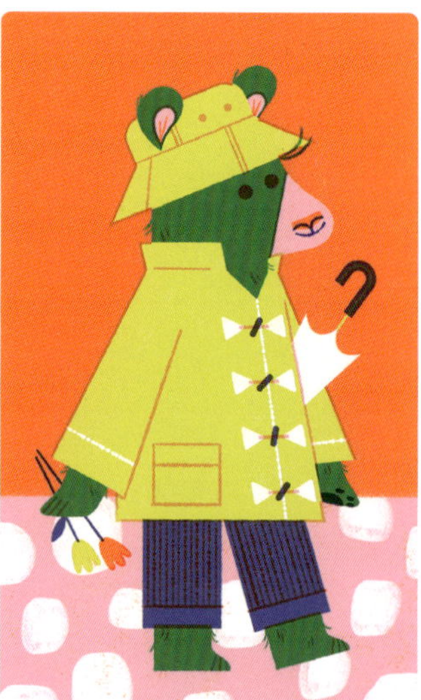

SMALL CHANGE, GIANT IMPACT

This series of four seasonally-themed illustrations started with the gorilla eating ice cream in summer. I didn't originally conceive of this as a series and, as such, started with a warm, summery colour palette. Note how the palette is almost the same as the previous image – red, yellow, blue, pink, and green – but in much punchier shades. Even small changes can have a huge impact on the final image. In order to create a unified look, I kept the same colour palette for each season and adapted it by emphasizing certain colours and overlays. The result is a fairly non-traditional take on the seasons, but hopefully one that still communicates which season is which in a fun and unexpected way.

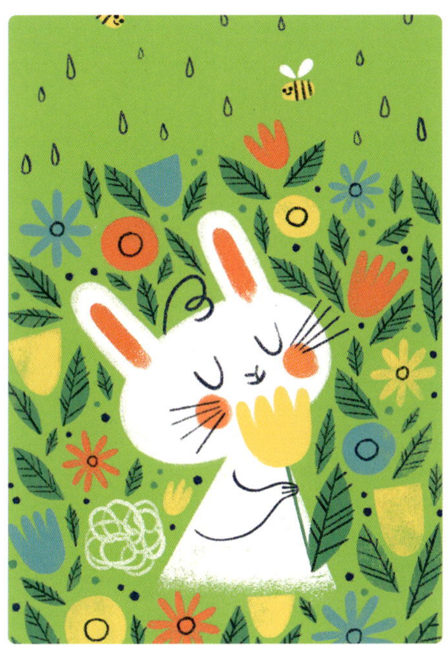

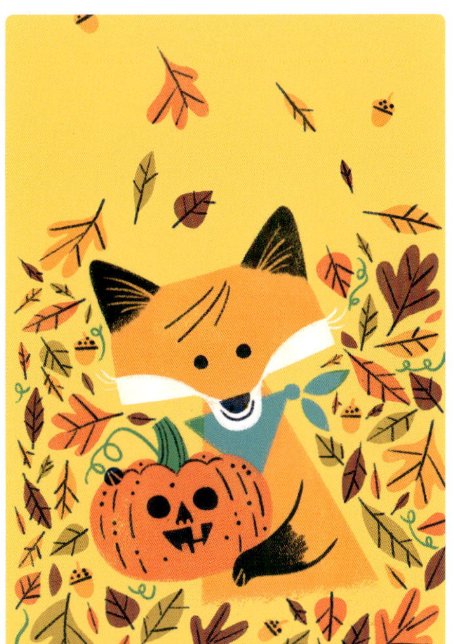

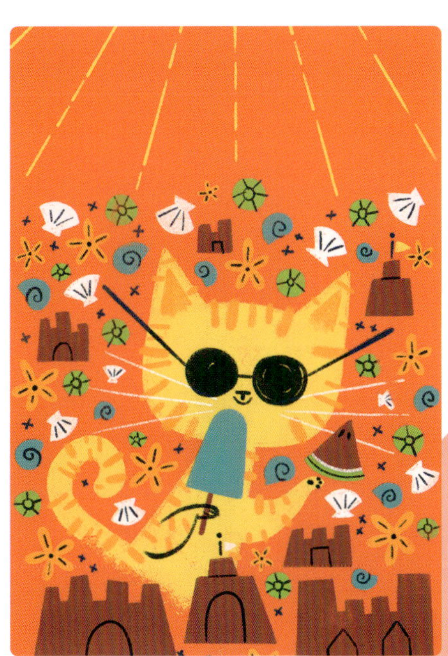

UNIFIED COMPOSITIONS

By contrast, this earlier series of seasonal illustrations is unified by composition and use of patterning rather than palette. The colours for each are all fairly dense and opaque, with few overlays for depth. The results are slightly richer and heavier, but perhaps more pronounced in illustrating which season is which.

'Being rigid about colour theory closes off risk-taking'

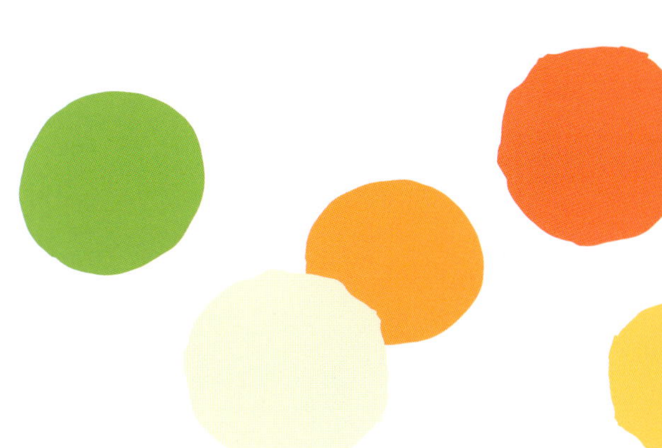

THINK OUTSIDE THE COLOUR WHEEL

Leave room for experimentation and intuition. Being rigid about colour theory closes off risk-taking. Without risk, your work may very well be technically proficient, but perhaps not as unique. Sometimes, unexpected colours can seem to work, even against all logic. And sometimes an 'unsophisticated' palette can be used in a way that lends depth to a piece.

Playing with colour

JAROM VOGEL

As a commercial illustrator my work is largely design-oriented and graphic, which means I am more concerned with achieving a strong composition and concept in an image than developing characters with accurate proportions or realistic rendering. My primary goal is to make a bold visual impact, and colour plays an immense role. In this chapter, I will cover tips on utilizing colour and contrast to produce attention-grabbing designs that hold the viewer's attention.

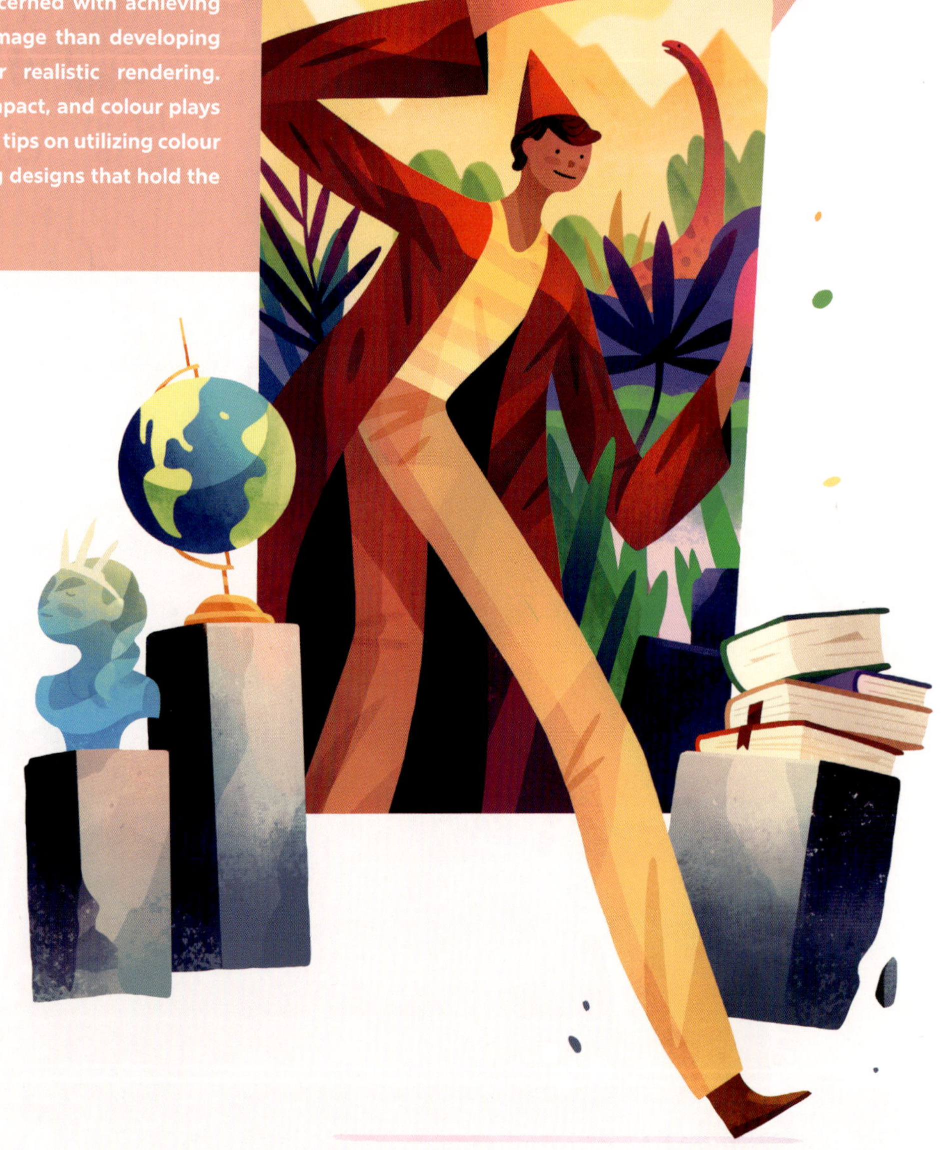

SET THE TONE

Choosing colours with intention to portray a feeling or vibe will help to set the tone of your character and the situation they are in. In this piece, I use primary colours – red, yellow, and blue – to convey a peaceful, innocent feeling.

'Primary colours – red, yellow, and blue – convey a peaceful, innocent feeling'

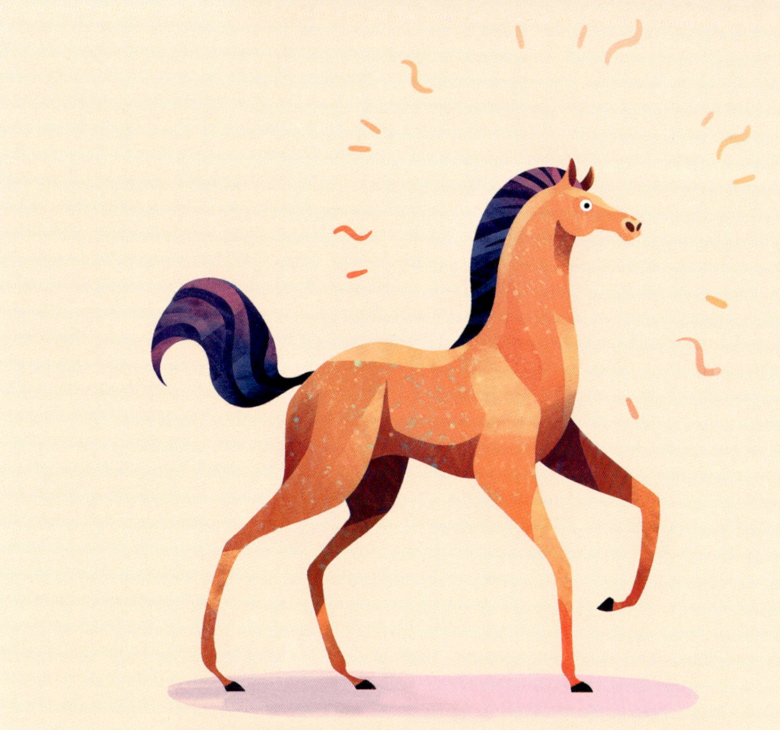

REVEAL THE BASE

Increase visual interest by starting a design with a complementary base colour, then allowing it to show through slightly. In this piece, a soft green can be seen shimmering beneath the orange surface of the horse's body.

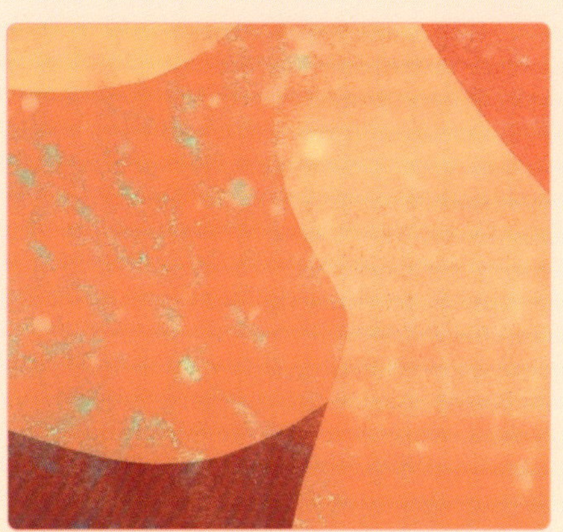

EMBRACE GRADIENTS

To establish the direction of the light source and add a touch of drama to a design, create gradients on a character that move from dark to light shades. Here, a solid dark background colour also sets off the gradient and adds further contrast and interest.

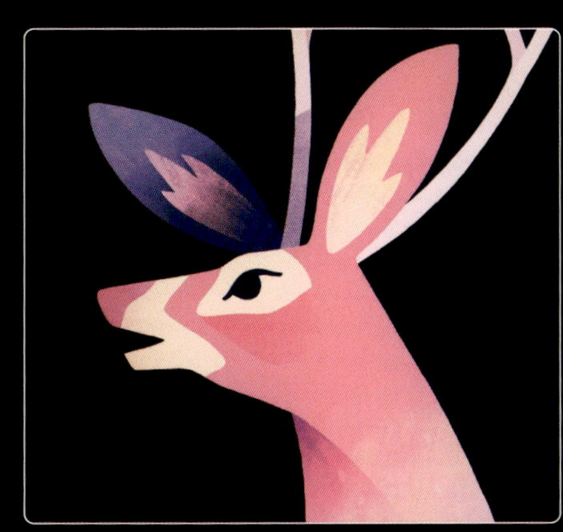

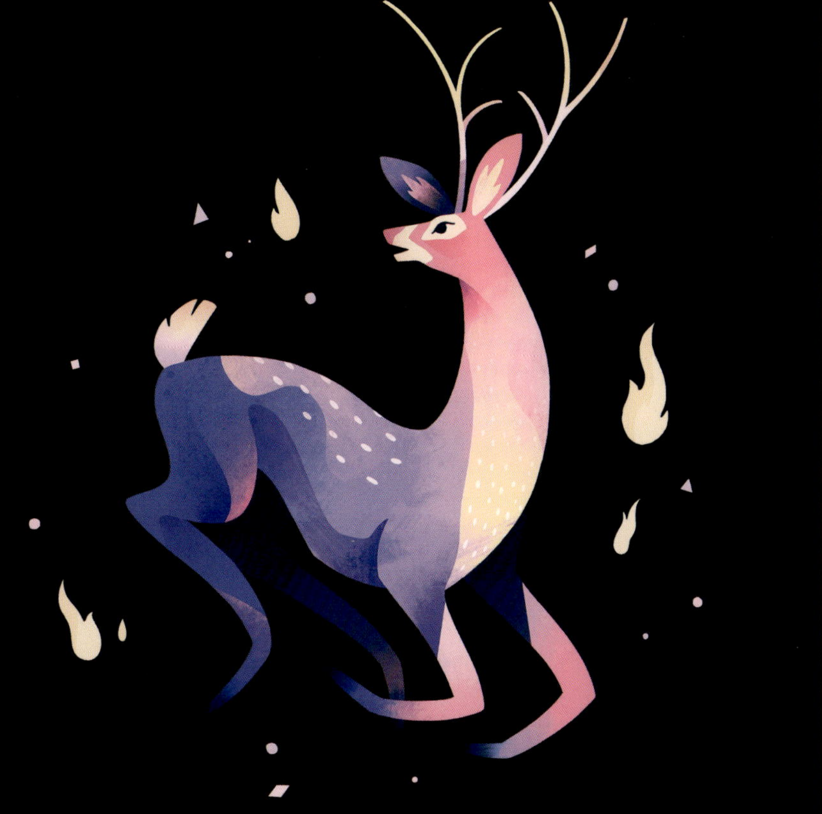

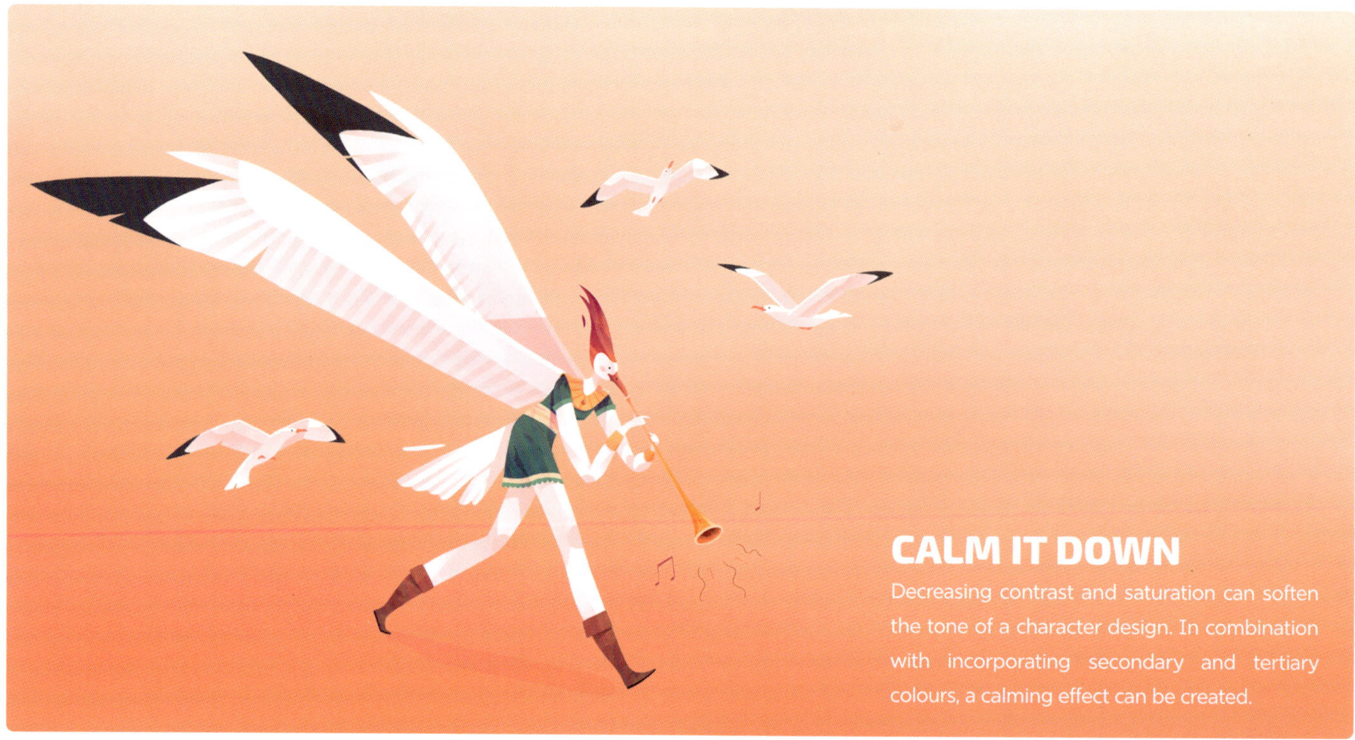

CALM IT DOWN

Decreasing contrast and saturation can soften the tone of a character design. In combination with incorporating secondary and tertiary colours, a calming effect can be created.

VALUE THOSE VALUES

Especially in lower contrast pieces, it's very important to check your values frequently to ensure they communicate the aesthetic and emotion you want to convey. Digitally this can be done by simply adding a black layer above everything else, then setting its blend mode to Saturation.

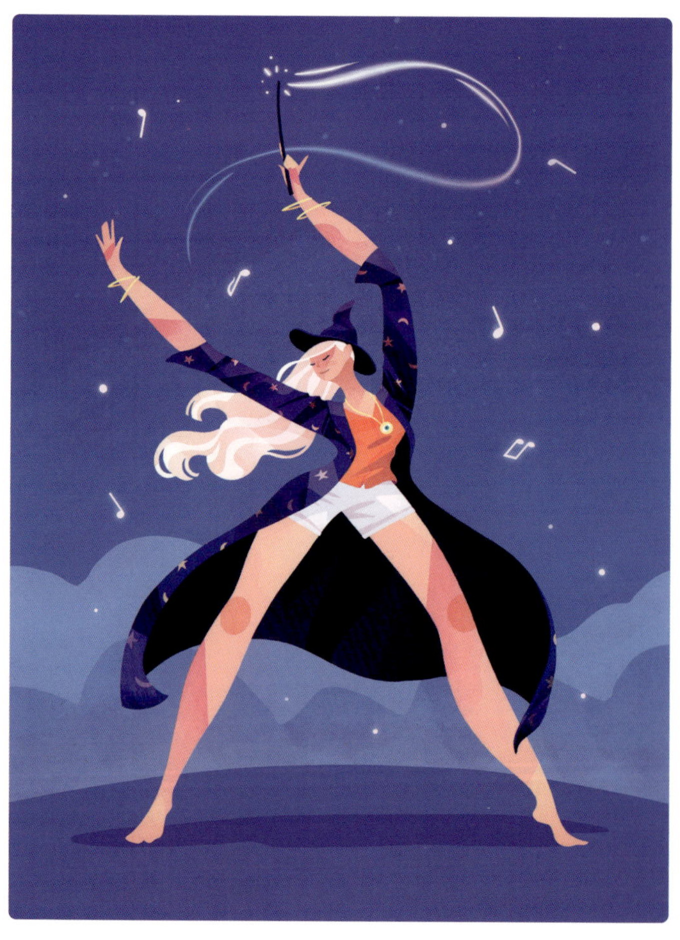

CONTRAST TEMPERATURES

Contrast in colour temperature can help make your character stand out from the scene. In this piece, the cool blue background and cloak are complemented by the contrasting warm tones of the character's skin and shirt.

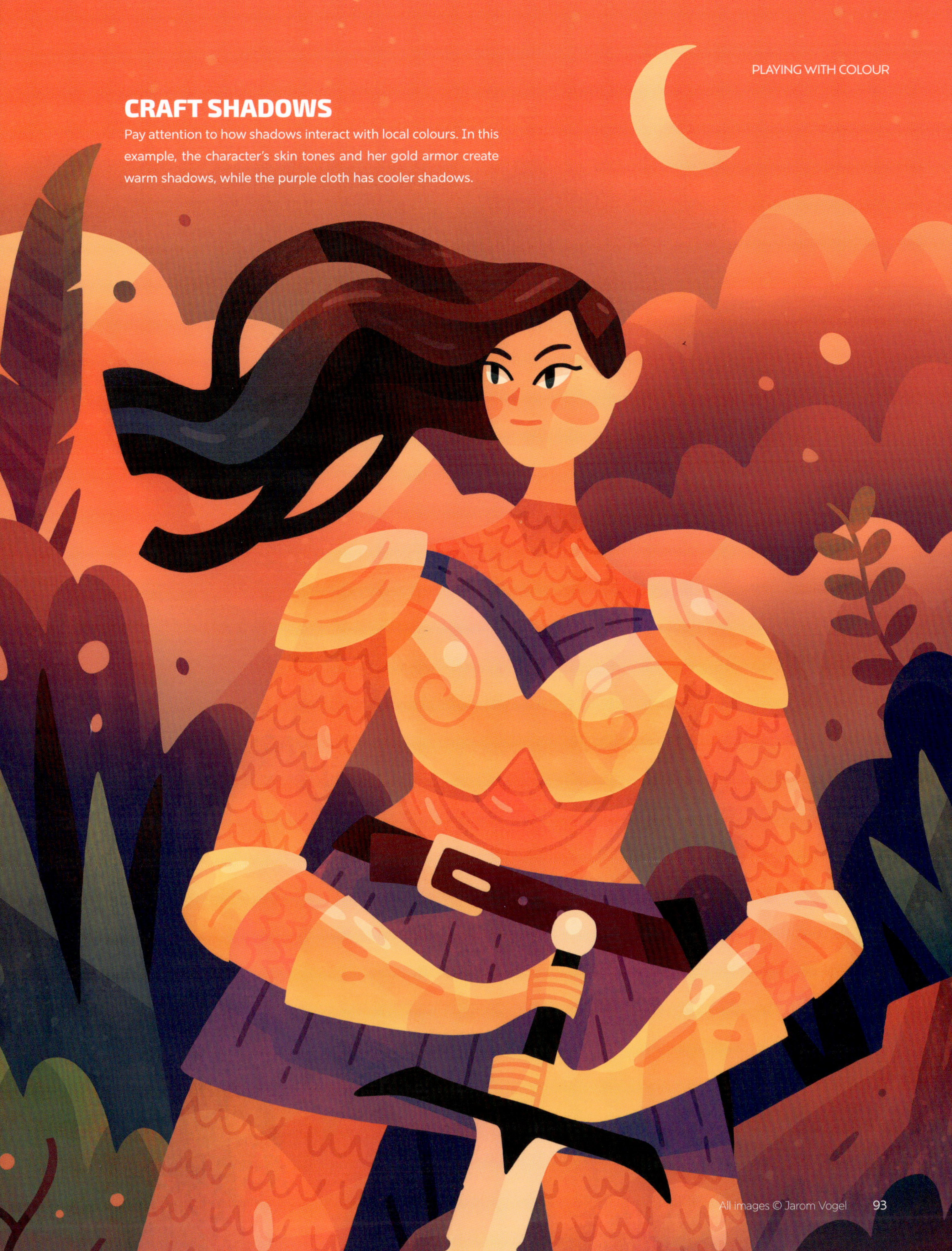

CRAFT SHADOWS

Pay attention to how shadows interact with local colours. In this example, the character's skin tones and her gold armor create warm shadows, while the purple cloth has cooler shadows.

The tiger's tale

JACKIE DROUJKO

Finding the perfect colours to emphasize mood and narrative is always an exciting challenge. Often, we think of colours as an afterthought, but I find colours to be as important as shapes and story. In this tutorial, I will show you my process: developing an idea, working through many iterations, settling on a concept, and creating a full and balanced composition – all while using colour as the centre of my design.

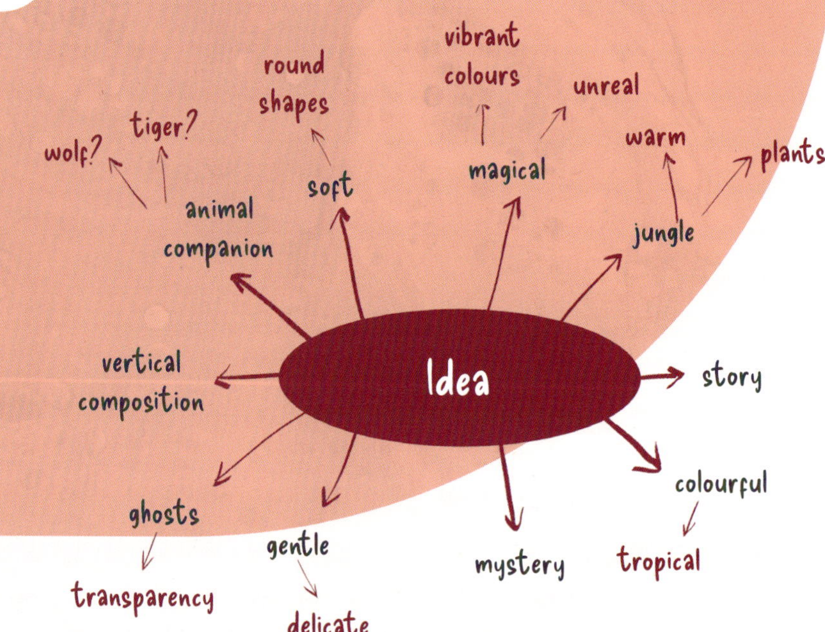

AN IDEA EMERGES

Let's start by brainstorming an idea for a new illustration. How do you want the piece to feel? What story do you want to tell? There are millions of directions a new painting can go, so I create a word map of all the words that come to mind when I think of what I would like to draw. I want to portray a gentle and magical feeling, so I consider how I can represent those qualities in my drawing. For 'gentle' I could incorporate round shapes and avoid harsh angles; for 'magic' I could use vibrant and unrealistic colours.

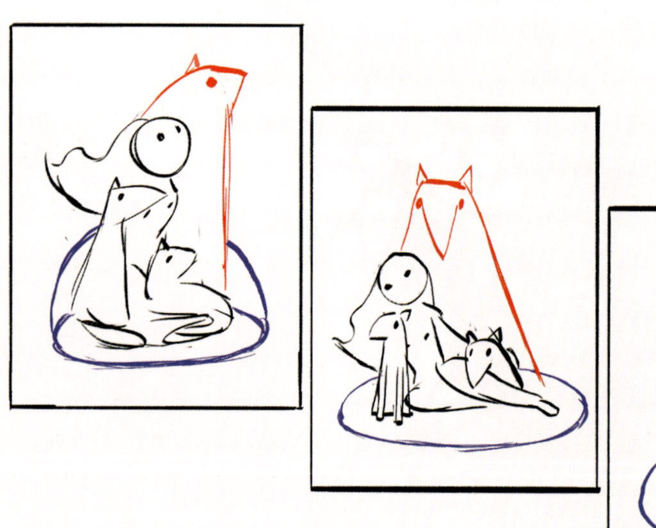

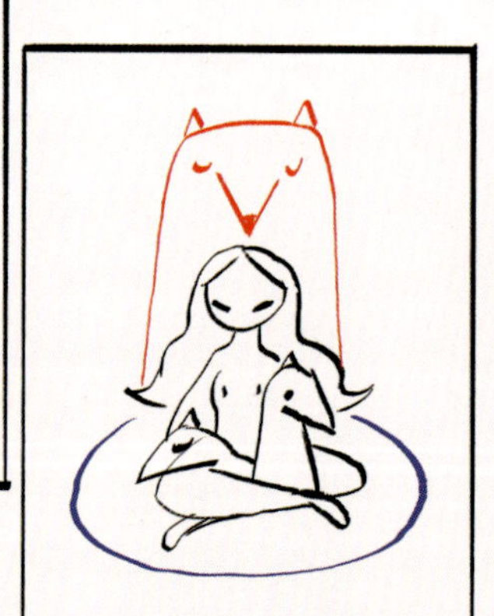

THUMBNAIL CONCEPTS

The next step is to create thumbnails of the composition. These thumbnails can be as rough as you want – the idea is to suggest where each character will be in the drawing, as well as representing the basic shapes you want to emphasize. Keep in mind the silhouette for a clear design. I know I want a central composition of three companion wolves surrounding an ethereal woman. A large wolf looming above the character will exude a feeling of protection. I want the ground visible in the illustration so the environment in which the characters live can further tell the story.

SKETCHING THE PACK

Sketch out your favourite thumbnail idea while keeping the mood board in mind. I draw a woman sitting with a pack of wolves, keeping her in the centre of the illustration so she feels safe, tucked within the pack. I keep the shape designs round to convey the idea of gentleness, and the detail levels low to maintain a sense of mystery around the animals. Are they real or part of her imagination? What are they all looking at? How could she have tamed wild animals? Is she a type of magical creature herself? I want the audience to have all these questions in mind when looking at this illustration – this will mean I've succeeded in creating mystery within the story.

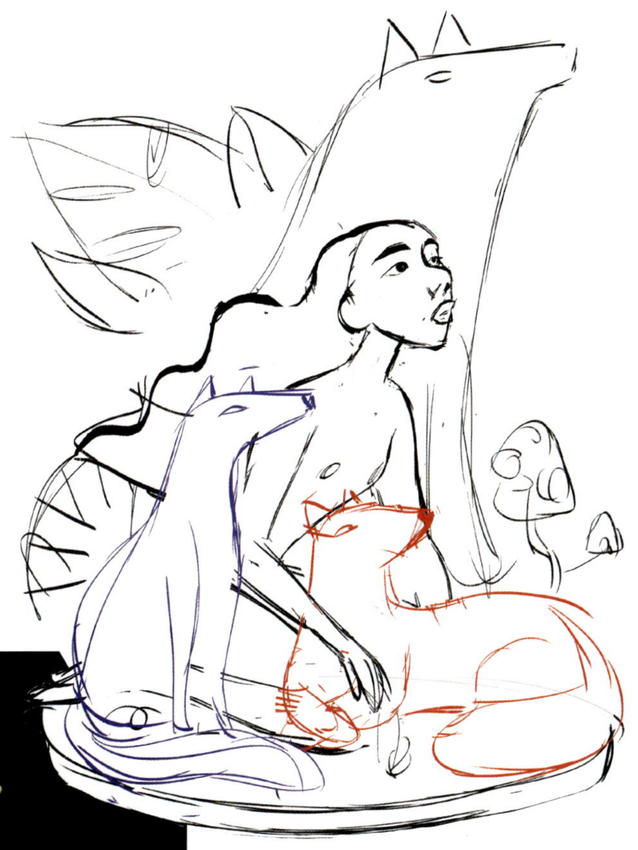

COLOUR & MOOD

I want colour to be the most alluring part of this illustration, so I add some rough ideas before continuing with the design. Against a black background, these colours feel so much more vibrant and ethereal. Using blues and yellows for the wolves adds to the unnatural feeling I'm trying to portray. The semi-transparent effect gives the animals a ghostly quality. The concept feels magical at this point – a naked woman with her wild companions isolated on the black page. Now, I need to define the lines to get a stronger idea of the final drawing.

DETAILED SKETCHING

I begin sketching more detailed wolf companions, because I know the line-free style I'll be using is already so simple that I will need a more structured design for the wolves. After trying this more detailed approach, I realize the animals don't fit with the soft, tropical mood I'm going for – they're too angular, and wolves typically represent threat and danger. Art is an evolving process – don't be afraid to work through many ideas before reaching the final design.

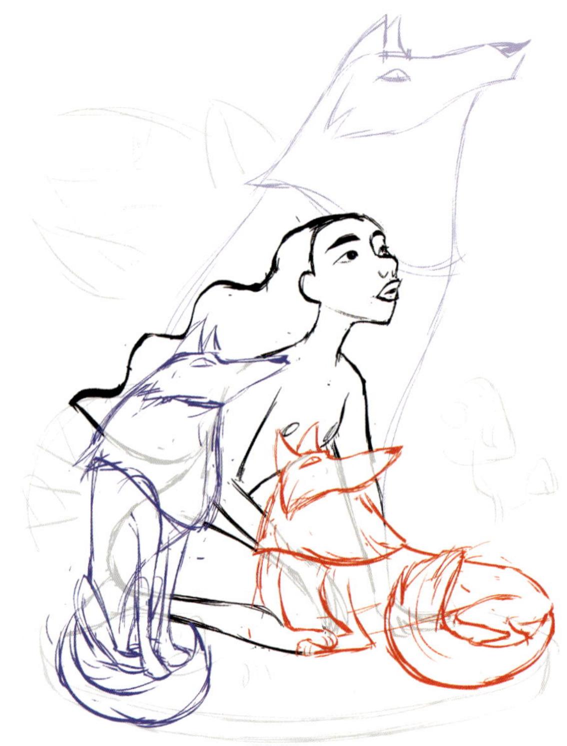

'I make sure all their heads are at different heights and their poses differ to create variety and interest in the composition'

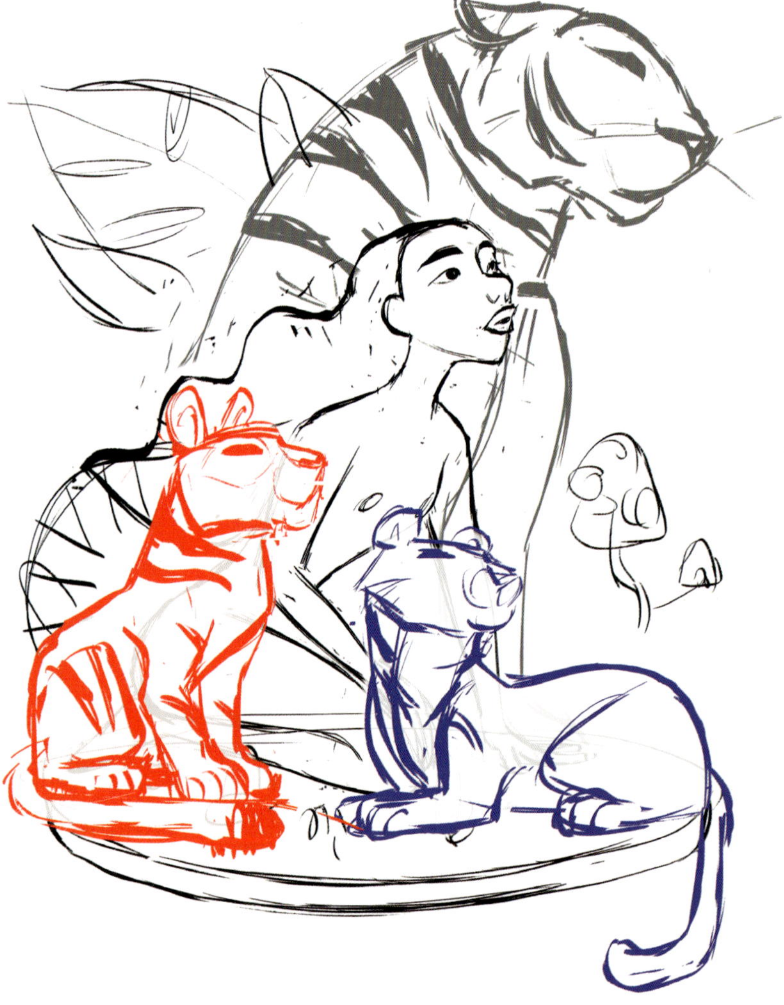

RE-EVALUATING THE CONCEPT

Instead of wolves, I decide to go with tigers – they fit my requirement for tropical animals that I can design using round shapes, and their stripes will add a playful design element. I draw two cubs to really emphasize the gentle nature of the illustration, with a large adult encompassing the other characters as if protecting them. I make sure all their heads are at different heights and their poses differ to create variety and interest in the composition. I'm happy with this thumbnail as the basis for my final composition.

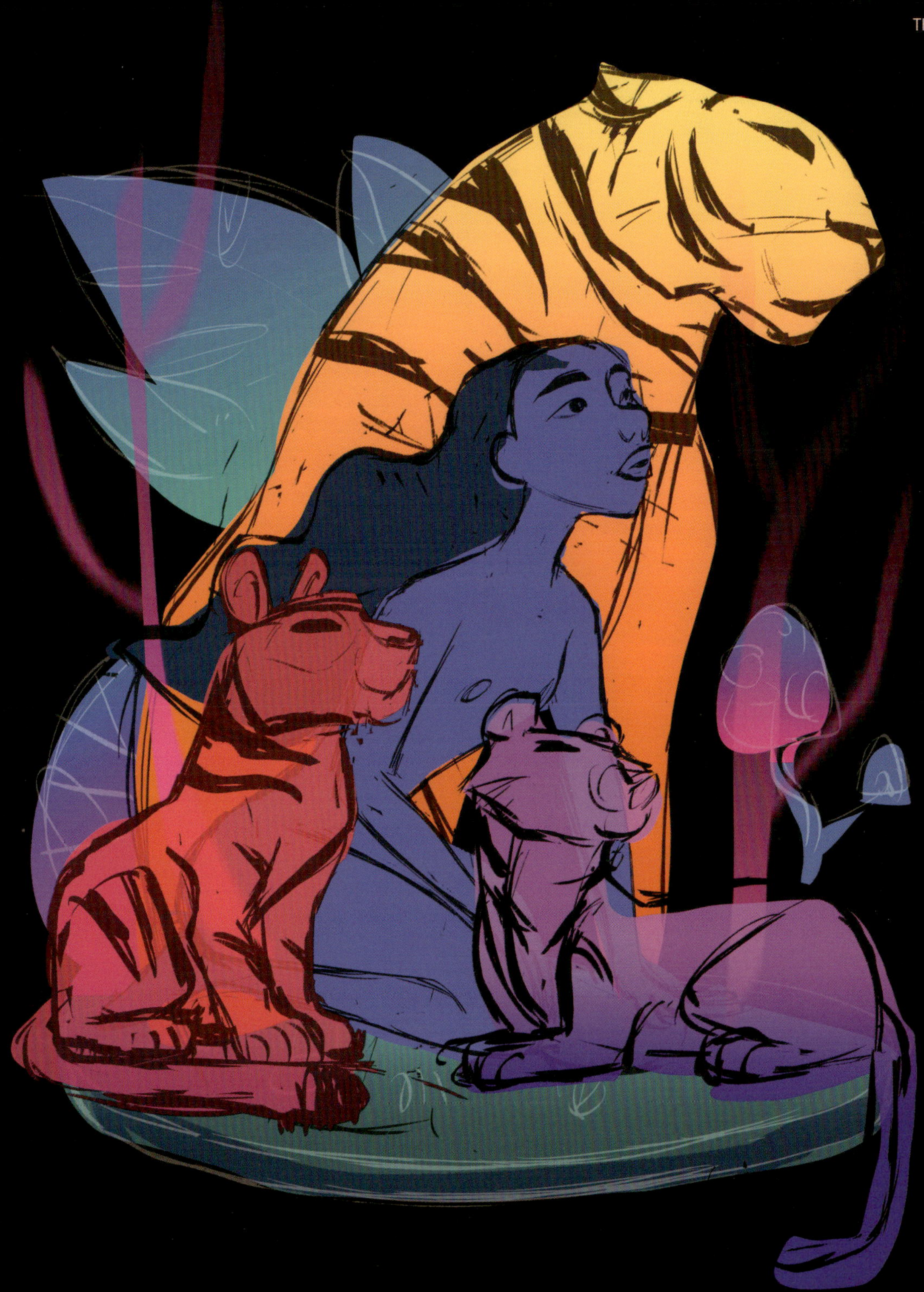

COLOUR CHANGE

After changing the animals I'm using, I can see that my colour choices could do with being more unified. I use the complementary colours blue and orange on the woman and main tiger to make them the focal point of the image. I intentionally paint the tigers with warm colours and use cool tones for the woman and background elements to create contrast throughout the design. I don't want the plants and ground to feel too far removed from real life, so I keep their colour as shades of green. I want the woman to feel unreal and magical, so I choose an unrealistic, monochromatic colour palette for her.

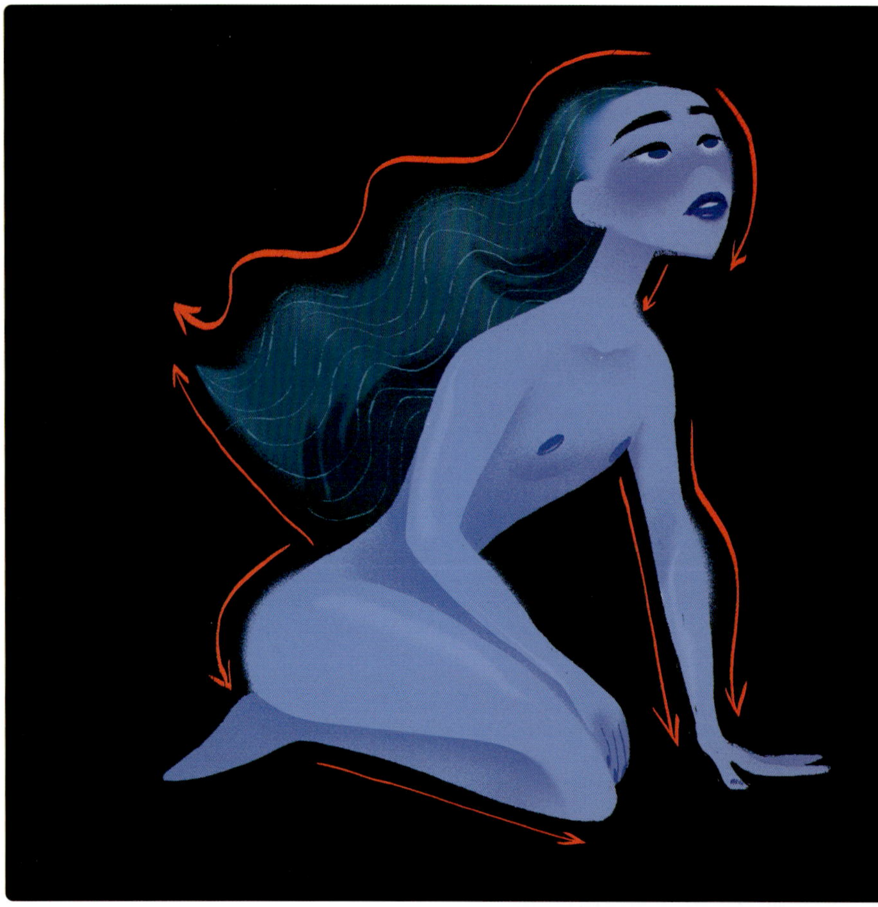

LINE DESIGN

Now we can work on developing the main character, incorporating the round lines and shapes that will create a gentle mood. It's important to offset the curved lines with straight ones. But how do you keep a rounded character design while also using straight lines? My trick is to ever-so-slightly curve those straight lines so they still give a round impression when looking at the overall character. Creating your first character sets a precedent for how you will approach the style of the rest of the illustration, so be sure you're happy with how they look.

BLOCKING THE BEASTS

I block in the tigers' silhouettes from the sketch to make sure the composition is strong. I'm also looking to clean up any issues that might weaken the design later on, such as tangents, a bad combination of straights and curves, or characters that don't appear properly planted on the ground. In this step, I usually try to simplify the shapes as much as I can to improve readability – it's very important that the viewer can instantly identify what they're looking at. I intentionally separate the tail, ears, and snout from the rest of the design to avoid overlapping groups and further clear up the shape of the silhouette.

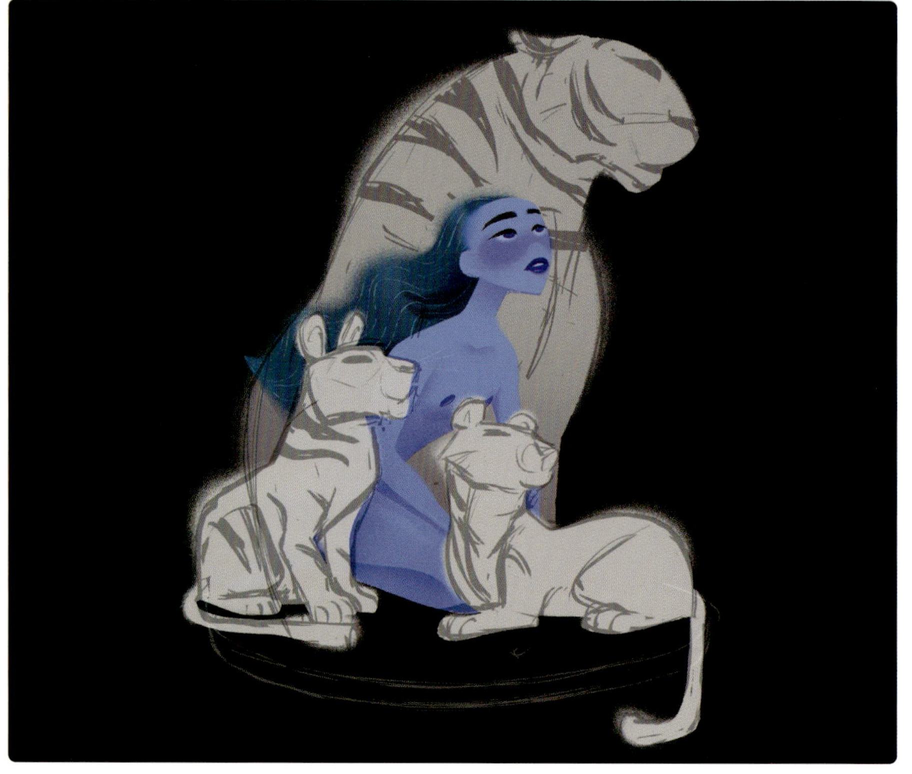

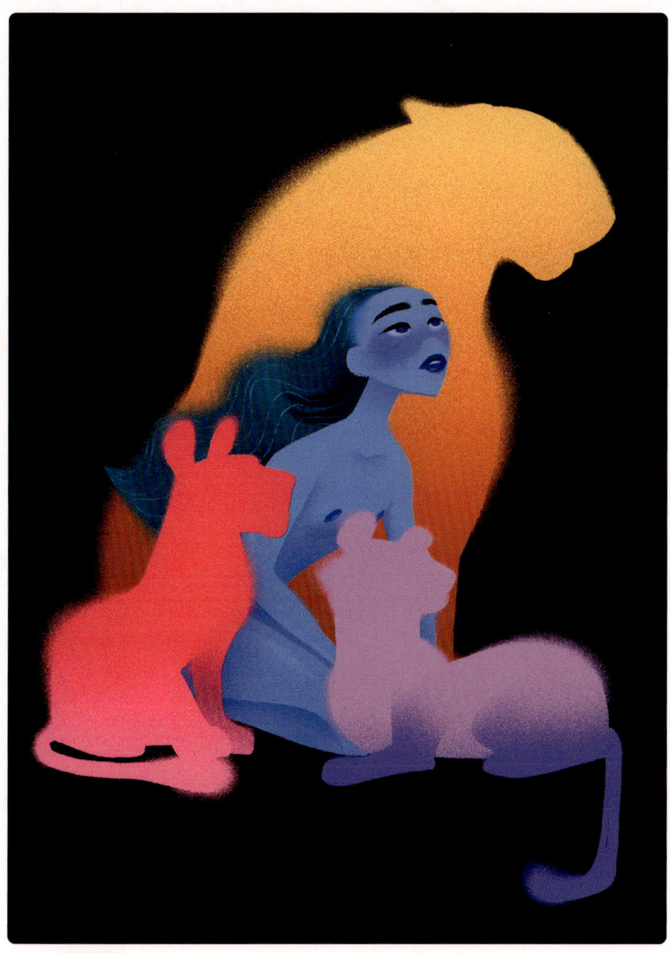

COLOURFUL CORRECTIONS

Next, I block the colours for the tigers. I have my rough colour palette from earlier to work with – I need to refine and adjust those colours for the final image. This means flipping between CMYK settings for print and black-and-white settings to check if the values are correct. To ensure the woman in the middle stands out, I keep the animals' warmer colours to contrast her cooler look. When choosing your colour palette, the design shouldn't be the only thing drawing the audience's eye to the focal point – colour is just as important.

There's a lot to consider, as all these decisions can quickly change the meaning of your piece. Is your drawing looking grimy and sad? Perhaps it's best to use desaturated colours. Or maybe you want your character to exist in a more realistic world – natural colours will help ground them in reality.

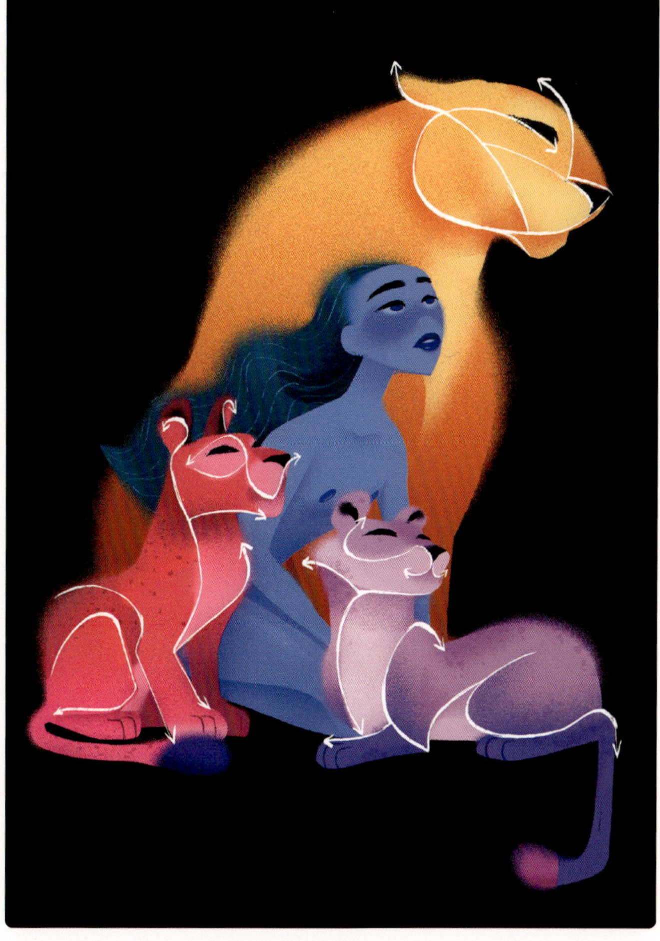

SHAPING THE DESIGN

Without lines, how do you separate shapes within a character? With blocks of varying colours and contrasts. Creating interesting shapes within the character's design is just as important as creating interesting silhouettes. I always make sure the shapes and sizes within my characters have variety – this adds dimension and volume to a design. Always try to avoid repetition to keep characters looking interesting. Follow the inner shapes of your design creating an invisible line and make sure that they all connect fluidly to one another. This is my technique for creating a harmonious character design.

TIGER BURNING BRIGHT

I add stripes to the tigers and the piece is really starting to come together. Using similar colours to those surrounding the tigers creates harmony throughout the design, keeping each element connected. I want the texture of the animals to feel fuzzy, so I keep as much grain in the design as possible. I add subtle transparency around their faces to accentuate the magical nature of these creatures and a ground plane in preparation for the next step.

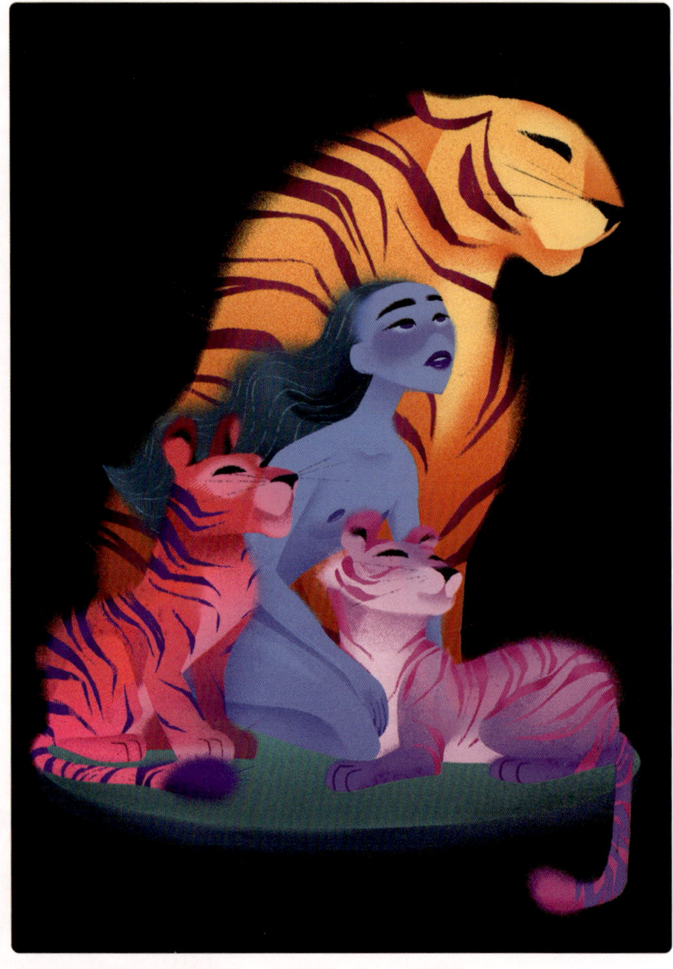

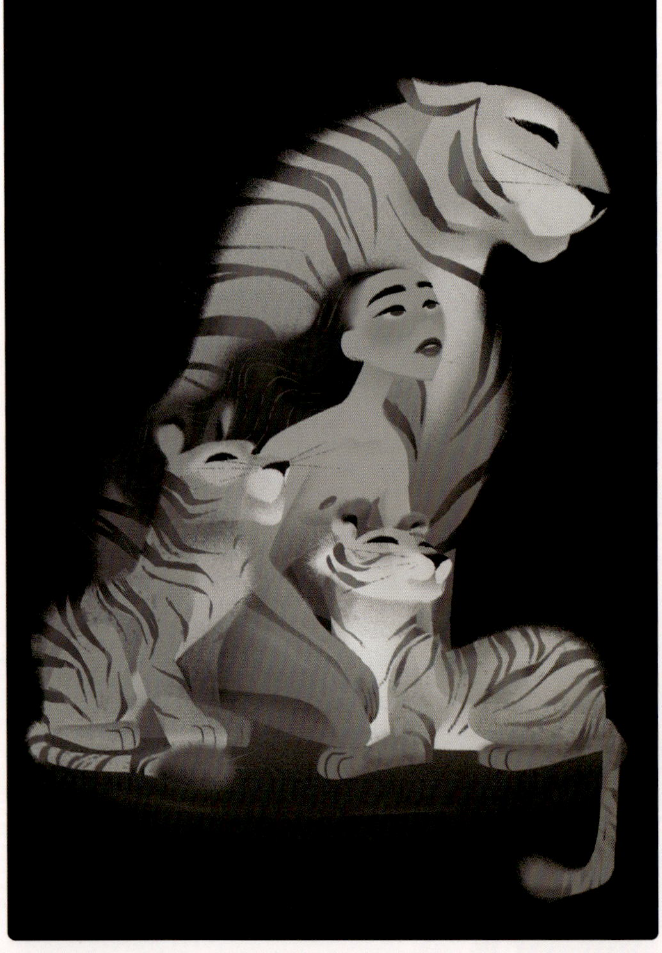

ALWAYS CHECK YOUR VALUES

Don't forget to check your values by looking at your piece in greyscale. This is a great way to see if there is enough contrast in your piece for your audience to clearly read the drawing. If some areas are nearly indistinguishable from others, make sure to play around with the values by adding Multiply and Overlay layers before finalizing your colours.

BUILDING THE BACKGROUND

When creating the background, I use my sketch as a starting point but give myself liberty to improve upon it. I create two trees to mimic the complexity of the tigers' stripes and round out the edges to a circle to simplify the design. The other foliage complements the focal point without drawing the viewer's attention away from the main character. The background is mostly green to very clearly ground the scene in a natural environment, creating a pleasant nook for the woman and tigers to rest in.

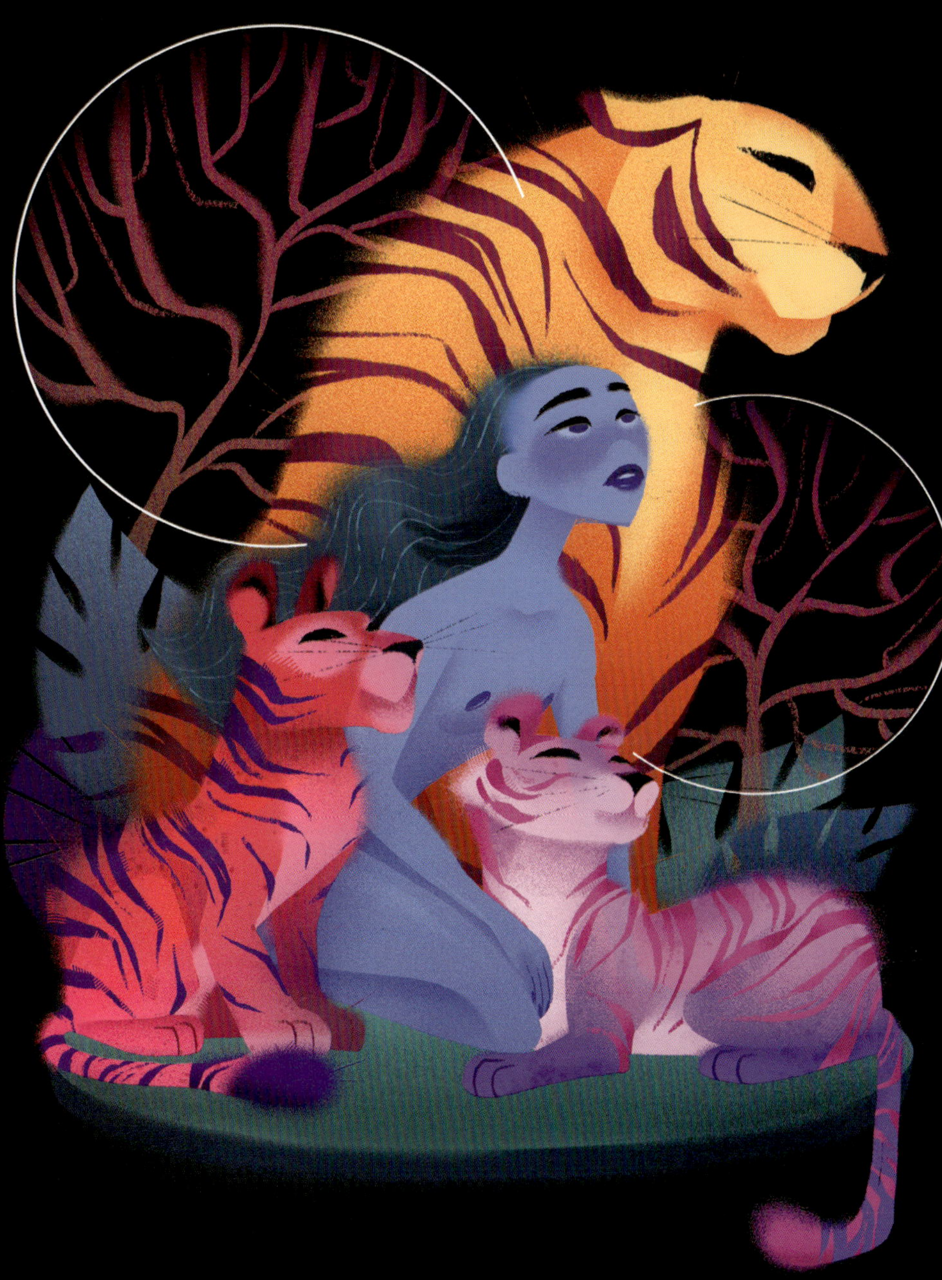

THE FINAL TOUCHES

Last but not least, I add the final touches and details to the illustration. At this point, it's very easy to go overboard with lots and lots of tiny details – after you've finished, take a second look and see what you can remove without losing the work's charm. I opt to add a few thick pieces of grass to add to the textured, cute aesthetic I'm going for. Remember, art is subjective and there is no right or wrong way to create a piece. The most important thing is to make conscious decisions about your design and learn how to improve for next time.

Final image © Jackie Droujko

EXPRES

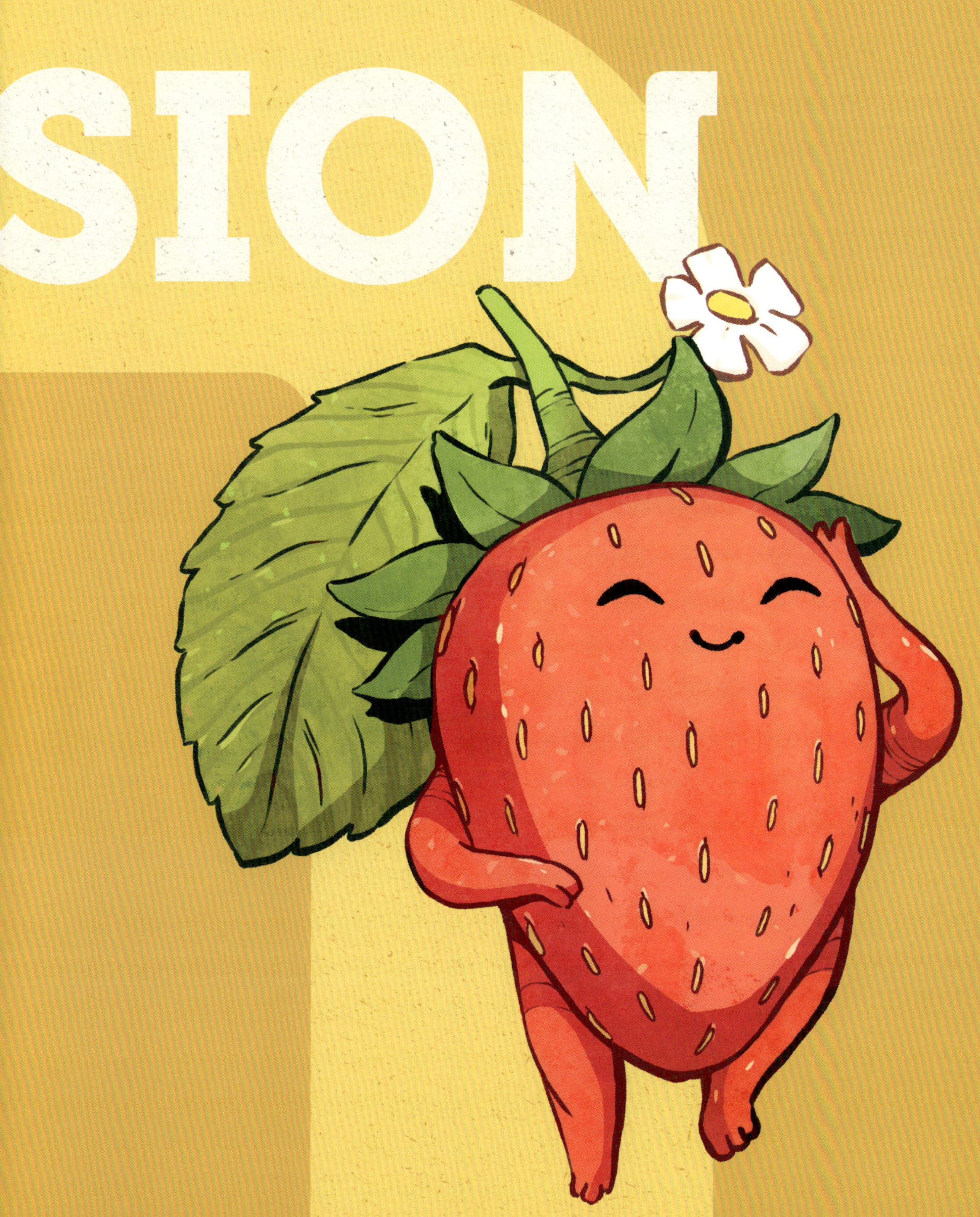

image © Johanna Forster

Expressing emotions

TRUST & FEAR

FELIPE RODRIGUEZ

To explore the emotions of characters, you must first understand the shapes of which the design is composed. In animation, each character plays a specific role, so each must have their own way of expressing themselves – your main character's fears may be different from your villain's. The tone of each emotion is also important – feeling trusted and arrogant can be different from feeling trusted and relaxed.

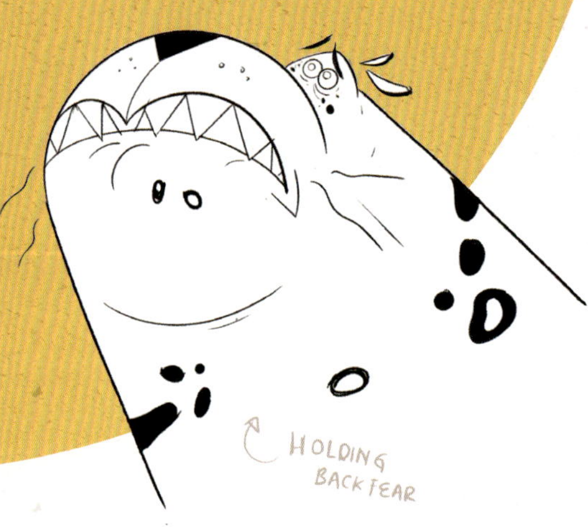

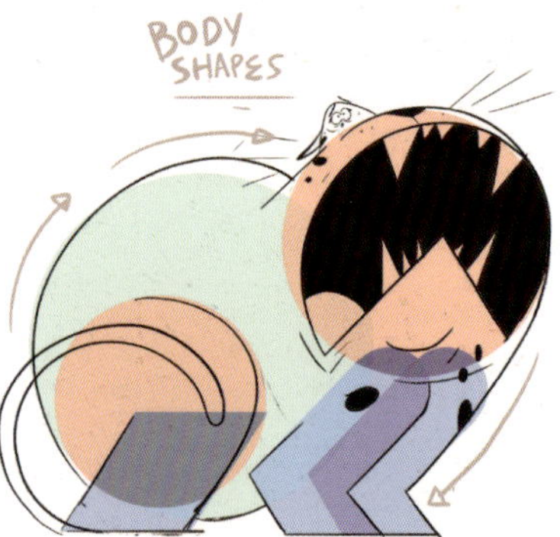

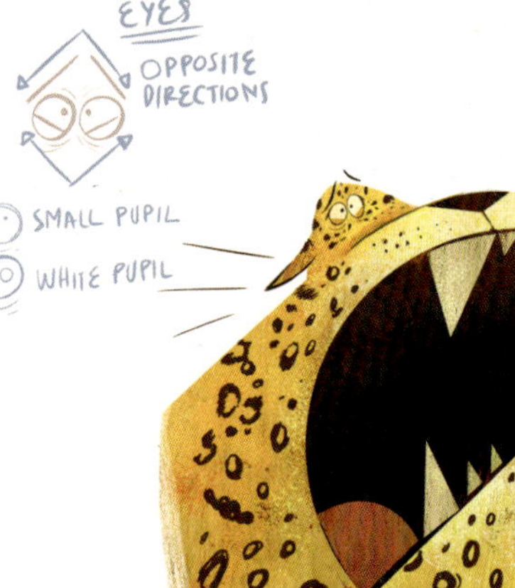

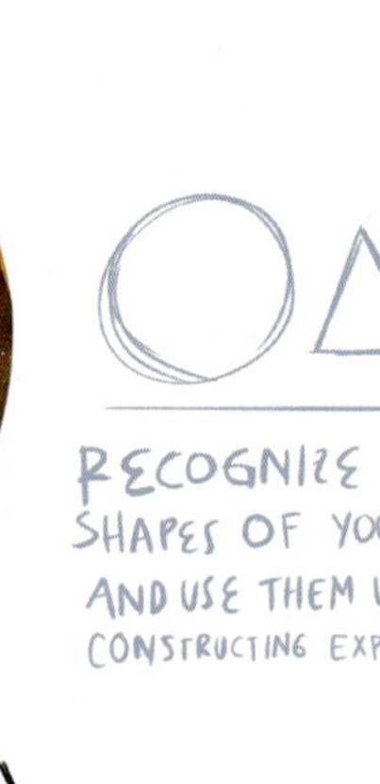

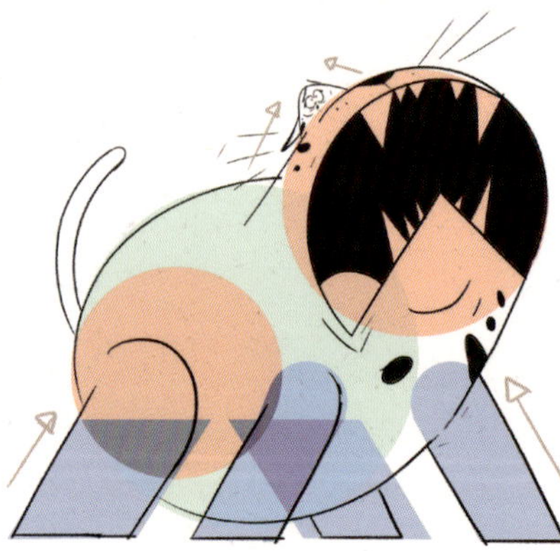

RECOGNIZE THE MAIN SHAPES

Start by analysing the shapes that make up your design in its simplest form and combine them according to expression. If you have triangles and circles as your main shapes, use them repeatedly in both facial and body expressions.

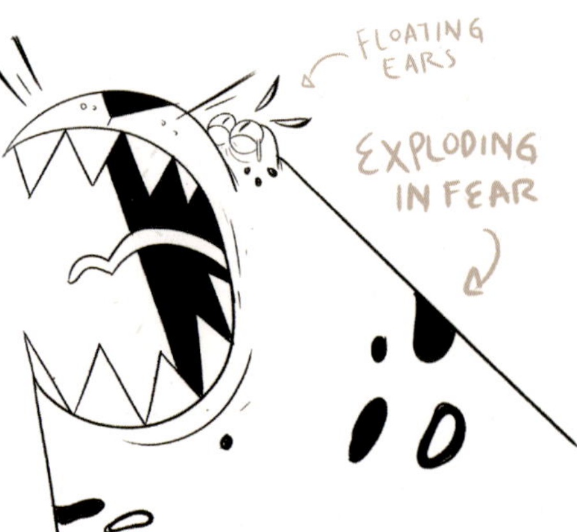

THINK ABOUT THE SITUATION

To recognize the different tones of an emotion, imagine the situation and the moment of reaction. When your character is anxious that something bad might happen, their expression of fear may be different from when that bad thing is actually happening!

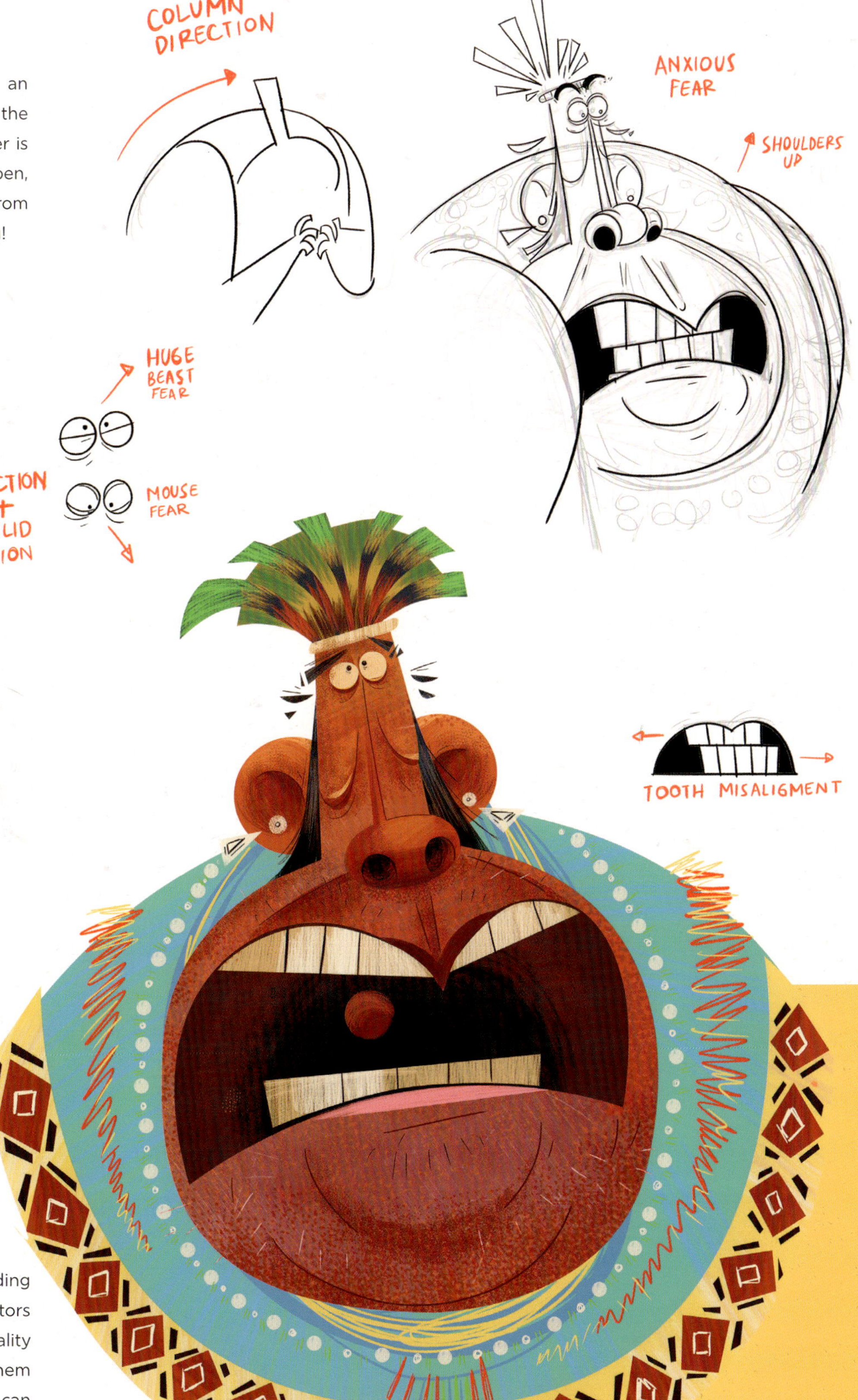

LEARN FROM FILM

One of the main resources for understanding how characters act is cinema. Look for actors and actresses that relate to the personality of your character and extract from them ways to express emotions. Film language can also help you understand how to place your character in front of the 'camera'.

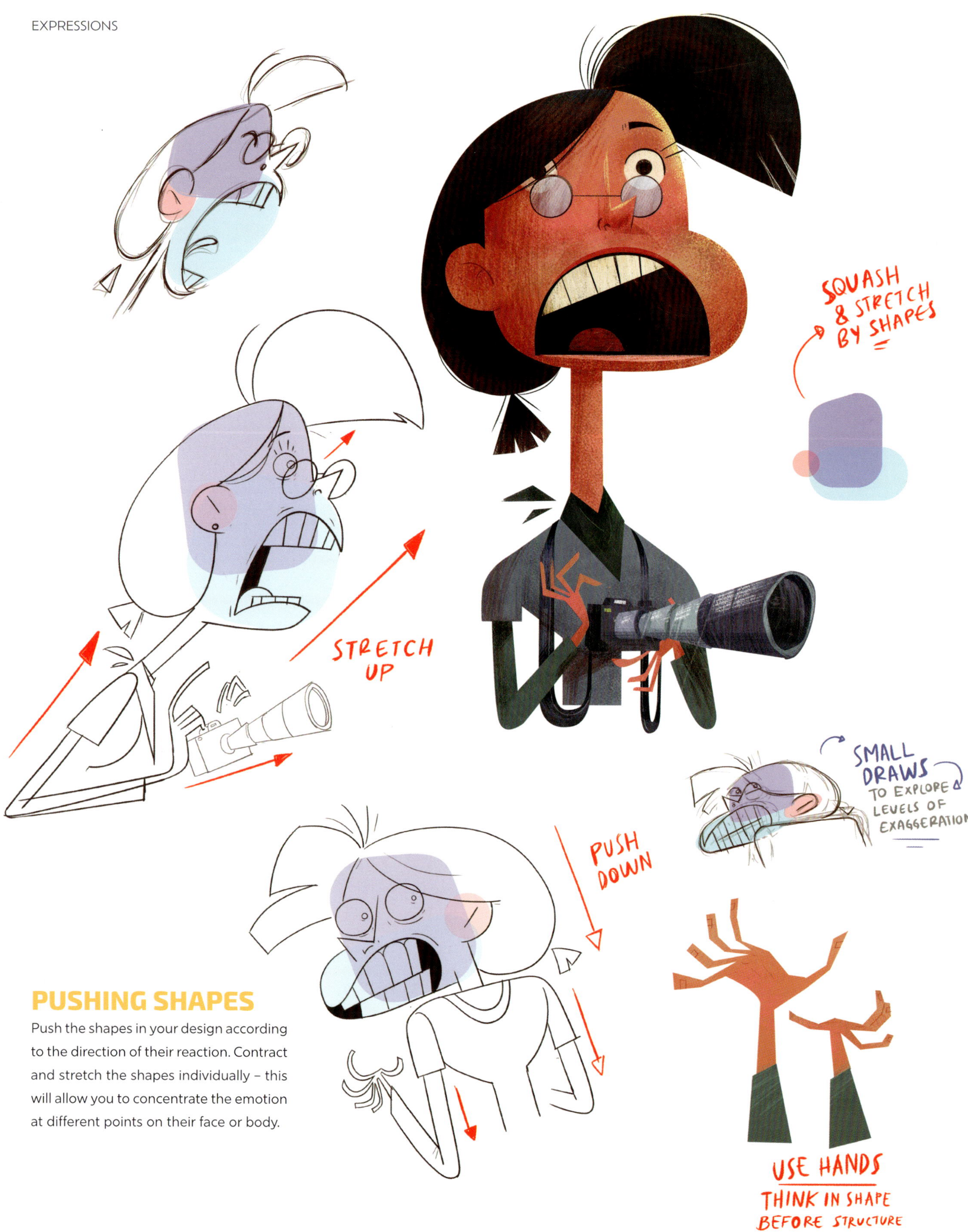

PUSHING SHAPES

Push the shapes in your design according to the direction of their reaction. Contract and stretch the shapes individually – this will allow you to concentrate the emotion at different points on their face or body.

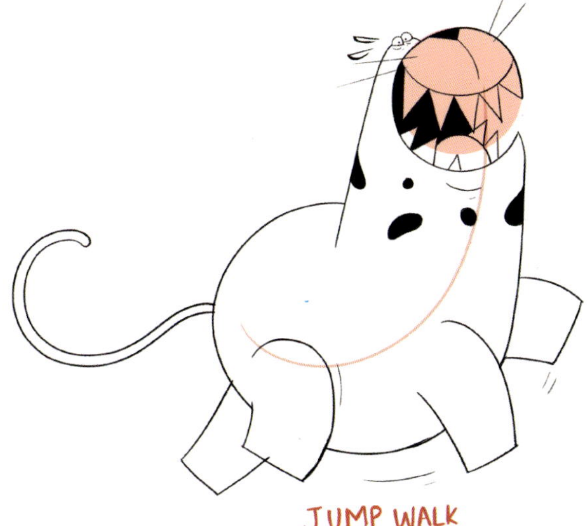

THINK THE EMOTION IN MOVEMENT

HOW IS THE CHARACTER BEHAVIOUR?

EMOTION THROUGH MOVEMENT

Understand how emotion would affect your character's behaviour and movements. Even the way they walk can tell the audience a lot about how a character feels.

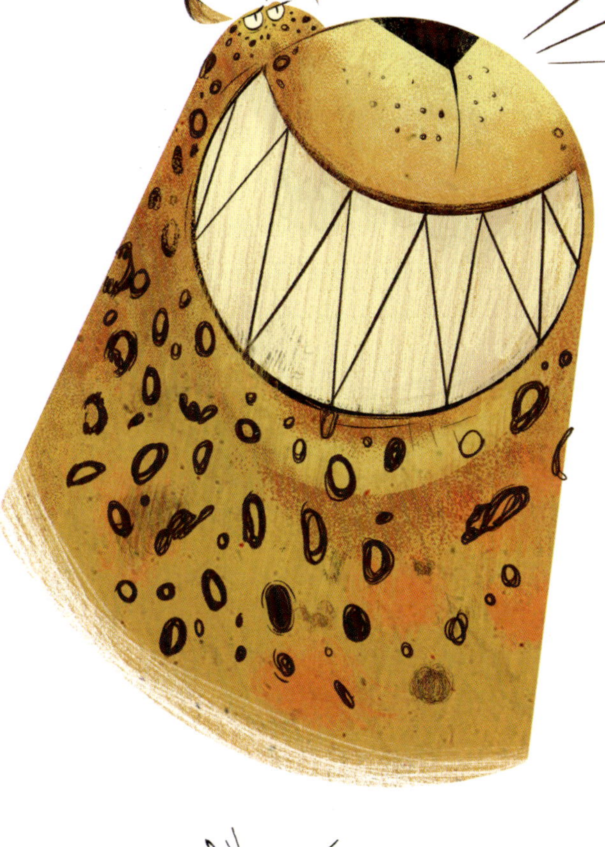

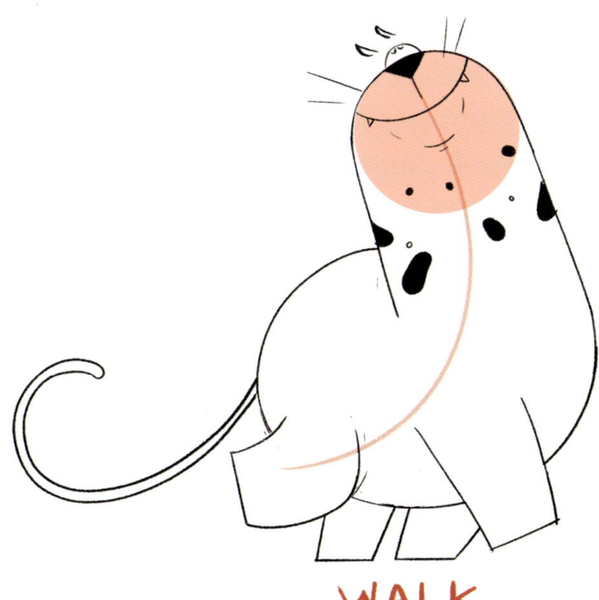

THINK SIMPLE

Start with simple shapes that express the emotion you want your character to feel. Once you have this essence of the emotion in place, then add layers of complexity. It can be useful to make miniature drawings very quickly to find the emotion that's right.

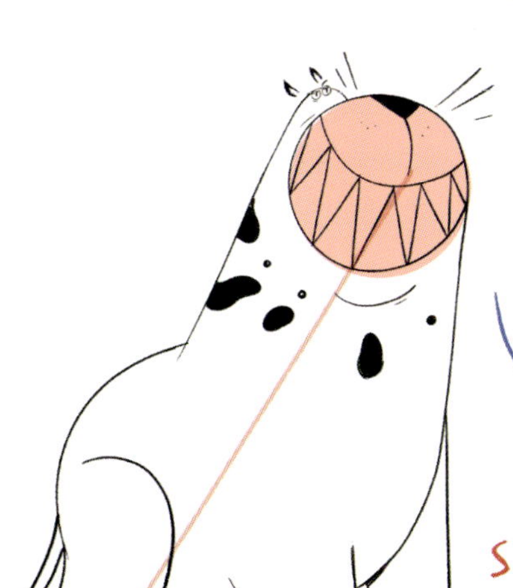

COMBINE EMOTIONS

USE HEAD + SHOULDERS DIRECTIONS

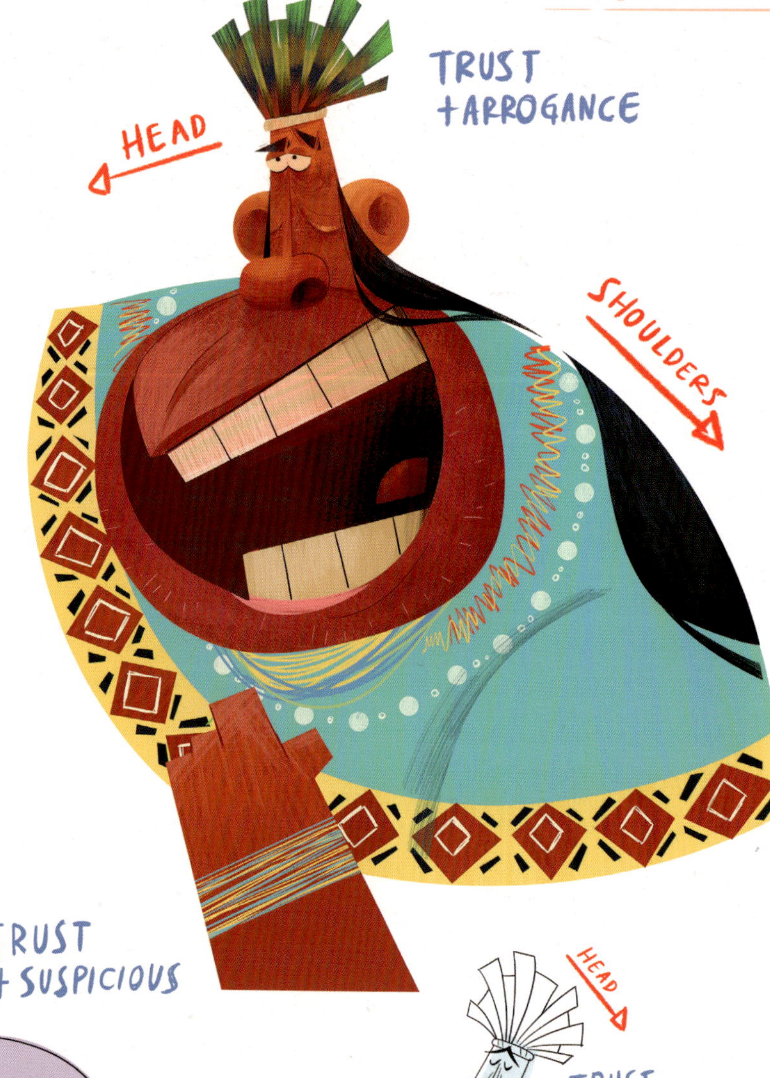

COMBINING EMOTIONS

Blend several emotions together to find new ways for characters to express themselves. Tilting the head and shoulders can add different tones to emotions.

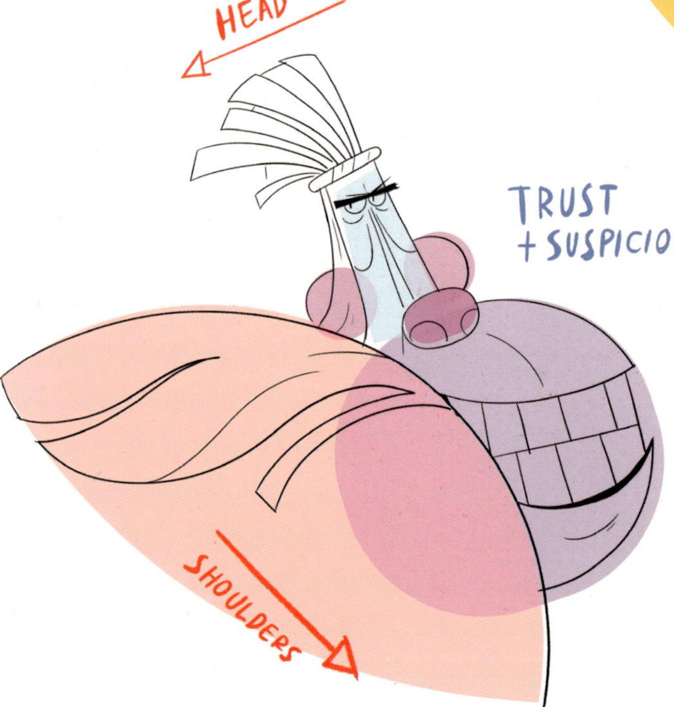

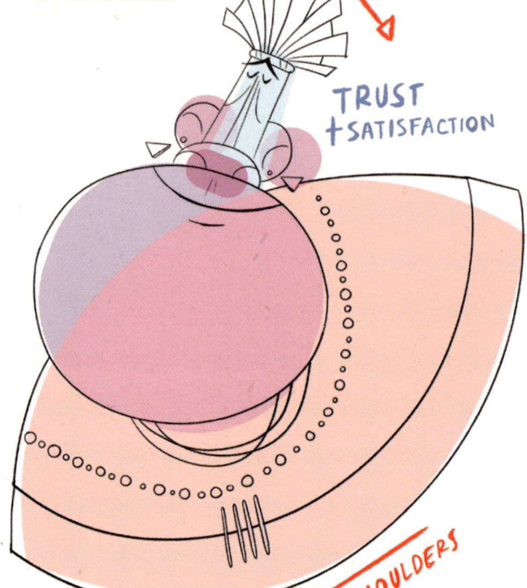

ENJOY IT!

Put yourself in the role of your character – if you want them to laugh, then you should try laughing, too! Acting out the emotions will help you get closer to the character and will make the whole process more enjoyable.

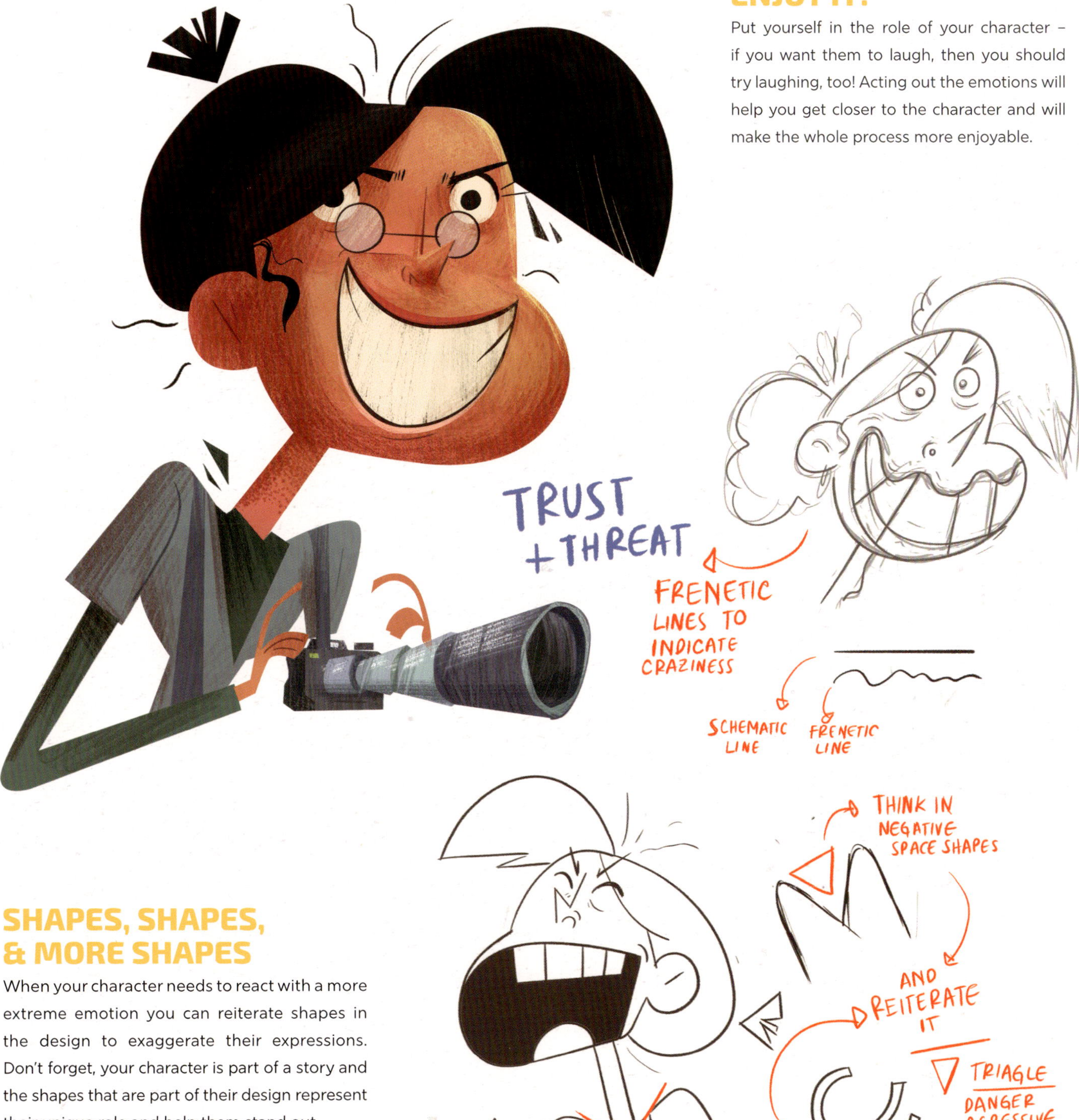

SHAPES, SHAPES, & MORE SHAPES

When your character needs to react with a more extreme emotion you can reiterate shapes in the design to exaggerate their expressions. Don't forget, your character is part of a story and the shapes that are part of their design represent their unique role and help them stand out.

Fruit... with feelings!

JOHANNA FORSTER

My most popular characters are probably my Grunlings – cute, anthropomorphic fruit and vegetable characters. To create your own expressive yet minimalistic characters like these, you need to break down the body language of an emotion to its essential components. When working on the initial sketch, imagine the character's body parts as being soft and flexible beans. Depending on the tension of a pose, they will lean in specific directions. By looking at some opposing emotions, we can see how playing with body parts can lead to strikingly different results.

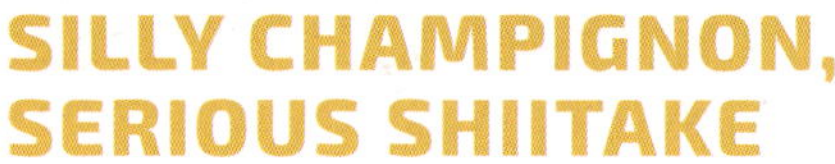

SILLY CHAMPIGNON, SERIOUS SHIITAKE

For a playful pose, push the character's chest forwards confidently and throw their arms and legs in different directions. Their body language should be very open. In contrast, a serious pose needs a straighter design, with body parts stiff and directed towards the centre of the body.

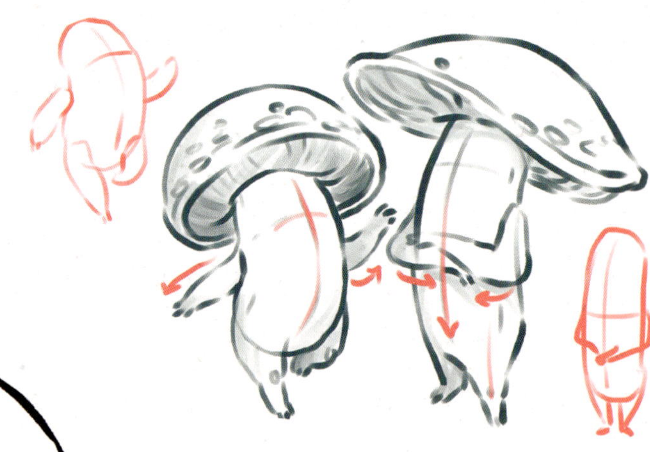

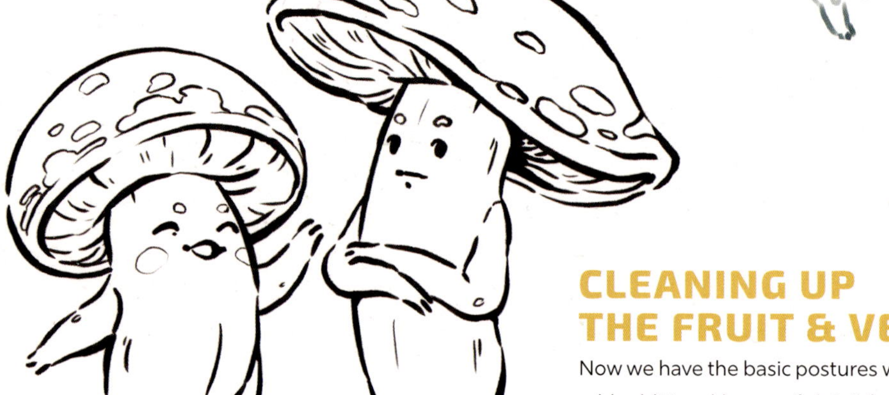

CLEANING UP THE FRUIT & VEG

Now we have the basic postures we're happy with, we can add additional layers of detail for a cleaner line drawing. At this stage, decide which details from the sketch to keep and further accentuate the shape of the characters.

SHY STRAWBERRY, BRASH BLUEBERRY

A self-confident body stretches outwards, with face and torso pushed forwards and open to the world. To show a shy posture, have your character hide their torso, pulling their arms, head, or both inwards towards their centre.

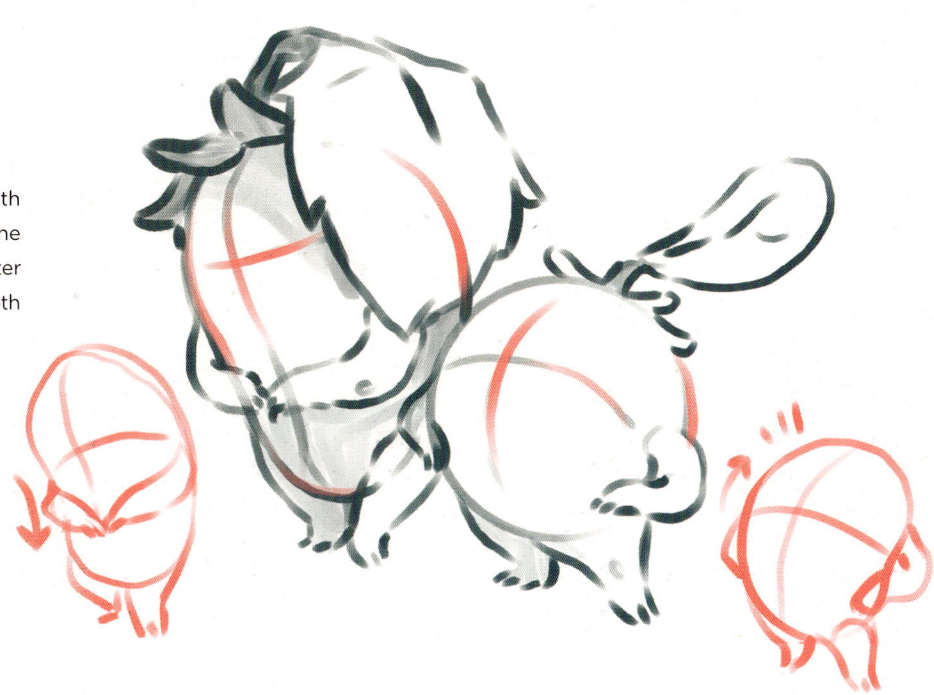

> 'Start by depicting the facial expression you're after in detail, and then reduce detail and remove as many elements as you can'

MINIMALIZING EMOTIONS

For minimalistic facial expressions, experiment with possible options on a separate layer. Start by depicting the facial expression you're after in detail, and then reduce detail and remove as many elements as you can while still conveying the desired emotion.

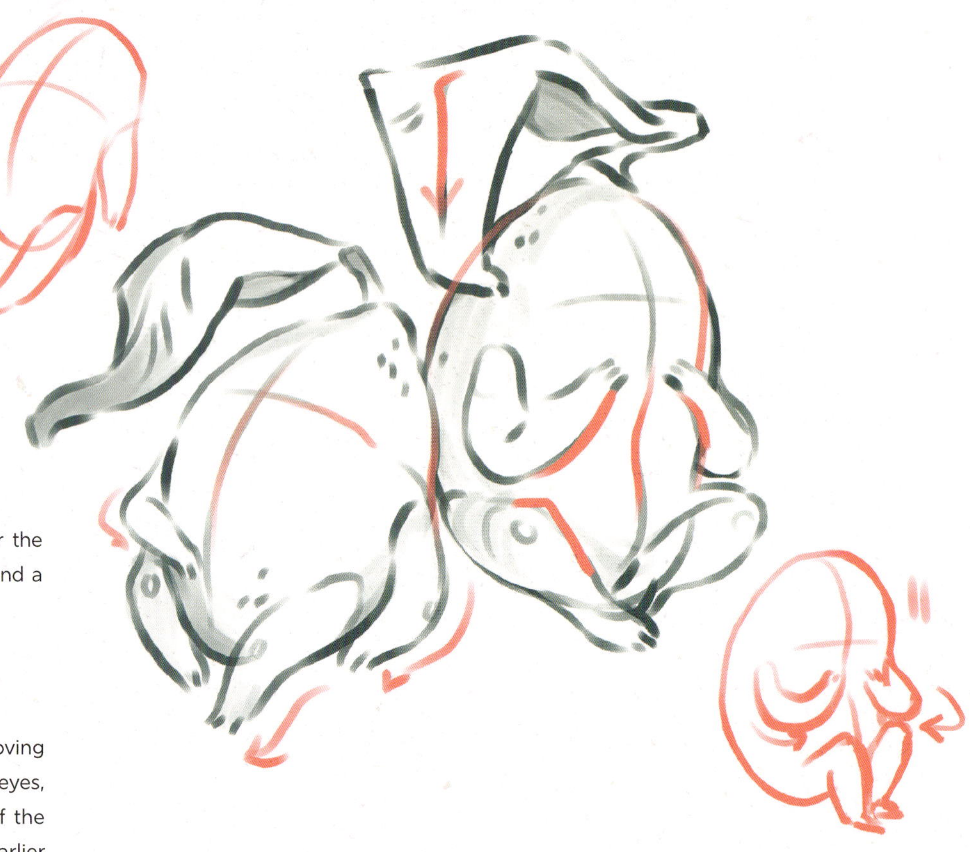

LOOSE LIME & TENSE LEMON

Despite being very different emotions, relaxed and tense poses can be quite similar – the difference is in how we choose to draw the lines. For the relaxed figure use flowing, smooth lines, and for the tense character go with sharper angles and a more defensive position.

CUTE FRUIT

For an extra cute facial expression, try moving your character's mouth close to their eyes, and put more weight on the corners of the mouth. Reusing the bean shape from earlier for the eyebrows will also help.

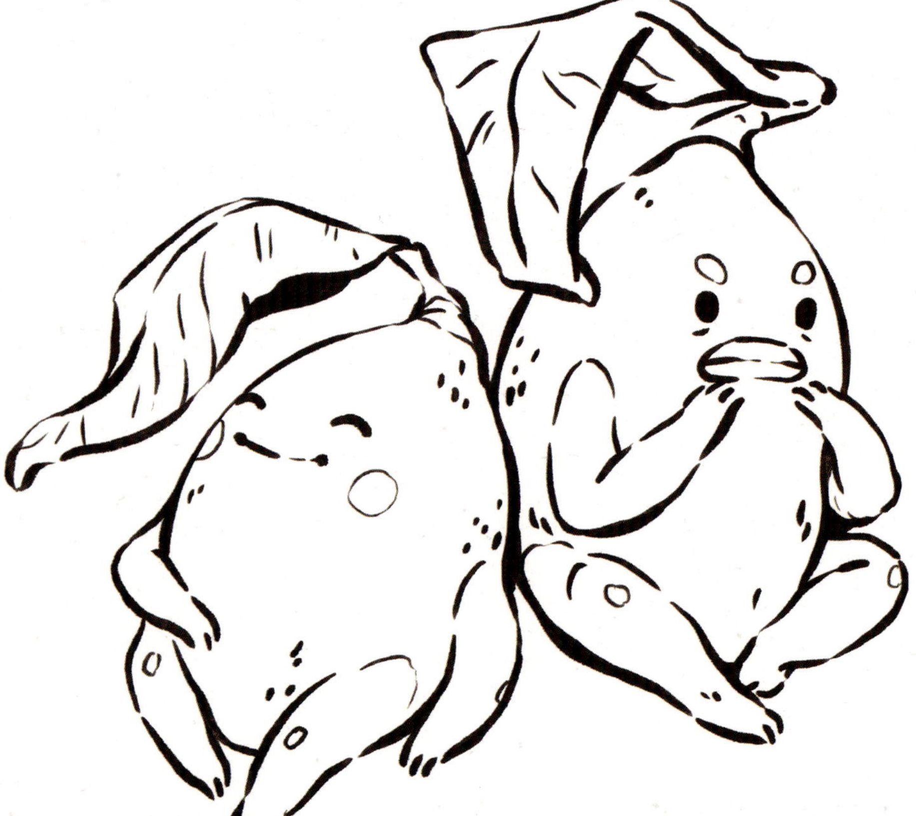

STAY LOOSE

It's important to avoid adding detail to your drawing for as long as possible, trying out several quick bean poses and facial expressions until you are happy the basic design captures the emotion you're going for. It helps to use a big, soft brush for the early iterations and only switch to a hard, ink-like brush for the final drawing.

EXPRESSING EMOTION IN HUMANS

The bean sketching technique I've used in this tutorial is best suited to minimalistic, chubby characters (like my fruit and veggies!) but it can also work with human proportions – just integrate a more detailed shape for the head and draw the limbs bigger.

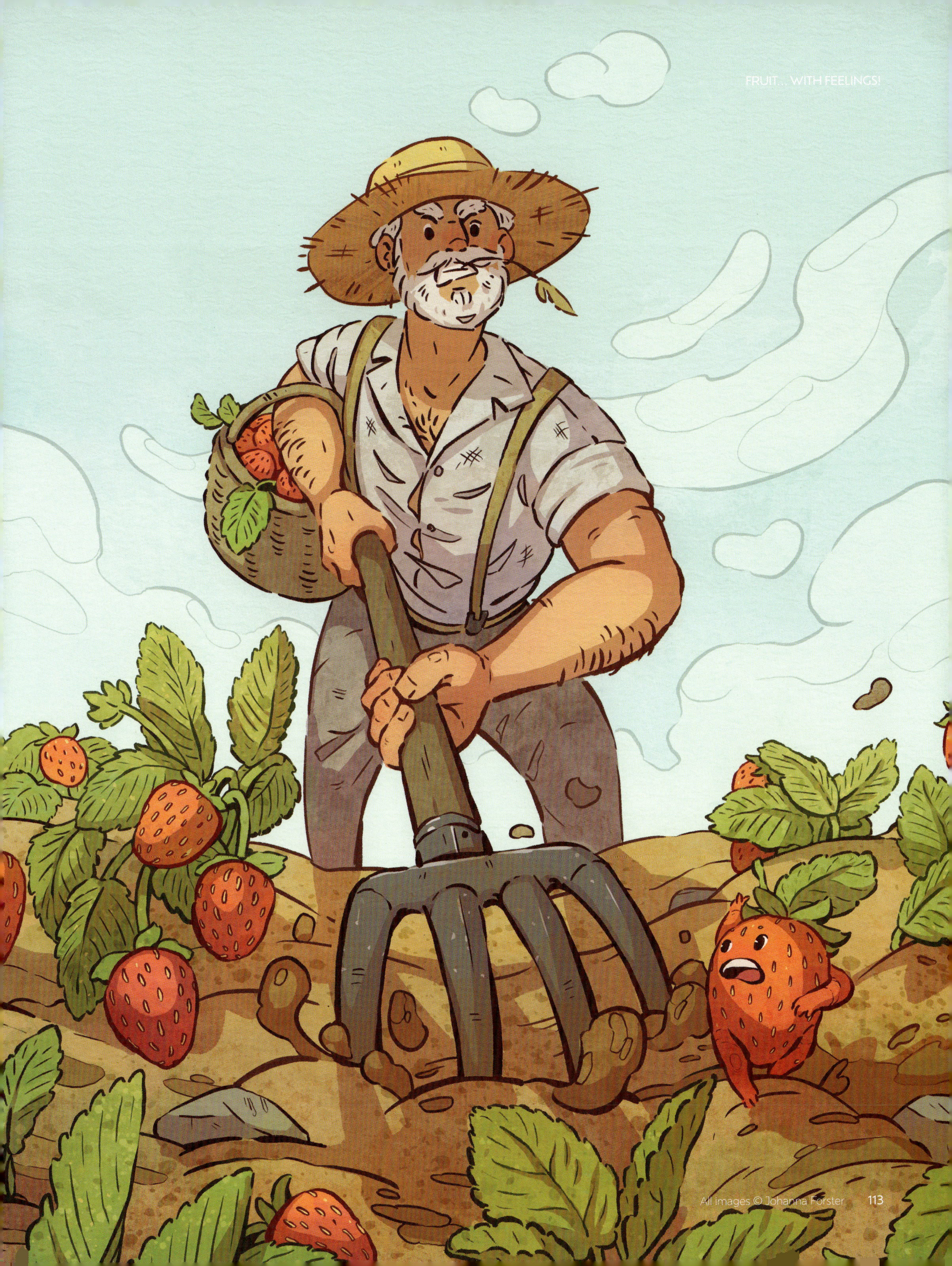

The powerless & the brave

RAQUEL OCHOA

It is so important to convey emotion through your character designs, to bring them to life and make them relatable to the viewer. Let me show you how I create characters expressing the emotions 'powerless' and 'brave', focusing on how to build body language and expressions.

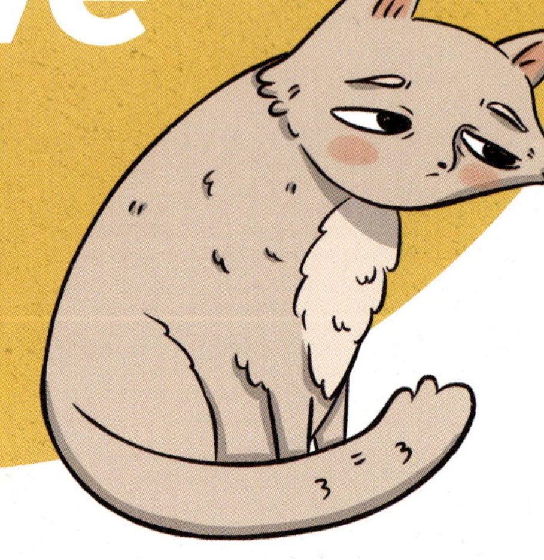

CAT'S CRADLE

To be powerless is to feel defeated or without ability, and this emotion affects the body by dragging it downwards. So, to make this cat appear powerless, I draw the body with a concave curve to it, conveying the weight of the feeling physically. I also draw the tail tucked in close to the body and tilt the head down, showing tiredness and uncertainty.

DOWN IN THE DUMPS

Now that we have established some signifiers of powerlessness, we can translate them to a female character. Reflecting the downward curve of the cat, I draw the woman hunching her shoulders forwards and lowering her arms. This helps show a lack of strength within the character as it visually draws the eye downwards. Focusing on the face, I pay attention to the curve of her eyebrows and mouth, and give her a downcast gaze to further communicate hopelessness and exhaustion.

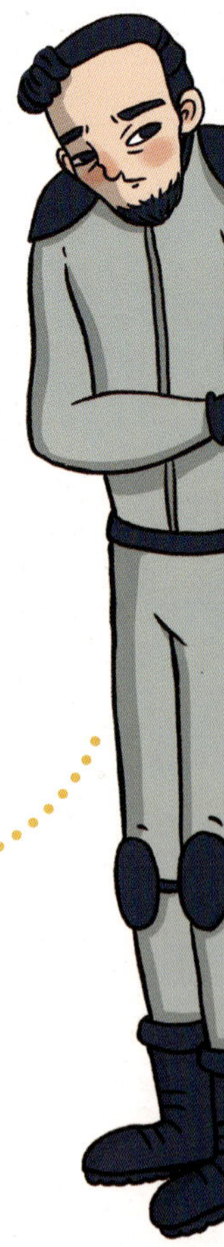

OUT OF SORTS

Now we can transfer these same characteristics to a male character, with some subtle variations. To help show an insecure and defensive attitude, I show him closing in on his own body. I use the arm to cover his body as a sign of helplessness, and lower his head. By combining this with a slack look upon his face, we evoke the feeling of powerlessness.

COOL CAT

In contrast to powerlessness, bravery is to be courageous and confident. To illustrate this within our character design, we need to contradict the body language of powerlessness and show conviction. We can do this by drawing the body in a convex position, with the face and chest lifted high. This position helps show self-confidence and a provocative attitude.

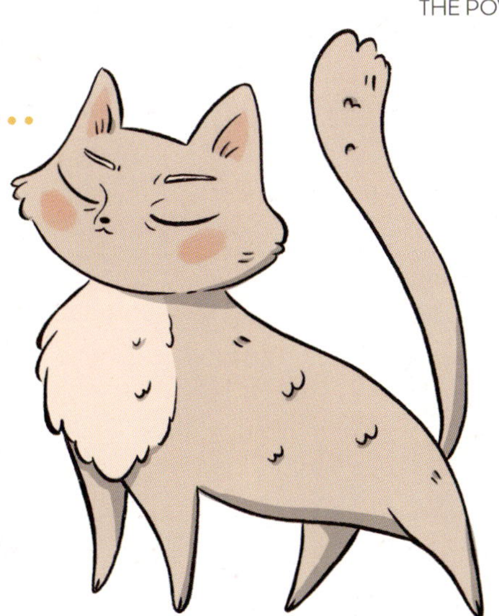

GIRL POWER

For our female character, we want to pose her in a way that helps showcase bravery and self-assurance. By drawing our character with her foot placed on top of a rock, with a clenched fist, we are able to denote an attitude of action, in line with the feeling of bravery. This, combined with her direct gaze, makes her appear confident and fearless.

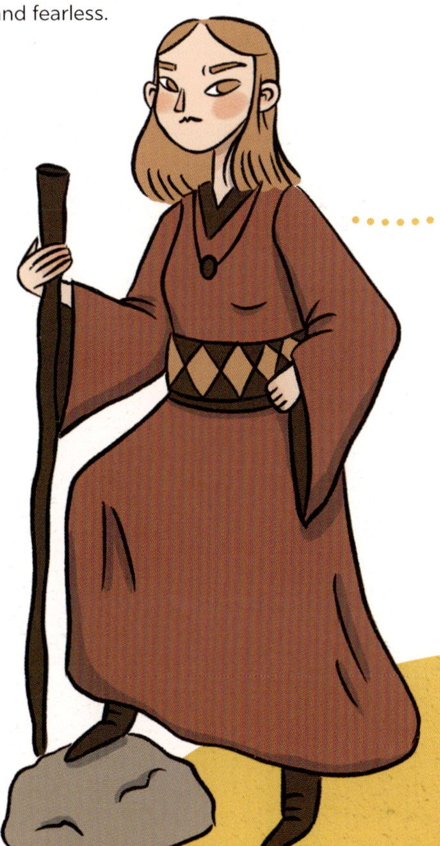

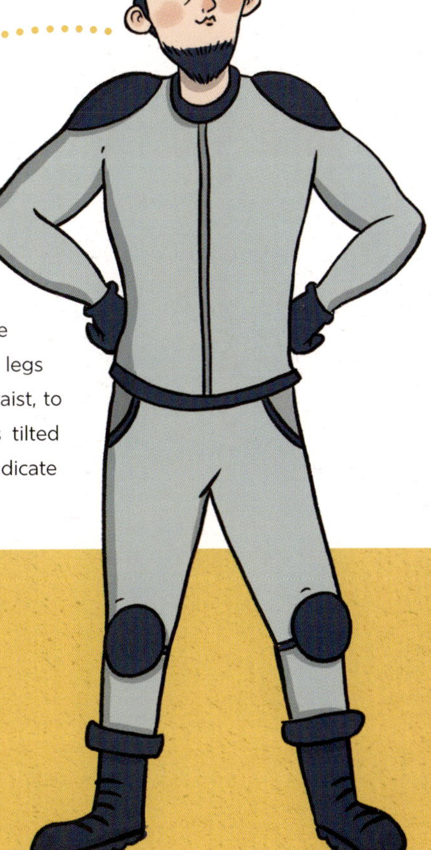

MAN OF THE HOUR

Compared with his powerless version, this brave male character has a more open pose. I place his legs apart in an assertive stance, with his hands on his waist, to evoke feelings of security and bravery. His chin is tilted upwards and his satisfied facial expression helps to indicate his confidence.

WORKING TOGETHER

Having the ability to successfully express emotion in characters is the goal of every character designer. Emotions increase the appeal of characters and help tell their story. The most successful way to do this is by ensuring that both the facial expressions and body language work harmoniously together. Having a strong reference image to work from can help – you can generate your own by posing and taking photographs, or prepare sketch studies from real life. This way, the audience will instantly recognize the emotion and be able to relate to your character.

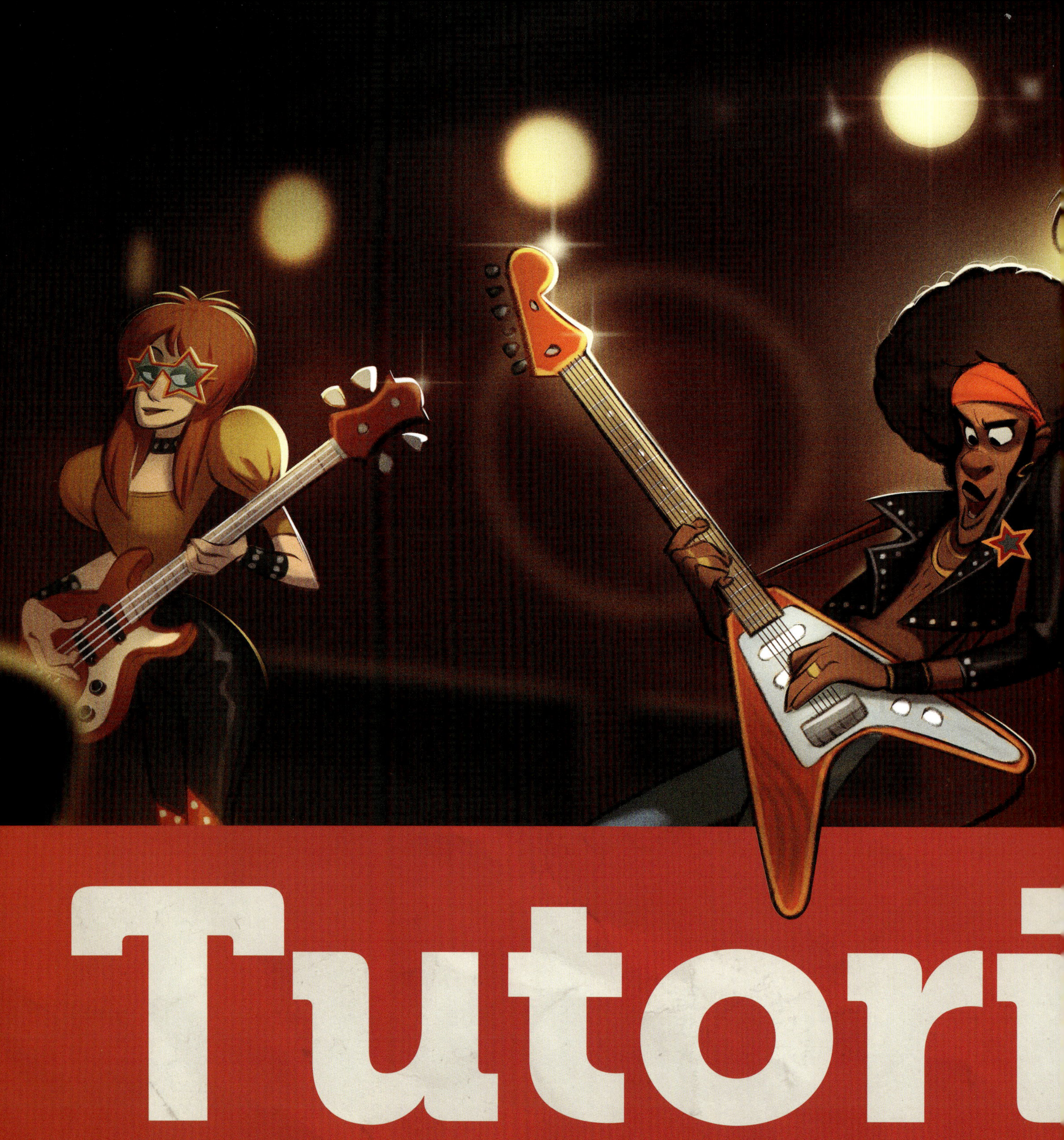

Tutori

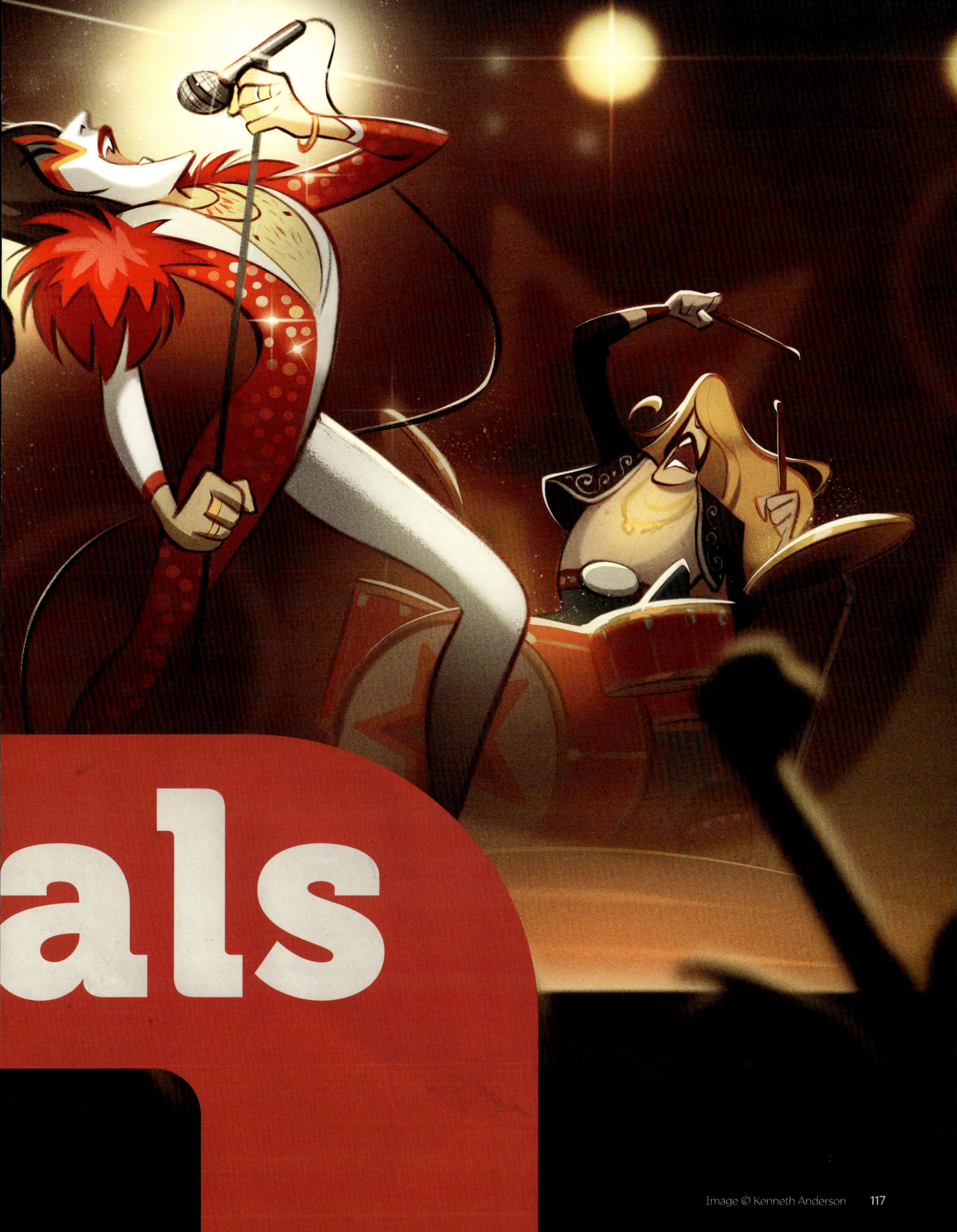

Image © Kenneth Anderson

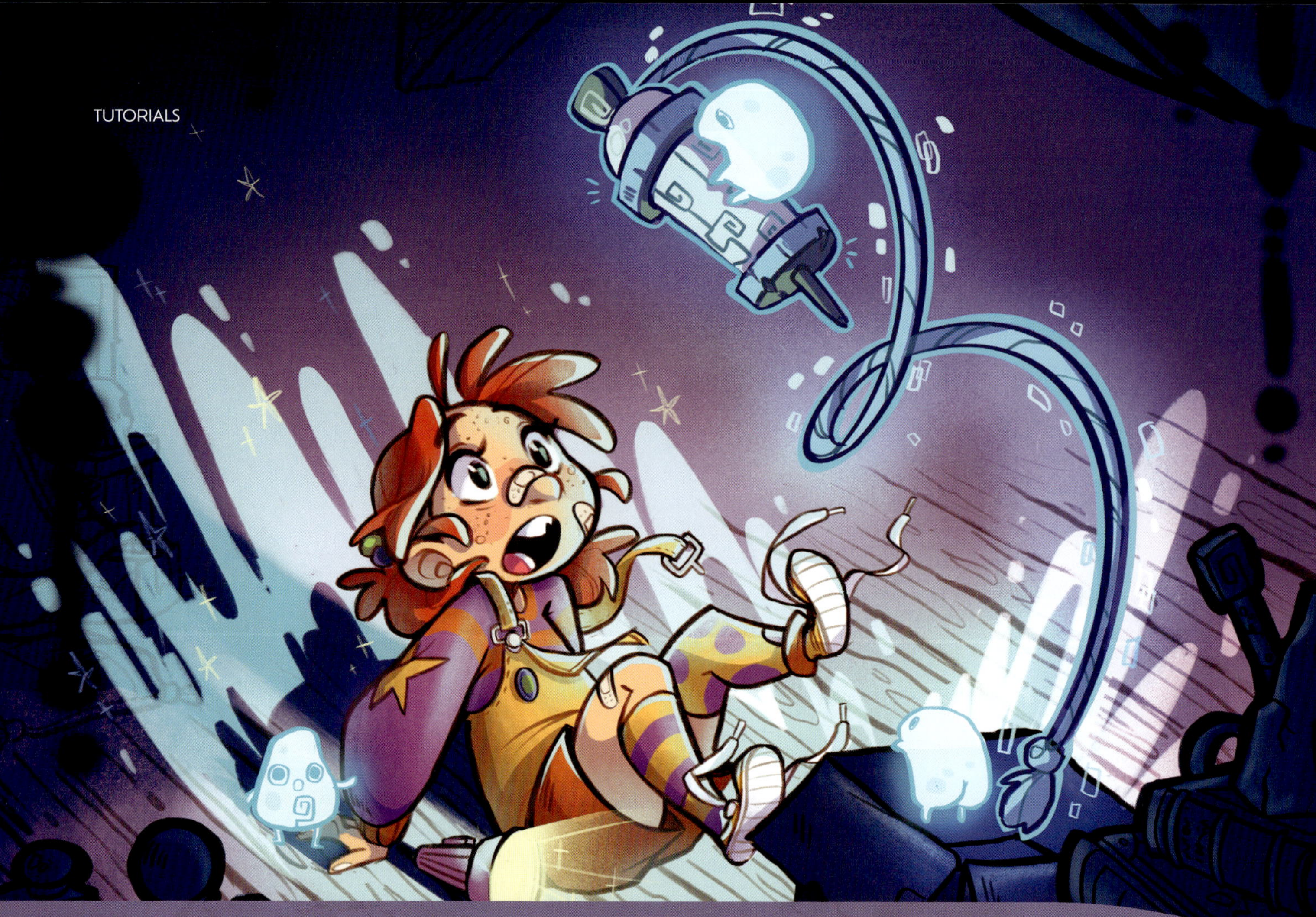

A mystery in the making

EVA STÖCKER

Creating your own character design is always an exciting journey, but the final appearance is only one part of a successful design - to truly bring your creations to life you need to consider their background story, feelings, behaviours, and especially their interactions with others. In this tutorial I'll talk you through my creative process for the realization of a character following a narrative brief. I will discuss well-known design techniques, such as shape language, composition, line of action, and colour. I'll also explain how to build up a strong personality and create an eye-catching illustration that tells a story that will captivate your audience.

01 BRAINSTORMING

Before starting with the actual character design, we need to brainstorm. Consider what your first thoughts were when reading the brief, and ask yourself who (or what) you'd like to draw. Other important questions are where, why, and what you need to consider in regard to the intended audience. Scribble down every idea that comes to mind after reading the creative brief. I think this first step is probably the most creative part of the whole process. I always carry a sketchbook with me (and even keep one beside my bed) so I can capture every thought and idea.

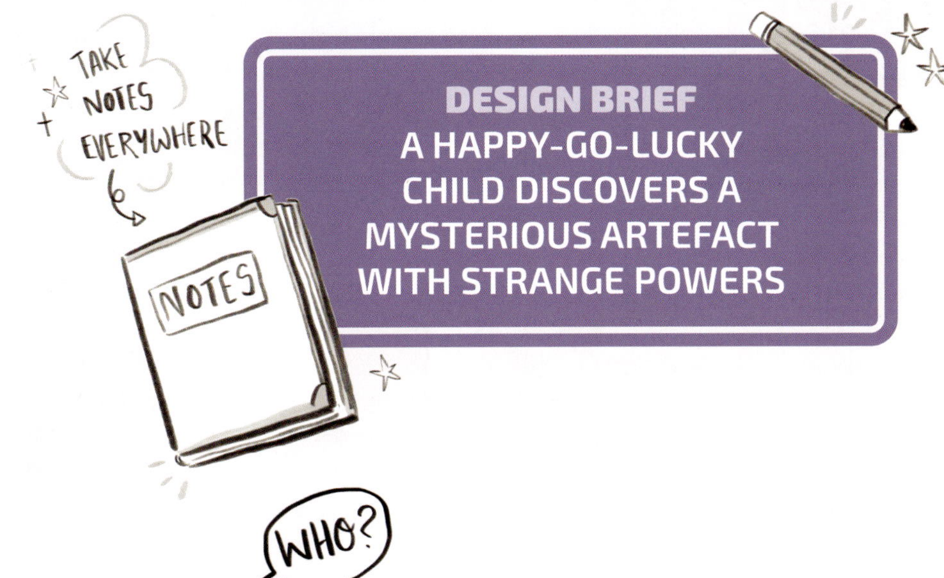

HAPPY-GO-LUCKY CHILD
LOVES ADVENTURES!
EASILY BORED
FRECKLES
OPEN-MINDED
CAREFREE/ NOT WORRYING TOO MUCH
FRIENDLY
CURIOUS
CHEERFUL
NAIVE
7-8 YEARS OLD
GIRL
HUMAN?
ALIEN?

02 MAPPING THE MIND

I collect and sort my initial thoughts around the three main elements of the brief I have been given: 'A happy-go-lucky child', 'mysterious artefact', and 'strange powers'. I start with the character itself, scribbling down some keywords and specifics about the character I'd like to create. I consider what 'happy-go-lucky' means, and what words I associate with it, and then do the same for 'artefact' and 'powers'.

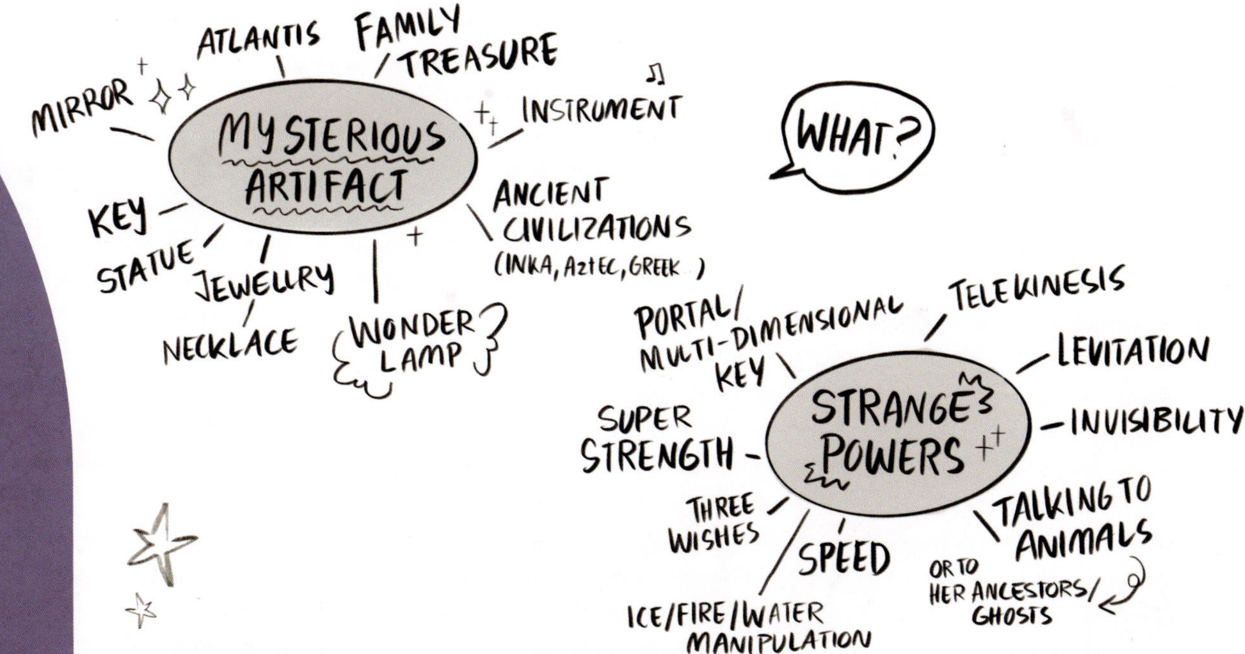

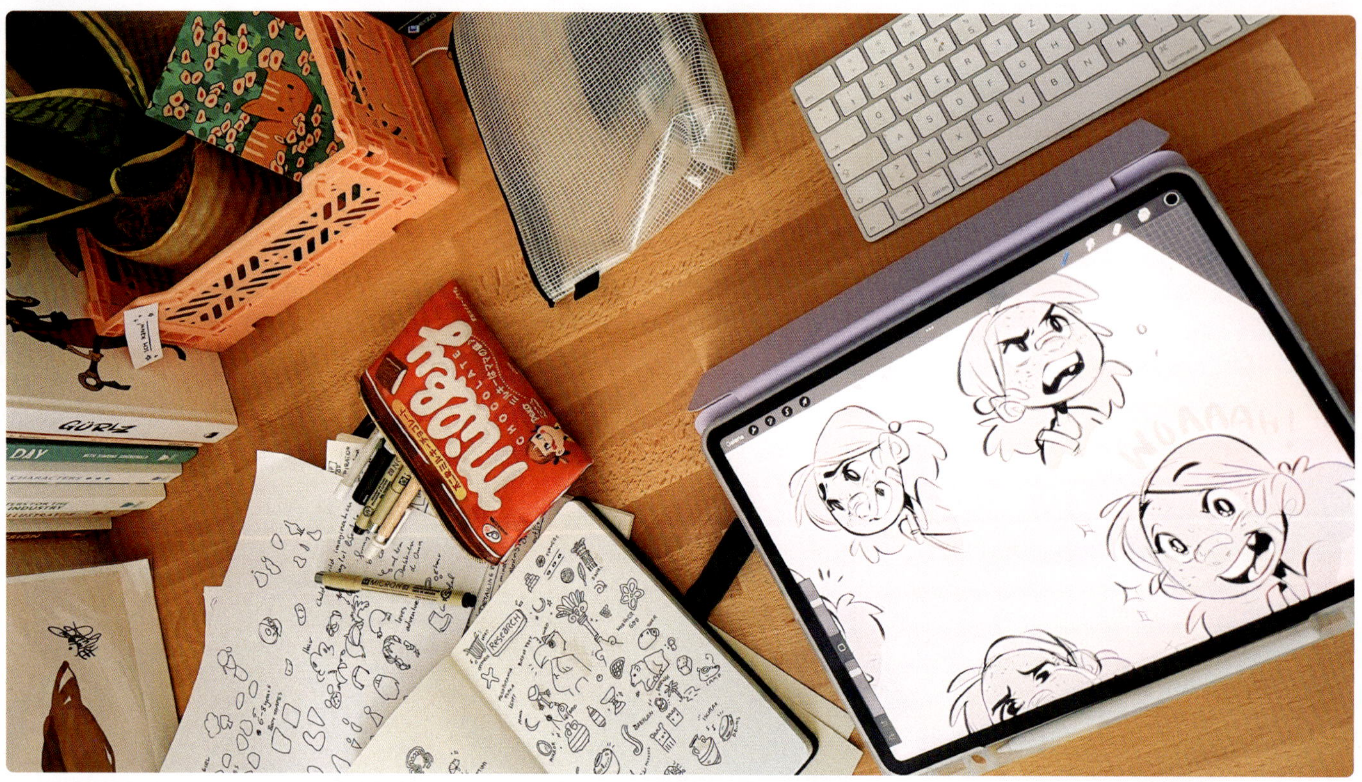

03 WRITING THE NARRATIVE

With a simple brief, you are free to create a deeper narrative around your characters before the design process begins. This will make it easier to create a fully realized design later on. With a background story in my pocket and a mind-map full of keywords, I start to look closer at the world I've created. I decide what aspects of the story will be the most fun to draw, what makes sense for the character, and what scene I want to compose. Now I can start to visualize.

A HAPPY-GO-LUCKY CHILD DISCOVERS
A MYSTERIOUS ARTEFACT
WITH STRANGE POWERS

A girl is visiting her grandmother during her school holidays. Bored by the slow pace of life at her granny's, she starts to explore the house. One day she ends up in the attic where she finds all the treasures her granny (once an archaeologist) collected from around the world. In one corner the girl discovers a mysterious artefact with strange powers – carefully hidden by her grandmother – which will change her life forever.

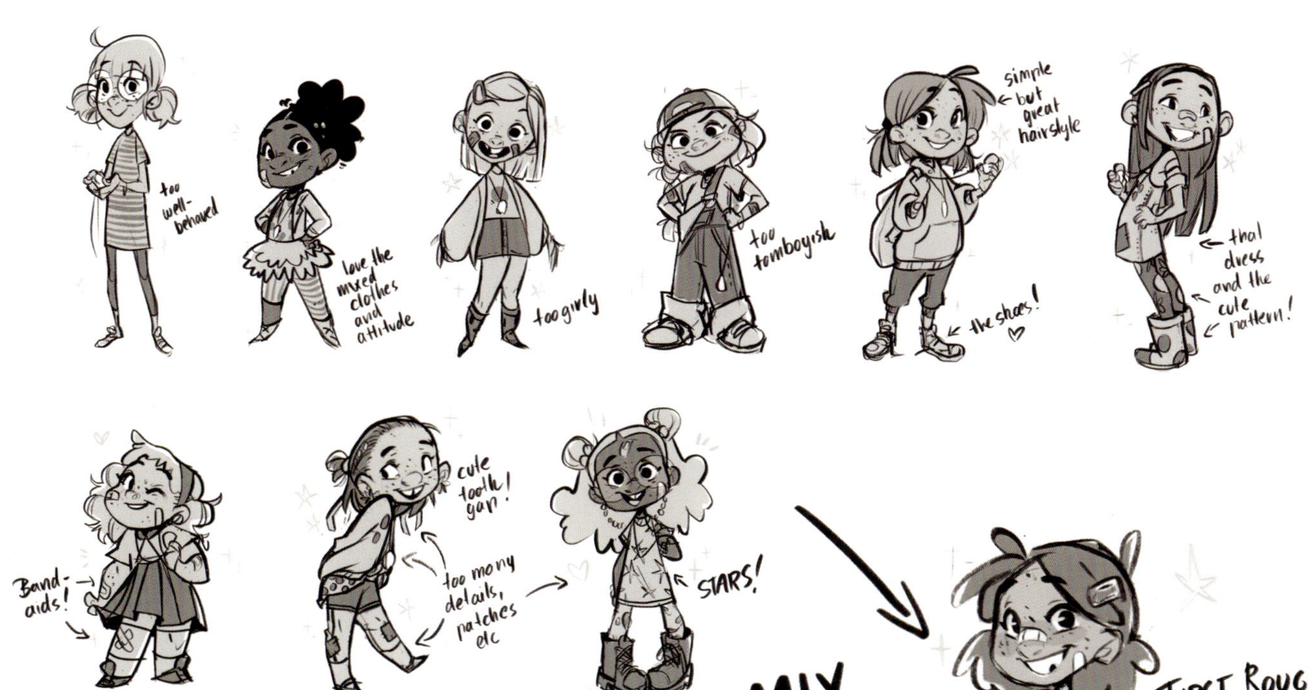

04 LET THE FUN BEGIN

I draw some rough character sketches based on the traditional shapes: square, triangle, and circle. Feel free to play with as many different body types as you like, but don't forget the original brief, and keep your mind-mapped keywords in mind. Start mixing and matching features until you settle on a design that encapsulates everything you want your character to be.

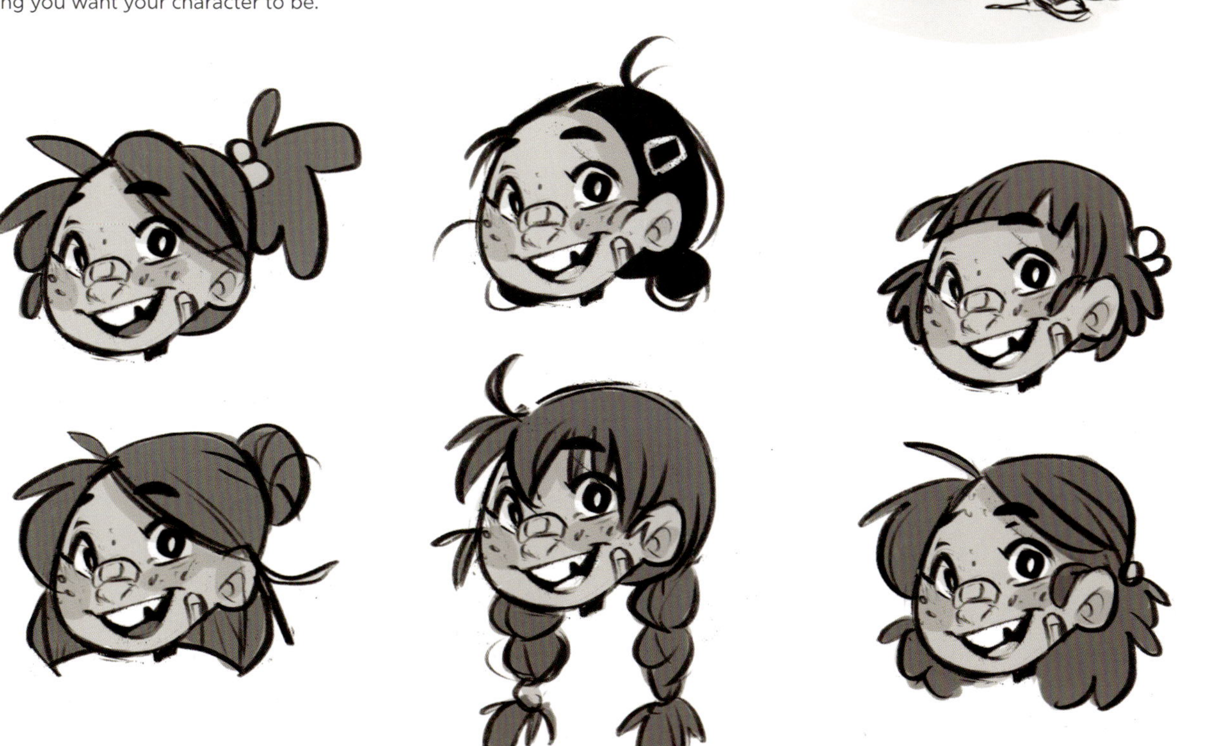

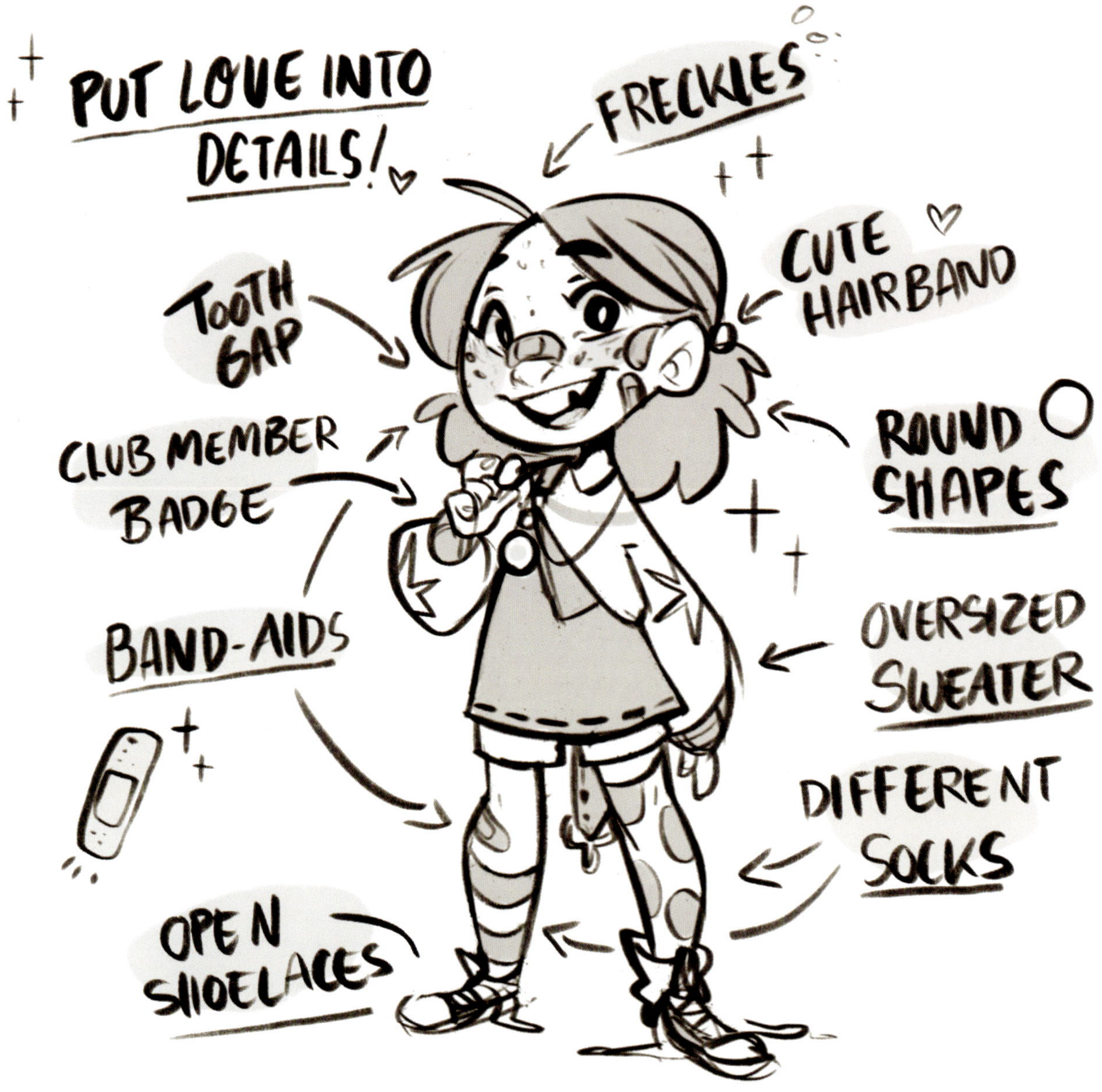

'Make sure the character remains simple, functional, and without any distractions'

05 THE FINAL DESIGN

With a design chosen, I now add details to make my character more complex and believable. As you add extra elements to the design always keep in mind that less is more. Make sure the character remains simple, functional, and without any distractions.

I give my girl a cute, bright smile, and cheeky freckles to show that she's a 'happy-go-lucky' child. Her funny combination of clothes shows that she's not worrying about much, and has a playful outlook on life. The Band-Aids and gap in her teeth show that she loves adventure, has a curious mind, and loves taking risks.

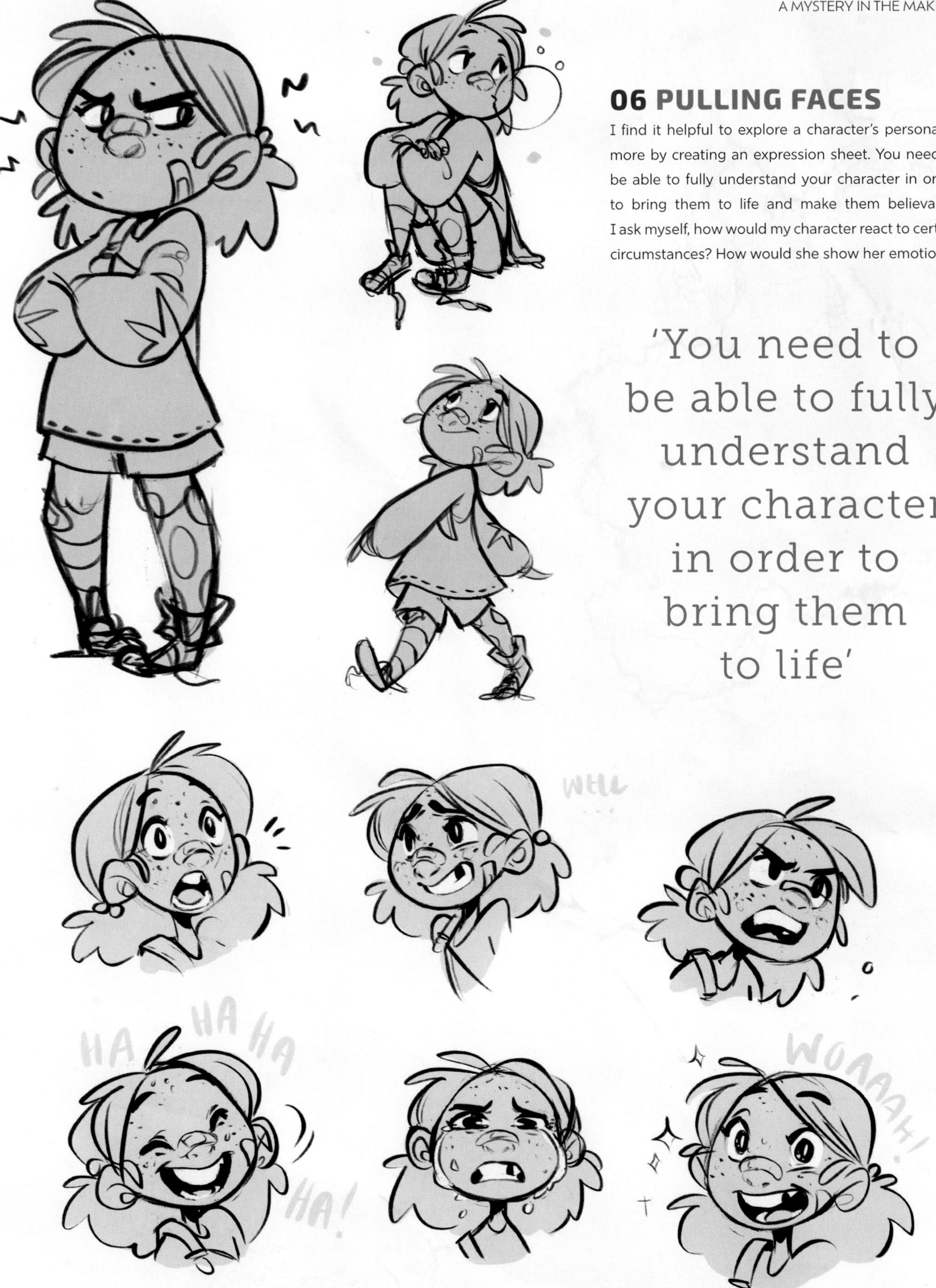

06 PULLING FACES

I find it helpful to explore a character's personality more by creating an expression sheet. You need to be able to fully understand your character in order to bring them to life and make them believable. I ask myself, how would my character react to certain circumstances? How would she show her emotion?

'You need to be able to fully understand your character in order to bring them to life'

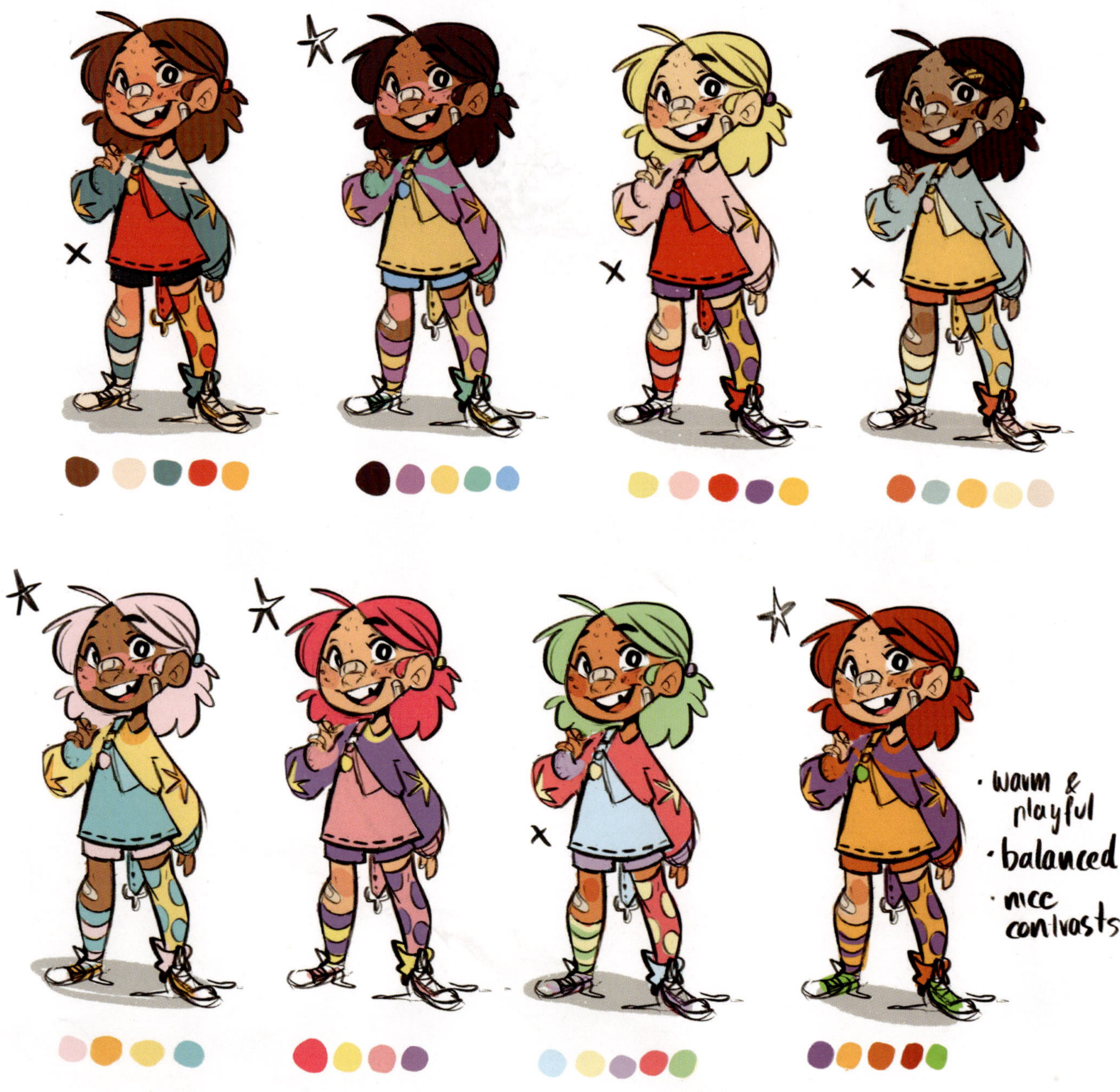

07 A PALETTE OR TWO

Now I explore different colour palettes for my character. I choose bright, vibrant colours as they read as happy and energetic, the characteristics I want for my girl. These colours are also appealing to the young audience I'm targeting and complement the character's personality. The most iconic character designs use only four or five colours, so try to keep your palette as limited as possible. The simpler, the better!

COLOURS AT A DISTANCE

If you're unsure which colour scheme you should choose, it can be helpful to look at your colour palettes from a distance – it will be easier to recognize which has the best contrast.

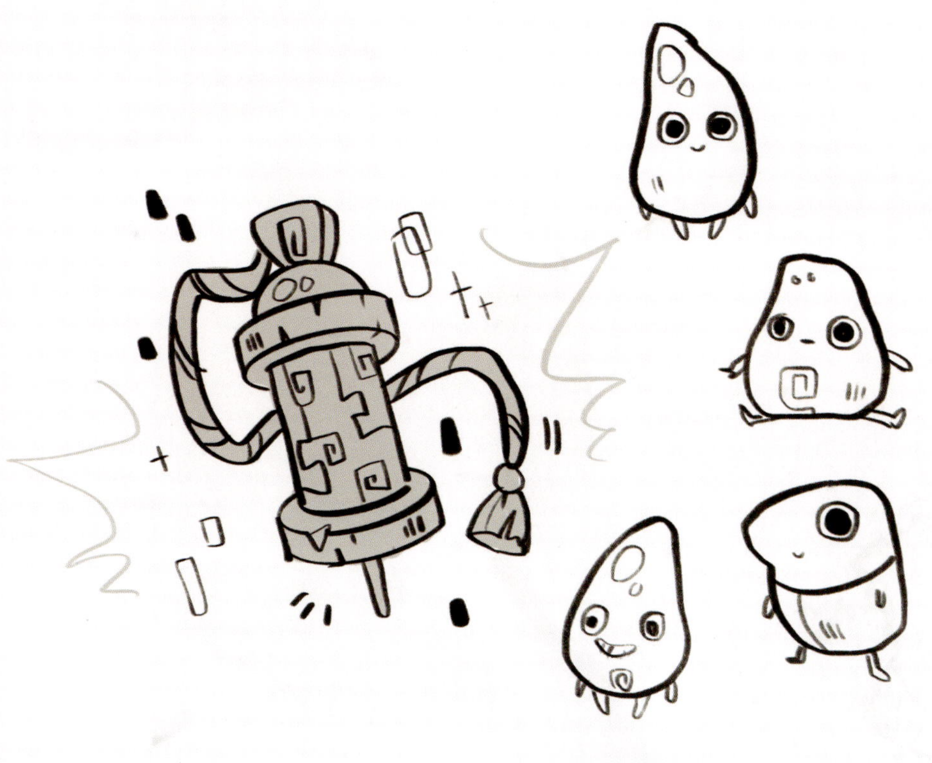

08 MYSTERIOUS MUSINGS

I need to work out what form the 'artefact' from the brief will take. My initial thought is to create a magical lamp that my character's grandmother brought home from one of her adventures. I don't like the idea of a little girl having three powerful wishes, though, and I don't think there's much potential in the story I can tell.

I think again and decide on a multi-dimensional key that opens portals to other worlds! A normal key still seems a little boring, so I add a twist to the design. With children's toys in mind, I turn the key into an ancient spinning top. I try out different shapes and add runes, which I found during my brainstorming phase.

FINDING THE ARTEFACT

As you can see, I changed the appearance of the artefact a lot! Don't get discouraged if your first, second, or third idea doesn't work – throwing ideas out is a normal part of the creative process

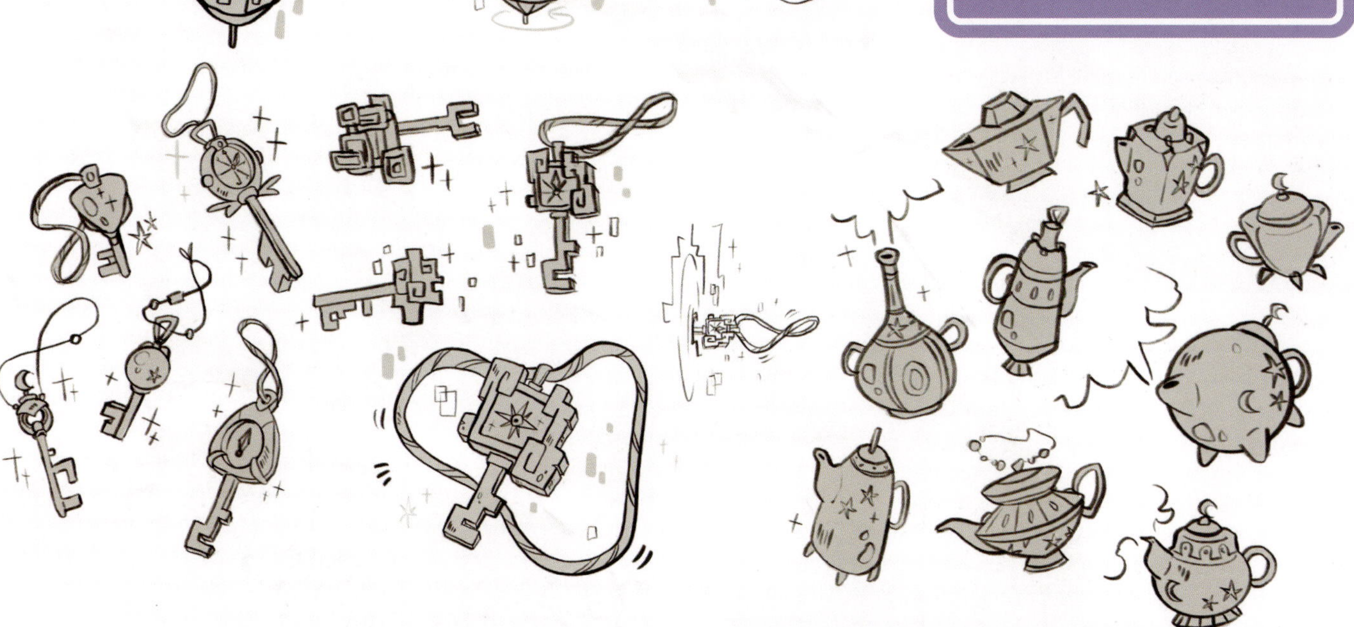

09 ACTING & REACTING

Now I've settled on a design that fits the brief and that I'm happy with, I can start exploring poses. The body language of the character and interaction with any objects should be the focus through this part of the process. The central question I need to answer is, 'How will my character react to the artefact?' Are they surprised, afraid, curious, or something else?

I start with some loose sketches – it doesn't matter if the perspective is off or details are missing. We can fix everything later.

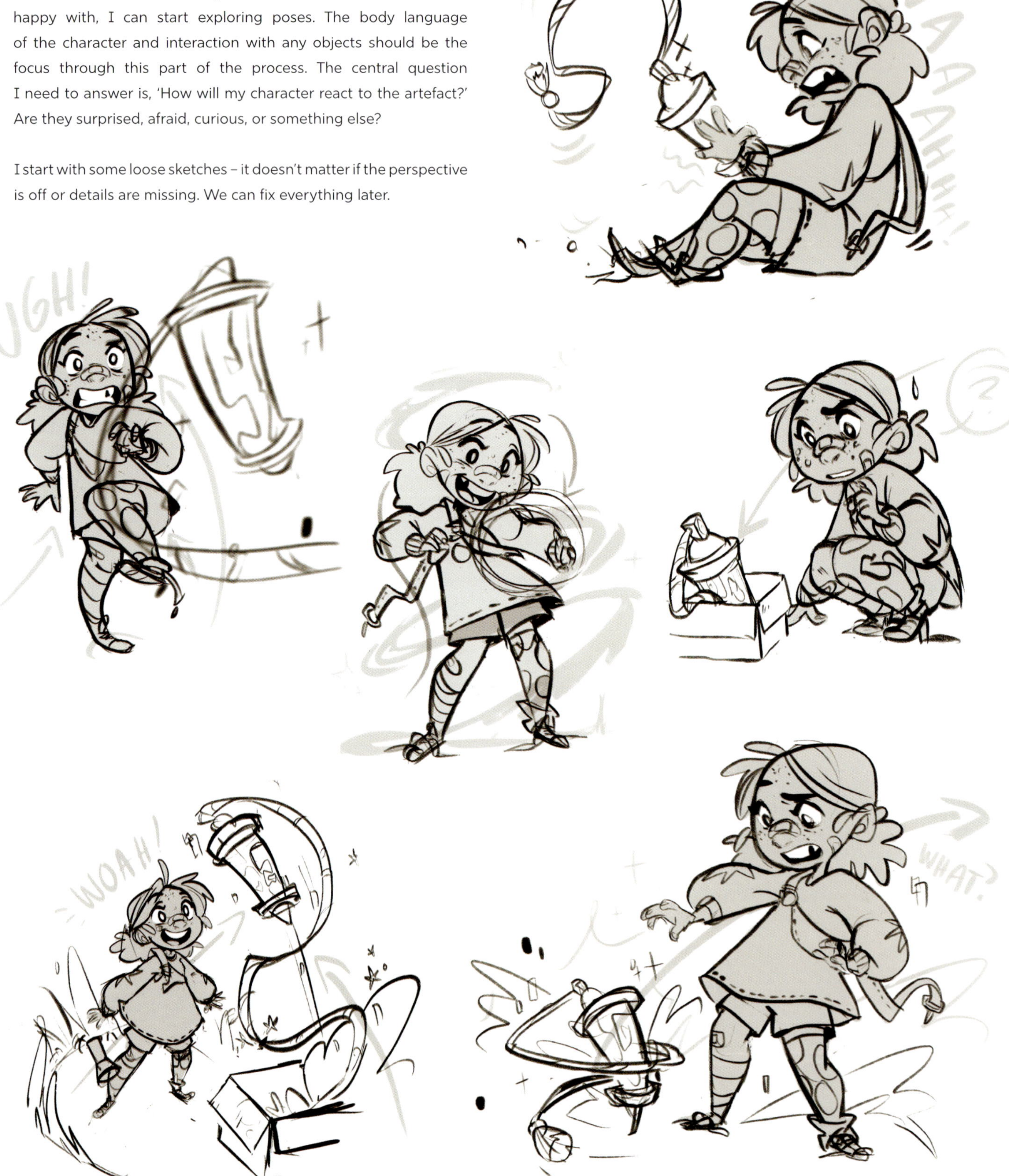

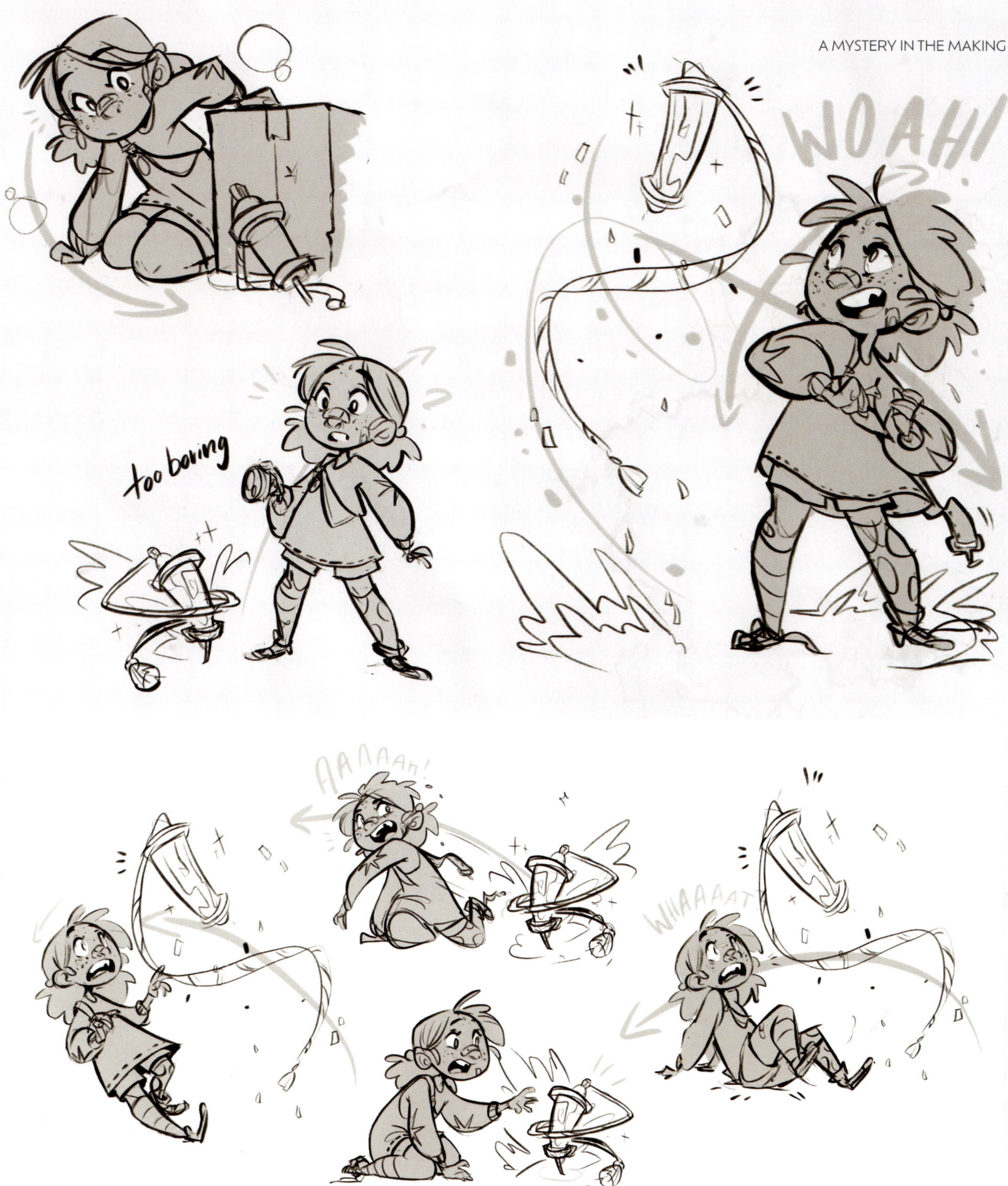

ACTION LINES

Adding action lines to an image reinforces the movement that you're trying to portray and can make a boring pose seem much more exciting. The action lines help me choose which pose to move forwards with. The image I settle on shows my character falling on her bottom, surprised and overwhelmed by the artefact appearing right in front of her.

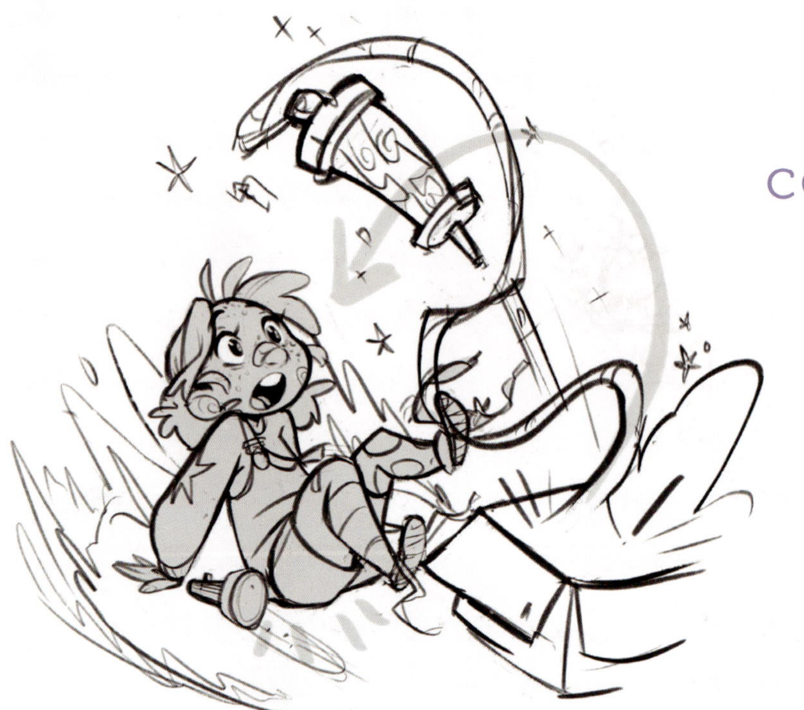

'I choose the composition with the strongest emotional connection between the character and the object'

10 THE FINAL SKETCH

I choose the composition with the strongest emotional connection between the character and the object, which also fits the story I'm trying to tell. For the final sketch, I decide to change my character's expression to something between surprise and amazement, instead of the fearful look in my earlier design. It's like you can hear the girl saying, 'Woah!' I also think the perspective of this pose is definitely the most interesting I came up with.

11 BACKGROUND CHECK

It's time to start putting all our ideas and concepts together and explore composing the whole scene. What information do we want the background to convey? Earlier, I decided the narrative brief would be the young girl discovering the artefact in her grandmother's attic. I want to show the location is packed with old souvenirs and trinkets but still keep the focus on the character. I add objects to both the foreground and background of the image that will guide the gaze of the viewer to the centre.

THE SCENE

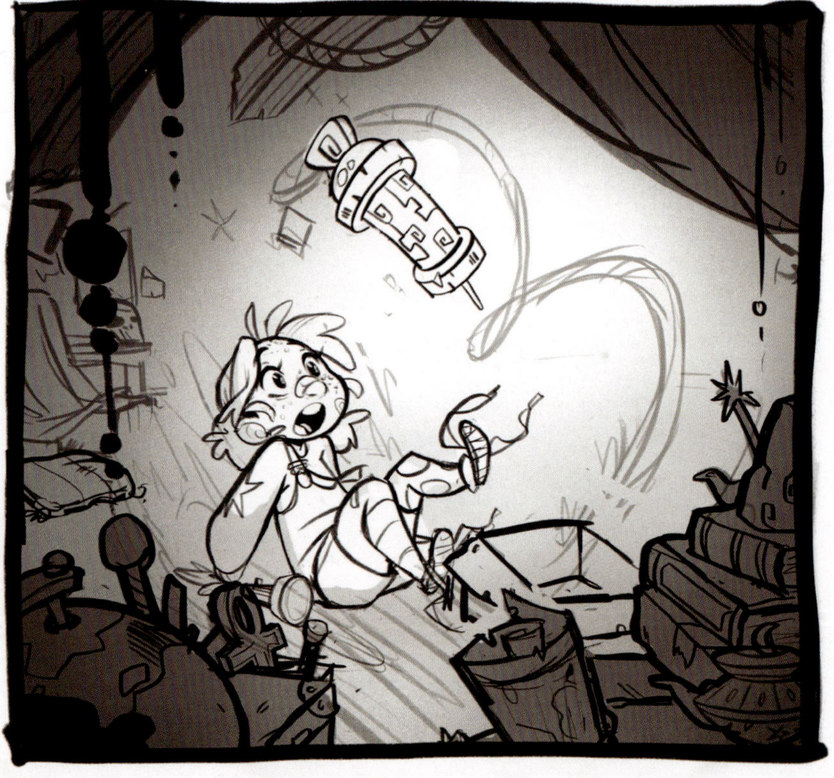

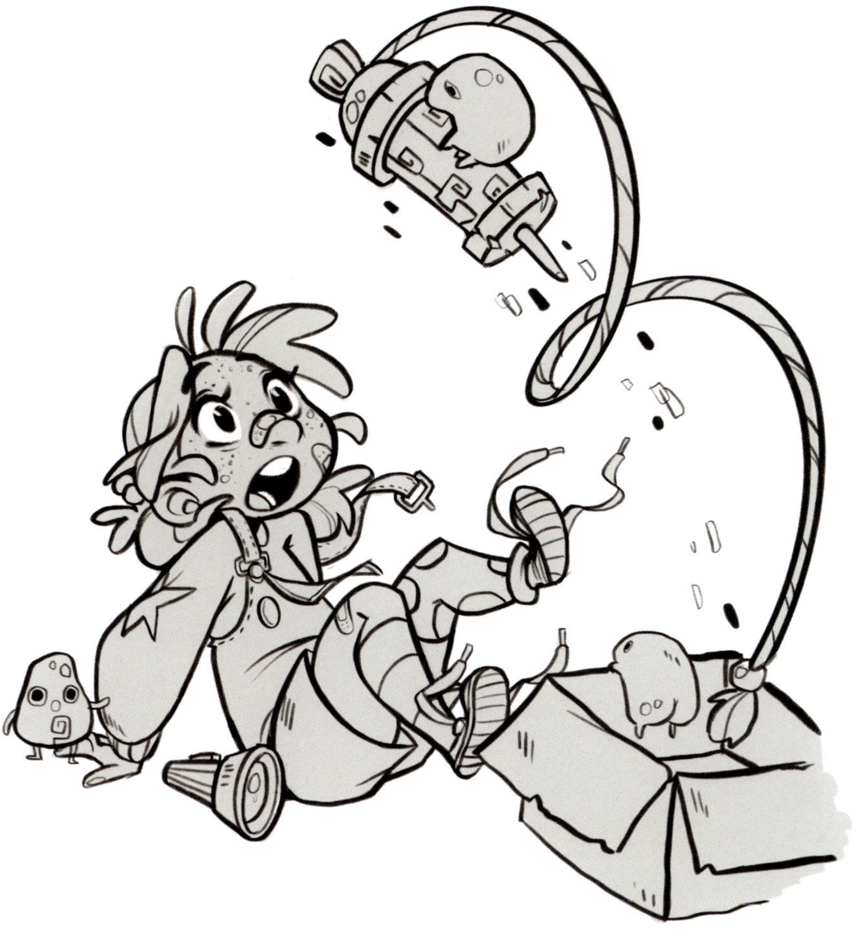

12 CLEANING UP THE MESS

With everything coming together nicely, it's time to clean up the sketch. I start by flipping the design for a fresh perspective – this helps make sure every part of the design is working well. I open up a new layer, choose my favourite line-art brush, and create the finished design. The secret for dynamic line art is creating a variation of thick and thin lines. Get loose and just let it flow!

13 COMING INTO FOCUS

I'm happy with my character's line art, so I move on to cleaning up the background. As well as finalizing the line art, I add Gaussian blur to the foreground objects so they appear out of focus. I add a thicker outline for the other foreground elements and lower the transparency of the background objects. These steps will automatically add depth to the line art.

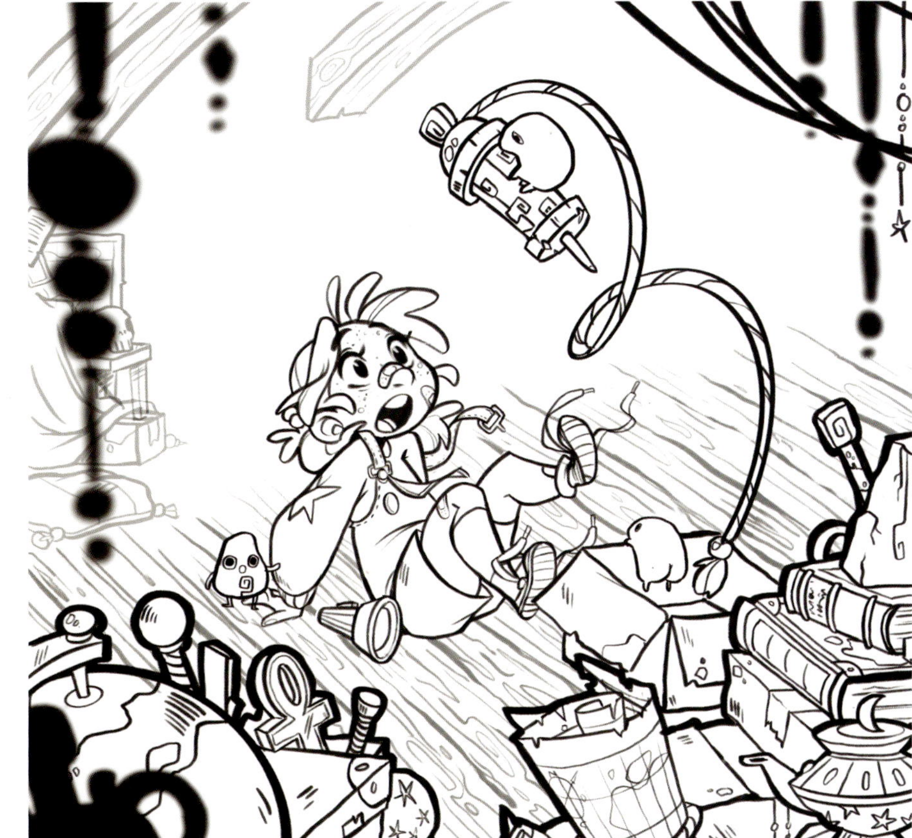

14 BRINGING IT ALL TOGETHER

Finding the perfect colours can be tough – choose a palette that serves what you're trying to convey in your scene. I take four of my favourite colour palettes from earlier and place them alongside the artefact. I choose the scheme that best contrasts the cool colour scheme I chose for the artefact. I create a new layer, under the line art, and add the flat colours to my character. I add some finishing touches and one final layer to overpaint some little details, add more highlights, and fix a few mistakes. And with that, the piece is complete!

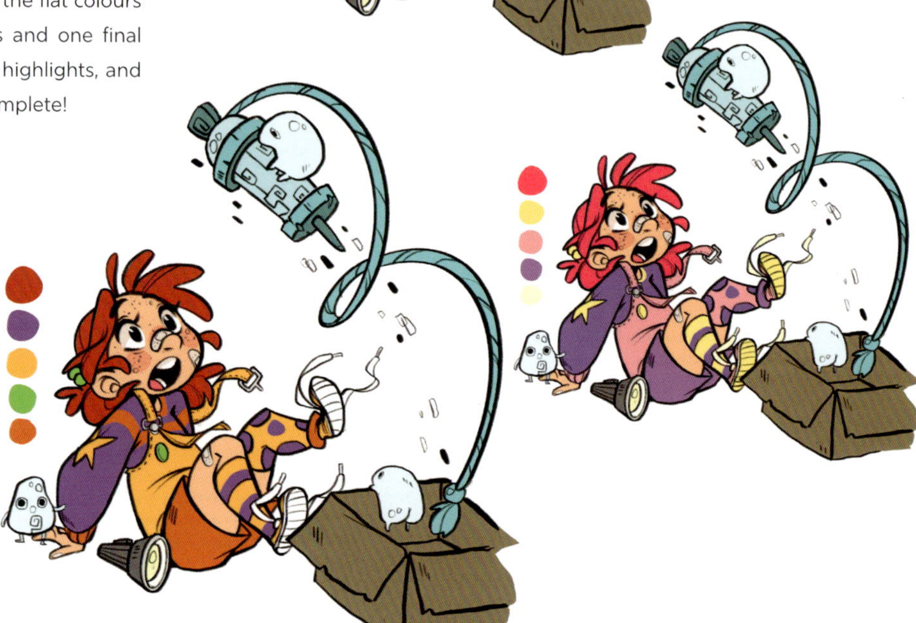

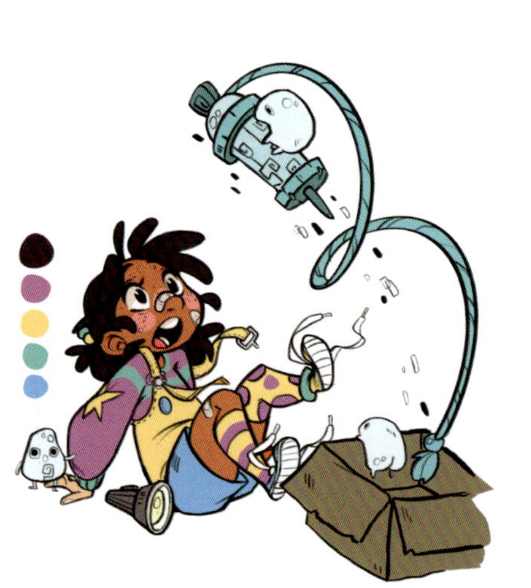

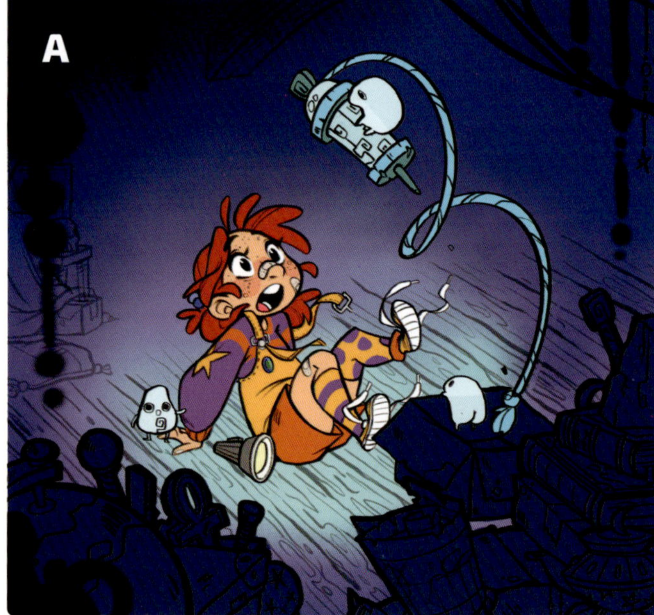

I want the character to stand out so I decide on cold colours for the background

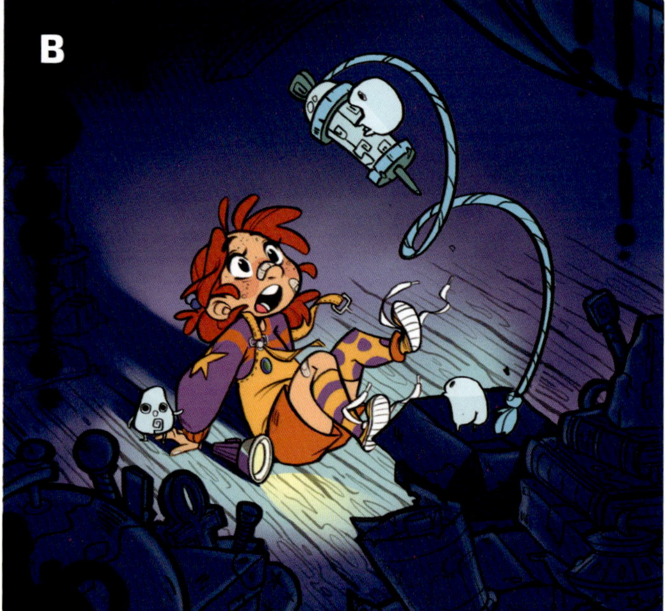

I restrict the background colour palette to monochromatic blues, adding a few dark and light highlights

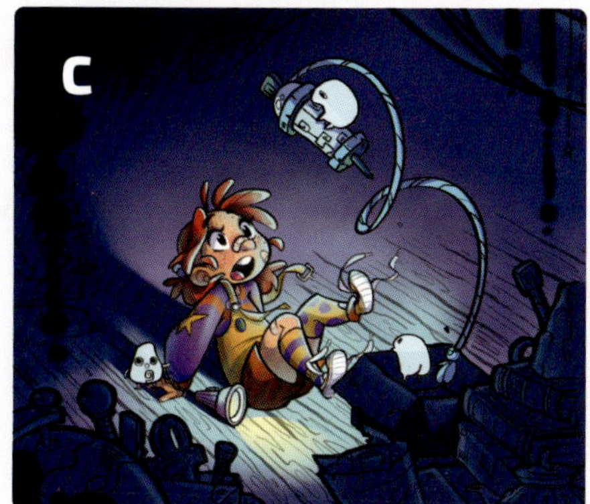

I add some shadows to the character to give the scene more depth

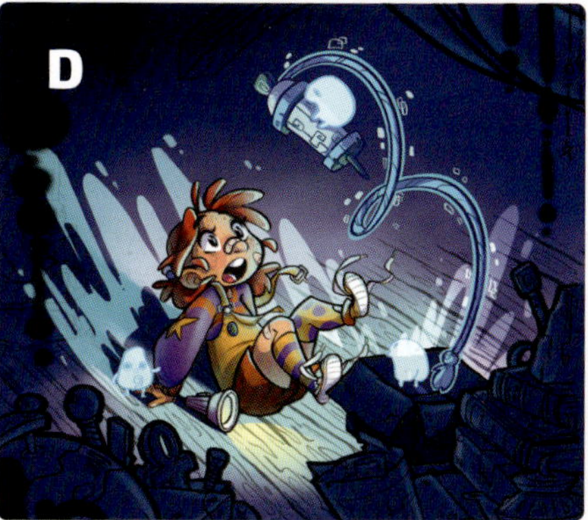

Special effects make the scene look more dramatic

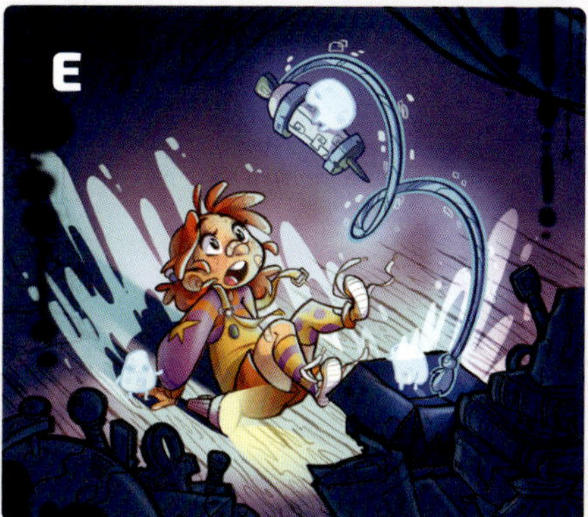

Finally, I add highlights and a warm colour layer for a coherent atmosphere

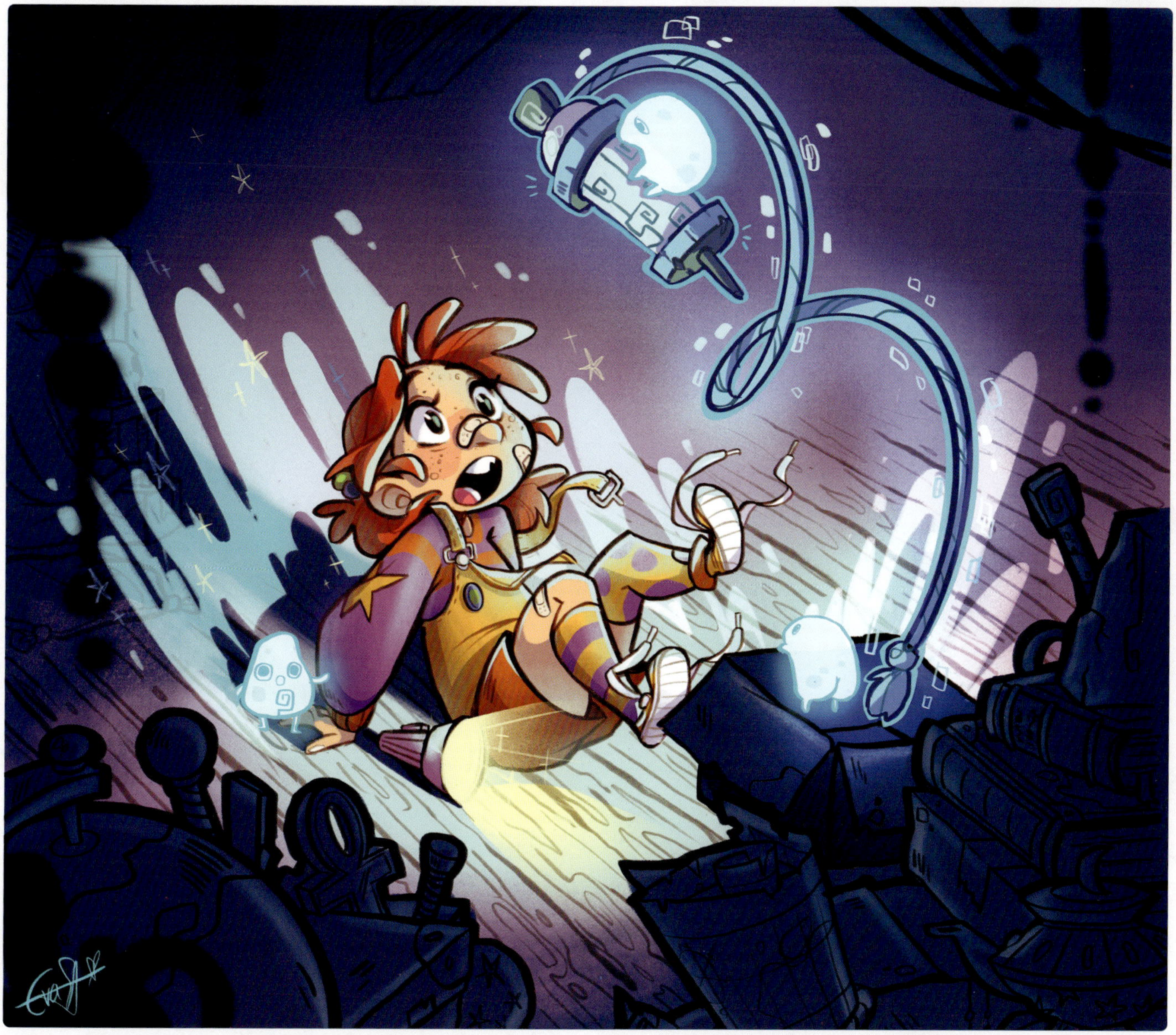

Final image © Eve Stöcker

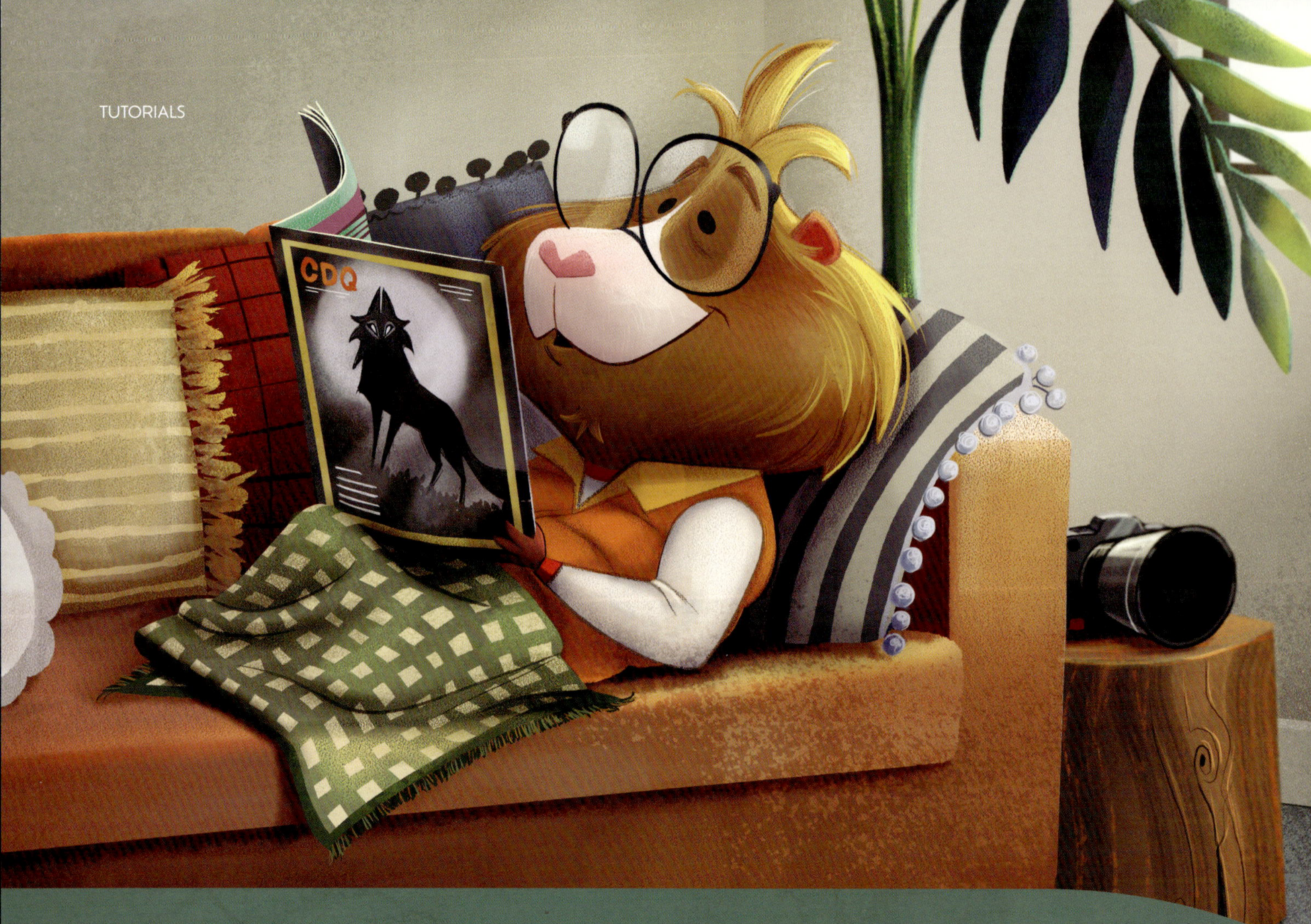

The guinea pig & the wolf

MELANY ALTUNA

I'm going to share with you my process for creating appealing, stylized characters. For me, designing a character has always been like solving a puzzle, with many, many pieces. If I look at the whole project at once, it's easy to become overwhelmed, and my creativity will be blocked. If I split the work up and focus on a few pieces at a time, then progress will be fun and give us great results. I will be working with traditional pencils and a sketchbook to warm up, and then my professional tools for research and character development – a Wacom Cintiq, an iMac, and Photoshop.

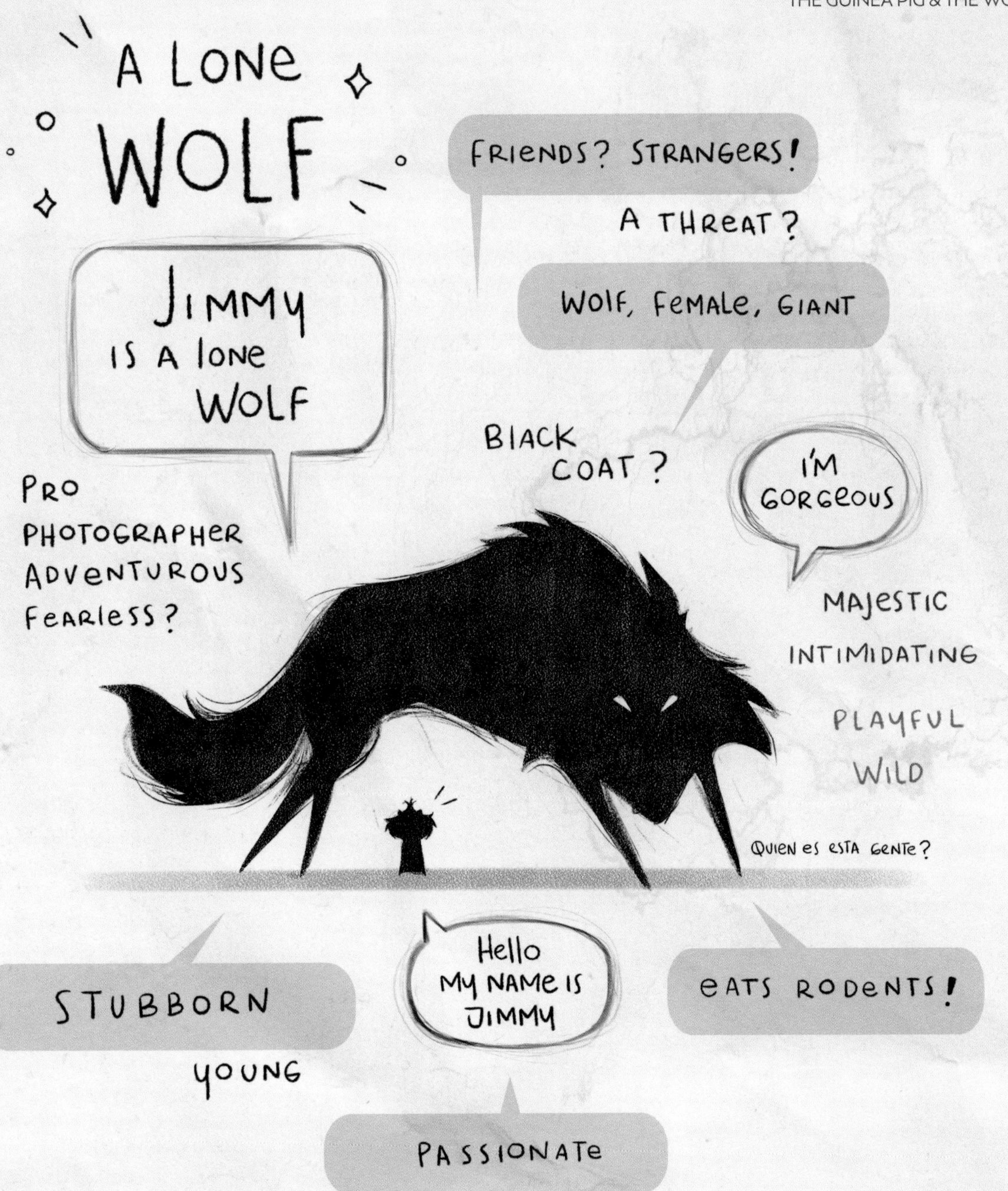

FINDING THE STORY

The brief for this project is very open – we will design two characters, a guinea pig and a wolf, and that's pretty much all we know about them. It's important we create a backstory for the characters first which will guide the rest of the process.

Looking online for references is a good starting point. Search for things that grab your interest and get your ideas flowing. Inspiration can come from anywhere. I was shopping online for outdoor clothing for my next camping trip before this project, and that sparked an idea. I decide I want my main character to be a guinea pig, and for the story to focus on him. Let's call him Jimmy. Jimmy will be a professional photographer who has a unique encounter with a giant wolf. His job is to take the best picture of the wolf possible, but that might be easier said than done!

ASKING QUESTIONS

With our characters in place, now we need to get a better sense of the 5 Ws – Who are the characters, What do they want, Where are they located, When is the story taking place, and Why? These questions are a great place to start your research and will help you find all the visual elements needed to make your characters unique. I know this might seem like it takes quite a lot of time, but it's an important step in the process, and one you should never skip.

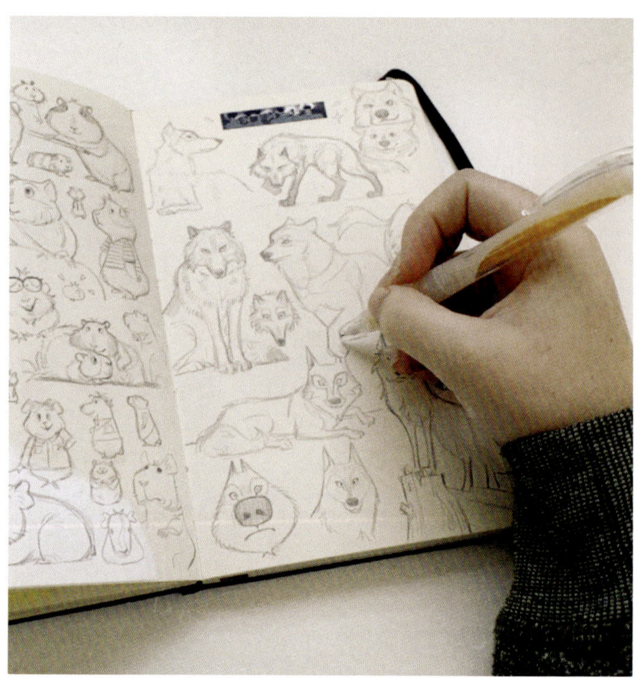

LET'S START SKETCHING!

When I draw animals, I like to start by sketching from photos. I go online and collect lots of references of wolves and guinea pigs of all shapes, sizes, and colours. This helps me get a feel for the shapes that make this animal unique. Don't worry too much about making anything pretty at this point – just try to experiment, learn, and pay attention to the proportions and characteristics. You never need to show this step to anyone if you don't want to. Keep that in mind and the pressure is off – enjoy the process!

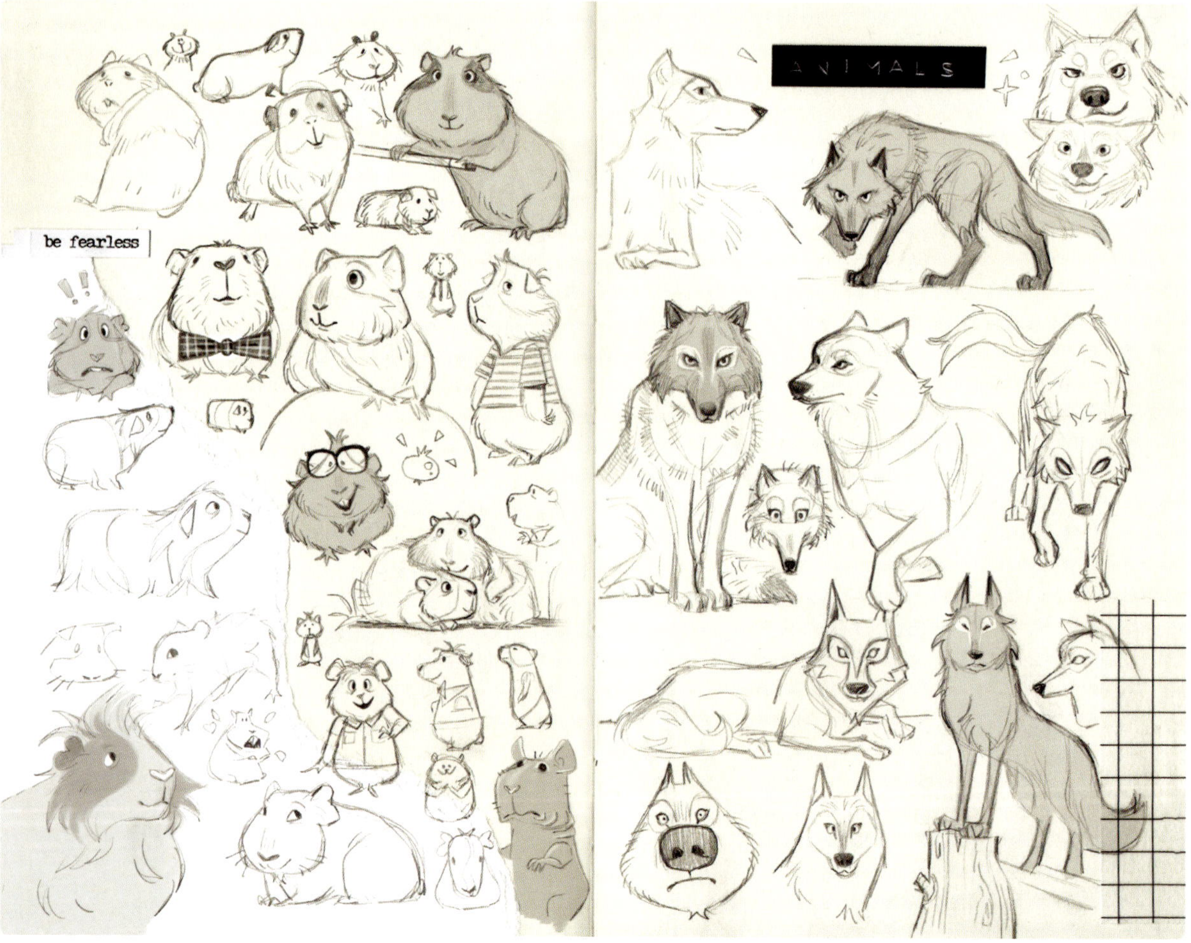

'I consider the balance between the body and face, and how large, medium, and small shapes can affect the design'

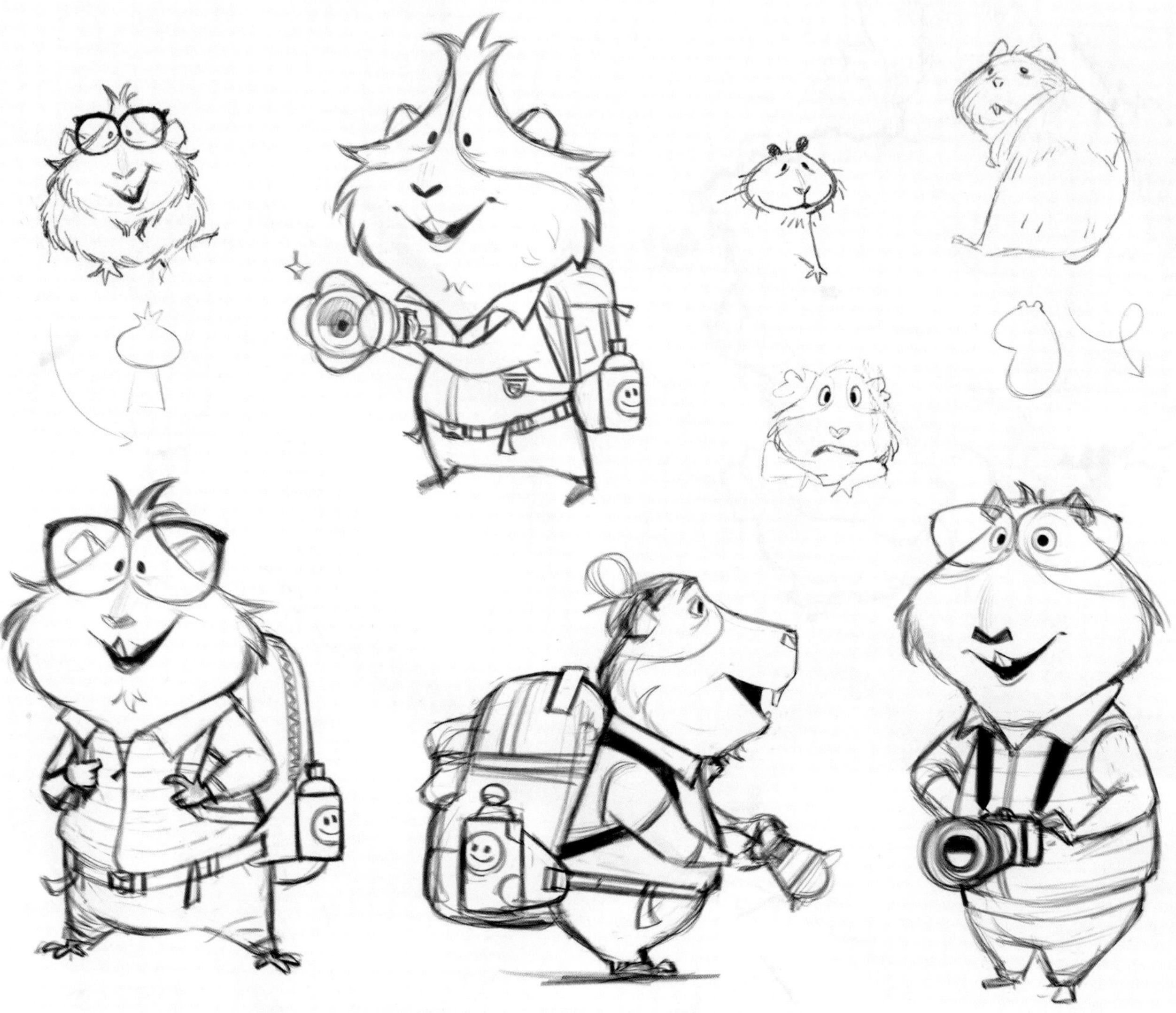

SHIFTING SHAPES

After warming up in the sketchbook I like to look at all my drawings and find a few that I really like, then start playing around with the proportions and shapes. I consider the balance between the body and face, and how large, medium, and small shapes can affect the design. I push the shapes and play with size to find an appealing look.

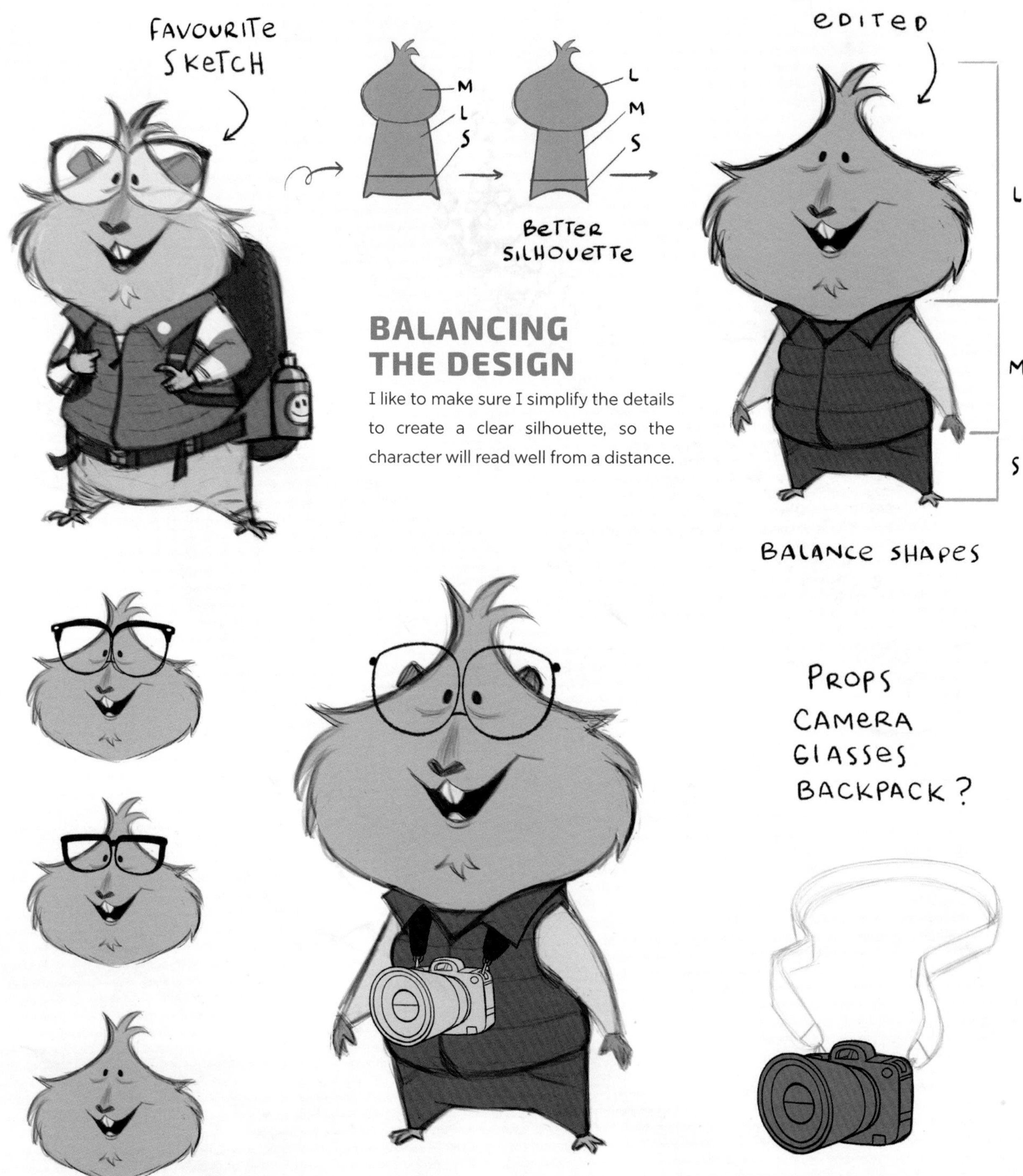

BALANCING THE DESIGN

I like to make sure I simplify the details to create a clear silhouette, so the character will read well from a distance.

PROPPING UP THE STORY

Adding props to a character can help express a little more about their personality. In this case, we need to make it obvious that Jimmy is a photographer on a mission, maybe by adding a camera or backpack. I also give him some glasses to compensate for his tiny dot eyes and to help the audience understand who he is right away.

Working on this step, I realize that people may mistake Jimmy for a tourist, and that's not the look I want for this character. I need to make sure I stay away from anything that suggests 'tourist' when moving on to colour and poses.

COMPLETING THE JIGSAW

Previously, I mentioned how I view the process of designing a character like putting a puzzle together – the more you practice, the faster your brain will start to put the pieces together all by itself. And just like with a jigsaw or puzzle, if you get stuck then the best thing you can do is take a break. Go for a short walk, clear your mind, and when you come back try a different approach.

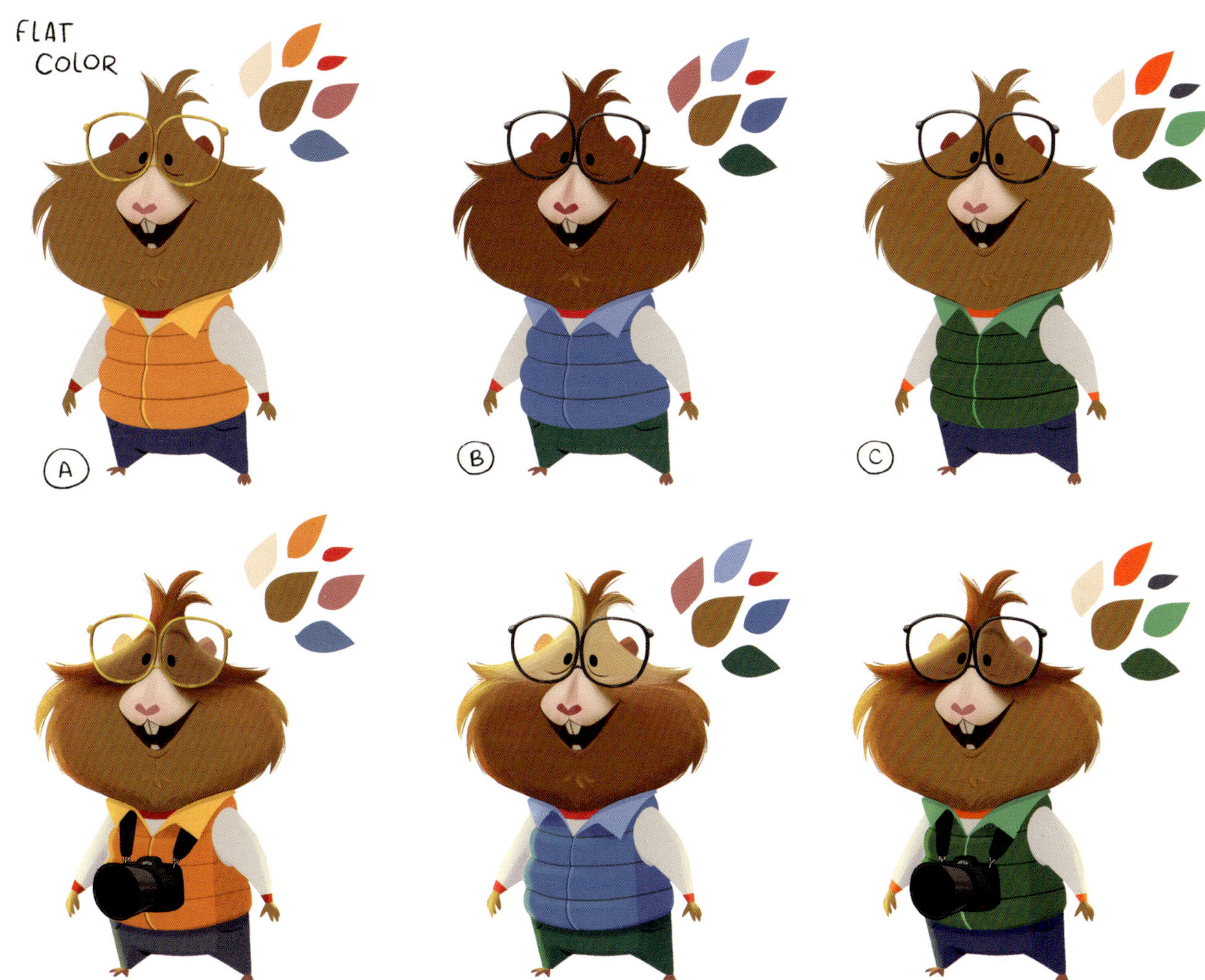

DRESSING JIMMY FOR THE JOB

At this point I go back to my references and look for consistent colours in their clothing. Looking at online stores helps you know what's on trend at the moment and what look could stand out. It might even help you to find a more unique colour combination than you originally imagined.

I want Jimmy to have warm colours in his hair – a mix of medium browns will look really pretty. We can then use the hair as a base and choose colours for his outfit that complement him. While working through different variations I start to notice that certain colour combinations make Jimmy look older than I want. Keep in mind the story you are trying to tell at every step of the process – every visual element influences what the audience will take from your design.

THE WOLF AT THE DOOR

Now, let's start working on the wolf. Again, I pick my favourite early sketches and start pushing shapes to create a good balance. I want the wolf to feel big and elegant – I'm looking for a rhythm that flows from the tip of her foot to the last hair on her tail. I'm imagining the final design as almost a full silhouette, with bright eyes and lots of texture, so I focus on poses that read easily.

Keeping a small silhouette of the other characters in your scene close to hand can help you build contrasting shapes and keep a nice sense of scale.

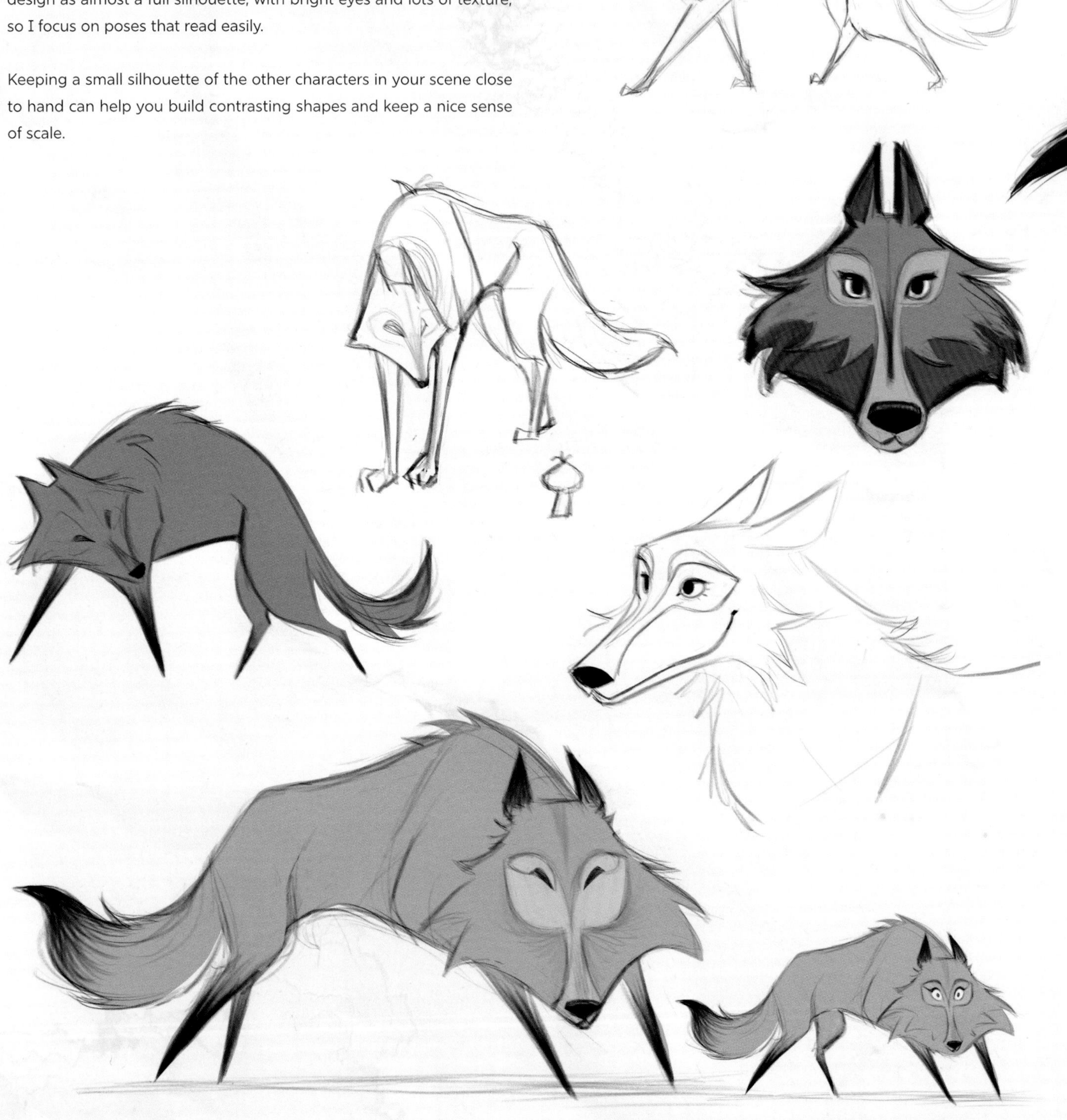

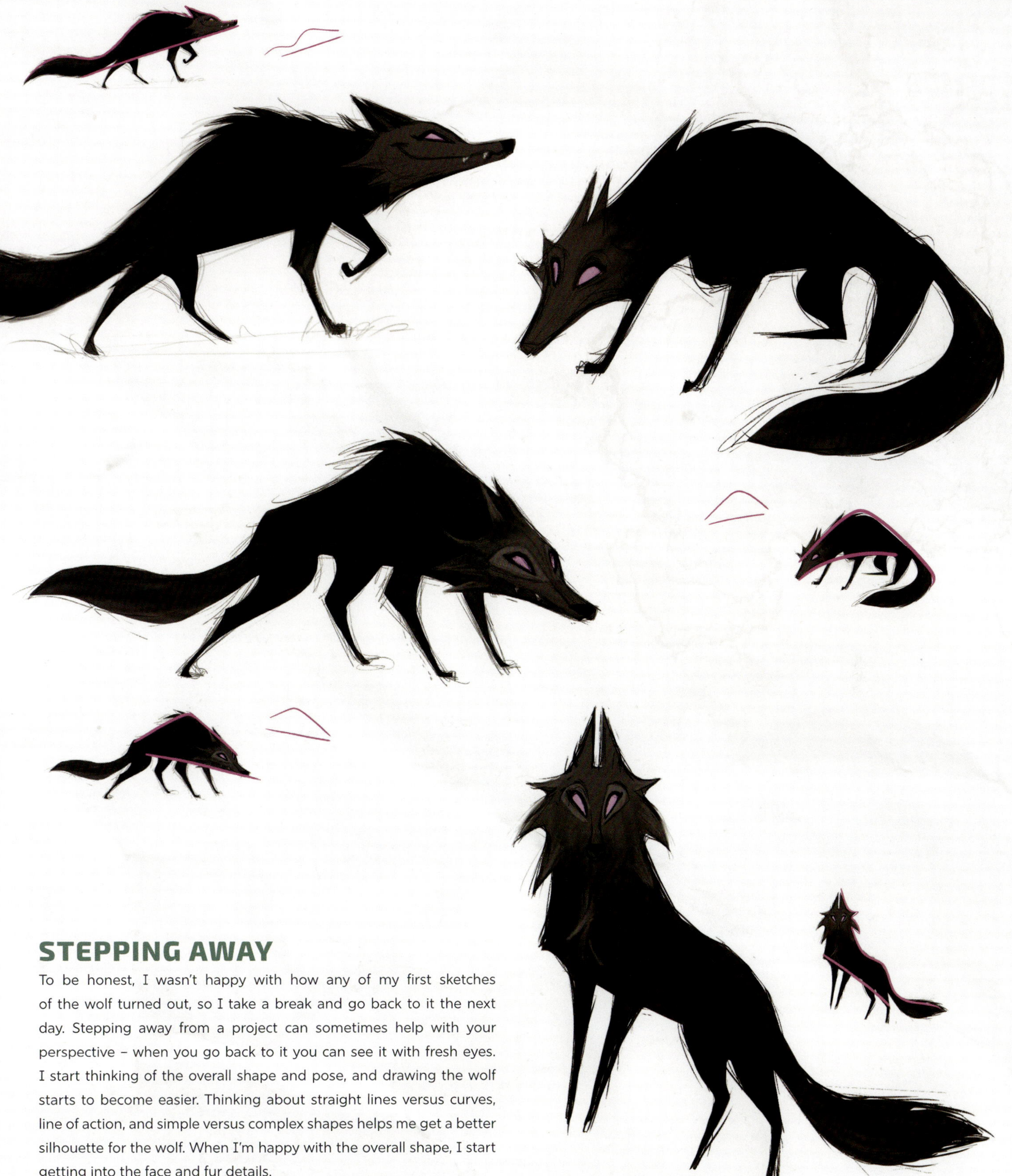

STEPPING AWAY

To be honest, I wasn't happy with how any of my first sketches of the wolf turned out, so I take a break and go back to it the next day. Stepping away from a project can sometimes help with your perspective – when you go back to it you can see it with fresh eyes. I start thinking of the overall shape and pose, and drawing the wolf starts to become easier. Thinking about straight lines versus curves, line of action, and simple versus complex shapes helps me get a better silhouette for the wolf. When I'm happy with the overall shape, I start getting into the face and fur details.

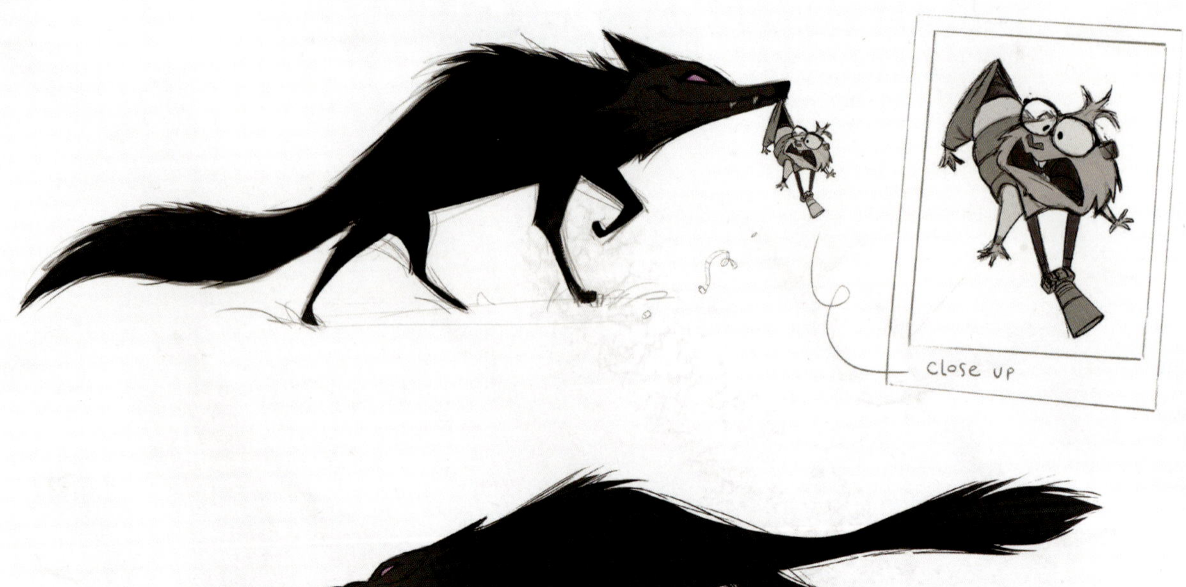
close up

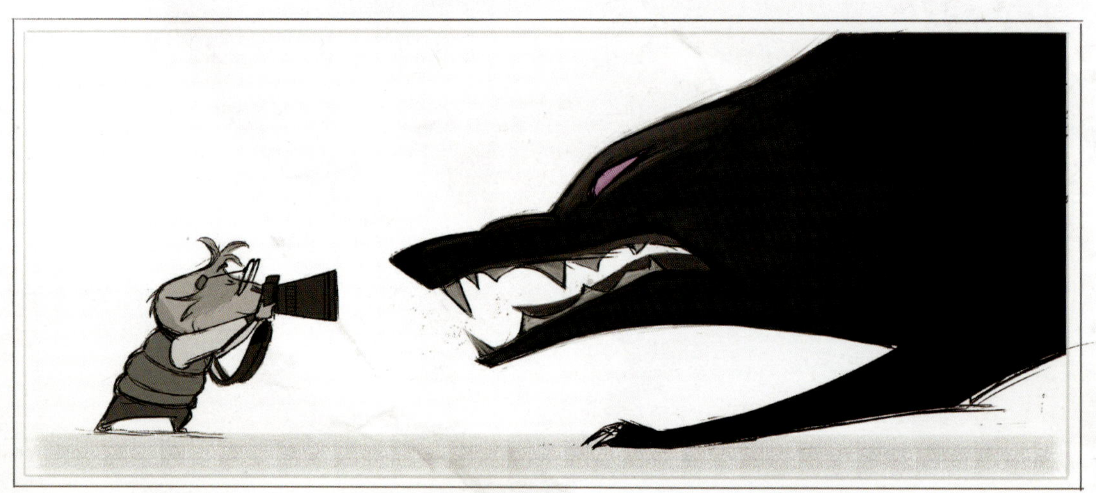

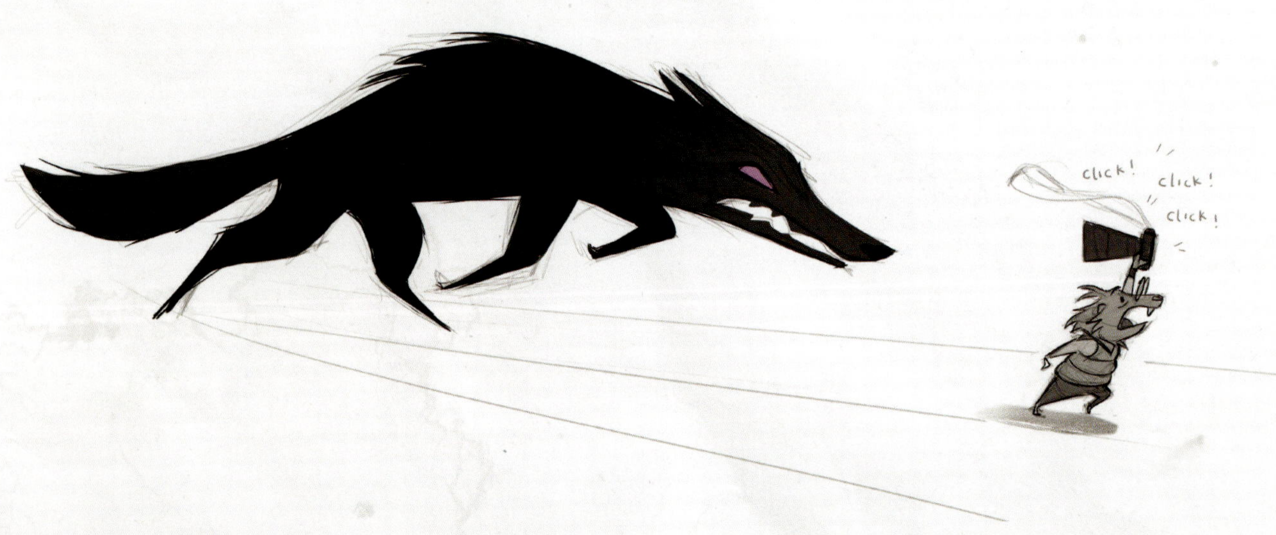
click!
click!
click!

'When cleaning the lines, we want to make sure the energy and overall feeling of the sketch doesn't get lost'

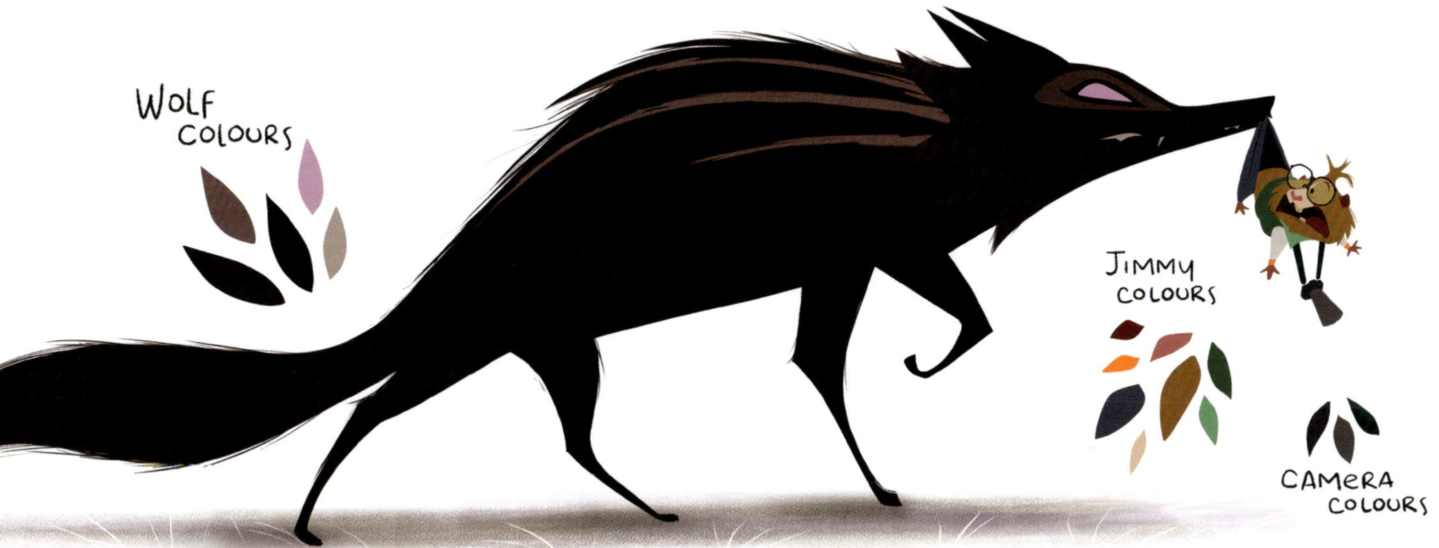

TELLING THE STORY

Now we know how both characters look, we can start playing with posing them. I want the poses to show who they are and what's going on in the story. Try to start this step really loosely – think about the energy and the story moments more than technicalities right now. I decide on a few poses to show – I want the characters face to face. I want to see how they look running from one another, and I want the wolf to catch Jimmy. Just feel free to play with different ideas, keeping in mind who the characters are and what they would do in any given situation.

You can take this step as far as you like, making as many poses as you want and picking your favourites. You can even clean them up and colour them, but this step isn't about creating anything clean and perfect – you just want to tell the story and keep the characters on model.

It's important to remember that character design should always be in support of the story. Without a story, a design can look good, but it won't be a real character.

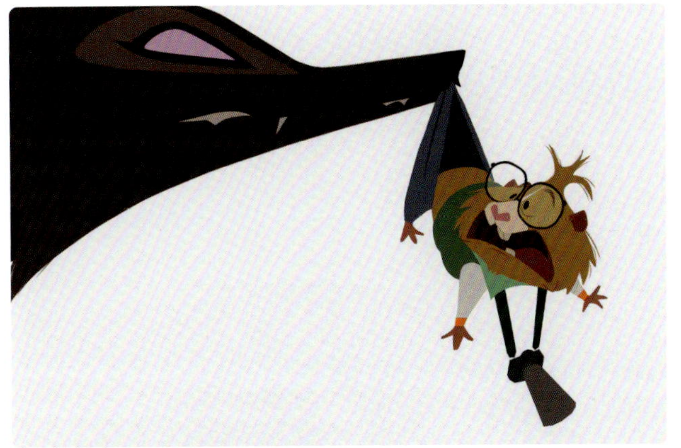

CLEANING UP & COLOURING

When cleaning the lines, we want to make sure the energy and overall feeling of the sketch doesn't get lost. It can be hard and a bit frustrating, but if you make sure you keep the important pieces, you can make it work. You can do the clean-up with just basic shapes to prep for rendering, or with line art.

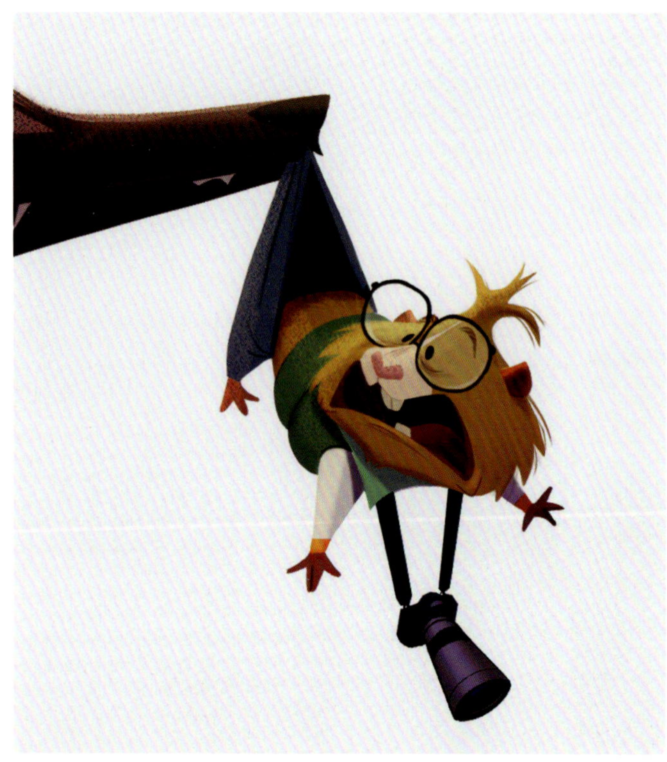

A COLOURFUL ENCOUNTER

Once we're happy with the flat colour shapes, we can start adding textures, detail lines, and shadow and light. I like to keep it simple and not get too crazy with the rendering when the shapes and expressions are already reading well. I add a close-up of Jimmy so the audience can see him better, without losing the contrast in size between him and the wolf.

And that's pretty much it. I love the story and characters I've come up with and will continue drawing them and see where the story ends. I hope Jimmy makes it out of the situation and manages to deliver his work on time!

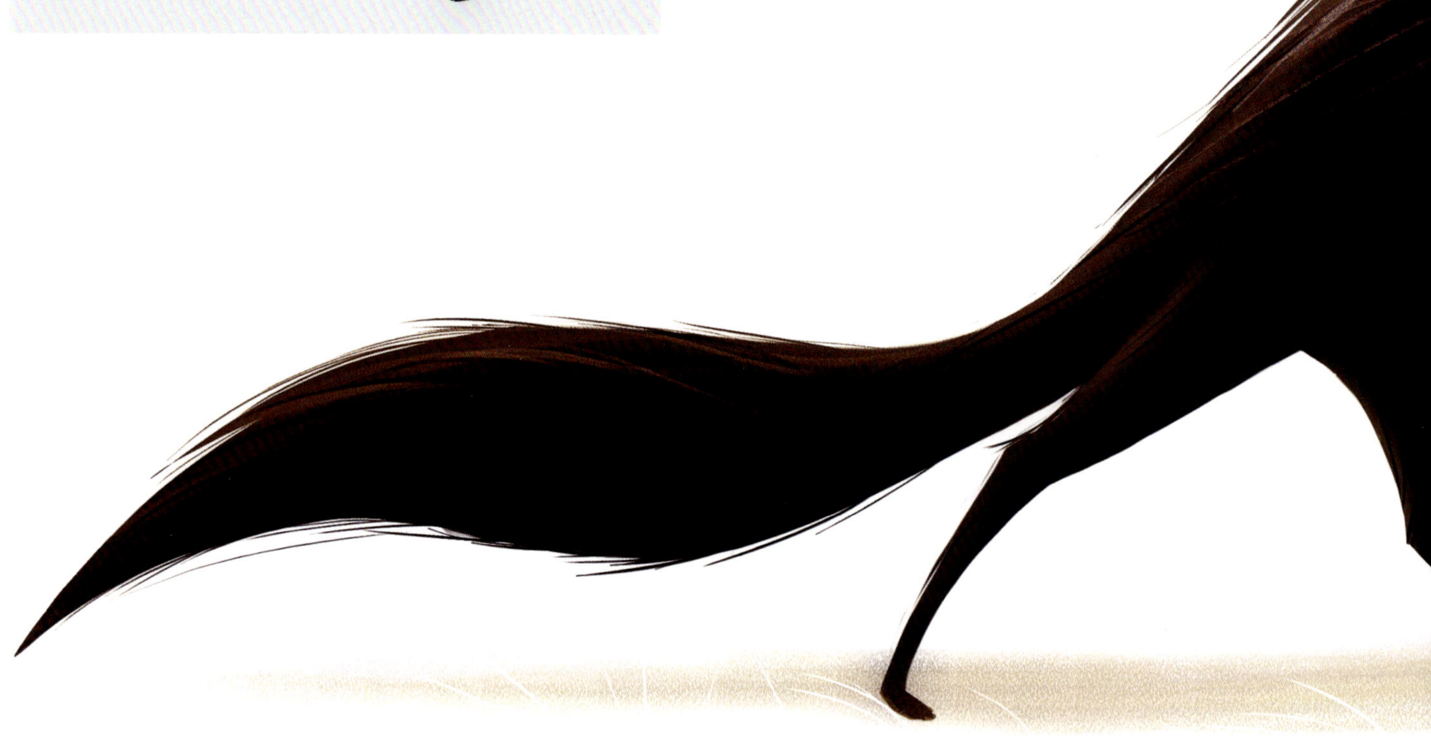

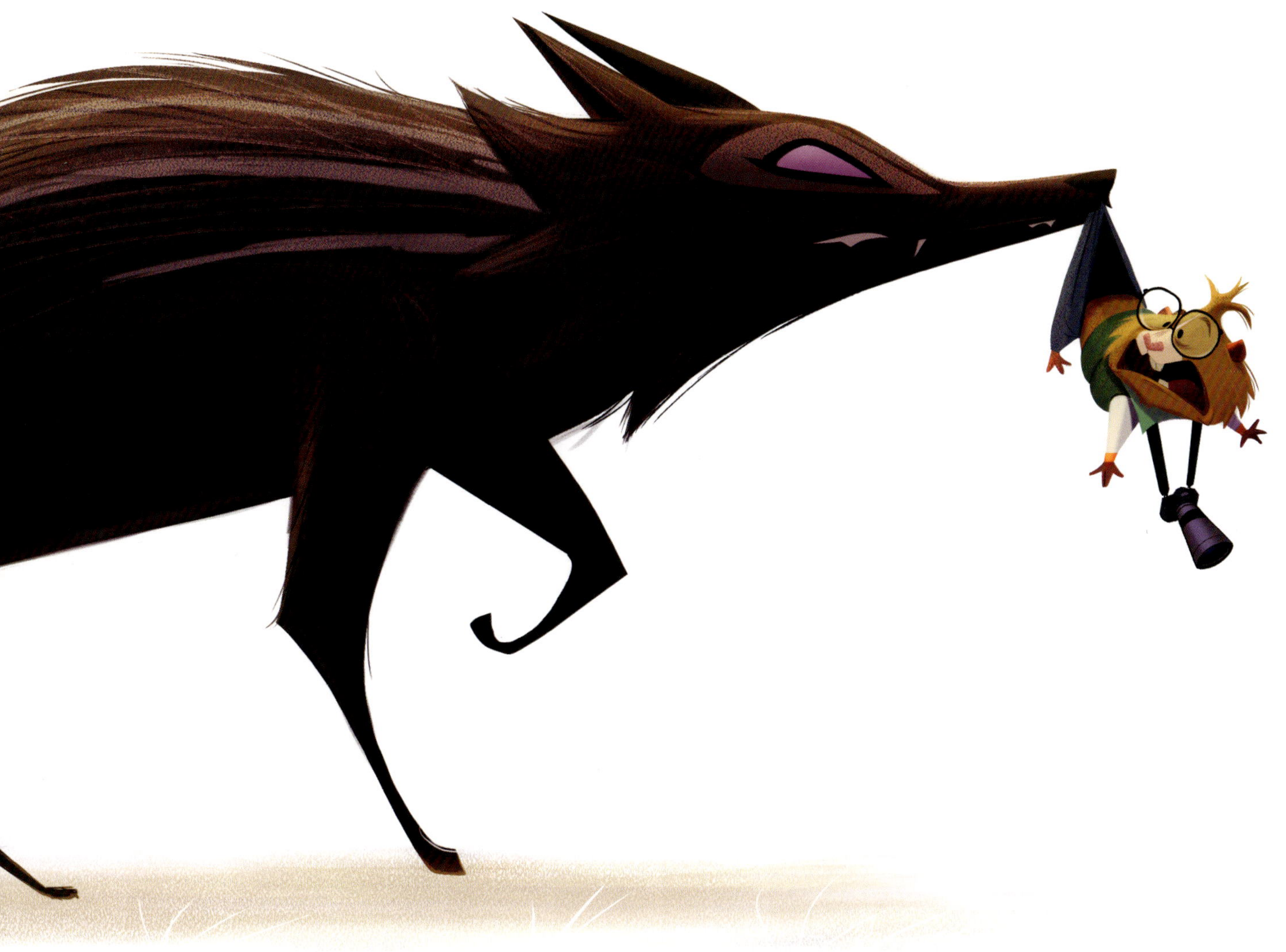

Final image © Melany Altuna

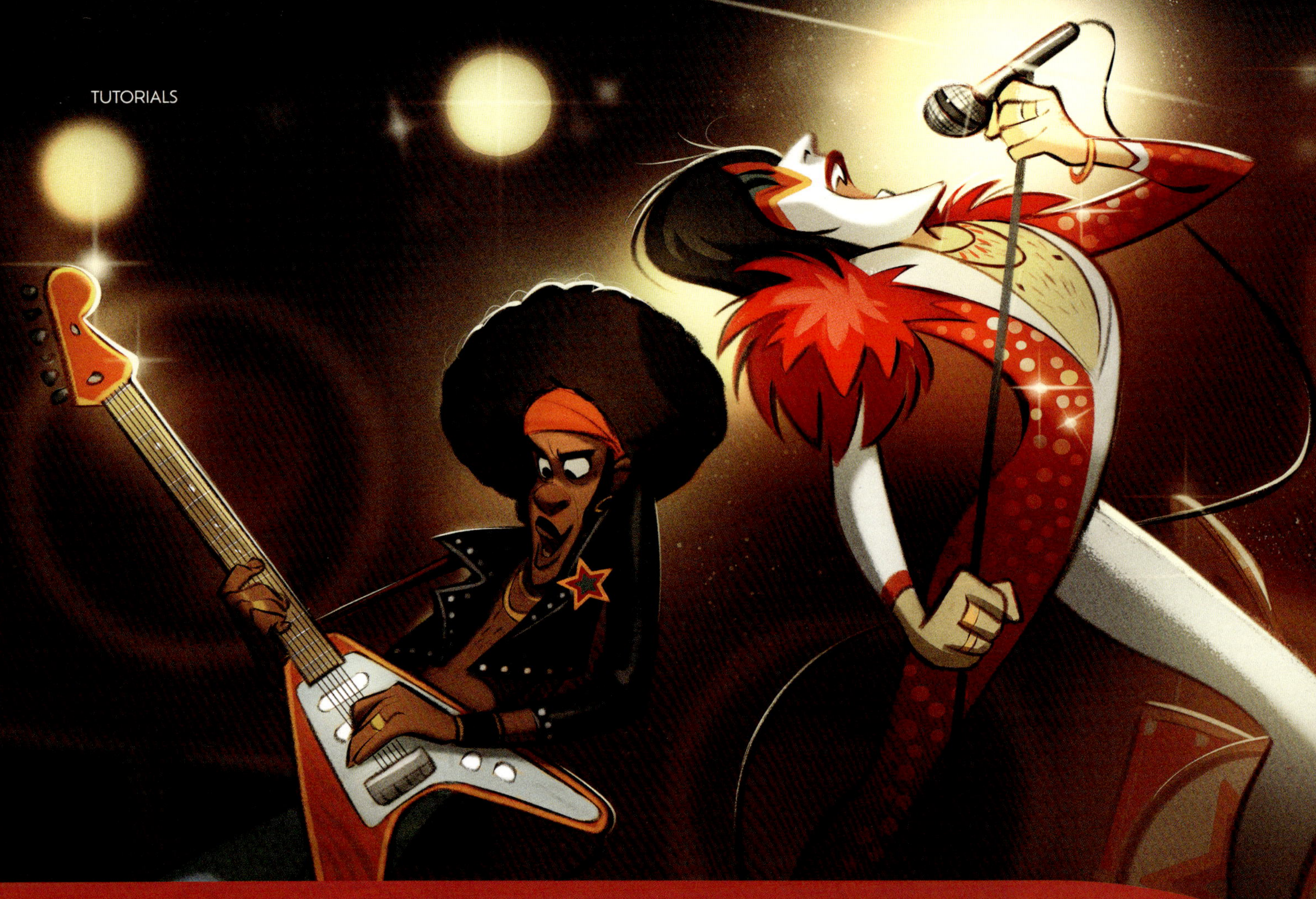

If you want rock, you've got it

KENNETH ANDERSON

Ah, the seventies! A decade of flares, platform shoes, and awesome rock music! Queen was the soundtrack to my childhood; later I discovered my dad's Led Zeppelin collection, and a friend introduced me to the wonders of Van Halen. Needless to say, I'm a huge fan of seventies rock and the potential for cool and unique characters it provides.

This tutorial follows the process of creating a small group of characters, making each design unique while still unified as a whole. I use Photoshop, but there is no special equipment required – just a pencil and paper will do! Grab your instrument of choice, turn the volume up to eleven, and let's rock!

'There's no shortage of amazing reference material to draw upon'

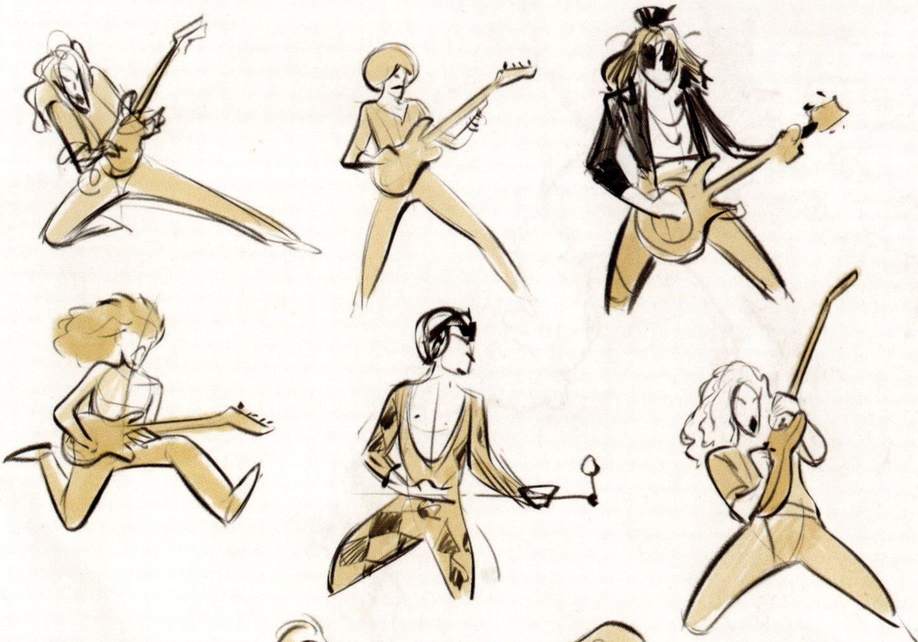

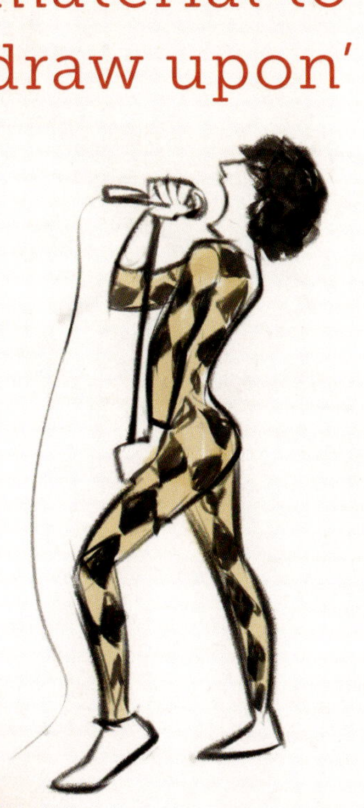

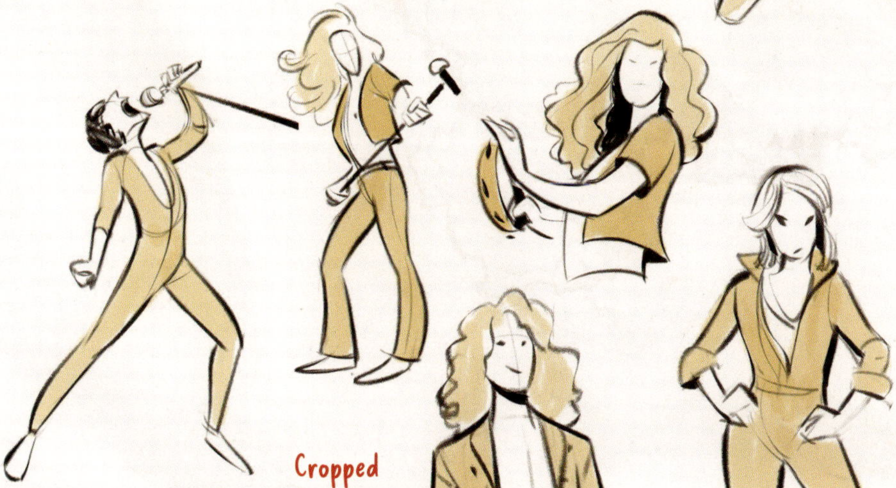

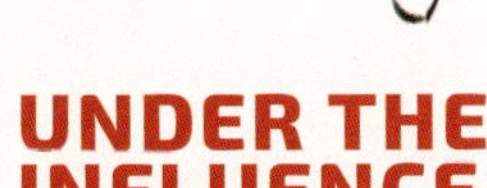

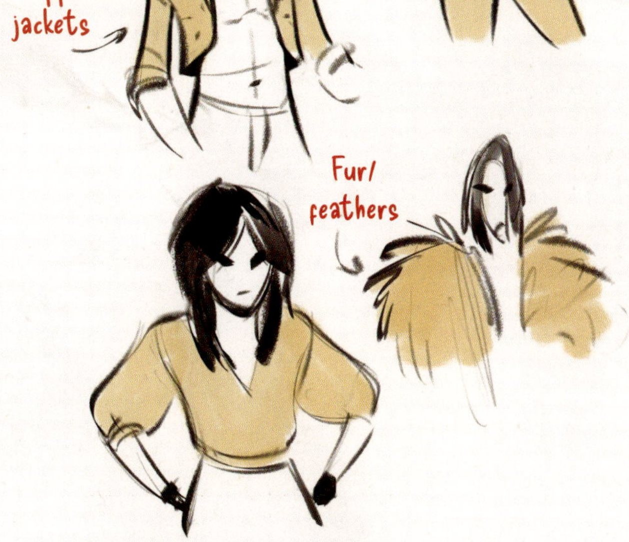

UNDER THE INFLUENCE

Designing a seventies rock band means there's no shortage of amazing reference material to draw upon. I gather together photos of Queen (of course!), Thin Lizzy, AC/DC, Black Sabbath, Fleetwood Mac, and more, and make some reference drawings. At this stage I'm not concerned with making anything perfect – it's about finding the essence of the theme, and what aspects of the fashion and vibe of the source material I want to recreate. Through my research, some common ideas start to form: big hair, moustaches, platform boots, flares, glamorous attire, and generally tight clothing with exposed, hairy chests!

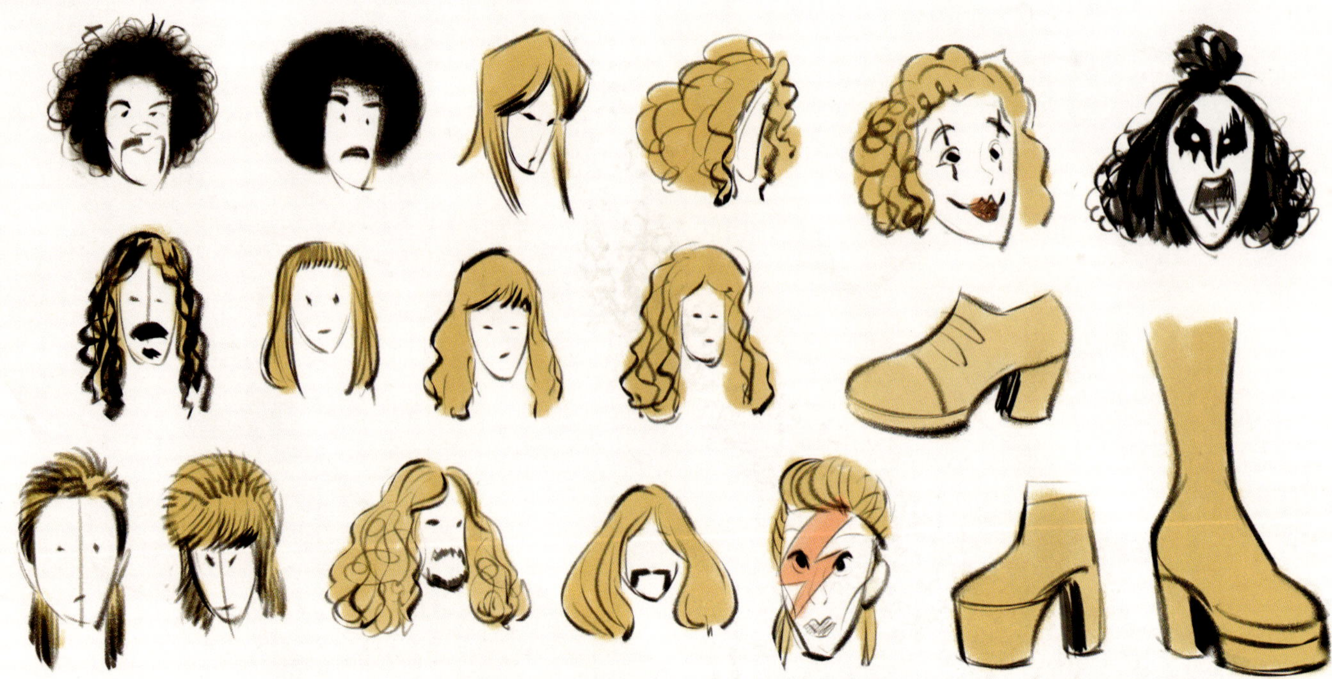

GETTING THE BAND BACK TOGETHER

70's ROCK BAND
- SINGER
- GUITARIST
- BASSIST
- DRUMMER

Gathering references won't only provide you with a visual springboard to design from, it will also help establish your cast of characters, or, in this case, bandmates. Most of the bands I'm referencing kept their lineup raw and simple: a guitarist or two, a bassist, a drummer, a singer, and we're ready to rock!

I decide to stick with this formula and aim to create four characters, each with a unique instrument. I decide on a guitarist, a bassist, a drummer, and a singer.

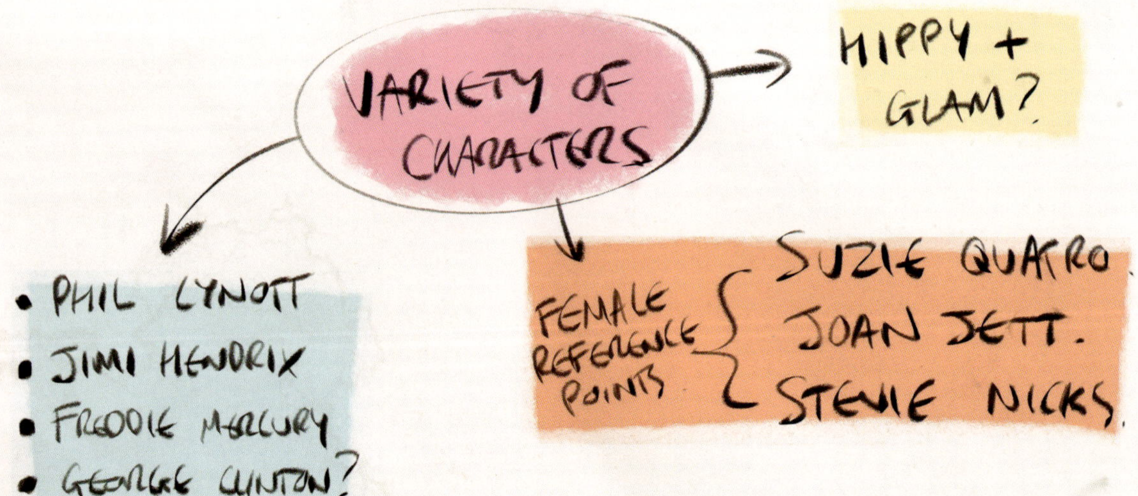

'We just want a clear starting point from which we can play around and see what works'

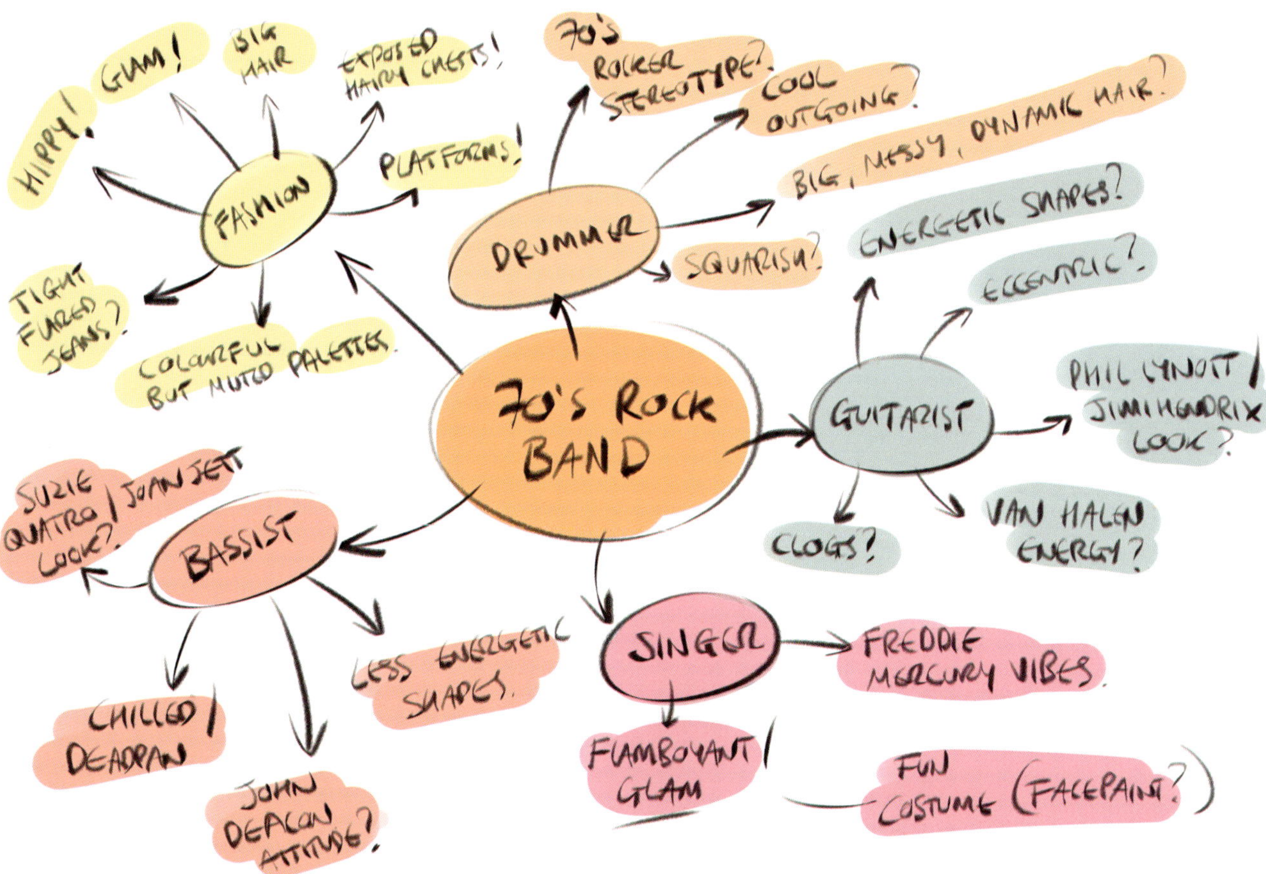

VARIETY SHOW

When drawing a cast of characters, it's important to make sure there's variety in the designs. Although seventies rockers were mostly male, there were some notable exceptions: Stevie Nicks, Suzi Quatro, and Joan Jett all had strong, unique looks we can pull from. And while the male seventies rock look was fairly homogenous, there are still plenty of interesting characters to consider: Phil Lynott from Thin Lizzy, Freddie Mercury, and Jimi Hendrix all have quirks that will be fun to reference.

Whatever your subject, try to find trends in design. Seventies rock seems to fall into two broad categories: the hippy vibes of Led Zeppelin or Fleetwood Mac, and the more glam look of Queen, Kiss, or David Bowie. I think I can bring both these styles together and create a really interesting look for my characters.

AUDITIONS ARE OPEN!

An idea of my cast of characters is starting to come together. I decide to loosely base the band on Queen: a flamboyant frontman, a chilled-out bassist, a cool, outgoing drummer, and a virtuoso guitarist. Let's mix things up, though – I want to bring some of Eddie Van Halen's energy to the guitarist, while referencing Phil Lynott and Jimi Hendrix for their look. For the bassist, I'm thinking of a Suzi Quatro vibe. And let's not forget to add plenty of glam!

Nothing is set in stone at this point and a lot of these ideas will fall by the wayside – we just want a clear starting point from which we can play around and see what works.

'A character's personality is mostly conveyed through their actions, but we can suggest meaning through design language as well'

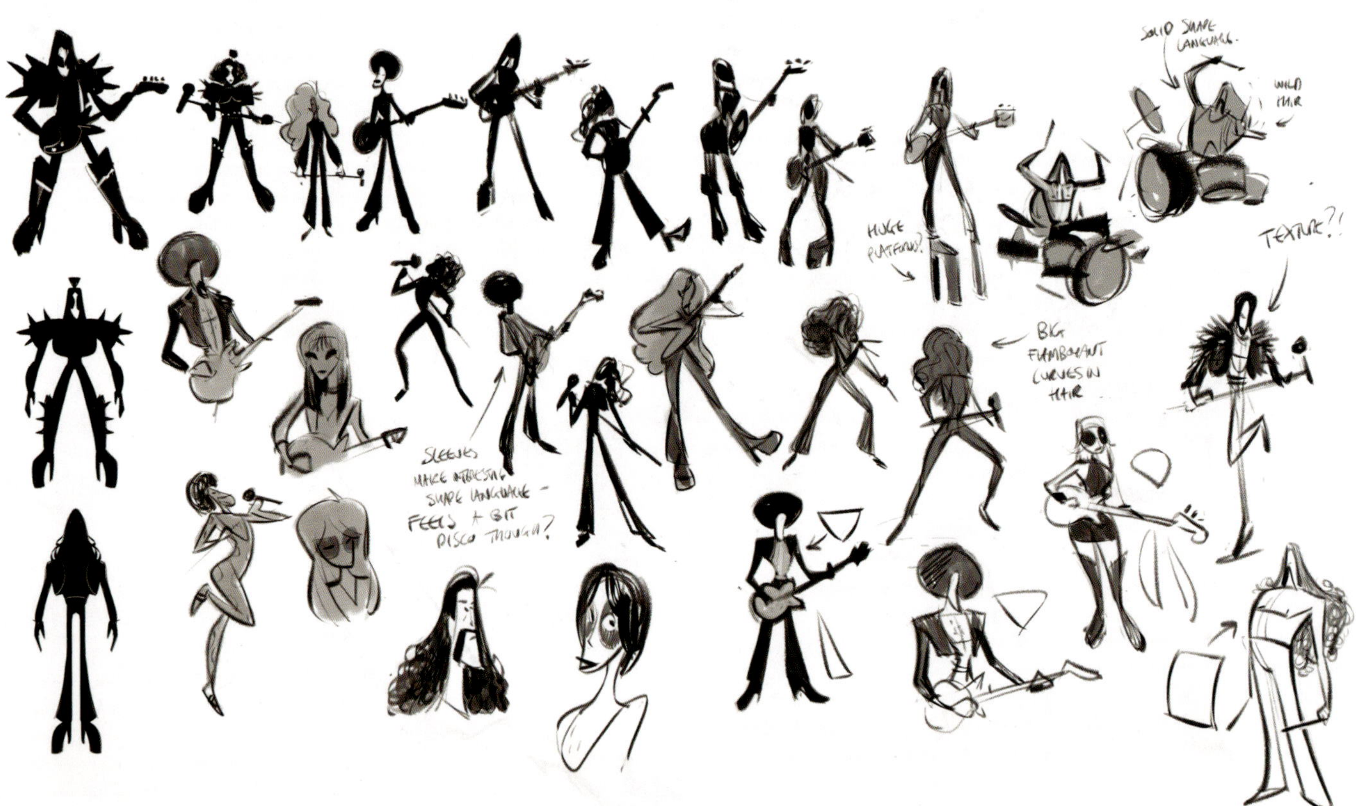

THE FIRST REHEARSAL

By now the brain should be buzzing with ideas and we're ready to start drawing. Start with thumbnails – loose, quick sketches exploring a variety of ideas. Any references collected can be used for inspiration here, so keep them to hand.

Thumbnails serve three goals. First, they help warm up the drawing muscles. Second, they start the problem-solving process. And third, they are a chance to explore, go wild, and have fun playing with contrast, shapes, silhouettes, and proportion. It's important that individual characters read instantly – their silhouette and shape design will help achieve this. At this stage, there is no such thing as a wrong drawing, so let it all out!

THROWING SHAPES

A character's personality is mostly conveyed through their actions, but we can suggest meaning through design language as well. I avoid making any of my characters too jagged and spiky in their design as that feels more suited to an eighties thrash metal band. I do think my energetic guitarist will benefit from some triangular forms. I use squarer shapes for the drummer as he is the grounding force in the band.

I've noticed that seventies rockers mostly had the same body type – tall and wiry. I want to keep this idea in my work so I explore using costume and hair silhouettes to really set them apart from each other. For example, one character might have an afro, while another has wild hair, or a long, crazy beard.

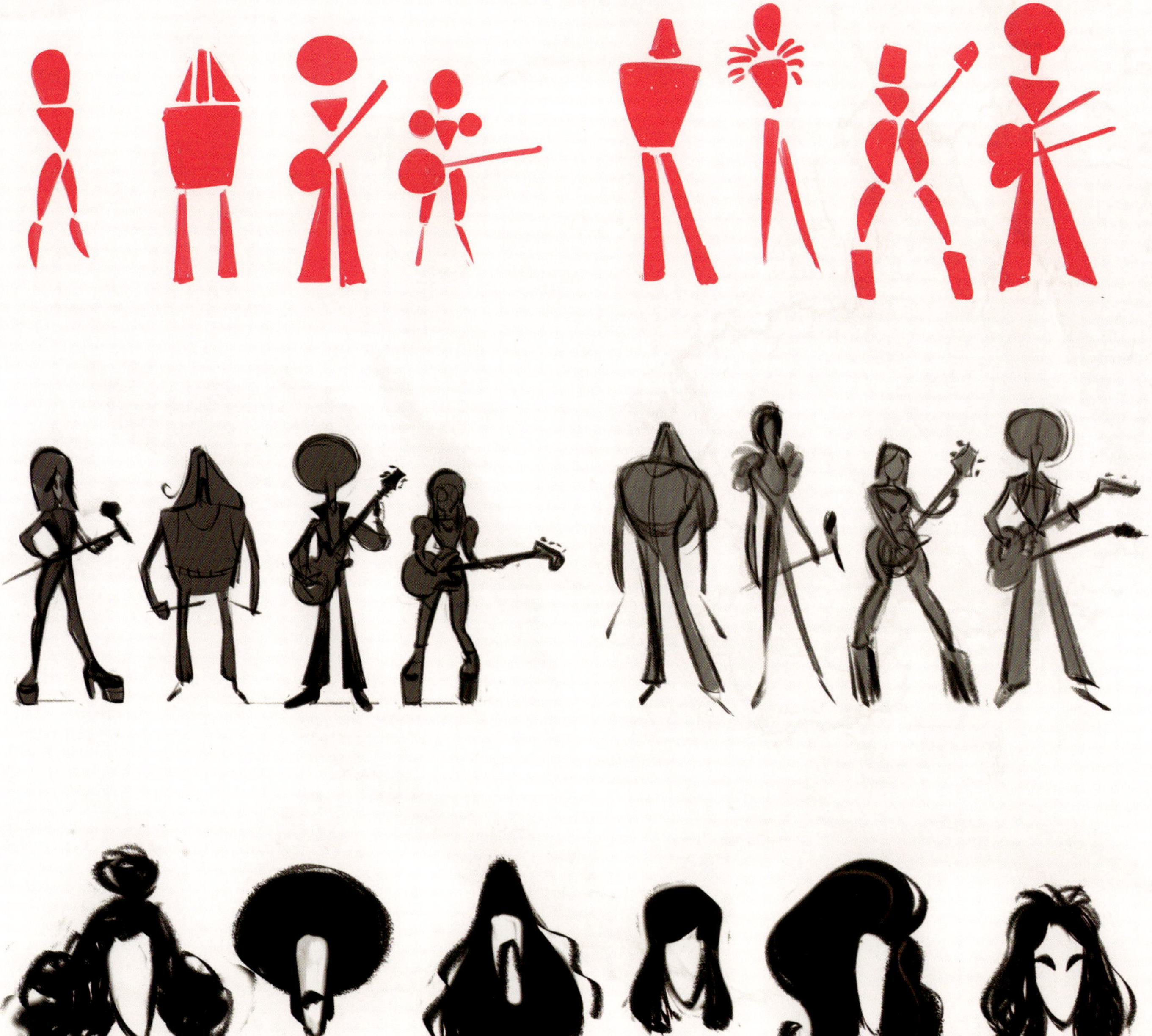

SHAPING CHARACTERS

When creating characters like mine that look 'realistic' while still being stylized, you don't always need to be heavy on the shape design. We can push shapes within a character's costume or hair to differentiate our character's silhouettes and suggest meaning, while still being relatively close to realistic human proportions.

'We can use costumes to differentiate the bandmates from each other, while also creating a unifying theme between them'

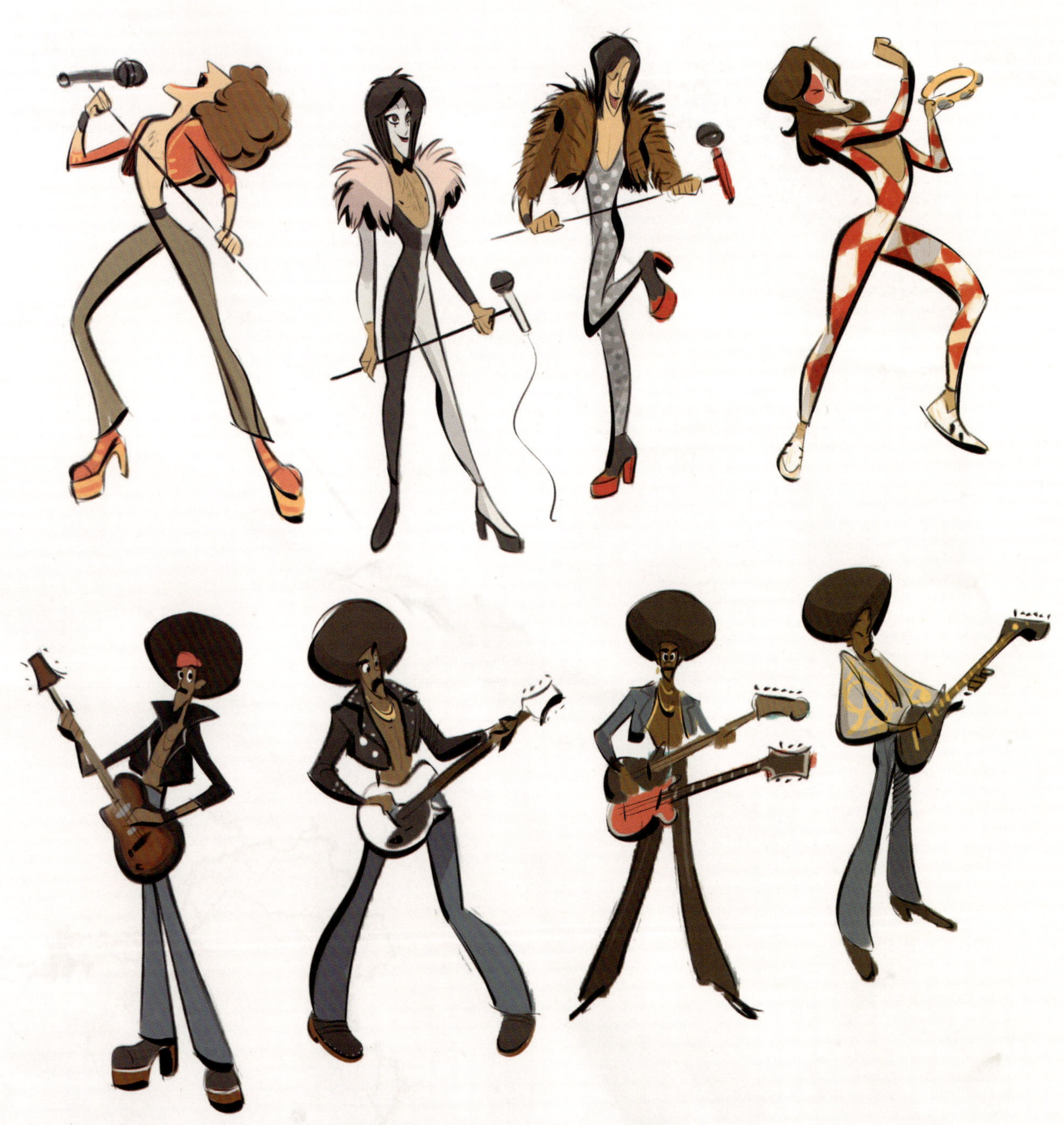

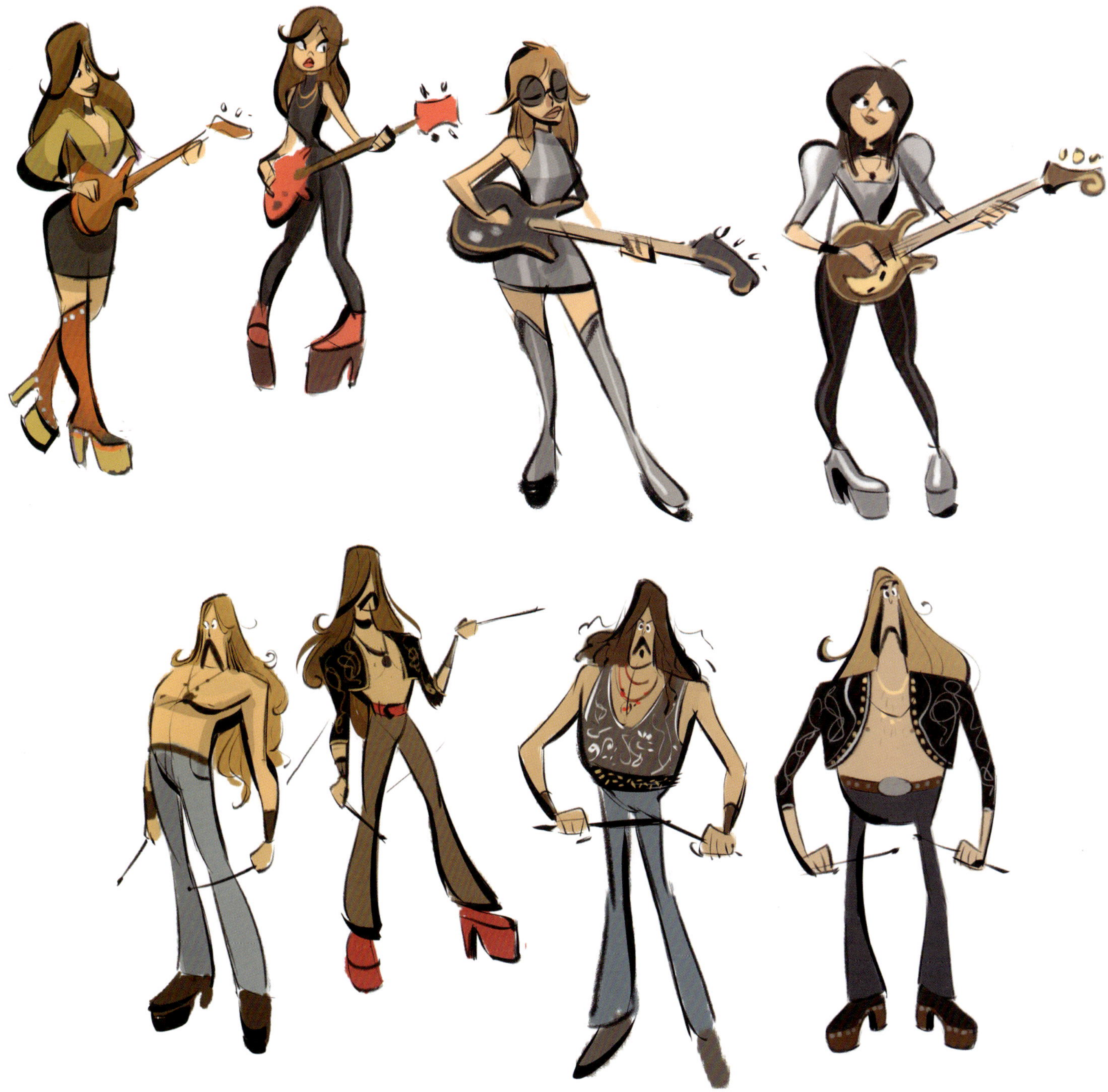

EXPERIMENTAL ROCK

Seventies rocker fashion was incredibly eclectic, giving us plenty of material to work with. We can use costumes to differentiate the bandmates from each other, while also creating a unifying theme between them. For my singer, I combine the wardrobes of Freddie Mercury with the face paint of Kiss, David Bowie, and Zal Cleminson. The fur jacket helps add some extra pizzazz and texture to the design.

Let's dress our guitarist next. Leather trousers or tight, flared jeans combined with platform shoes are a seventies standard. I try some flowery Jimi Hendrix style shirts, but he starts to feel more disco than rock. A cropped leather jacket seems to work well.

I'm going for Suzi Quatro and Joan Jett vibes for my bassist – I want her to look cool! Last but not least is the drummer, who I decide I'm going to draw as a completely stereotypical seventies rocker.

HEADS UP!

A character's face is the most important part of a character design – it's the main point of focus for the audience, where they connect and empathize with a character. With this in mind, it's a good idea to explore head designs in a little more detail.

Starting on a fresh page, I riff off my reference material, playing with hair and facial features. I want to nod to some well-known musicians, but at the same time not just draw caricatures of them.

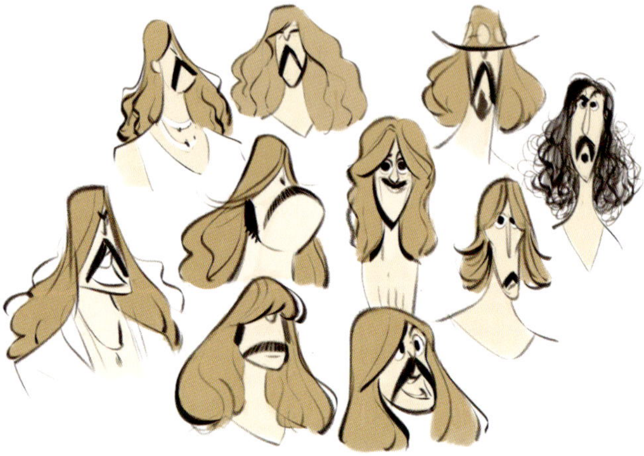

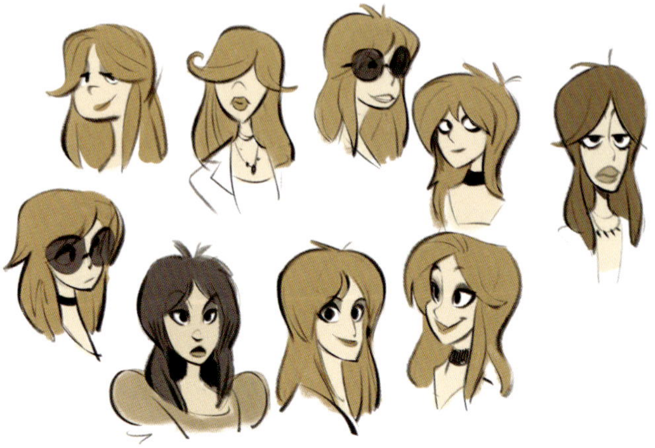

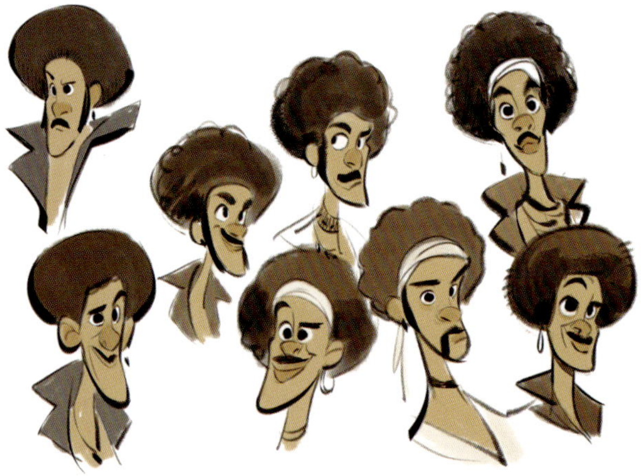

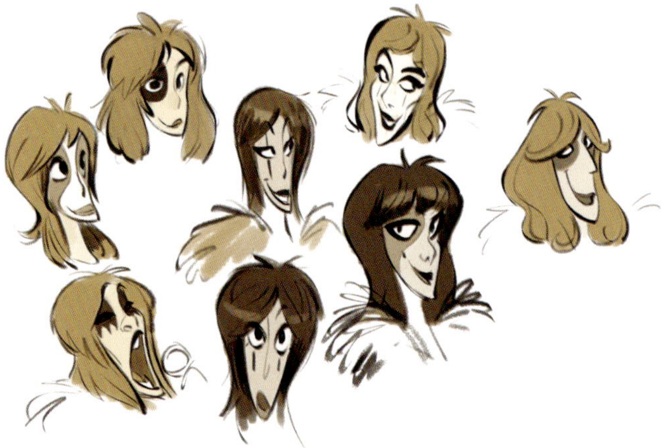

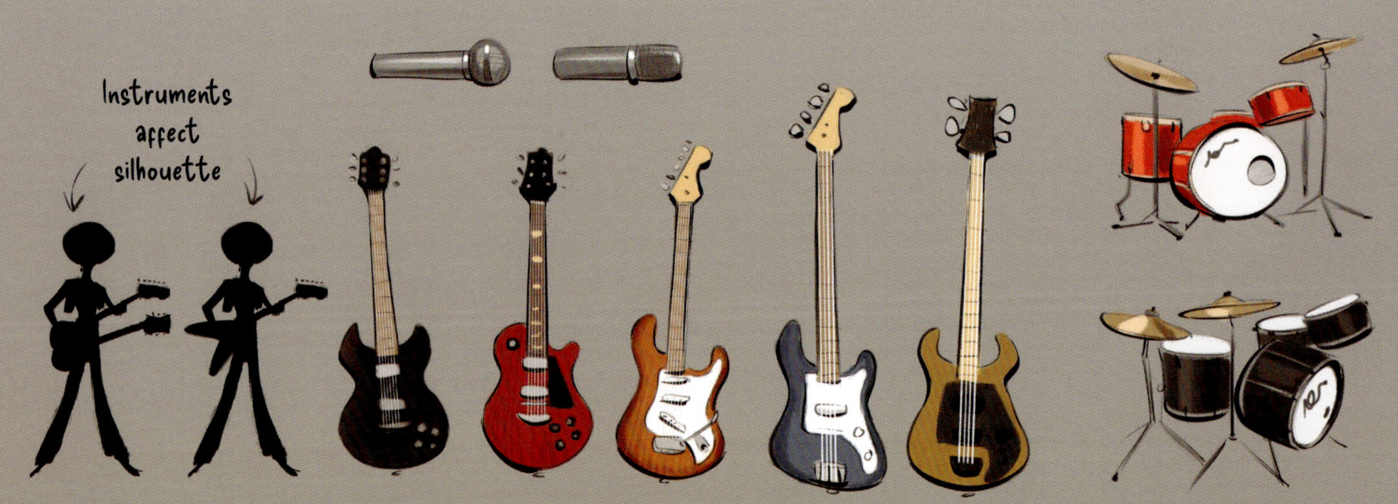

TUNING THE INSTRUMENTS

Let's not forget the characters' instruments – they can be an extension of their personalities. Brian May built his iconic Red Special from scratch out of an old fireplace with his dad, while Eddie Van Halen combined different guitar parts to form his infamous Frankenstrat! A rock band's instruments clearly mean a lot to them, so let's treat them with the care and attention they deserve.

Instruments are a great place to play with shapes that can completely change a character's silhouette. Think outside the box – it could be fun if my guitarist plays a double-necked guitar that he built himself, a nod to so many greats of seventies rock all in one go. Bringing these ideas into design can really help add backstory to your characters.

THE UNUSUAL SUSPECTS

While my characters are starting to work as individuals, they don't yet feel as though they're part of the same band. To fix this, I mix and match some elements from other sketches and add some common costume elements between them, such as the stud detailing.

Colour will help synthesize the characters into one coherent band while also allowing us to add some variety between them. I lock down a seventies-inspired colour palette and tweak my characters to match. I want my singer to be the most vibrant – he is the frontman of the band so he should really stand out. The other three bandmates I think work best as more subtle variations on the theme – leather, denim, and colours taken from the palette.

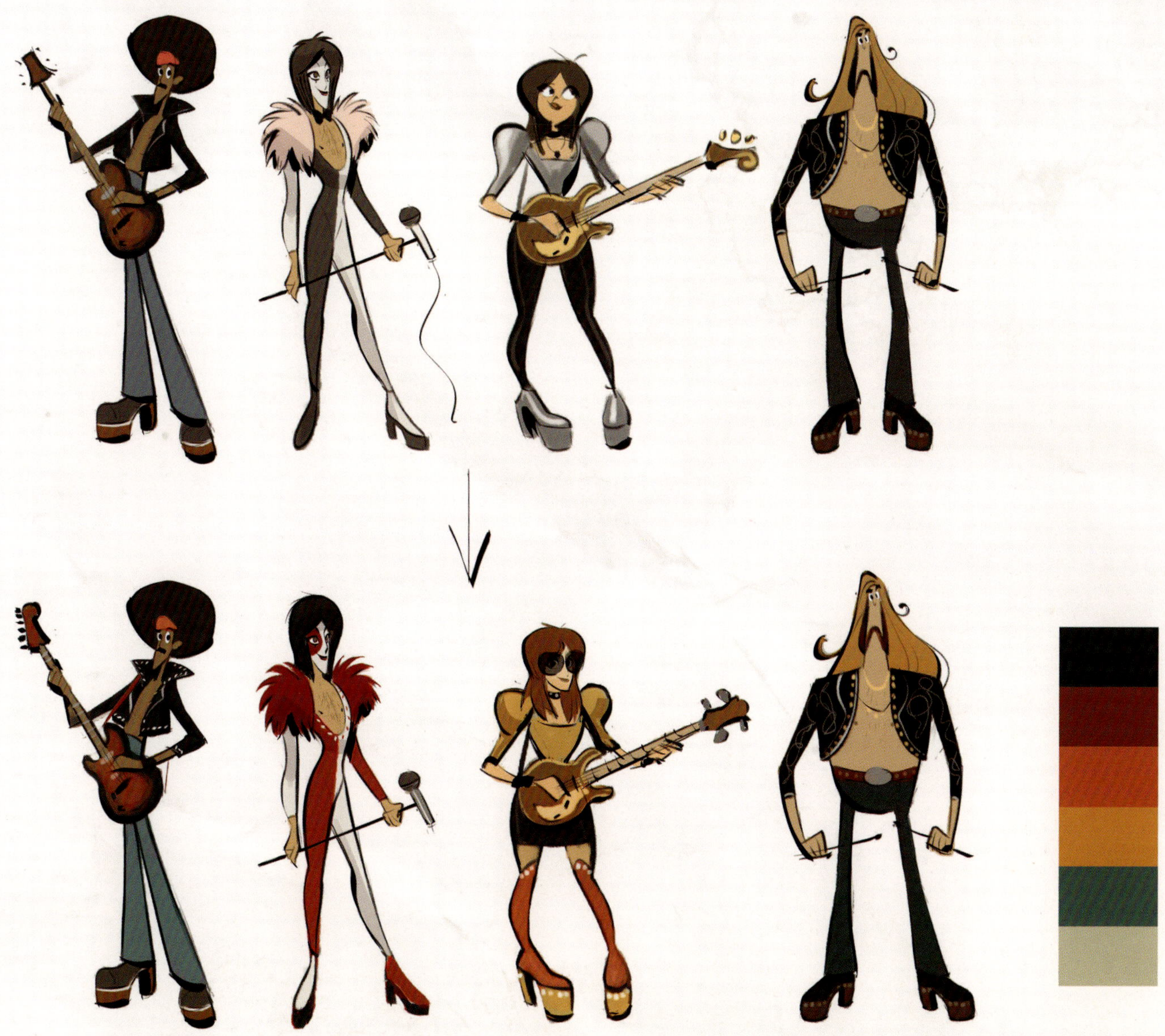

REFINE THE DESIGN

By now the bandmates are starting to jam well together! I double-check that they each have a clear silhouette and good proportions, that their costumes are unified but varied, and that their individual personalities are starting to shine through. Now we can finesse the designs and tweak them to perfection.

I revisit my reference material to think of ways to enhance my characters, and add a bit more visual interest, such as well-placed details in the costumes. These edits can be subtle, but still effective. Be careful with where you place detail, though – it shouldn't distract attention from the character's face.

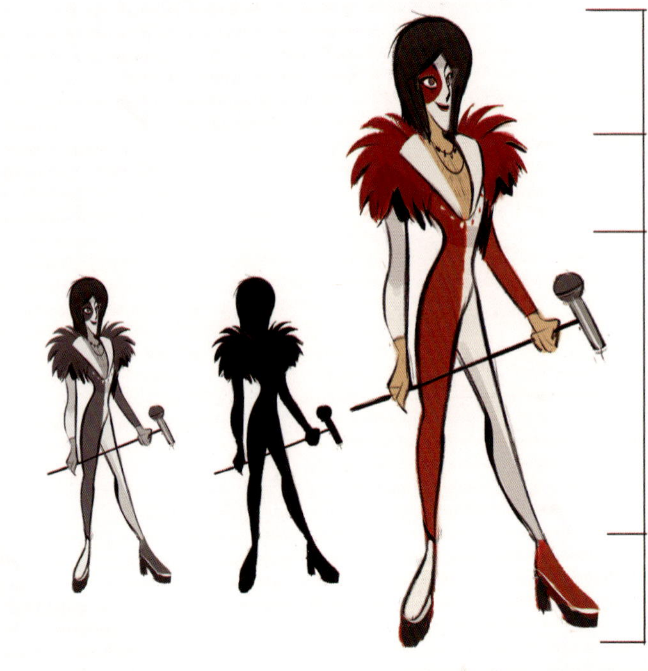

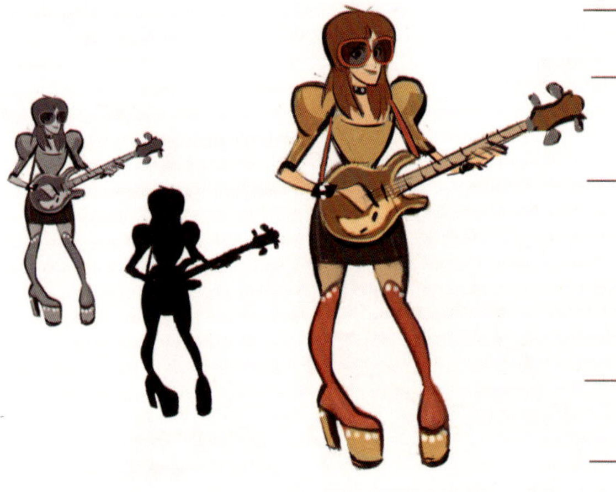

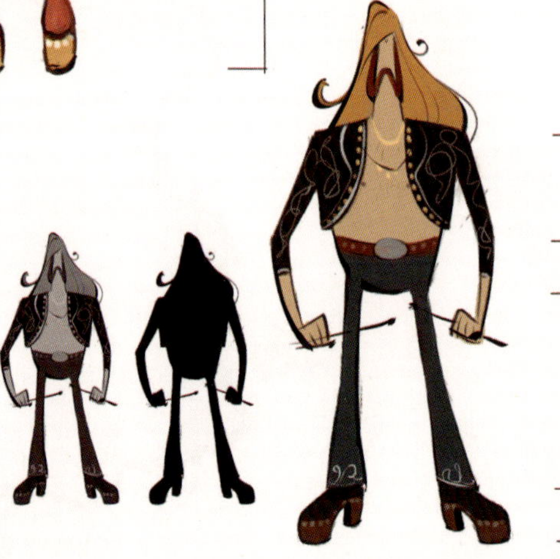

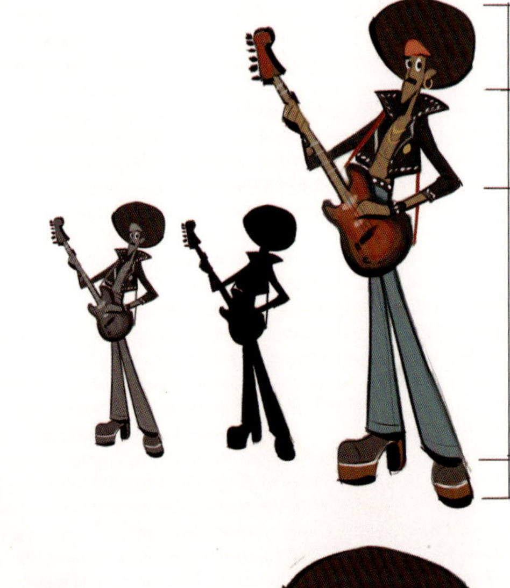

THE GUITAR THAT GOT AWAY

I was tempted to give my guitarist his own double-necked 'Frankenstrat' guitar. While I liked the idea, I worried it was a bit too niche of a reference. Clarity in design is important – don't forget that sometimes the simplest idea can also be the best one.

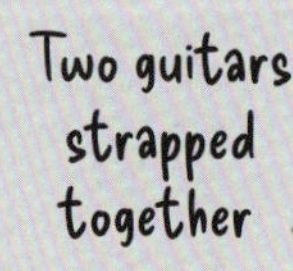

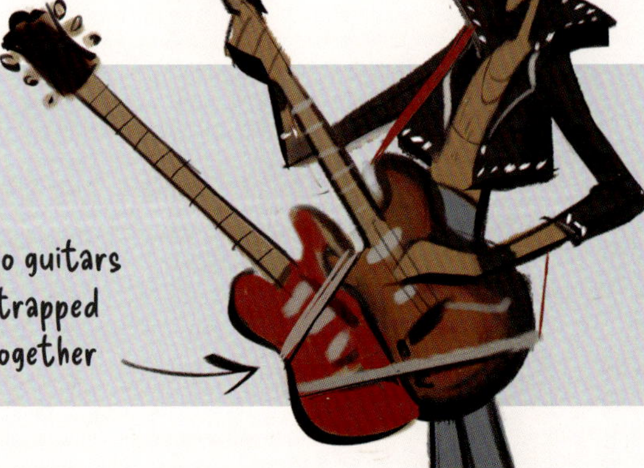

OPENING NIGHT

The platforms are on, the instruments are tuned – it's time for the band's first gig. I want the viewer to feel like they're in the crowd, so I establish a basic backdrop for the scene, choosing a lower camera angle that looks up towards the band on stage.

I want the characters to look like they're really playing, so I need to figure out how best to group them. I want my singer and guitarist to feel like they are connected visually somehow, playing together in the moment. I work out poses which feel in harmony with one another.

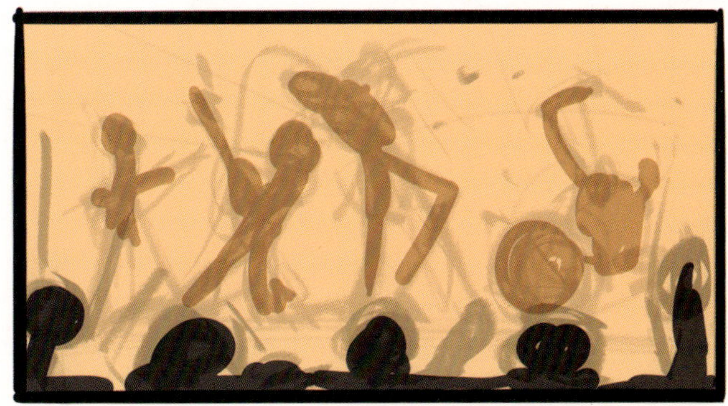

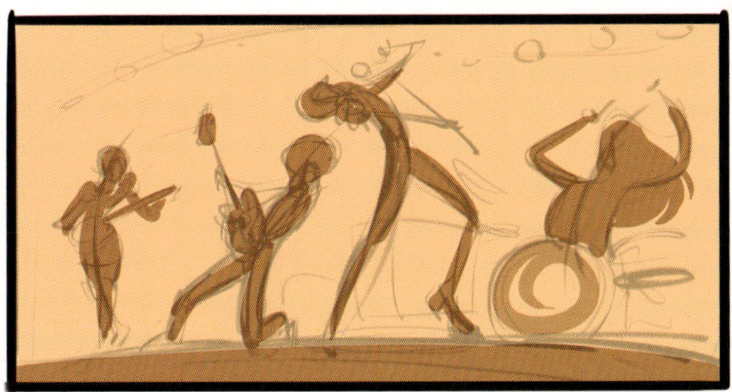

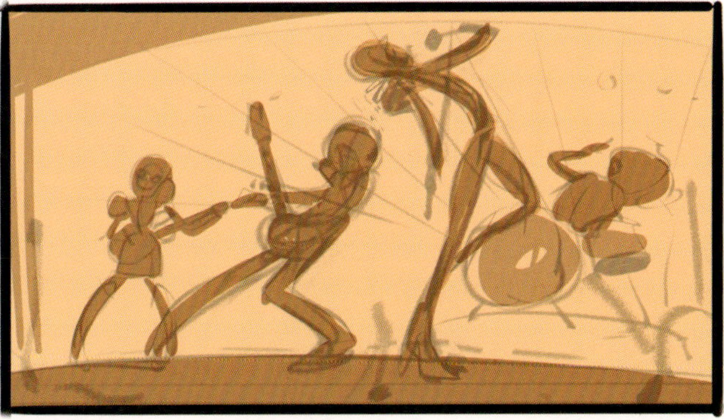

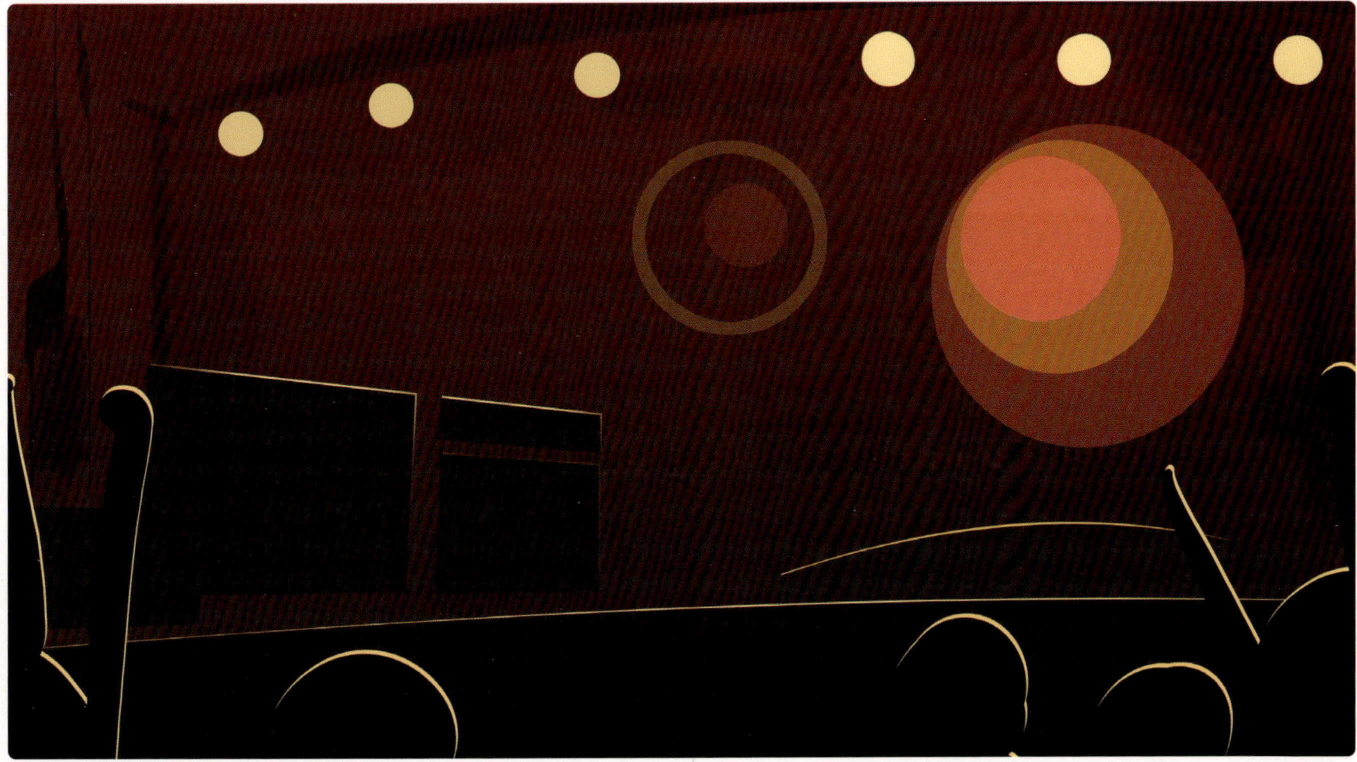

'Attention to detail adds so much personality to a character's design'

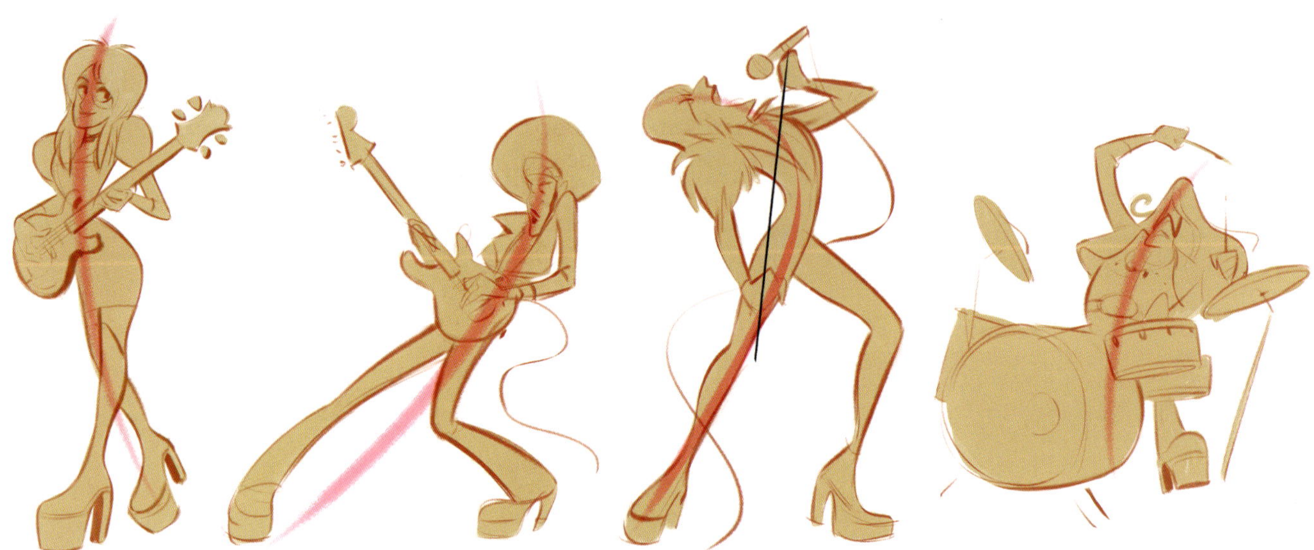

GUITAR HEROES

I want my band to feel like they are performing together while also conveying their individual personalities. Maybe my guitarist plays guitar with his teeth, Jimi Hendrix-style, or with a violin bow like Jimmy Page? I settle on giving him a hint of Eddie Van Halen's enthusiastic energy in his pose. Sometimes the best idea is the simplest.

It might be a nice nod to Jimi Hendrix to have my guitarist playing left-handed on an upside-down, right-handed guitar. This detail might escape most people, but attention to detail adds so much personality to a character's design.

For my singer, I want to channel Freddie Mercury's flair. I can see the drummer being a bit wild, his crazy hair going all over the place. And for the bassist, it would be nice to contrast her energy with the others and keep her chilled out, giving off John Deacon vibes.

THE SHOW MUST GO ON

With the difficult bit of the performance and composition out of the way, I can now focus on bringing everything to life. I lock down my characters' poses, making sure they are clear and work well with each other, while still conveying the right statement. I pay special attention to silhouettes and line of action.

I add colour and ensure each character pops out from the background. Lighting effects can add visual interest and make the characters stand out further.

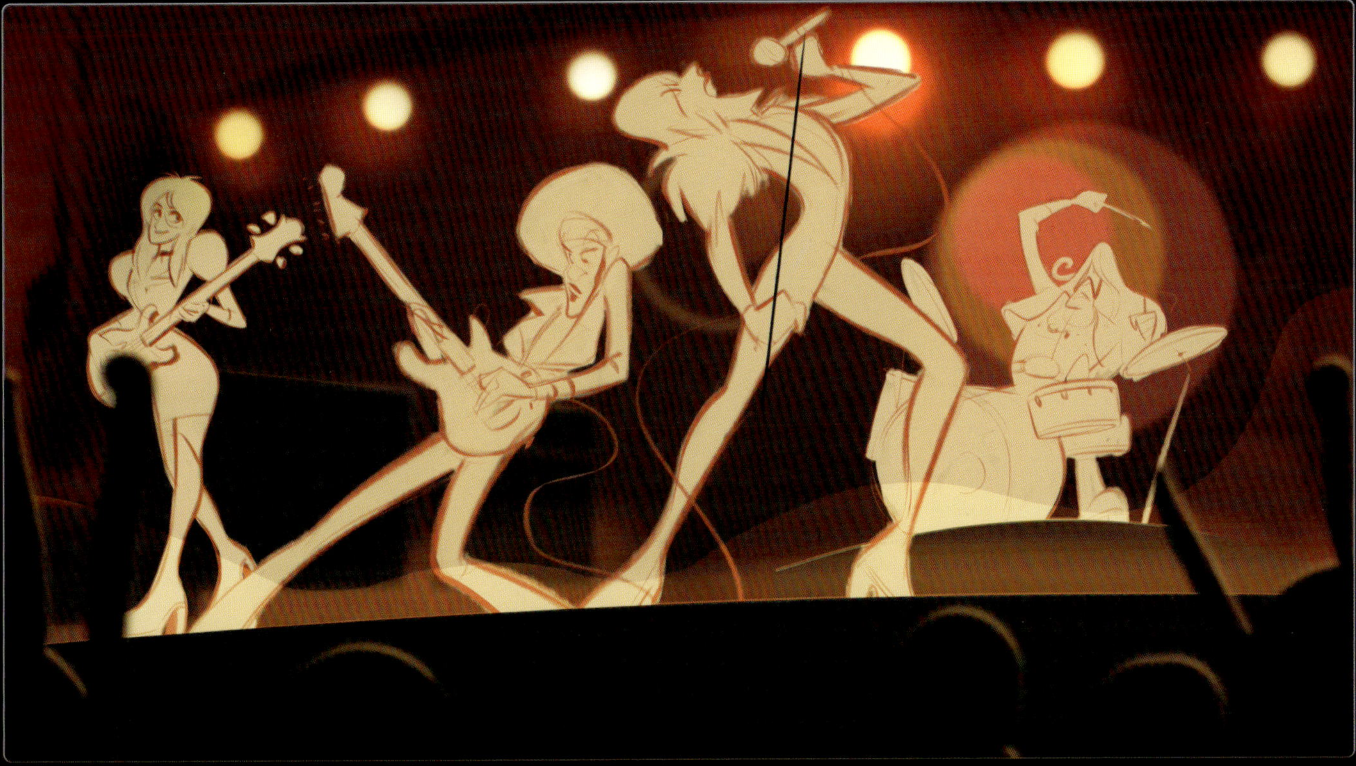

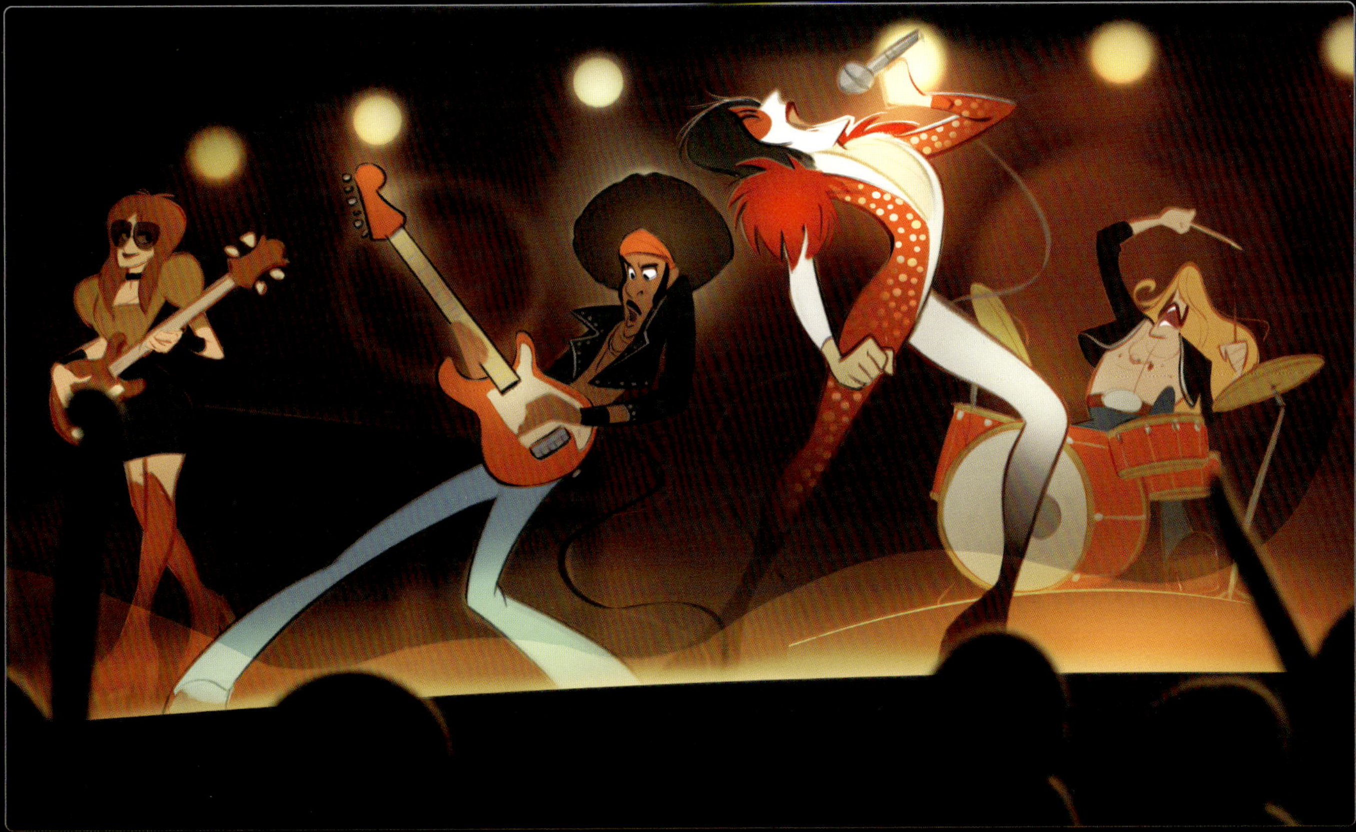

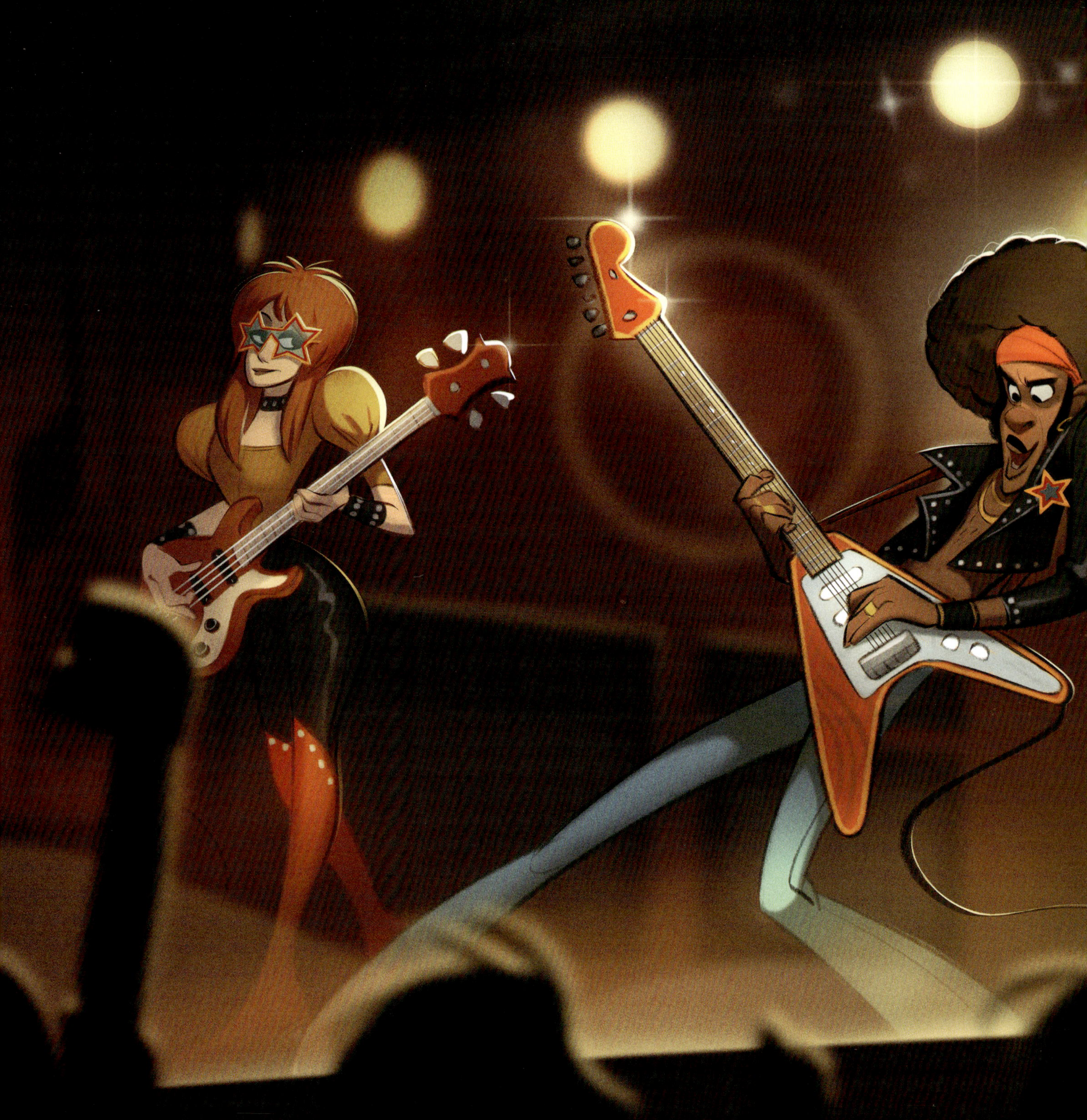

THE LAST WALTZ

At the very last minute I invent a star logo for the band, using the colour palette and seventies-inspired repeat pattern. I add it to the background and incorporate it into my characters' designs – the bassist's sunglasses, the guitarist's badge, the singer's face paint, and the drummer's kit. I also decide that a Flying V-style guitar suits the band better – the shape language connects with the star motif and creates visual harmony with the triangles in the guitarist's design.

With a few final tweaks, the band is making sweet music together. I've only just scratched the surface of the world of seventies rock –

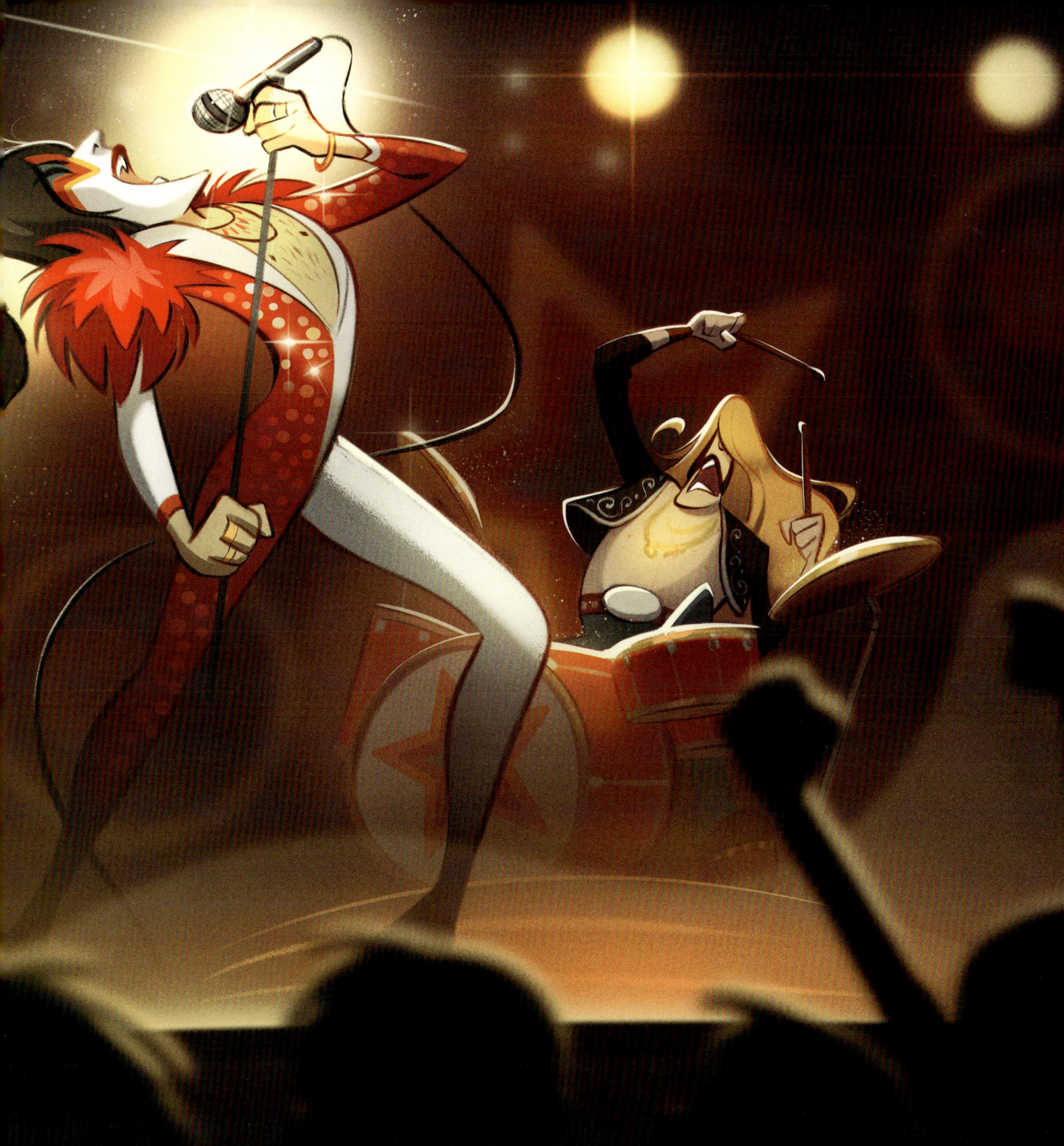

I could redo this process a hundred times and invent an entirely different band lineup each time as there's so much excellent reference material to choose from. Design is a bit like making music – it's about unifying ideas, playing with contrast, while maintaining harmony. But most of all, it's about feeling – conveying an emotion, a vibe, and finding it through improvisation. Start from there, see where the process takes you, and before too long you'll have your own lineup of rock superstars!

CONTRIBUTORS

MELANY ALTUNA

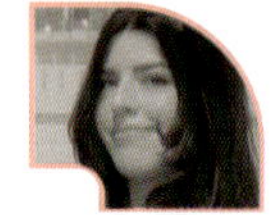

CHARACTER DESIGNER FOR DISNEY TVA
MELANYALTUNA.NET

Melany is a character designer and visual development artist. For the past ten years, she has worked on a variety of animated TV shows for Warner Bros. Animation, Netflix, Nickelodeon, and more.

KENNETH ANDERSON

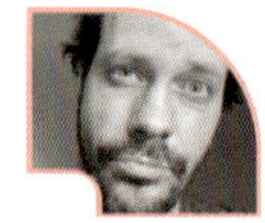

CHARACTER DESIGNER & ILLUSTRATOR
CHARACTERCUBE.COM

Kenneth is a freelance artist specializing in character-driven work across children's publishing, animation design, and more. Based in Scotland, he loves bringing quirky characters and imaginative worlds to life.

LYNN (QIANLIU) CHEN

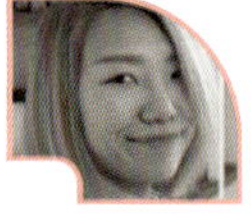

ART LEAD AT MOON ACTIVE
ARTSTATION.COM/LYNNCHEN

Lynn is a Los Angeles-based visual development artist and currently works at Moon Active as an art director. She loves painting with light and colour and creating whimsical illustrations of her corgi.

JACKIE DROUJKO

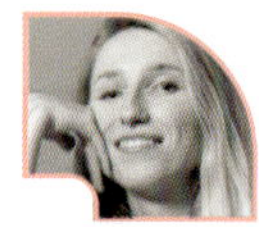

CHARACTER DESIGNER
JACKIEDROUJKO.COM

Jackie is a Canadian character designer, filmmaker, and educator. She creates award-winning animated shorts, runs a popular YouTube channel, and mentors artists worldwide in storytelling and character design.

JOHANNA FORSTER

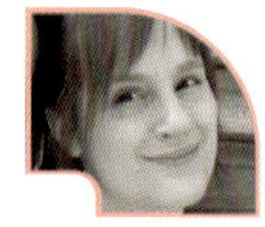

INDEPENDENT ILLUSTRATOR
JOHANNAFORSTER.COM

Johanna is a German artist drawing fantastic scenes and characters inspired by nature. She sells her creations online and at markets, but also focuses on game and colouring-book projects.

TOM HÄNNI

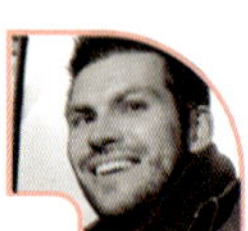

ILLUSTRATOR & ANIMATOR AT PIXELFARM
PIXELFARM.CH

Tom was born in 1979 in Bern. After studying at the College of Arts there, he founded the design studio Pixelfarm with two friends, where he works to this day as a character designer, illustrator, and animator.

RAAHAT KADUJI

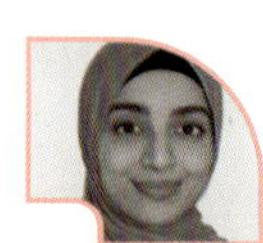

ILLUSTRATOR & AUTHOR
RAAHATKADUJI.COM

Raahat is a children's book author and illustrator. She makes art in the Oxfordshire countryside, where she finds inspiration in nature, wildlife, and the quiet comforts of everyday life.

AURÉLIE LISE-ANNE

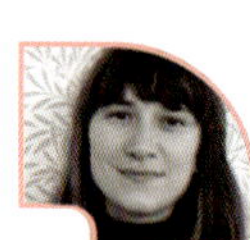

ILLUSTRATOR & VIS DEV ARTIST
AURELIELISEANNE.COM

Aurélie is a freelance artist. While her previous experience includes vis dev and art direction in animation, she now mainly focuses on bringing worlds to life in children's books.

JOHN LOREN

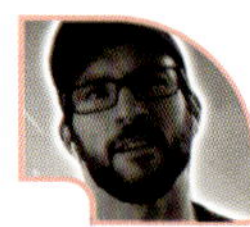

FREELANCE ARTIST
JOHNLOREN.COM

John is an artist from New England. Recent projects he has worked on include *Spyro Reignited Trilogy*, *Crash Bandicoot 4: It's About Time*, *Hearthstone*, and *Disney Lorcana*.

AMANDA MACFARLANE

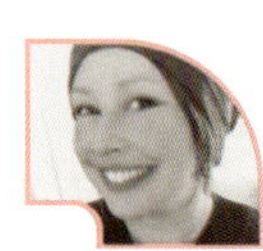

FREELANCE CHARACTER DESIGNER & VISDEV ARTIST
AMANDAMACFARLANE.COM

Amanda has worked as a a visual development artist and character designer for clients such as Warner Bros. Television, Warner Animation Group, *Disney Lorcana*, and Walt Disney Imagineering.

VANESSA MORALES

FREELANCE ILLUSTRATOR & CONCEPT ARTIST
PHONEMOVA.COM

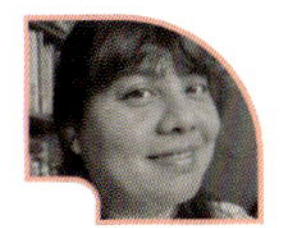

Vanessa is a Mexican illustrator, character designer, and concept artist, with a deep love for nature and all things whimsical, who works in children's illustration.

LYDIA NICHOLS

ILLUSTRATOR
LYDIANICHOLS.COM

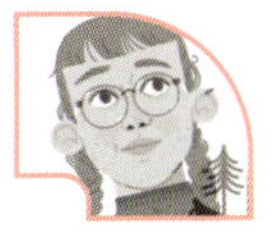

Lydia is an image-maker with a penchant for printmaking processes and anthropomorphic touches. She once dreamed of being either a cartoonist or vet, but now happily illustrates animals (among other things!) instead.

RAQUEL OCHOA

FREELANCE ILLUSTRATOR AT RACHEL WINKLE
RACHELWINKLE.COM

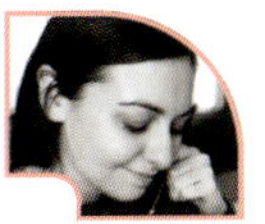

Raquel is an illustrator from Spain, currently working in children's books and passionate about bringing wonderful stories to life through art. She enjoys creating magical characters and imaginative worlds.

SARA PAZ

GRAPHIC DESIGNER & ILLUSTRATOR
SARAPAZDESIGN.WORDPRESS.COM

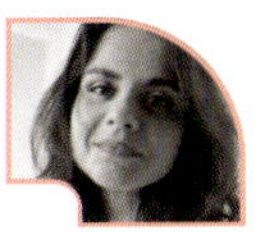

Sara is a designer and illustrator with extensive experience in educational and editorial projects. She specializes in character-driven artwork, merging clear visual storytelling with a distinctive, colourful style.

ANASTASIIA PLATOSHYNA

CHARACTER ART DIRECTOR AT NETFLIX
ANASTASIIAPLATOSHYNA.PORTFOLIO.SITE

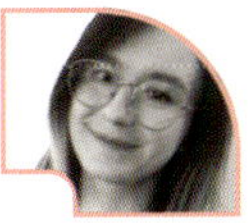

Anastasiia is a Ukrainian-Canadian artist based in Vancouver. She has been working in the animation industry for seven years, with experience ranging from character design to art direction.

ALEX RELLOSO

STORYBOARD ARTIST AT SONY PICTURES ANIMATION
ALEXRELLOSO.COM

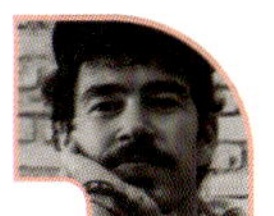

Alex is an Annie-nominated storyboard and character-design artist from Madrid, working currently at Sony Pictures Animation, and previously at DreamWorks, Skydance, Netflix, and The SPA Studios.

JOAKIM RIEDINGER

LEAD ANIMATOR AT FORTICHE
INSTAGRAM.COM/JOUA.K

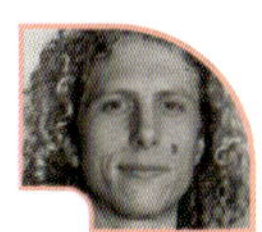

Joakim is a French animator and illustrator who has brought a dynamic style to projects including *Spider-Man: Into the Spider-Verse*, *Minions*, and *Arcane*, focusing heavily on motion and gesture.

FELIPE RODRIGUEZ

CHARACTER DESIGNER & DIRECTOR
FELIPERODRIGUEZART.COM

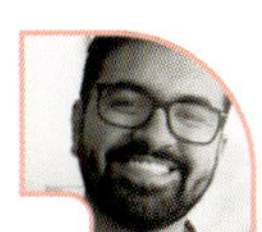

Felipe is a Colombian character designer and illustrator. He has worked on projects such as *Krapopolis*, *Trolls Band Together*, and *Momoguro*. He is the co-creator of the series *Astropackers* for Cartoon Network LA.

EVA STÖCKER

CREATIVE LEAD ART
INSTAGRAM.COM/EVAYABAI

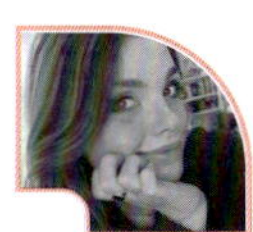

Eva works as a designer in advertising agencies and shaping brand stories. In her free time, she's an artist, creating unique characters and exploring creativity in countless imaginative ways.

MELANIE TIKHONOVA

CONCEPT ARTIST AT MIGHTY CANVAS
MELANAMOBES.COM

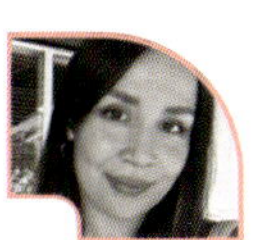

Melanie is an artist who loves storytelling and making silly things with shapes, colours, and memories. Her goal is to stay curious, keep exploring, and always keep creating!

RAQUEL VILLANUEVA

FREELANCE ARTIST
RAQUELVILLANUEVA.ES

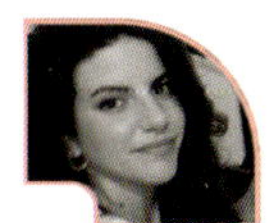

Raquel is a visual development artist, background painter, and 2D lighting artist who loves creating worlds and telling stories through light and colour.

JAROM VOGEL

FREELANCE ILLUSTRATOR
JAROMVOGEL.COM

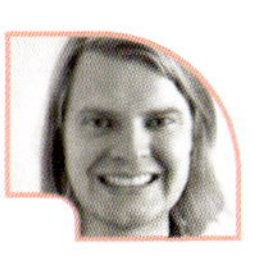

Jarom is a freelance illustrator based near Portland, Oregon. He completed a BFA in illustration in 2015, and has since created artwork for a wide variety of clients and illustrated several children's books.

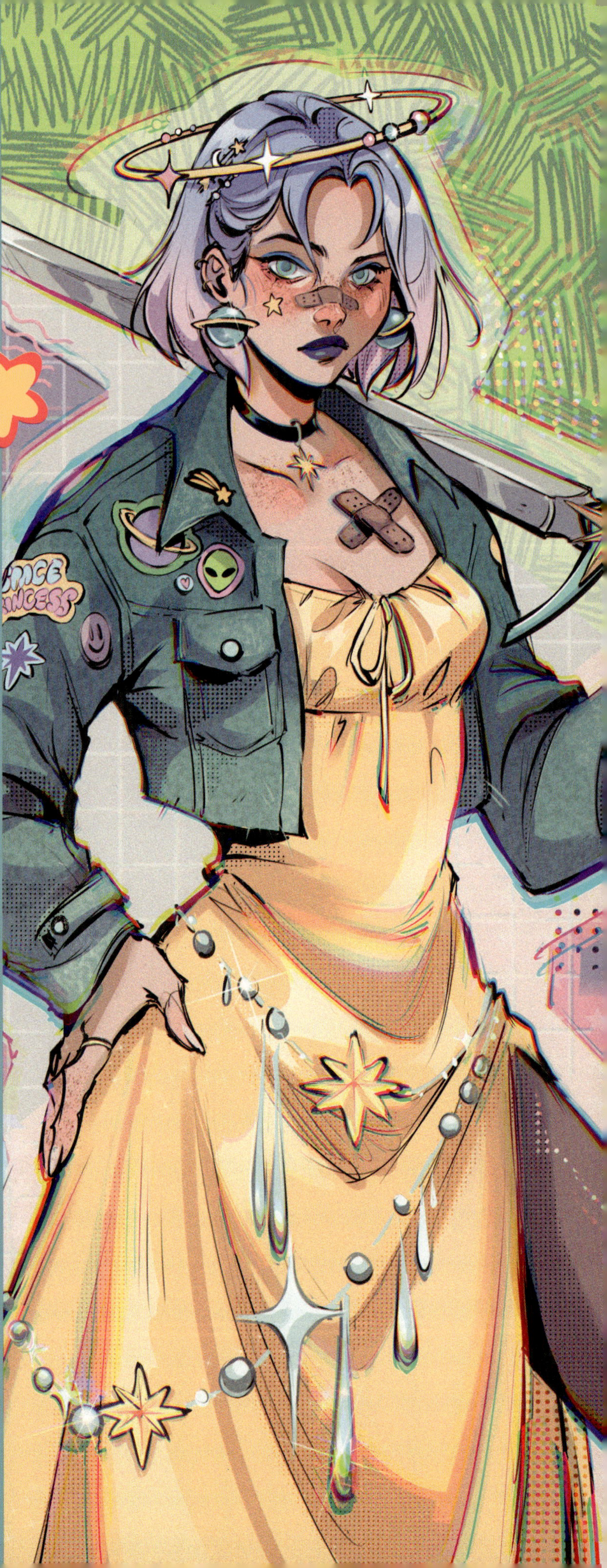

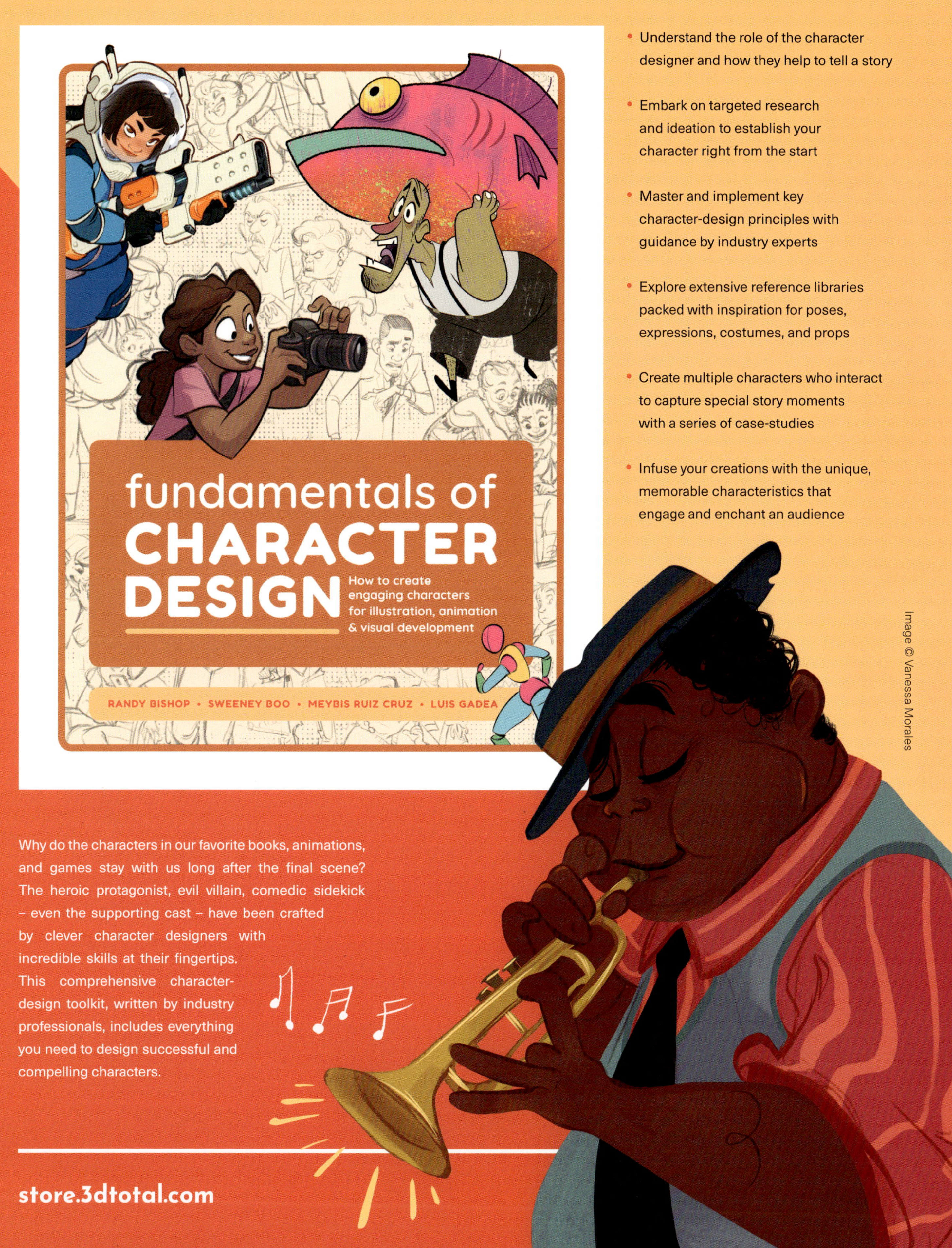
fundamentals of
CHARACTER
DESIGN
How to create engaging characters for illustration, animation & visual development
RANDY BISHOP • SWEENEY BOO • MEYBIS RUIZ CRUZ • LUIS GADEA
Image © Vanessa Morales

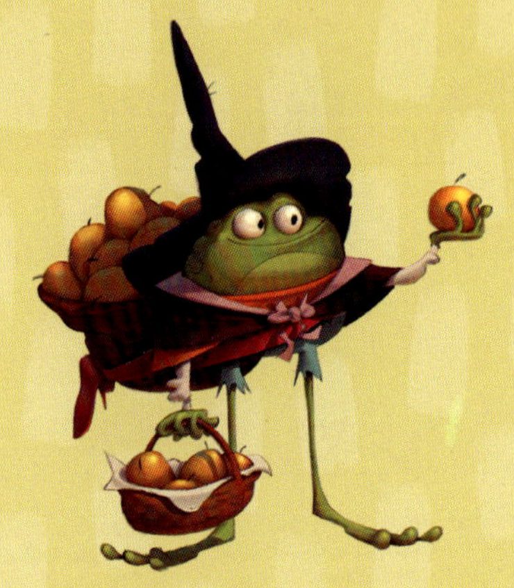

3dtotal Publishing

3dtotal Publishing is a trailblazing, creative publisher specializing in inspirational and educational resources for artists.

Our titles feature top industry professionals from around the globe who share their experience in skilfully written step-by-step tutorials and fascinating, detailed guides. Illustrated throughout with stunning artwork, these bestselling publications offer creative insight, expert advice, and essential motivation. Fans of digital art will enjoy our comprehensive volumes covering Adobe Photoshop, Procreate, and Blender, as well as our superb titles based around character design, including *Fundamentals of Character Design* and *Creating Characters for the Entertainment Industry*. The dedicated, high-quality blend of instruction and inspiration also extends to traditional art. Titles covering a range of techniques, genres, and abilities allow your creativity to flourish while building essential skills.

Well-established within the industry, we now offer over 100 titles and counting, many of which have been translated into multiple languages around the world. With something for every artist, we are proud to say that our books offer the 3dtotal package:

LEARN • CREATE • SHARE

Visit us at store.3dtotal.com

3dtotal Publishing is part of 3dtotal.com, a leading website for CG artists founded by Tom Greenway in 1999.